Computer Based
Information
Systems

**The Irwin Series in
Information and Decision Sciences**

Consulting Editors
Robert B. Fetter   **Claude McMillian**
Yale University   *University of Colorado*

Computer Based Information Systems

Thomas J. Murray

Syracuse University

1985

RICHARD D. IRWIN, INC.
Homewood, Illinois   60430

ISBN 0-256-03164-9

Library of Congress Catalog Card No. 84–81417

Printed in the United States of America

1 2 3 4 5 6 7 8 9 0 MP 2 1 0 9 8 7 6 5

Preface

The field of information systems has been undergoing changes in content and an expansion in interest as an academic major. Because the field has expanded rapidly, the courses comprising a major vary, and as a result, there may be significant differences in the content of various academic programs.

In most instances, the content of programming language courses is relatively well-defined. The introduction to data processing course is also fairly standard with a wide selection of excellent textbooks to consider for adoption. Most programs also offer a systems analysis and design course. In some cases, one course may be offered in analysis and another in design. But there is little definition of non-programming courses between introduction and analysis and design. There is a need to provide a bridge between these courses and to other advanced courses. This textbook is an attempt to fill this niche. In addition to serving as a bridge, the book may serve as the basis for a second, technically oriented course alone.

The material assumes knowledge of the fundamentals usually covered in an introductory course. In addition, it is helpful if students have been exposed to a programming language. However, the book is language independent, and almost any higher language could be used as a vehicle to learn the concepts.

The book can be used at either the undergraduate or the graduate level. The difference in courses at each level lies in the depth of the material covered and the nature of the assignments made. Earlier versions of many of the chapters have been used at both graduate and undergraduate levels. Courses using this text would be most typically found in schools of business administration or management, departments of industrial engineering, or departments of engineering management. In addition, the book may be a useful and readable source of information for professionals in the field.

Chapter 1 is meant to provide a quick overview of the field. Although students will encounter an introduction to hardware and software in the introductory course, this text will, in addition, emphasize data, models, and procedures. This emphasis may be new to many students, but it provides a necessary balance. Chapter 2 reviews the purpose of an information system. The system supports decision making, and the type of decision making affects many design considerations. Chapter 3 discusses information theory. Although this chapter may be skipped without serious damage to the succeeding material, the information theory model is a particularly rich one. The theory sheds light on a wide range of topics encountered in later chapters. Chapter 4 emphasizes data and their handling. In most introductory courses, data are assumed to be readily available, correct, timely, etc. In the *real world*, this can never be assumed. Chapters 5 and 6 cover hardware and software. Some of this material may have been covered in the introductory course; if so, it may be scanned quickly or skipped. Chapter 7 covers the two main families of secondary storage devices: magnetic tape and magnetic disk. Chapter 8 covers sorting. Although sort/merge utilities are usually available in a mainframe environment, they are not always available in a microcomputer environment. Sometimes it makes more sense to build a simple sort into an applications program rather than to utilize the available sort/merge package. Chapter 9 divides file searching into two levels: the logical and the physical. This approach seems to help student understanding. Chapter 10 is a continuation of searching, and many of the chapter's concepts are applied in Chapter 11, which introduces data base management systems. Chapter 12 discusses data compression. Chapter 13 introduces telecommunications. Although students are often exposed to some of these concepts in the introductory course, their understanding of the material is usually rather hazy. The amount of time devoted to this chapter can be adjusted to take students' backgrounds into account. Chapter 14 discusses the broad area of integrity and security. This is a newsworthy area, and examples can be gleaned from newspapers and magazines to illustrate most points. Chapters 15 and 16 look forward to systems analysis and design and very quickly provide an overview of this area. These chapters can be optional in most courses.

A list of additional readings is included at the back of each chapter for those who wish to pursue a topic in greater detail. These lists are not comprehensive—they are selected readings I recommend as a good starting point for further study.

Many people have contributed in one way or another to this text and should be thanked. A number of secretaries over the years have typed and retyped parts of the manuscript. They all deserve a sincere thank you. Of these, I especially want to thank Patricia Sullivan.

I have used parts of the manuscript in courses, and student feedback has helped me add examples and remove ambiguities. Former students who read the book will, I hope, see a point they first made or an exception they first recognized incorporated into these pages.

Dr. Jack D. Becker used parts of the manuscript in a course at the University of Missouri—St. Louis and provided many useful comments. I thank him.

Finally there are a number of people who reviewed the manuscript for the publisher and who provided a wealth of comments, suggestions, and recommendations. A number of changes for the better have been included based on these reviews. These reviewers included: Durward Jackson, California State University at Los Angeles; Leonard J. Garrett, Temple University; John A. Willhardt, Alabama State University; Milton J. Alexander, Auburn University; and Ronald Teichman, The Pennsylvania State University. They also deserve thanks.

No text is in a final, unchangeable form. This is especially so in a field as volatile as computer based information systems. I would appreciate receiving any suggestions or recommended changes from the text's users. I will take these into account in any future revisions.

Thomas J. Murray
Syracuse, N.Y.

Contents

Chapter 1

Overview

Introduction

The concept of information systems is one that is receiving increasing attention by both researchers and organizational users. It is an outgrowth of, and attempt to deal with, what has been termed an information explosion. All organizations require flows of information that assist the managers in these organizations to make the numerous decisions required of them. Information systems serve a wide spectrum of organizational decision making ranging from supporting day-to-day operations to supporting long-term planning.

The basic philosophy of information systems differs from the more traditional concept of data processing. Whereas the older concept is oriented around the processing of data, the newer concept is oriented around the providing of information to the system's users. There is an essential difference between data and information. This difference will be made clearer in the succeeding pages. Because of this difference, many of the practices used in data processing systems may be necessary but not sufficient in the design of an information system.

A digital computer is not essential to an information system. In organizations using manual systems, information is still provided to those needing it. As the requirements for information have expanded and increased in sophistication, digital computers have commonly formed the heart of many information systems. This book is oriented around the concepts associated with computer based information systems.

Information is received by a user through both formal and informal channels. **Formal channels** are set up by an organization to officially link sources of information with the users of such information. A formal structure may be exemplified by the authority relationships represented in an organization chart. Formal channels are the established paths of communication among units or individuals in an organization. **Informal channels** involve all other patterns of communication. It should be clear that information systems may be a sophisticated tool for establishing an efficient formal structure of communication. Such a formal structure complements but does not replace informal structures. Thus, a study of computer based information systems is incomplete since it does not include a study of these complementary and essential informal channels.

The organized study of information systems has been a result of the increasing sophistication and interdisciplinary nature of such systems. It is no longer enough for the designer of a computer based information system to be competent in using the basic principles of computer science. Now a designer must also incorporate knowledge from such disparate fields as the business functional areas, the behavioral sciences, information theory, programming, and many others. A successful computer based information system involves a careful blending and merging of elements from all of these fields.

The users of computer based information systems must also have greater knowledge of these systems. On the one hand, computer power has become more and more available and access to the computer has become easier. This powerful and flexible tool is a means of obtaining information and assistance for the user who has the knowledge to take advantage of it. On the other hand, the user needs a level of computer expertise so that he or she can work with the technical staff to meet his or her needs. The user must also have a greater understanding of the assumptions built into the computer based systems available and their limitations and potentialities. Without such an understanding, the output provided by the system may be misapplied with unexpected consequences. Only a knowledgeable user can judge the workings of a computer based information system, and only a knowledgeable user can see the changes and modifications needed to make such a system even more useful.

The first applications of computer systems involved data manipulation and arithmetic operations. They were usually computerized versions of earlier manual systems. The earliest examples involve census, scientific, and payroll applications. If the processing capabilities of the computer are seen in a broader context, then the computer itself may be recognized as a potential communications link among users. Not only can numeric data be rapidly manipulated, but data of any kind can be processed, summarized, combined, recombined, stored, and formatted as the need arises. Thus, the computer can be viewed as a powerful tool with very generalized capabilities. It is this broadened view of the computer that has contributed in part to the growing study and implementation of computer based information systems.

Another evolutionary feature of the use of computers lies in decentralization of processing power. The earliest configuration can be termed **local batch,** that is, both the processor and all peripheral equipment were located at the same site. In a **remote batch** configuration, communication between a central site and a remote terminal became possible. This remote terminal generally served as a somewhat sophisticated card reader, printer, and sometimes card punch. With the introduction of a **time-sharing** capability, multiple remote users could share the central site's processing power concurrently. **Distributed processing** involves the interconnection of multiple processing centers. In such a configuration, the total processing workload is shared. In recent years, terminals have incorporated some limited processing capability in their design. Thus, there has been a steady move toward a dispersal of processing power throughout a computer network.

Advances in large-scale integration (LSI) chip technology have allowed computers to become less expensive and, as a result, available to more potential users. Small business and personal computers are now being introduced into smaller and smaller organizations for ever more varied applications.

The availability of increased processing power at a lower cost has made possible the manipulation of more complex representations of a problem. With such a capability, better solutions to problems in many application areas become possible.

Rapid access to, updating of, and inexpensive storage of data allow retrieval of current information. In some applications, such capabilities have become an essential part of daily operations. Airline reservations systems and some inventory control systems are only two such examples.

In parallel with the above developments, efforts to allow easier use of computer based systems have been initiated. This has been, in part, an outgrowth of a shift in the relative cost of computer time and human user time. Computers of the first generation were relatively costly in processing time. As a result, systems were designed to minimize processing time at the expense of the less costly user time. This imbalance has now shifted to the opposite end of the spectrum (that is, computer time is relatively inexpensive whereas user time is relatively expensive). As a result, efforts are under way to allow more efficient use of user time even if it is at the expense of less efficient use of processor time. A number of user-oriented packages now allow an easier user/machine interface. In addition, careful design of output reports and flexibility in allowable inquiry formats contribute to user convenience.

A desire for more efficient use of the output of a computer based information system and an awareness of numerous failures in the design of such systems in the past have also triggered studies involving the behavioral sciences. This research may result in more effective design. The results of some early studies have already been incorporated into some new systems.

At the present time the field of computer based information systems is an interdisciplinary one that combines the tools, techniques, and research of many fields with the more traditional concepts of data processing and computer science. As computer communications expand and computing power is distributed throughout an organization, the network becomes more of a generalized communications system. Thus, electronic mail shares the network with data processing, simulation and forecasting models share the system with data base access and retrieval, and voice shares the telecommunications lines with data.

Components of an Information System

A computer based information system may be viewed as consisting of a number of components. It is in the effective integration of these components that the success or failure of such a system is determined. It is important to recognize that a successful computer based information system is not a function of computer technology alone. The components of such a system include hardware, software, data, models, procedures, and users.

Hardware

Hardware consists of the physical equipment used in an information system. It includes not only any central processing units but also all input/output equipment used to interface with the processors. Various secondary storage devices controlled by the processor and used to store programs or data are also included in this category.

Terminals and microcomputers are linked by means of telecommunications lines to central sites or by means of local area networks to other local equipment. Hardware includes this equipment and the communications equipment needed to interface with a telecommunications line. The characteristics and capabilities of such equipment have taken on greater importance as distributed processing and remote access networks have come into more common usage.

Various data preparation and offline data input devices should also be included. These devices are not under the control of the central processing unit but carry out a critical step in the entire information processing cycle.

Software (or Programs)

Software (or **programs**) are sets of instructions that are to be executed by the hardware. Programs are intangible; nevertheless, without them the computer can do nothing. Programming involves rigorously defining the logic required to accomplish a given task. This is followed by the actual writing of the individual instructions, which is called **coding** the program.

A **bug** is an error in a program. **Debugging** is the ongoing effort to correct such errors. There is no practical way to prove that a reasonably complex program is error free. On very large programs, it is not uncommon to discover errors even after years of operation. The use of various structured techniques and a commitment to quality may significantly reduce these.

Programming is a highly labor-intensive activity. As a result, the costs of programming are increasing whereas the cost of hardware is decreasing. In many installations, programming costs have come to dominate all others.

The trend in software has been toward higher level (or more powerful) languages, greater user friendliness, and ease of use.

Software development has been described as everything from an art to witchcraft. There has been an increasing effort to make it more of a science. Structured programming and the various structured analysis and design techniques have pushed software development in that direction. These structured tools not only aid in the development of software but also result in improved reliability and simpler maintenance.

Software has grown in complexity and sophistication as computer based systems have expanded into the area of real time applications and into telecommmunications and distributed networks. In addition, software is increasingly required to coexist with other software in a close working relationship for an information system to work successfully.

Data

Data serve as the input to an information system. They are processed and information is produced. Data may be stored within the system and then retrieved whenever needed. When placed on secondary storage devices, data must be organized so that they can be updated and retrieved efficiently. In addition, measures should be taken so that data integrity and security are maintained.

The amount of data required to be stored depends not only on the volume of data accepted as input to the system but also on the retention policy used in the system. In some applications, only summarized data may be stored after an initial period; in other applications, storage of the full set of data may be required. Of course, different retention policies may be used for different types of data. Neither is on-line storage required for all data during their useful life.

These data must be organized into useful relationships, accessed and retrieved efficiently, and sorted into useful sequences. There are alternative approaches to each of these requirements. The advantages and disadvantages of each of these alternatives must be understood and weighed carefully for a successful information system.

Data must also be entered into the computer and stored without permanent damage or unauthorized modification or deletion. As a result, the rejection of invalid data and the availability of error correction procedures are critical. Considerations of data protection and integrity also cannot be ignored.

Models

A **model** is an abstract representation of the assumptions built into the information system. Data are processed in accordance with the constraints and rules of a model. A model represents a *picture* of the information system environment within which information is produced. It is also within the constraints of the relevant models that data are collected. As a result, it cannot be concluded that because data have the characteristics of accuracy, timeliness, etc. that useful information is produced. The quality of the information produced also depends on the relevance and meaningfulness of the processing models.

Models used have tended to be normative rather than descriptive. A **normative model** provides an output which ought to be followed. It is frequently a model of management science that produces an *optimum* solution. A **descriptive model** produces an output which is similar to what, in fact, a decision maker would produce. There is a place for both types of models, but normative models have tended to dominate information system design.

Procedures

Procedures are directions for the personnel working with a computer based information system. These instructions must be written down and made available to all involved. They must be clear and unambiguous. Responsibility for each required action must be clearly established. Procedures address a wide range of concerns including but not limited to the following examples:

1. Data input preparation.
2. Operator instructions.
3. Backup and recovery procedures.
4. Manual handling of documents.
5. Disaster procedures.
6. Report distribution.
7. Error correction and control.
8. Data, source document, and report retention policies.
9. Systems development guidelines.

Procedures are concerned with the many manual operations required to complement the computer based operations of an information system. It is necessary that they be thought out as carefully as hardware and software decisions are.

Users

The ultimate judgment of the effectiveness of any information system must be made by the system users. An information system must be designed in such a way that the relevant information needed by its users to assist in decision making is provided in an accurate and timely manner.

It cannot be concluded, however, that high use of a computer based information system by itself is an indication of success. Cheney,[1] for example, summarizes three variables as surrogate criteria for measuring the success of an information system. These are:

1. Information satisfaction (i.e. how satisfied are the users with the information received).
2. Job satisfaction (i.e. how compatible are the users with the organization as evidenced by attitudes toward the job before and after implementation).
3. Utilization (i.e. is the information actually used to make decisions).

An important aspect of information system design is the division of tasks between the human user and the computer. A good system allows the user to perform those tasks that he or she can do in a manner that is superior to the computer and also allows the computer to carry out those tasks that it can do better. The computer can best be allocated to those tasks requiring manipulation of a large volume of data, speed, accuracy, or relatively complex computations. The human user can best recognize complex data patterns, solve ill-structured problems, or handle exceptional situations.

A well-established principle frequently used in information system design is the **exception principle.** In many applications the user needs only to be informed of those cases in which the data deviate from a norm or fall outside of a range. Only those cases, the exceptions, are reported to the user. This can be a defense against information overload.

The design of a computer based information system must take into account its users. In fact, most failures of such systems have occurred not for technical reasons but because of a serious mismatch or incompatibility between the system and its users' needs.

Cost/Benefit Analysis

A cost/benefit justification is usually required by most organizations before a major investment is approved. Capital goods such as machinery, trucks, and expensive tools usually require a cost/benefit analysis. A **cost/benefit analysis** is a study of the potential investment which estimates the relevant costs associated with the investment and the estimated benefits or value expected to result from its use.

Information is an intangible asset used within the organization. It bears some similarity to other intangibles such as patents, copyrights, and goodwill. The benefits of any information system or any additional increment to an existing information system must be weighed against the associated costs. *Information is not a free good.*

Information is used to support decision making. In practice, all decisions are made with imperfect information. The value of information lies in the value of the decision made. The incremental value of additional information is based on the value of the improved decision made as a result of that additional information. Of course, perfect information results in the best decision and, therefore, the value of perfect information serves as an ideal.

The following simplified example serves to clarify these concepts. Assume that a decision maker must select one from four possible alternative courses of action as follows:

Alternative	Outcome
1	0
2	0
3	$1000
4	0

Only alternative 3 results in any benefit. The decision maker, however, does not know which one of the four alternatives is the *correct* one. The expected value associated with the decision (assuming an equal probability of selecting any alternative) is $250. If information that eliminates alternatives 1 and 2 is available to the decision maker, then the expected value of his decision is $500. The value of the information was $250. Perfect information is clearly worth an additional $500.

The above example also makes the point that information is only of value if it is actually used in making a decision. A report produced by an information system that is not read is of no value. It is only of value if it potentially can influence the outcome of a decision.

Costs incurred in a computer based information system are a function of a number of variables. Four usually highly significant variables are volume, complexity, timeliness, and data storage requirements.

Volume simply refers to the number of data transactions required to be processed in a given period of time. Cost increases as volume increases.

Complexity refers to the amount of processing required for each data transaction. Cost increases as complexity increases.

Timeliness refers to the degree to which data are not outdated when available to a user. Cost increases as timeliness becomes greater. There are a number of factors that affect timeliness. These include response time, batching interval, and the data collection cutoff lead time.

Response time is concerned with the amount of time between the request by a user for information and the receipt of that information, assuming that it is available in the system. The response time may vary from seconds in an on-line, real time, computer based system to hours in a batch-oriented system to days in a manual system. Cost increases as the response time decreases.

Batching interval refers to the time between updating runs in a batch-oriented computer system. Cost increases as the batching interval decreases. As the batching interval decreases, the updating runs occur more frequently and, as a result, the data available to the user are, on the average, more up-to-date. In the extreme, a real-time, updated system incurs the highest costs but provides the most current information to its users.

There is a period of time in a batch-oriented system between the point when data collection for an update is terminated and when those data are entered into the system. This is called the **data collection cut-off period.** Although timeliness is clearly a function of this period, there is no direct relationship between the length of this period and cost.

Data storage requirements are dependent not only on the volume of data required to be processed by the information system, but also on the data retention policy. Cost of data storage increases as the amount of data retained increases. Data may be discarded after a certain period of time has elapsed, or they may be relegated to less expensive (but longer retrieval time) types of storage.

Some costs and benefits may be difficult to translate into a monetary amount. This is especially true in evaluating benefits, e.g. it may be difficult to place a dollar value on increased customer goodwill resulting from faster delivery or from fewer billing errors. In some cases, a computer based information system (or an addition to it) can be justified on a purely monetary basis. If it cannot be so justified, it should not yet be rejected. A careful and objective evaluation of the less tangible (but no less real) benefits should be made before a final decision is made.

To further complicate the analysis, the use of computer based information systems tends to so permeate the organizational structure that it is frequently difficult to allocate costs and especially to define and allocate benefits.

Information System Characteristics

Although there are many possible characteristics that can be used to describe a computer based information system, the following are some of the more commonly used.

The **range** or **scope** of activities that the information system supports may vary. In one application, a highly specialized system may support investment decision making; in another organization a computer based information system may support decision making across a wide range of interrelated business functional areas.

The **capacity** of the system may be represented by several possible measures such as number of data transactions processed in a given period of time, number of inquiries answered in a given period of time, volume of data stored, or amount of processing that can be handled.

Accuracy of an information system refers to the lack of errors in its output. Errors can occur in the original collection and entry of the data, in its processing, or in its output.

Accessibility refers to the availability of information to the system's users when it is needed by them and without an unreasonable amount of effort.

Age of data refers to the currency of the data. In some applications, data must be very current, e.g. an airline reservations system; in other applications data may not require great currency, e.g. a planning/forecasting system for a marketing group. Of course, different sets of data in a system may differ in age.

Usefulness of information must be measured in terms of its users. This is a function of factors such as format, clarity of presentation, etc.

Consistency means that information provided to different users or to the same user does not contradict itself and reconciles correctly. This is primarily a function of using homogeneous data and of updating stored data in an internally uniform and compatible manner. Consistency does not, however, imply accuracy.

Clearly this list of characteristics is not all inclusive. In addition, many of these characteristics are not completely independent of each other.

Conclusions

A successful computer based information system requires an almost symbiotic relationship among hardware, programs, data, models, procedures, and users. Past experience shows that all too often such systems have tended to be oriented much too strongly around the capabilities of the hardware and program components. Instead of a design in which the other components adapt to the user, the user has been forced, in many situations, to adapt to an uncomfortable (and ineffective) way to the available technology.

A computer based information system cannot be viewed as simply a system oriented around and dominated by a number of hardware-based building blocks or as the processing of input data to produce output. An information system must be designed so as to provide information in a usable form, in a timely fashion, and in an efficient manner to the information consumers of an organization, that is, the decision makers.

It should not be assumed, however, that a successful computer based information system should supply all of the information needed by its user. An information system may be designed to support decision making in one or more narrow, specialized areas based on cost/benefit analysis. The concept of a total information system, i.e. one that supports all decision making in an organization, is not a viable one.

Although a formal system may be an essential source of information, it generally cannot be the only one. Various informal sources of information exist in any organization. A computer based system should complement and not attempt to completely replace these alternative sources of information.

An information system is a tool to aid its users. Individual characteristics of various computer based information systems may vary, but the purpose of all such systems is to serve some of the information needs of its users.

The following chapters will discuss in more detail the various components and characteristics of computer based information systems.

Reference

1.   Cheney, P. H. "Measuring MIS Project Success." *Proceedings 9th Annual AIDS Conference*, Chicago, Ill., October 19–21, 1977, pp.141–143.

Additional Readings

Alloway, R. M. "User Managers' Systems Needs." *MIS Quarterly* 7, No. 2 (June 1983), pp. 27–41.

Benson, D. H. "A Field Study of End User Computing: Findings and Issues." *MIS Quarterly* 7, No. 4 (December 1983), pp. 35–45.

Brooks, F. P. Jr. *The Mythical Man-Month*. Reading, Mass.: Addison-Wesley Publishing, 1975.

Burch, J. G. Jr.; F. R. Strater; and G. Grudnitski, *Information Systems: Theory and Practice*. 2d ed., New York: John Wiley & Sons, Inc., 1979.

Davis, G. B. *Management Information Systems*. New York: McGraw-Hill, 1974.

Hirsch, R. "The Value of Information." *The Journal of Accountancy* 125, No. 6 (June 1968), pp. 41–45.

Keen, P. G. W., and M. S. S. Morton, *Decision Support Systems*. Reading, Mass.: Addison-Wesley Publishing, 1978.

King, J. L., and E. L. Schrens, "Cost-Benefit Analysis in Information Systems Development and Operation." *Computing Surveys* 10, No. 1 (March 1978), pp. 19–34.

Kleijnen, J. P. C. *Computers and Profits: Quantifying Financial Benefits of Information*. Reading, Mass.: Addison-Wesley Publishing, 1980.

McLean, E. R., ed. "Information Systems and its Underlying Disciplines." *Data Base* 14, No. 1 (Fall 1982).

Morrison, R. R. "A Survey of Attitudes Toward Computers." *Communications of the ACM* 26, No. 12 (December 1983), pp. 1051– 57.

Weinberg, G. M. *The Psychology of Computer Programming*. New York: Van Nostrand Reinhold Co., 1971.

Review

1. Briefly differentiate between the orientations of data processing and information systems.
2. Discuss why programming is still more of an art than a science.
3. What is the ultimate test of any information system?
4. Relate the data collection cut-off period and the batching interval to timeliness. Ignoring response time, what is the average delay in a batch-oriented system?
5. What may be some intangible benefits of a computer based information system?

Chapter 2

Systems, Models, and Information Systems

Introduction

An information system is a sophisticated tool for accepting data as input and producing information in various forms as output for the system users. An information system does not exist in isolation but as an integral component of a functioning organization. It exists to provide support to various units of that organization. A clear understanding of the objectives and uses of an information system can be had only in terms of the organizational functions supported by that information system. The information system should exist not as an end in itself but as a powerful support tool for decision making by its users.

The concept of *system* is a broad, abstract one, but one that allows a number of insights. It is useful to draw some parallels between the abstract concept of a system and the reality of a working information system.

At the heart of any information system is the concept of a model. An understanding of the importance and limitations of models is important for a clear understanding of the functions of an information system.

Since information is used to support decision making, an understanding of the various general types of decision making is also required. Characteristics of different decision making classes vary, and, as a result, have major implications for the design of information systems.

Systems

A **system** is a set of elements operating within a boundary and interacting with each other to achieve one or more objectives. This is
certainly a very general concept. What tie the system together are
the relevant relationships among the elements. There may be many
relationships that exist among the system's elements and other elements. The system is defined by the selection of some relationships
as relevant and the ignoring of others as irrelevant. The problem at
hand, that is, the purpose for defining the system, determines which
relationships are relevant.

Implicit in the definition of a system is the assumption that it can
be determined for any element whether or not that element is a
member of the given collection and, therefore, whether or not it is a
part of the system. In other words, a boundary can be drawn around
the system. This boundary will enclose those elements that are a
part of the system and exclude those that are not a part. What is
outside the system is called the **environment.**

Systems may theoretically be of two types, closed systems and
open systems. A **closed system** is one that is isolated from its environment (i.e. no interaction across the boundary of the system occurs). An **open system** is one in which interaction with the
environment occurs. An open system is affected by its environment
and, in turn, affects it. A practical system can be closed only in a
very limited way. For example, a system may be closed with respect
to material but open with respect to information. Systems may be
viewed as existing on a continuum ranging from completely closed
to completely open. Neither extreme exists in practice. However, the
characteristics of a system will vary with its location on this open/
closed spectrum. As a result, openness and closedness of systems
must be viewed as relative concepts, that is, one system is more open
(or closed) than another.

If a system is relatively closed, it does not readily react to changes
in its environment. This is because most changes are filtered out at
the boundaries of the system. A closed system may remain relatively
stable and may change very slowly.

If a system is relatively open, it senses changes occurring in its
environment and can adapt (within limits) to them. The adaptation
occurs in a way that is favorable to the continued operation of the
system. A relatively open system, as a result, maintains a more dynamic stability.

A system cannot react and adapt to every change. To do so would
distract it from its primary objectives. To avoid handling minor

changes, filtration occurs at the boundaries of even an open system. Complete insulation, however, would result over a period of time in a system completely out of touch with its environment and no longer carrying out relevant or meaningful objectives.

The degree of openness required for any system depends on the purpose of the system. One system may require for best operation great openness while another may require less interaction with its environment.

A system adapts to its environment also by modifying its output. It does this through feedback. A system accepts input from its environment and produces output. **Feedback** involves sensing this output and providing the results of this monitoring as additional input, which changes the output.

Control is a concept of measuring performance against some predetermined objective. Feedback is a means of control used in systems of many kinds.

An organization is a system existing in an environment. It affects and is affected by that environment. In addition, the organization itself consists of a number of **subsystems.** Each subsystem has its own environment consisting of some other subsystems and, perhaps, part of the environment of the whole organization. For example, although advertising (a subsystem) may have no interaction with facilities maintenance (another subsystem), production will be closely tied to sales.

Any of these organizational subsystems and the organization as a whole must strive to ensure control (i.e. to adjust their operations to more closely achieve their objectives) and to adapt to their environment. The flow of information originating both within the organizational unit and from outside the unit is the mechanism by which control can be exercised and adaptation can be achieved. Thus an information system serves a purpose analogous to that of a nervous system.

Information is required on the results of current operations carried out by the organization. This information then allows the organization to measure what variation exists between its actual performance and its planned performance. In other words, the organization controls its own operations, and it does this through the use of information. Based on the information received, its decisions are made to bring the actual state of the organization closer in line with its planned state.

At the same time, the organization exists in an environment which changes. The flow of information across the system boundaries allows the organization to make those changes in its objectives or methods that will allow it to operate more successfully, that is, it adapts.

If each organizational subunit *optimizes* its operation, then, in general, the whole organization does not necessarily optimize its operation. This is the problem of **suboptimization.** For example, if each department in a manufacturing company optimizes its primary goal and these goals are not very carefully selected, then the performance of the entire company may be jeopardized. If a warehousing department is judged on the basis of minimized costs, then inventory should be reduced to zero (clearly a minimum), but sales will clearly be affected and perhaps disastrously. If the sales department is judged on the number of units sold, prices may be cut to the point where losses are incurred. Although this example presents extreme cases, more subtle examples of suboptimization with organizational subunits operating at cross purposes abound.

An information system is an organized mechanism for channeling these information flows to those decision makers exercising control and making needed adaptations.

Models

An infinite amount of data faces a decision maker. Clearly, not all of the available data are relevant to any given decision. There is also a degree of relevance, e.g. highly relevant, helpful, somewhat relevant, etc., associated with these data. In order to deal effectively with these data, the decision maker must abstract a finite (and manageable) subset of data from this potentially infinite collection. Data are the elementary units of experience but of necessity most must be discarded. This abstraction (or filtering) is accomplished by the application of a model.

Figure 2–1 illustrates the concept of a model. Some limited aspect of reality is circumscribed. Its boundaries, however, may be somewhat unclear or ambiguous at points. A **model** abstracts from that subset of reality and represents it in a simplified version. This version is capable of manipulation and the production of a solution or answer that in turn is applied back to the real world.

Examples of models include:

1. Equations in physics, e.g. $E = M \cdot C^2$ or $F = M \cdot A$.
2. The Capital Asset Pricing Model in finance.
3. Learning models in psychology.

Figure 2–1
The Modelling Process

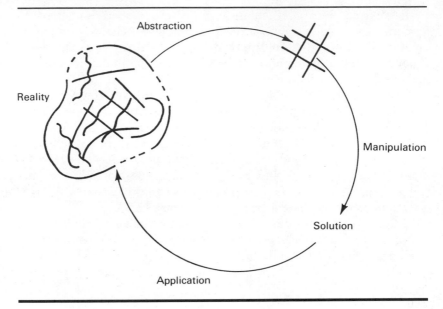

Abstraction

Reality

Manipulation

Solution

Application

4. Linear programming models.
5. The double entry bookkeeping model.

A computer program will incorporate a model in its logic sequence and, as a result, all of the assumptions inherent in the model become part of the program.

There are two general sources of error in the use of any model. These are the errors associated with the abstraction of the model and the manipulation of the model.

Because every model represents a simplified view of reality, error exists in the difference between reality and the model's view of the same reality. The model has built-in assumptions that are only approximately true. It assumes that some variables are not relevant or that there are no interactions between variables when, in fact, these variables or interactions do have some effect. Because it filters out data, some error inevitably exists.

An error in the manipulation of the model may be the result of a computer program error, a logic error, a mathematical error, etc. It is also possible that the model is too complex and, as a result, cannot be effectively manipulated. A simpler model might ease this problem.

Errors associated with the manipulation of the model should be eliminated. Errors associated with the abstraction itself are inherent in the use of any model.

A model is a simplified *view* of reality. It imposes an order or pattern on a disordered mass of data. Outside of a model, data are meaningless. The model organizes a subset of these data into a useful pattern. Data do not contain only one possible interpretation. Different models imposed on the same data may result in different interpretations.

The model accepts as input selected (or filtered) data and produces as output information, that is, what is needed by a decision maker to select among alternatives.

The model is not the reality. The information produced by the model is based on the inherent assumptions of the model. To the extent that the assumptions are reasonable and are, at least, approximately true, the information produced is valuable. To the extent that these assumptions are not reasonable and approximately true, the information produced is less useful and may even be misleading. With experience, a model may be modified so as to more accurately reflect the reality it represents.

All information systems contain built-in models. It is essential that the users of such systems have an understanding of these models. This understanding must include a recognition of the underlying assumptions inherent in the models.

It is also important to understand that since the *real world* changes, the models imbedded in an information system to represent aspects of that *real world* may become obsolete. The models used in the information system inherently contain assumptions—these assumptions may with time no longer prove reasonable. Thus models should be reviewed regularly for continuing appropriateness.

The ultimate test of any model lies in its value to the user. The model that produces output which is either ignored or not capable of making a difference in decision making is worthless.

There are other desirable characteristics in any model, e.g. ease of use, ability to produce insight, economy in the use of resources. Certainly in comparing two models the one that is easier for its users to understand, to manipulate, and to apply its output is the potentially better model. Some models may produce a deeper insight into the interrelationships among the relevant variables. This ability may allow a better understanding of the *real world* aspect under study and, as a result, allow the decision maker greater control and more sophisticated application of the model's output. One model may make more efficient use of available resources than another. For example, one model may require less data (or easier to obtain data) than another. One computer based model may require less central processor time than another or may manipulate fewer variables than another. One model is theoretically better than another if it provides better information to the decision maker. Practically, one model is better than another if it is more useful to the decision maker than another.

Decision Making

An information system should support decision making. Decision making, however, is not an activity that can be described by a fixed set of characteristics. It is, in fact, an activity that covers a wide spectrum, and at any point on this spectrum the characteristics of the decision-making activity differ. For clarity of presentation this spectrum can be divided somewhat arbitrarily into a number of decision-making levels. The dividing line between levels is not, however, a clear and unambiguous one but a *fuzzy* one. Hare[5] refers to operational, tactical, and strategic levels. Davis[4] describes the four levels of transaction processing, operational control, management control, and strategic planning. Anthony[1] uses operational control, management control, and strategic planning. Other more multidimensional approaches have also been proposed. Hare's taxonomy will be used in the following discussion. Figure 2–2 illustrates the relationship of these levels, with the typical orientation for applications.

Figure 2–2
Decision-Making Levels

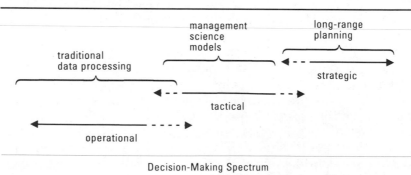

Decision-Making Spectrum

The three levels of decision making can be broadly described in terms of the typical decision characteristics encountered at each level.

Operational decision making is oriented around the day-to-day, well-established, well-structured, and repetitive decisions encountered in any organization. Simon[6] has described a spectrum of decision making ranging from *programmed* to *nonprogrammed*. Operational decision making lies at the programmed end of this range. Models are relatively simple at this level and remain relatively stable over time. Decision making at this level is highly structured and information can be derived from available data in a relatively straightforward manner. In system theory terms, the decision maker is faced with a relatively closed system. Most of the traditional, well-established data processing systems have been designed to support operational decision making.

Tactical decision making is concerned with decisions that can be reasonably structured but are influenced by miscellaneous, unstructured elements. These are the decisions frequently made by middle management. At this level, the models become more sophisticated. The decision making is carried on within a less structured environment. Greater uncertainty permeates not only the data collected but the assumptions inherent in the models. Management science models and techniques are frequently used to support this level of decision making. In systems terms, the decision maker is faced with a more open system.

Strategic decision making is oriented around long-range plans. It is concerned with events and relationships frequently outside of the direct control of the decision maker. At this level, the system under study is a rather open one. In Simon's[6] terms, decision making is nonprogrammed and is usually a function of an organization's top management. To date, computer based information systems have not been of significant direct assistance at this level. Decision support systems offer some promise as tools at this decision-making level.

Figure 2–3 summarizes some of the different characteristics of these three decision-making levels. These characteristics change as one moves across the spectrum from the operational through the tactical to the strategic. Models increase in complexity, and the system under study changes from a relatively closed one at the operational level to a relatively open one at the strategic level. The decision makers also change from operating personnel through middle management to top management. The relevant time span at these differ-

Figure 2–3
Characteristics of Decision-Making Levels

	Level		
	Operational	Tactical	Strategic
Models	Simple————————▶	Complex————————▶	Very complex
System studied	Relatively closed——————————————————▶		Relatively open
Management	Operating——————▶	Middle————————▶	Top
Data used	Recent past——————▶	Recent & older——▶	Older
Orientation	Immediate future——————————————————▶		More distant future
Emphasis	Control——————————————————————————▶		Planning
Methodology	Well-known————————▶	Emerging————————▶	Ill-defined

ent decision-making levels also differs. The data used at the operational level are from the very recent past, and decisions are made centered on the present or immediate future. At the tactical level, recent data may be combined with older data to support more future-oriented decisions. These decisions, in general, have direct implications over a longer period of time, e.g. one or two years. At the strategic level, timeliness of data is of less importance and the decisions supported are oriented around the more distant future, e.g. five to ten years. Since decisions at the strategic level are long-range, it is usually not essential to have very recent data. The manipulation of large amounts of data accumulated over longer periods of time may be used to support decision making. It is very doubtful that up-to-the-minute (or second) data can have an impact on such decision making. (An exception occurs in such situations as an unexpected court decision, a governmental overthrow, etc.) Although the full impact of a strategic decision is not felt for some time, its implications may be enormous when it is felt. At the operational level the emphasis is on control, whereas at the strategic level the emphasis is on planning. Since traditional data processing systems have been used at the operational level, the methodologies for the design and implementation of such systems are well-established. At the tactical level, techniques are being improved as such systems are now being implemented. However, at the strategic level the appropriate methodologies remain either ill-defined or unknown.

Figure 2–4 illustrates the increasingly integrative nature of the decisions supported by an information system as one progresses across the decision-making spectrum. As information systems cover a broader area of support, they must integrate information more. This integration is possible only if the data inputs are consistent. In addition, it becomes necessary at the higher levels to filter and summarize the

Figure 2–4
Information System Integration

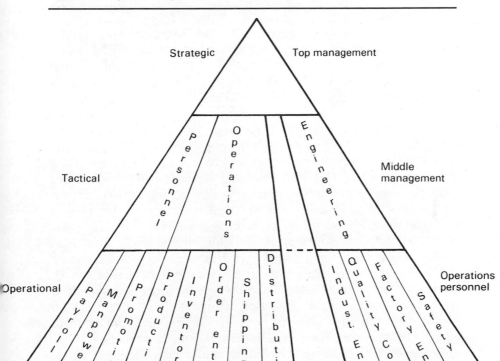

information system output to a greater extent than is required at the operational level.

A conclusion that must be reached is that: *Since information systems are designed to support decision making, the characteristics of any information system are dependent on the level of decision making supported.*

Information Systems

In the 1960s it was not uncommon for computer-oriented professionals to advocate the concept of the **total management information system,** or **total MIS.** This approach implied that one well-organized and well-structured information system could supply the information needs of all decision makers in an organization (or, at least, could fulfill all of the requirements of a formal information system).

A clear advantage of such a system would be that information would be integrated, consistent, and available. Early steps taken in this direction were unsuccessful. As a result, the concept of the total MIS has been discredited.

The present (and more practical) thinking in this area envisions a number of information systems supporting various areas of decision making within an organization. There is, at least, a two-dimensional aspect to this: Various functional areas (e.g. marketing, finance) may be supported, and the level of decision making (i.e. operational, tactical, or strategic) supported may vary.

Although there are clearly some overlaps in the data utilized by different functional areas, there will, in general, be different information requirements since the decisions required are dissimilar. Thus the concept of the total MIS has been replaced with a concept of multiple formal information systems coexisting within an organization. Some of these systems may be tightly or loosely coupled. Others may operate independently of each other. Some may be highly computerized; others may be manual. In addition, the levels of decision making supported by different information systems may be different.

Not only must the output of an information system be understood, but the set of potential outputs that the system could have produced must also be appreciated. Swanson[7] illustrates this in terms of a humorous but incisive story of a professor doing research on a remote island. His information system simply tells him that things at home are either OK or disastrous. His failure to understand the limitations of the system leads to a complete misunderstanding of the conditions at his home.

Another phenomenon associated with some information systems is that of information overload. **Information overload** implies that a user receives more information in a period of time than can be absorbed and therefore used in making a decision. Because the human being can process only so much information per unit of time, any information over this limit cannot be used. Beyond a loss of information, the overload may severely impair or degrade the user's ability to process any information. Conditions of information overload, however, are frequently conditions of data overload. The user is provided with a mass of data that has not been processed in a manner that produces relevant information. Not infrequently, information systems have been designed to produce voluminous reports that may have historical interest but little usefulness for current decision making.

Argyris[2] points out that even though a proposed or new information system may be recognized by its users as an aid to rational decision making, it may still be opposed. He attributes this to the facts that frequently users do not understand new computer based technology, and radical changes are sometimes required in managerial style. In short, it is not uncommon for managers facing the introduction of new information systems to feel threatened by this new technology. It is generally true that if the users of any information system are opposed to its use, the effectiveness of the system may be completely compromised.

Recent approaches to the design of computer based information systems have attempted to incorporate various organizational and behavioral factors. These factors would appear to play a more important role at a higher level of decision making. The role of cognitive style, that is, a user's characteristic or usual approach to problem solving, has been pursued as a research area.[3]

Information Use Pathology

In any organization there are always dangers that an information system will not be used in an effective manner. It might be said that the conditions creating these dangers are pathological.

Because information systems use models that must implicitly limit the number of factors taken into consideration, there is a danger that those factors or variables which cannot be readily quantified will be ignored. For example, management science techniques may give an illusion of rigor and comprehensiveness. Those factors that cannot be conveniently fitted into such a model may be assumed away; but sometimes it is the nonquantifiable or the intangible that spells the difference between success and failure. It is also in the area of complex *pattern recognition* that human experience and expertise become crucial. Therefore, the output of many formal information systems must be supplemented by human judgment before a decision is made.

The future is always difficult to forecast. As a forecast involves the more distant future, the greater the degree of uncertainty that will surround the forecast. There may be an organizational tendency to overdiscount the future because of this uncertainty. The organization may rely on various features of the present and come to assume that these features are permanent and unchangeable. This tendency is a pathological reflection of the normal and generally wise heavier weighting of the immediate future over the distant future, and of the tried and true channels of information both from within and without the organization.

Information that does not fit the expectations of the user may be filtered out or distorted. It is not only overconfidence in the familiar that leads to failure in an organization's information use. Someone who has made an intellectual commitment to an idea publicly will frequently reject what refutes it.

The very nature of hierarchy with its reward structure is conducive to bias in the entry of data into an information system. Because of the system of rewards and penalties associated with the performance of an individual, there will be pressure (perhaps subtle) to conceal unfavorable data and provide perhaps optimistic reports of the status of various projects or tasks. For example, it is not uncommon to discover only very late in the design stage that a complex and sophisticated design project is behind schedule and over budget.

Information may be processed through several levels in an organizational hierarchy. Repeated filtration and summarization may conceal significant variations in the original data. As a simple example, a division may market two products. If one product results in a loss of $500,000 per year and the other product results in a profit of $800,000 per year, the information that the division produces a profit of $300,000 per year is correct but also seriously misleading.

It can be summarized that an information system must be used wisely to produce organizational benefits. If an information system is not managed properly, and its potential and limitations understood clearly, it can be the source of problems and confusion rather than assistance to its users.

Decision Support Systems

The concept of a **decision support system (DSS)** is a relatively new one, although its antecedents can be traced back to the early 1970s.

Figure 2–5 shows an expanded view of the information systems model presented in Figure 2–4. An additional dimension based on problem structure has been added. Whereas operational decision making is made in a predominantly well-structured environment, strategic decision making occurs in a predominantly unstructured environment. However, unstructured problems exist across the full spectrum of decision making.

A DSS is a computer based system designed to assist a decision maker in a semistructured environment. The system is oriented around using the power of the computer on structured aspects of the problem

Figure 2–5
Expanded Information System Model

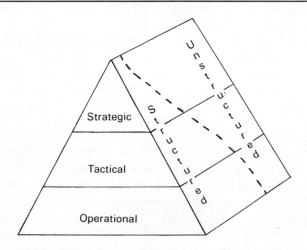

under study while reserving to the decision maker the unstructured aspects of the problem. The DSS provides an organized methodology for the integration of analytical, computer based models with qualitative, subjective inputs.

A DSS is interactive, and perhaps the most important characteristic of a successful DSS is the ease and simplicity of the user interface with the system. The DSS must be designed for a nontechnical user. This implies that technical terminology in the interface must be minimized, if not avoided completely. Error messages must be simple, and the corrective action required must be clear. The system interface must also be written in the terminology of the user, e.g. a physician requires the use of medical terminology, a banker requires financial terminology, etc.

A decision support system must also take into account the various decision styles of its users. It is the user that must dominate and control the DSS. A decision maker will have adopted, over a period of time, certain styles of analysis and decision making. If the DSS does not allow the user to remain reasonably close to that built up (and proven) chain of analysis, the user will find it too counterintuitive or difficult to use the system. It then becomes almost inevitable that he or she will make very limited use of it. It is when the DSS amplifies the user's own analytical approach that it is most successful.

Not only must the DSS provide access to various data required for analysis, but the availability of multiple models is necessary. The models may be generated as needed, perhaps, through the use of a very high level user-oriented language, or be stored and available to the user on a selection basis.

Traditionally, computer based information systems have utilized more and more sophisticated models. It is frequently true that decision support systems utilize less sophisticated models. Yet the DSS may be successful because these models are easily used by the decision maker and mesh comfortably with his or her own decision style.

Finally, a decision support system is evolutionary by nature. A DSS may also serve an educational role for its users. With experience, the decision maker becomes more sophisticated in the use of the DSS. This can result in an improved design and even greater usefulness. Modifications and extensions can be incorporated into the DSS, which allows the decision maker an even greater flexibility and depth of analysis. The design of the DSS is an ongoing effort that combines knowledge from diverse fields into a useful, working tool.

Conclusions

An information system should be an aid to decision making. It accepts as input data, processes those data by means of one or more models, and produces as output information. Information is a resource used to narrow down the number of alternatives (or, at least, changes the probabilities of these alternatives) facing a decision maker.

Informal sources of information always exist and necessarily supplement the output produced by formal sources. Computer based systems are a sophisticated form of formal information systems.

A number of information systems will coexist at any given time within an organization. Some may be tightly coupled (i.e. may share many resources), others may be loosely coupled, and others may operate independently. Not only are the information systems supporting various functional decision-making activities within an organization different, but the level of decision making supported may be reflected in strikingly different designs.

A decision support system is a highly interactive computer based system that is designed to assist decision making in a semistructured environment. It attempts to merge the strengths of the computer with the strengths of its user in a synergistic fashion.

A good information system provides strong support in the form of information for decision makers but does not replace managerial judgment.

References

1. Anthony, R. N. *Planning and Control Systems: A Framework for Analysis.* Boston: Harvard Business School, 1965.
2. Argyris, C. "Resistance to Rational Management Systems." *Innovation,* No. 10 (1970), pp. 28–35.
3. Benbasat, I., and R. N. Taylor. "The Impact of Cognitive Styles on Information System Design." *MIS Quarterly* 2, No. 2 (June 1978), pp. 43–54.
4. Davis, G. B. *Management Information Systems: Conceptual Foundations, Structure and Development.* New York: McGraw-Hill, 1974.
5. Hare, V. C. Jr. "Communication and Information Systems." in *Contemporary Management: Issues and Viewpoints,* ed. J. W. McGuire. Englewood Cliffs, N.J.: Prentice-Hall, 1974, pp. 192–216.
6. Simon, H. A. *The Shape of Automation for Men and Management.* New York: Harper & Row, 1965.
7. Swanson, E. B. "A Parable on the Understanding of a Management Information System." *Interfaces* 3, No. 2 (February 1973), pp. 51–53.

Additional Readings

Ackoff, R. L. "Management Misinformation Systems." *Management Science* 14, No. 4 (December 1967), pp. B140–56.

Alter, S. L. *Decision Support Systems: Current Practice and Continuing Challenges.* Reading, Mass.: Addison-Wesley Publishing, 1980.

Ashby, W. R. "Analysis of the System to be Modelled," in *The Process of Model Building in the Behavioral Sciences,* ed. R. M. Stogdill. New York: W. W. Norton, 1970, pp. 94–113.

Dearden, J. "Myth of Real Time Management Information." *Harvard Business Review* (May-June 1966), pp. 123–32.

————. "MIS Is a Mirage." *Harvard Business Review* (January–February 1972), pp. 90–99.

Deutsch, K. W. *The Nerves of Government.* New York: Free Press, 1966.

Emery, J. C., and C. R. Sprague. "MIS: Mirage or Misconception?" in *Computers and Management in a Changing Society,* ed. D. H. Sanders. New York: McGraw-Hill, 1974, pp. 162–66.

Golomb, S. W. "Mathematical Models: Uses and Limitations." *IEEE Transactions on Reliability* (August 1971), pp. 130–31.

Keen, P. G. W. "Decision Support Systems: Translating Analytic Technique into Useful Tools." *Sloan Management Review* (Spring 1980), pp. 33–44.

Keen, P. G. W., and M. S. S. Morton. *Decision Support Systems: An Organizational Perspective.* Reading, Mass.: Addison-Wesley Publishing, 1978.

Murray, T. J. "Data, Information and Intelligence in a Computer Based Management Information System." *Journal of Applied Systems Analysis* 6 (1979), pp. 101–5.

Rappaport, A. "Management Misinformation Systems—Another Perspective." *Management Science* 15, No. 2 (December 1968), pp. B133–36.

Sprague, R. H. Jr. "A Framework for the Development of Decision Support Systems." *MIS Quarterly* (December 1980), pp. 1–26.

Sprague, R. H. Jr., and E. D. Carlson. *Building Effective Decision Support Systems.* Englewood Cliffs, N.J.: Prentice-Hall, 1982.

Wilensky, H. L. *Organizational Intelligence.* New York: Basic Books, 1967.

Review

1. Why can there be no completely closed system?
2. What is a model?
3. Why are models used?
4. There is only one true model to represent any aspect of reality. Do you agree or disagree? Justify.
5. Differentiate the three levels of decision making.
6. Briefly explain the concept of the total MIS.
7. Explain how information flows may be distorted in an organization because of hierarchy.
8. Explain how information flows may be distorted in an organization because of specialization.
9. What is a decision support system?

Chapter 3

Information Theory

Introduction

Information theory is concerned with measuring quantitatively the amount of something called *information.* The source of information lies in the interaction of model and data. Information theory is concerned with the question: *how much information?*

Information theory limits itself to a rather narrow, specialized view. In this theory, *information* is a term with a precise, technical meaning. Information as used in this sense is not the same as in the colloquial usage of the word. Perhaps the use of the same word to convey both a popular meaning and a narrower, more specialized meaning is unfortunate. However, this is encountered in a number of other situations.

The theory is concerned only with the amount of information. It is not concerned with the content, value, use, or even the truth of the information. Thus, information theory is concerned with an abstract (but quantitative) concept of information that is unrelated to any specific use.

Information theory was originally developed by Shannon[2] and extended by Weaver[2]. Although originally oriented toward telephone communications, it has since provided a framework for studies in many other fields. The theory has not only proven useful in engineering applications but also has provided insights and understanding in a number of other areas. It can be viewed as *a useful way of looking at things.*

Before defining information explicitly, the subject will be approached indirectly. It is hoped that this approach will provide an intuitive feel for the concept of information and some of its implications.

Communication

Communication is the transmission of information from a source to a destination. Figure 3–1 shows a block diagram that illustrates a generalized communication system.

Figure 3–1
Communication System

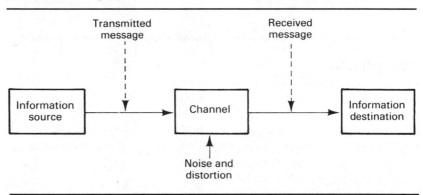

The output of the information source is the transmitted message. For example, if the information source is a person talking, the transmitted message consists of the words spoken. If the information source is a CPU, then the transmitted message consists of digital pulses on an output communication line.

The **channel** is the medium used to transmit the message from the information source to the information destination. For example, it may be the air itself when communication occurs between two people in each other's presence, or it may be the public telephone network.

While the message is passing through the channel, noise or distortion may modify it. In principle, noise and distortion may be differentiated on the basis that **distortion** is a fixed modification of the signal (and thus can be compensated for), while **noise** involves a random perturbation of the signal. In practice, there is really a continuum from pure noise to pure distortion.

The information destination is the person or thing, e.g. a computer terminal, for whom the message is intended. Ideally, all of the information originating at the source arrives at the destination. Practically, noise and distortion reduce the amount of information arriving at the destination.

Assume that the following puzzle is presented. An individual is asked to determine a five-letter word beginning with Q, that is Q ___ ___ ___ ___ is given, and he or she must determine the missing letters. It is known that the word is in the English language. What is the second letter? Phrased another way: How much information is needed to determine the second letter? (Information is used here in an intuitive sense.) In fact, all words (not including acronyms) in the English language beginning with the letter Q have as a second letter U. Q is always followed by U. Thus, there is no uncertainty about the second letter—there is only one possibility: U. No information is needed.

If communication is viewed as the transfer of information, then communication implies the existence of a number of alternatives. Thus, information is gained when one of a number of alternatives is selected. In the above example, since only one possibility exists for the second letter, no information is received when the individual is informed that the letter is a U. Since he or she already knows that there is only one possibility, no information is gained.

By reducing the number of alternative possibilities facing an observer to one, information is reduced to zero, that is, communication is blocked. Ashby[1] offers a greatly simplified example to illustrate this. A prisoner is to be visited by his wife. He is anxious to learn if a confederate in his crime has been apprehended yet. His wife, however, cannot be allowed to send him such a message. The complication is that they may have agreed on a simple code before his capture. At the visit, she asks to send him a cup of coffee. The warden realizes that this may be a code. The canteen normally sells tea and coffee. The warden has coffee delivered, but indicates that the only beverage available is coffee. The code might be contained in the fact that sugar is placed or not placed in the coffee. The warden adds sugar and tells the prisoner that he hopes he did not put too much in. Communication might have been arranged through sending or not sending a spoon. The warden says that regulations forbid any spoons.

In each case in the above example, the warden has attempted to reduce the number of alternatives to one: only coffee, always sugar, and never a spoon. In each case, as the alternatives are forced to one, communication is blocked and no information is gained by the prisoner.

Figure 3–2 shows a more generalized block diagram describing a communications system. In this figure a transmitter/encoder and a receiver/decoder have been added to the system. The transmitter/encoder transforms the message in some way and produces a signal suitable for transmission over the communication channel. The input to the transmitter/encoder is the transmitted message, and the output is the transmitted signal. For example, if the transmitter/encoder is a telephone the transmitted message consists of spoken words. The transmitted signal is a series of electrical oscillations on the telephone line. Another example could involve the transmission of data between a central processing unit and a remote terminal. Data are output by the CPU, and encoded for transmission over a telecommunications line. The receiver/decoder transforms the received signal and attempts to reproduce the original message in the same, or perhaps a different, form.

Communication is the transfer of information between the source and the destination in the system. The encoder may be used to transform the message into a more efficient form in the signal. At the same time, the same amount of information is maintained in the signal as in the transmitted message. The signal may contain it in a more compact form, however. This will be discussed below in more detail.

Figure 3–2
Generalized Communication System

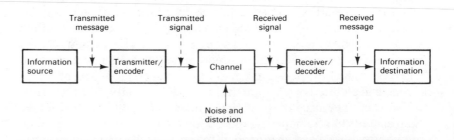

Information Defined

Information is essentially a function of a set of alternatives. The statement that the sun will rise tomorrow contains no information since only one alternative exists, that is, the sun will in fact rise. The statement that it will rain tomorrow contains information since the weather is variable.

Thus, an inherent property of information can be described: *Information is a function of a set of alternatives.*

From this basic idea flows a corollary that, at least on the surface, is quite surprising. *The information conveyed is not a property of the message communicated.* For example, two managers receive the message: profitable. Do they both receive the same information? The answer is: *not necessarily.* If the first individual received the message from the set of alternative messages:

> profitable
> loss

and the second individual received the message from the set of alternative messages:

> very profitable
> profitable
> low profitability
> break even
> small loss
> loss
> high loss

then information theory says that the second individual received more information, since his or her message came from a larger set of possible messages. The reader would probably intuitively feel the same way.

It was stated that the information conveyed is not an intrinsic property of the message. It is a function of the entire context or situation. For example, although the weather is variable, a rainy season exists in some geographic areas, and the statement that *it will rain tomorrow* is expected during that season. The weather forecast contains little information. When two persons who know each other meet or pass each other, the message *hello* or *how are you* may be passed. On someone's birthday, the phrase *happy birthday* is far from unexpected. These phrases all contain very little information. They are expected. In all of the above described situations, one is not surprised. These phrases are expected under the given circumstances. They are considered highly probable.

The amount of information contained in a message is a function of the probability of that message. Thus, a message that is expected and can be predicted with high probability contains little information. The message that is unexpected contains much more information. It is the most infrequent messages that contain the most information.

Information reduces uncertainty, or selects some alternatives as more probable than others. It has been defined as a function of probability only, that is, the information provided by a message is a function of the probability of that message being received out of the ensemble of total possible messages that could have been received.

Appendix 3–1 provides a somewhat more mathematical discussion of the information theory equations. The interested reader is referred to this appendix for further detail. Knowledge of the contents of this appendix is not required for the following discussion.

If the probabilities of the n alternative messages are equal, the amount of information (H) contained in a message is:

$$H = \log_2 n \tag{3–1}$$

If the probabilities are not equal, i.e. message i occurs with probability p_i, then the expected amount of information (H) contained in a message is:

$$H = - \sum_{i=1}^{n} p_i \log_2 p_i \tag{3–2}$$

subject to

$$\sum_{i=1}^{n} p_i = 1$$

Appendix 3–2 shows that these two forms of the basic information definition are equivalent. Equation 3–2 reduces to equation 3–1 in the case of equal probabilities. The basic unit of information has been defined as the **bit.**

As an example, how much information is provided by the flip of a fair (i.e. the probability of a head = the probability of a tail = .5) coin?

$$H = \log_2 2 = 1 \text{ bit}$$

Thus, one bit of information reduces the number of alternatives by half. The original two equally probable alternatives (head and tail) in the example are reduced to only one.

As another example, how much information is needed to answer the question: Will the sun rise tomorrow? There is only one outcome possible: yes.

$$H = \log_2 1 = 0 \text{ bits}$$

As another example, suppose there are eight equally likely outcomes.

$$H = \log_2 8 = 3 \text{ bits}$$

Suppose that these eight equally likely outcomes resulted from three flips of a fair coin. Calculating the information obtained from each flip independently:

$$H = \log_2 2 + \log_2 2 + \log_2 2 = 3 \text{ bits}$$

The result is the same.

As an additional example, consider a standard deck of 52 playing cards. See Appendix 3–3 for logarithms of selected integers. If one card is selected at random from this deck, $\log_2 52 = 5.7$ bits of information are required to answer the question: Which card was selected? If it is revealed that the card is red, then $\log_2 26 = 4.7$ bits of information are still required. Notice that by halving the number of cards under consideration (from 52 to only 26 red cards), one bit of information has been used. If in addition it is revealed that the card is a diamond, $\log_2 13 = 3.7$ bits more are needed to answer the question. In general, any constraint placed on a problem reduces the number of alternatives and therefore reduces the information content of the messages received. The constraint itself may be viewed as information possessing. In the example above, the constraint that the card selected was of a red suit represented one bit of information.

Maximum information is provided in the equally probable case. As the probability distribution of the alternative messages becomes more skewed, less information on the average will be provided with each message received. In the extreme, when one message takes on a probability of one and all other messages take on a probability of zero, zero information is provided. In the two-message case, information provided is distributed approximately as shown in Figure 3–3.

Figure 3–3
Information Distribution in Two-Message Case

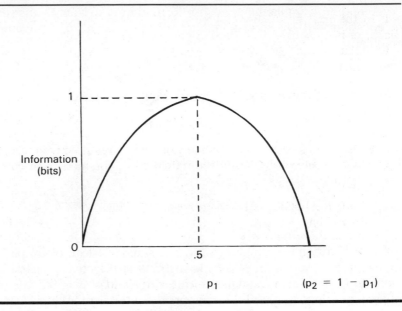

As an example, an information source emits four characters: A, B, C, and D. If they are equally probable:

$$H = \log_2 n = \log_2 4 = 2 \text{ bits}$$

The appearance of one of these characters provides two bits of information. In other terms, two bits of information, that is, pieces of information of the yes and no type, are needed to determine which will occur. We could look at the questions as follows: Dividing these four characters into two groups:

A

B

C

D

we ask: Is it in the first group?(first question). If the answer is *no*, for example, we ask looking at the second group:

C

D

Is it in the first group?(second question). If the answer is *yes*, the character is, of course, C; if the answer is *no*, the character is D.

Calculating the information content of the same source but with the characters appearing not equally probable and assuming:

$$p(A) = 0.4$$
$$p(B) = 0.3$$
$$p(C) = 0.2$$
$$p(D) = 0.1$$

See Appendix 3–4 for logarithms for fractions.

$$H = -0.4\log_2 0.4 - 0.3\log_2 0.3 - 0.2\log_2 0.2 - 0.1\log_2 0.1$$
$$= -0.4(-1.322) - 0.3(-1.737) - 0.2(-2.322) - 0.1(-3.322)$$
$$= 1.847 \text{ bits}$$

Again assume:

$$p(A) = 0.7$$
$$p(B) = 0.1$$
$$p(C) = 0.1$$
$$p(D) = 0.1$$

$$H = -0.7\log_2 0.7 - 3[0.1 \log_2 0.1]$$
$$= -0.7(-0.515) - 3[0.1 (-3.322)]$$
$$= 0.3605 + 1.0066$$
$$= 1.357 \text{ bits}$$

Note that by simply changing the probability distribution of the source messages, the information content is changed.

There are a number of assumptions made concerning the information source. To the extent that these assumptions are at least approximately true, the information calculated as shown above is meaningful.

The probability distribution of the output of the source must be stable, that is, it cannot change with time.

The source must be **ergodic;** in other words, if observed over a reasonable period of time the sequence of output messages will be typical of the distribution.

It should also be observed that if the successive messages produced by the source are not statistically independent, then a reduction in average information per message results.

Redundancy and Efficient Encoding

It has been shown that as soon as some alternative messages become more probable than others, the average information per message decreases.

Consider an unfair coin that will result in 90 percent heads and 10 percent tails. The average information obtained from a flip of this coin is:

$$-.90 \log_2 .90 - .10 \log_2 .10 \quad =$$
$$-.90\,(-0.152) - .10\,(-3.322) =$$
$$0.469 \text{ bits}$$

As expected, this is less than the maximum information that would have been obtained from a flip of a fair coin, i.e. $\log_2 2 = 1$ bit. This means that with 1,000 flips of the unfair coin 469 bits of information are obtained, whereas with a fair coin 1,000 bits of information would have been gained. Another view of this is that the same amount of information, i.e. 469 bits, should have been obtainable with only 469 flips of a fair coin. There is redundancy, or excess, in the flips of the unfair coin, since 1,000 flips produce the same information that ideally only 469 flips could produce.

Redundancy is defined as:

$$1 - \frac{H_{\text{actual}}}{H_{\text{max}}}$$

In the example redundancy is:

$$1 - \frac{469}{1,000} = 53.1\%$$

Any stream of messages from a source in which the messages do not occur with equal probability can be recoded in such a way that fewer symbols may be used without any loss of information.

For simplicity, assume that the source emits only two symbols: A and B. The encoder accepts as input a string of these two symbols and produces as output a string of 0s and 1s.

If the symbols A and B appear with equal probability, then each occurrence contributes one bit of information. The simplest encoding scheme, e.g. encode A as a 0 and B as a 1, is also the most efficient. A string of 1,000 such binary digits transmits 1,000 bits of information over the channel.

If the symbols occur as 90 percent A and 10 percent B, then the source is producing 469 bits of information per 1,000 symbols. A *brute force* but simple method would use the same encoding scheme as above. A more efficient method might be to encode the symbols in accordance with the following scheme:

Symbol Pair	Code	Probability	Weighted Average
AA	0	0.81	0.81
AB	10	0.09	0.18
BA	110	0.09	0.27
BB	111	0.01	0.03
			1.39

In this scheme the most frequent pair is replaced by the shortest code and the least frequent by the longest. As a result, the average code length per symbol is reduced.

In the simple coding scheme one binary digit contains only 0.469 bits of information, or 469 bits require 1,000 binary digits.

In this scheme an average of 1.39 binary digits are required for each pair of symbols, or each symbol requires, on the average, 0.695 binary digits. The 469 bits of information are now carried by 695 binary digits.

To summarize:

Coding Scheme	Binary Digits/Symbol	Bits of Information/Binary Digit
Simple	1	0.469
Complex	0.695	0.675

The coding scheme can be made even more efficient, that is, each binary digit can carry more information and therefore fewer binary digits are required per symbol. The cost is that the coding/decoding scheme becomes more complex.

In the ideal scheme, each binary digit carries one bit of information. As a result, in the example only 469 binary digits are needed to carry all of the information generated by the source. In this example 469 is an absolute minimum. No coding scheme can do better than this.

It is interesting to note that Samuel Morse, in developing his code for the telegraph, realized that letters of the alphabet do not occur with equal frequency. A count of the number of pieces of type for each letter found at a printer's shop gave him an estimate of relative frequencies. He then assigned the shortest codes to the most frequent letters.

Figure 3–4 is another way of viewing redundancy. The information contained in message 1 is represented by the shaded area / / / . The information contained in message 2 is represented by the shaded area \ \ \ . But not all of the information received from message 2 is new—some of it has already been received with message 1. Thus redundancy is represented by the overlap area.

It should not be assumed that redundancy is necessarily an undesirable characteristic in any communication. Redundancy serves as the basis for error detection and correction. For example, the English language (or any natural language) is highly redundant. Letters can be correctly recognized more easily within the context of words; words can be recognized more easily within the context of sentences.

If all 26 letters of the alphabet and a space were equally probable, each symbol would provide $\log_2 27$, or 4.755 bits of information. Experiments seem to indicate that each character in standard English offers, on the average, approximately 1.4 bits of information. Thus redundancy in the language may be approximately:

Figure 3–4
Relationship between Information and Redundancy

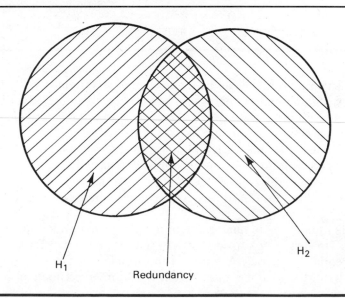

H_1

Redundancy

H_2

$$1 - \frac{1.4}{4.755} = 71\%$$

If the language were not redundant, then any error in a sequence of characters would transform that sequence into another equally legitimate sequence of characters. Redundancy reduces significantly the probability of that mistake.

Error detection and correction schemes are used both in the computer and with data transmitted over a telecommunications line. These schemes are implemented by introducing redundancy into the coding schemes used. Chapter 5 discusses some aspects of this topic. Some data compression schemes simply reduce the redundancy contained in a set of data to achieve a more compact data representation. Chapter 12 discusses this in more detail.

Channel Capacity

A characteristic of all practical communication channels is that there is a maximum amount of information per unit time that they can

Figure 3–5
Channel Capacity

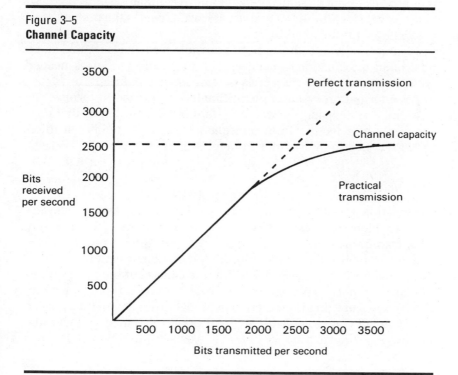

transmit with high reliability. This upper limit is called the **channel capacity (C).** As long as the amount of information (H) transmitted is less than the channel capacity (H <C), it can be received with an arbitrarily small number of errors. An increasing number of errors is inherent in transmission at a rate higher than C. Figure 3–5 illustrates channel capacity.

Channel capacity as an upper reliable limit seems to describe the operation of channels of many types. As the pulse rate transmitted over a telecommunications line increases, distortion and attenuation of the pulses eventually cause the reception of a meaningless signal at the far end of the line. Information overload in human beings may also be viewed as an exceeding of the individual's channel capacity. A well-designed information system must take into account the many forms of channels within the system and their capacities.

Information and Decision Making

The purpose of an information system is to provide information to a decision maker. The decision maker must select from a number of alternatives. Information is what either eliminates some of these alternatives (ideally all but one) or, at least, changes the probabilities associated with the alternatives.

Clearly if only one alternative is possible for a decision maker, no additional information is needed. The most information is needed when multiple alternatives of equal probability are faced.

An information system must ultimately be judged in terms of its assistance to decision makers. A system producing output that does not assist in selecting from multiple alternatives (i.e. is not information) is not an information system.

Conclusions

Information theory is not so much a methodology as a framework within which some aspects of information systems can be viewed. This framework can lead to a more in-depth understanding of various relationships facing the information system designer.

It must be emphasized that within the context of the theory information does not imply meaning, truth, value, etc. It is purely a quantitative measure that is a function of probabilities alone. Information theory is not concerned with any real world relationship or with the meaning of information to users. It exists in an abstract form in isolation from either meaning or user. Yet it has proven to be an extremely useful tool in practice.

The information theory is able to offer a means of understanding a number of topics in otherwise widely separated fields. The revealing of the underlying information theory structure in these fields means that only one model, i.e. information theory, is needed to provide explanations. Without information theory, multiple explanations are needed. The framework provided by information theory may clarify topics in the fields of:

decision making (Chapter 2)
sorting (Chapter 8)
binary search (Chapter 9)
data compression (Chapter 12)
cryptography (Chapter 14)

References

1.   Ashby, W. R. *An Introduction to Cybernetics,* chapter 7. London: Chapman and Hall, Ltd., 1956.
2.   Shannon, C. E., and W. Weaver. *The Mathematical Theory of Communication.* Urbana, Ill.: University of Illinois Press, 1949.

Additional Readings

Cherry, C. *On Human Communication.* Cambridge, Mass.: MIT Press, 1957.
Hamming, R. W. *Coding and Information Theory.* Englewood Cliffs, N.J.: Prentice-Hall, 1980.
MacKay, D. M. *Information, Mechanism, and Meaning.* Cambridge, Mass.: MIT Press, 1969.
Singh, J. *Great Ideas in Information Theory, Language, and Cybernetics.* New York: Dover Publications, Inc., 1966.

Review

1.   How many bits of information are needed to select 1 out of 30 equally probable alternatives?
2.   How many bits of information are needed to reduce the number of equally probable alternatives facing a decision maker from 20 to 5?
3.   Assume that the basic unit of information had been defined as that required to select one from three equally likely alternatives.

    (a) How many units of this *information* would be required to select
        1 from 27 equally likely alternatives?

    (b) How many questions with three possible answers would be
        needed to select 1 from 81 equally likely alternatives?

4.   If a report to a decision maker is in error, does it provide information
    to that decision maker? Justify your answer.

Appendix 3–1
Information Theory Background

In addition to being dependent on probability alone, the information function should also be:

1. Continuous.
2. At probability $= 0$ should be infinite.
3. At probability $= 1$ should be zero.
4. Monotonically decreasing as the probability takes on values from 0 to 1.

Such a function is shown in Figure 3–6.

Figure 3–6
Graph of the Information/Probability Relationship

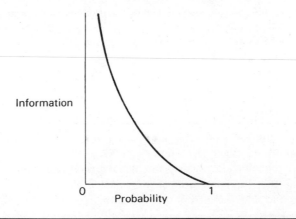

The function that has been used in the definition of information which meets the above criteria is logarithmic. The information received with the occurrence of a message with probability p is defined as:

$$h = \log_2 \frac{1}{p} = -\log_2 p$$

If two possible messages may occur with probabilities p_1 and p_2 then the information associated with message 1 is $-\log_2 p_1$ and the information associated with message 2 is $-\log_2 p_2$. The **expected information** obtained from the occurrence of a message from the set of message 1 and message 2 is:

$$H = -p_1 \log_2 p_1 - p_2 \log_2 p_2$$

In general, the expected value of the information obtained per message from a set of n messages is:

$$H = -\sum_{i=1}^{n} p_i \log_2 p_i$$

subject to

$$\sum_{i=1}^{n} p_i = 1$$

The choice of the logarithm to the base 2 (rather than another base) is discussed below.

Approaching the problem from another direction, the following argument (which is parallel to that of Raisbeck[1]) is presented.

Figure 3–7 shows a *black box*, that is, a system whose inputs and outputs may be observed but whose inner workings remain unknown. This box will be considered an information source. When the start switch is thrown, the box operates and one of n lights on an

Figure 3–7
Information Source

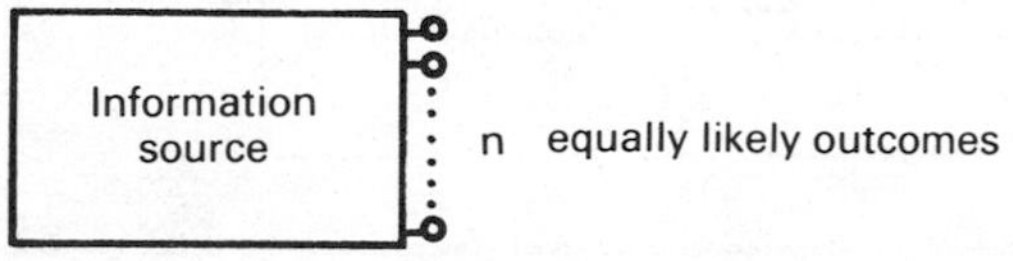

Information
source   n   equally likely outcomes

output panel comes on. Additionally, it is known that any one of the n lights may come on with equal probability. As n increases, more information is required to select the correct outcome or an outcome provides more information.

Figure 3–8 shows two independent information sources similar to that in Figure 3–7. Both are contained in another black box.

If there are n_1 possible outcomes from information source 1 and n_2 possible outcomes from information source 2, then the total number of possible output combinations is $n_1 \cdot n_2$. It would appear reasonable that if some amount of information is provided by source 1 and some amount of information is provided by source 2, then the amount of information provided by both should be the sum of the two. Thus, where $n = n_1 \cdot n_2$, $f(n) = f(n_1) + f(n_2)$ where $f(\ )$ is a function operating on the number of alternatives to give the information.

A number of solutions are possible for this problem. The one that information theory uses is:

$$f(n) = c \log n \qquad \text{(in general)}$$

Two questions remain: (1) what base logarithm should be used? and (2) what value for the constant c should be used?

Figure 3–8
Two Independent Information Sources

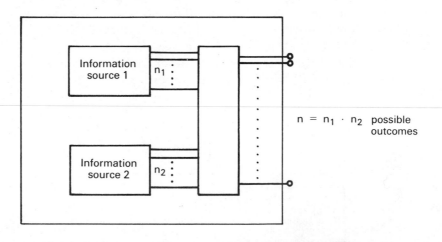

The simplest possible case is that of flipping a coin. Two outcomes are possible: heads or tails. The logarithm base 2 was chosen. In this simplest case, one unit of information is defined. The value for c was set equal to 1. The unit of information is called a **bit** and the symbol used is H.

Reference

1. Raisbeck, G. *Information Theory.* Cambridge, Mass.: MIT Press, 1963, chapter 1.

Appendix 3–2
Information Theory Formulas

$$H = - \sum_{i=1}^{n} p_i \log_2 p_i$$

subject to

$$\sum_{i=1}^{n} p_i = 1$$

When n outcomes are equally probable:

$$p_i = \frac{1}{n}$$

Substituting:

$$\log_2 p_i = \log_2 \frac{1}{n} = -\log_2 n$$

Substituting again:

$$\sum_{i=1}^{n} -p_i \log_2 p_i = \sum_{i=1}^{n} \frac{1}{n} \log_2 n = \log_2 n$$

which demonstrates the equivalence of these forms when the alternatives are equally probable.

Appendix 3–3

Logarithms (Base 2) of Selected Integers

n	$\log_2 n$	n	$\log_2 n$
1	0	24	4.585
2	1.000	26	4.700
3	1.585	27	4.755
4	2.000	28	4.807
5	2.322	30	4.907
6	2.585	32	5.000
7	2.807	36	5.170
8	3.000	40	5.322
9	3.170	44	5.459
10	3.322	48	5.585
11	3.459	50	5.644
12	3.585	52	5.700
13	3.700	55	5.781
14	3.807	60	5.907
15	3.907	64	6.000
16	4.000	70	6.129
17	4.087	75	6.229
18	4.170	80	6.322
19	4.248	85	6.409
20	4.322	90	6.492
22	4.459	100	6.644

Appendix 3–4

Logarithms (Base 2) of Selected Fractions

p	$\log_2 p$	p	$\log_2 p$
0.05	-4.322	0.55	-0.862
0.10	-3.322	0.60	-0.737
0.15	-2.737	0.65	-0.621
0.20	-2.322	0.70	-0.515
0.25	-2.000	0.75	-0.415
0.30	-1.737	0.80	-0.322
0.35	-1.515	0.85	-0.234
0.40	-1.322	0.90	-0.152
0.45	-1.152	0.95	-0.074
0.50	-1.000	1.00	0

Chapter 4

Data Input and Error Control

Introduction

No information system can be better than the data entered into it. Inaccurate data result in lower quality information, which can result in poorer decision making. Even a relatively low level of inaccurate data entering a system may result in a loss of confidence in the system by its users. In addition, some errors will be cumulative and result in a continuing deterioration in the quality of information produced. The acronym **GIGO,** that is, Garbage In Garbage Out, is used to convey the realization that confidence in the output of an information system can be no better than the accuracy of its input.

A three-step philosophy should exist for error control of input data:

1. Prevent erroneous data from entering the system.
2. Detect any such data that do, in fact, enter the system.
3. Eliminate from the system any erroneous data detected and undo the effect of using these erroneous data.

This philosophy recognizes an important aspect of such error control: *Errors cannot be completely eliminated, but their effect on the quality of the information produced by the system must be minimized.*

Most input data are processed by human operators. It is a fact of life that human beings are subject to error and, therefore, some errors must be expected in data input. Making the assumption that only accurate data will enter an information system is an invitation to failure. Since some error is inevitable, a general principle may be stated as follows: *The earlier an error is caught, the less expensive will its correction be.*

The details of the data input process depend on the method of processing. Different processing methods have different requirements for data input handling.

Methods of Processing

There are two general methods of processing data used in computer based systems: batch processing and on-line processing. The characteristics of these methods of processing differ in many ways, including the handling of data input. Both batch processing and on-line processing may be implemented on the same computer system, that is, some applications on a system may be batch processed while other applications are on-line.

In **batch processing,** data are grouped (or batched) outside the computer system and then entered into the computer as a batch. The program required and any instructions for the computer system are made available. The processing is carried out without user intervention, and the job is run to completion. Once a batch program begins execution, the user is returned either a successful run or an abnormal termination with no possibility for ongoing modification of the job.

Although batch processing is the older of the two methods of processing, it is still used for many applications. The arguments for batch processing include the following:

1. Programming a batch application is simpler.
2. Greater efficiency in computer time and the use of other resources can be had.
3. Less hardware, e.g. less teleprocessing-oriented equipment, may be needed.

Two modifications of batch processing may be encountered. These are remote batch and remote job entry.

A **remote batch** capability allows the transmission of the batched input data from a remote site over a telecommunications line to a central computer. A **remote job entry (RJE)** capability allows not only batched data but also programs and instructions for the system to be entered remotely and transmitted to a central computer. RJE hardware provides greater flexibility and capabilities to the remote site batch users.

In **on-line processing,** data are entered a transaction at a time into the computer for immediate processing. Data are not batched first but can be entered into the system as they become available. On-line systems may also transmit the results of processing directly to the locations requiring these results. For example, an order entry system may accept data on a new order from a sales office terminal and print out a picking slip at a warehouse terminal.

Real time processing is a form of on-line processing that provides a response back to the user within a period of time short enough (usually no more than a few seconds) to affect the user's next input. It is on-line processing with a low response time.

Time sharing is a form of real time processing in which a small amount of time, called a time slice and measured in thousandths of a second, is allocated to each of a number of jobs in a sequential fashion. As a result, multiple users obtain real time processing on an interleaved basis. Time sharing is highly interactive for each user.

On-line processing offers the following advantages:

1. Data may be processed rapidly.
2. Data input and search can be carried out in any order.
3. A series of job steps in a batch environment may be compressed into one step in an on-line environment.
4. Both input and output are extended out from the central site to those locations most appropriate (i.e. users interact directly with the system and do not require intermediate handling of input and output).

On-line processing necessitates that data files and programs required be on-line, that is, available directly to the system without human intervention. It also necessitates direct access (see Chapter 7).

Identification Codes

An **identification code** is an abbreviation used to identify a particular piece of data. As examples, identification codes may be used to specify a particular customer, patient, salesperson, manufactured or stocked part, product, student, course offering, etc. In essence the use of an identification code, such as 6317, instead of a full customer identification, such as World Wide Widget Company of St. Louis, Missouri, results in a number of efficiencies. It allows easier manipulation, e.g. sorting, of data in a computer based system. As an abbreviation it requires fewer characters for manual recording of data, for transmission, and data entry into the computer. As a result, less time is spent in the total data input phase. Identification codes are also important because they usually serve as the basis for searching and frequently are the basis for sorting data.

An identification code should ideally have the following characteristics:

1. It should be **unique** (i.e. the code should identify only one data item). The same code should not represent two or more data items.
2. It should be **expandable** (i.e. it should be possible to easily add new identification codes as new data items are added).
3. It should be **compact** (i.e. it should represent a set of data items in a minimum number of characters).
4. It should be **precise** (i.e. the rules for the creation of an identification code for a new data item should result in only one possible code).
5. It should be of **fixed size** (i.e. each identification code for a set of data items should contain the same number of characters).
6. It should be **meaningful** (i.e. the code should convey to a user at least some information on the data item represented).

It should be clear upon reflection that not all of the above characteristics are completely compatible with each other. For example, a code may not be completely compact, of fixed length, and also provide an opportunity for expansion. Similarly, the characteristics of compactness and meaningfulness are somewhat inconsistent. In fact, a reasonable balance of these characteristics is sought. Of course, in any given application one characteristic may be more desirable than another.

There is a tradeoff between compactness and flexibility. Costs of data capture, transmission, data entry, storage, and both human and computer processing increase as the length of the code increases. However, categorization, statistical analysis, and other types of data studies become easier as the code length increases.

The following discusses four general identification code schemes commonly used in computer based systems and one phonetically based identification code. Variations on these basic coding schemes may also be encountered.

Pure Serial Code

In a **pure serial code** the code is assigned in the sequential order of its characters as data items are added. For example, assuming that a numeric code is to be used as an employee number, the first employee is assigned identification number 1, the next number 2, etc. It is conceptually the simplest type of identification code.

Advantages of the pure serial code are:

1. It is short.
2. It is unique.
3. It is precise.

Disadvantages of the pure serial code are:

1. The data items cannot be maintained in any order other than that in which the code was assigned.
2. It is not very meaningful.
3. Insertions to maintain an inherent order cannot be made in the data item list without recoding at least part of the list.
4. Deletions in the data item list leave gaps in the code.

Assuming that there are N data items to be coded and n characters are to be used in the code, then the minimum number of code positions required is:

$$\lceil \log_n N \rceil$$

where the symbols $\lceil \ \rceil$ designate the integer value equal to or next highest over the argument.

For example, if 10,000 data items are to be encoded using the 10 numeric digits, then $N = 10,000$ and $n = 10$. In this case:

$$\lceil \log_{10} 10,000 \rceil = 4$$

This means that a minimum of four character positions is required to represent this data item list. The codes assigned would be 0000 through 9999. For most applications 0000 would probably not be used as a valid code.

If 500 items are to be encoded with the 10 numeric digits, then:

$$\lceil \log_{10} 500 \rceil = 3$$

and if the same 500 items are to be encoded using the 26 alphabetic characters, then :

$$\lceil \log_{26} 500 \rceil = 2$$

Pure Block Code

In a **pure block code** the full range of the code is divided into segments or blocks. Data items possessing some particular characteristic are assigned to the same block. For example, account codes in an accounting system might be assigned as follows:

Fixed assets	100 series
Current assets	200 series
Fixed liabilities	300 series
Current liabilities	400 series
Expenses	500 series
etc.	

Expense accounts in this example might be numbered:

Payroll	500
Overtime	510
Travel	515
Supplies	520
etc.	

Advantages of the pure block code are:

1. New data items may be inserted within a block as long as unused codes remain within that block (i.e the block is expandable).
2. The code contains some meaning.

Disadvantages of the pure block code are:

1. It is not as compact as the pure serial code.
2. Meaningfulness is limited.
3. Gaps exist in the code.

Multiple Block Code

In a **multiple block code** more than one set of blocks may be used to categorize the data items. The identification code is divided into blocked areas, each of which identifies a particular characteristic of the data item. For example, the U.S. Post Office's zip code is a multiple block code.

Figure 4–1 shows the makeup of a typical zip code. In the example 6 represents a major region covering the northern midwestern states of the United States, 31 represents the sectional sorting center at St. Louis, and 21 is a local post office.

Figure 4–1
Zip Code Interpretation

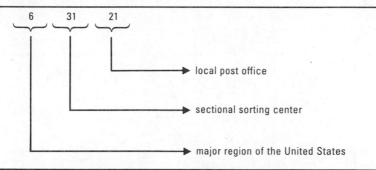

Advantages of the multiple block code are:

1. It is more meaningful than the single block code.
2. It is expandable as long as gaps remain within the appropriate sectors of the code.

Disadvantages of the multiple block code are:

1. It is not as compact as other codes.
2. Blocks must be very carefully defined, and the maximum length within each block must be very carefully estimated.
3. It is possible that some codes may not be unique.

Serialized Block Code

In a **serialized block code** a unique serial number is added to either a single or multiple block code. In some applications it is possible that a block code does not provide a unique identification. In such a case the code is made unique by the addition of a serial number. For example, one form of a men's clothing code consists of five parts as shown in Figure 4–2. Since there may be more than one size 40, regular cut, style 12, color 17 suit, the serial number 05 is added. This identifies specifically which suit is being referenced. Advantages and disadvantages are clearly similar to those of any block code, except that uniqueness is guaranteed as long as gaps remain in the serial number component of the code.

Soundex Code

The **Soundex** system is phonetically based. It is used to code surnames and is frequently used in connection with telephone or

Figure 4–2
A Serialized Block Code

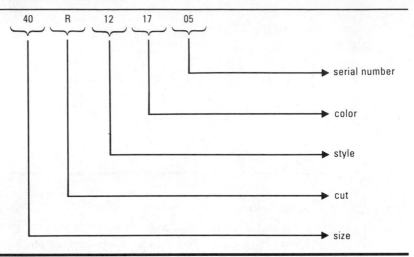

radio inquiries. The code contains one letter and three numbers. The objective of this coding system is not to produce a unique code, but to produce the same code for all surnames sounding alike. In some situations the spelling of a name is uncertain, yet a number of different spellings may be common. For example, SMID, SMIT, SMITH, SMYTH, and SMYTHE are all spelled differently but may be pronounced similarly.

The rules for creating the code are as follows:

1. Keep the first letter.
2. Delete the letters: A, E, I, O, U, Y, W, and H.
3. Assign the following numbers for the remaining letters—

    B, F, P, V   -   1
    C, G, J, K, Q, S, X, Z -   2
    D, T   -   3
    L   -   4
    M, N   -   5
    R   -   6

4. Add zeros, if necessary, to complete a code of one letter and three numbers.
5. Ignore any remaining letters.

Using these rules, the surname SMITH would be encoded as S530 (as would its four alternates in the example above). The surname MURRAY would be encoded as M660 and the surname BECKER as B226.

An operator retrieves data on all surnames identified by the code. An additional piece of identifying data (e.g. an employee number, a social security number, or a home address) is then needed to select the correct set of data from the collection of candidates.

Data Input

Though usually considered a rather prosaic operation, data input is a critical phase in the operation of any computer based information system. **Data input** is concerned with the steps required in the handling of data before it is ready for processing. The information provided in the output of the system is obviously no better than the data provided in the input.

Data Input in a Batch Environment

Figure 4–3 illustrates the steps making up data input in a batch environment. It shows the handling of a batch of data through the data input process.

Figure 4–3
Data Input in a Batch Environment

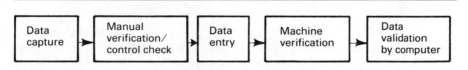

Data capture is concerned with the original entering of data on a source document. This is frequently done by hand and may be entered on a standard form by an operator, poll-taker, accountant, or other noncomputer-oriented personnel. After preparation these documents are usually manually verified for completeness, accuracy, reasonableness, etc. This manual verification may also form a part of a broader control system. For example, foremen, managers, or other supervisory personnel may exercise this control function.

The source documents are then transmitted to a location for data entry. Data may be transmitted by hand, internal mail, external mail (e.g. by the Postal Service), or other means. Data entry is concerned with the transformation of data from the form contained on a source document to a machine-readable form. After conversion, machine verification is usually carried out.

The machine-readable data are then preprocessed by the computer. The data are checked for errors or inconsistencies. This is called **data validation.** Data successfully passing this validation may then be processed further.

The sources of errors that may occur in the data entry step cover a wide range. Some typical sources are:

1. Data on the source documents are incorrect (e.g. the wrong part number has been entered).
2. Data on the source documents are illegible.
3. Data on the source documents are misread.
4. The data entry operator may enter data incorrectly (e.g. the operator strikes the wrong key on a keyboard).

Some factors which can tend to increase the incidence of the above sources of error are:

1. Poorly designed source documents.
2. Inconsistency in data recording procedures.
3. Nonstandardized formation of data characters (e.g. not clearly differentiating between the digit *zero* and the letter *o*).
4. Operator environmental factors (e.g. poor lighting, lack of adequate training, etc.).

Data input in a batch environment is usually made by means of punched cards. The **keypunch** is the basic data entry device that punches data into a punched card. The **verifier** is a device that accepts as input a deck of cards already punched. The operator reenters the data from the same source documents. A mismatch between the reentered data and punched data indicates a possible error calling for reentry.

The basic assumption in keypunch-verify operations is that the probability of two operators independently making the same error is small. It should be noted, however, that incorrect data entered on the source documents will not be caught. In addition, errors associated with illegible or easily misread data characters may not be significantly reduced.

Although punched cards were the dominant medium for many years, they are now rapidly decreasing in usage for data entry. Data may also be entered for batch processing through a terminal. The data are accumulated into a batch and then processed.

Turnaround documents are sometimes used in billing applications. The computer-produced bill includes a punched card containing the amount owed and the customer account number. The customer returns this card with the payment. If the payment submitted equals the payment due, the card is simply used directly as data input to the account updating program. Only if the payment received differs from the payment due is a new data input card prepared. By using correctly punched cards in the vast majority of payment cases, the possibility of data entry error is greatly reduced.

Data Input in an On-Line Environment

Figure 4–4 illustrates the steps making up data input in an on-line environment. It shows the handling of a single transaction through the data input process. A transaction may still be captured on a source document that is manually verified. The transaction is then entered into the system by a data entry operator, and validation is carried out on that transaction.

Figure 4–4
Data Input in an On-Line Environment

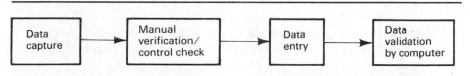

Source data recording combines the data capture and the data entry functions. As a by-product of the data capture function, data are produced in a machine-readable form. The improved meaningfulness of the data to the data input personnel and the elimination of intermediate steps in the data input process should result in increased accuracy of the data. The occurrences of some types of errors may be minimized, and the expense of operating two sequential data input functions may be reduced.

As an example, factory information systems accept data from badge readers. When an employee begins or ends a job, he or she inserts an individual badge into the reader. This employee identification allows the time of the employee to be allocated from one job to another for accounting purposes and for tracking jobs through the manufacturing process.

Data Entry Devices

There is a wide range of data entry techniques. A general principle in data entry is: *The operator should enter the minimum amount of data necessary. All data that can be provided by the computer should be.* If the amount of data entered is reduced, data entry time is saved and the number of data entry errors is reduced. The use of identification codes is one means of accomplishing this. Data entry devices include the following.

Buffered Keypunch

A **buffered keypunch** contains two small memory areas, or buffers. The operator punches the data directly into an input buffer rather than directly into a punched card. Data entered are displayed on a CRT. Corrections can be made simply by *backspacing* and replacing any incorrect characters in the buffer. When the operator has completed entry, the contents of the input buffer are transferred to the output buffer. The operator enters data for the next card into the now available input buffer and, in parallel, data in the output buffer are punched into a card.

Buffered keypunches may also operate in a verify mode. This eliminates the necessity of having two different types of equipment, that is, keypunch and verifier, and, as a result, provides greater flexibility in keypunch job assignments.

Advantages of a buffered keypunch over a standard keypunch include:

1. Ease of correction by backspacing.
2. Fewer wasted punch cards due to incorrect punching.
3. Greater speed in that data may be entered for one card while the previous card is still being punched.

The buffered keypunch is a batch environment data entry device.

Key-to-Tape

With a **key-to-tape system** data are entered directly onto a magnetic tape from a keyboard. Punched cards are eliminated as an interim storage medium. There is also usually a speed advantage over a keypunch.

Key-to-tape devices also offer some display capability so that the data entered may be viewed as a check. Another advantage of these devices over punched cards is that record lengths may be variable. The maximum number of characters that may be punched onto one punched card is 80. The number of characters that can form a record on tape may exceed this. As a result, greater flexibility and efficiency in input formatting is possible.

If a large number of different data entry jobs are processed, new tapes must be mounted frequently. If one large data entry job is entered on more than one key-to-tape device, the data will be contained on more than one tape. It is also possible that, although one data entry job may be spread over several tapes, parts of more than one job may be contained on any one tape. **Pooling** is a procedure that separates out and combines onto one tape the entries for a single job for input to a computer.

Key-to-Cassette

Key-to-cassette devices are really another form of the key-to-tape concept. These devices write the data entered through a keyboard not on a computer-compatible tape but on a cassette tape. The contents of these tapes must later be transferred (and converted) onto a computer-compatible tape before computer processing may proceed. The cassettes may be hand carried or mailed to a pooling/ conversion station. When located at a site remote from a central computing facility, their contents may be transmitted over a telephone line to the central site.

One advantage of such devices is the ease of changing tapes. A cassette may be easily removed and a replacement made within seconds, whereas a larger tape must be rewound and its replacement mounted.

Key-to-Disk

A **key-to-disk system** is also called a **shared processor system.** The heart of the system is a minicomputer. Figure 4–5 illustrates a typical configuration of such a system. Data entry is made by means of a keyboard device. Multiple keyboard stations are controlled by the single processor. Data are stored on disk. Batches of data for the same job may be entered at different keyboard stations. These batches are logically linked together on disk. Output for a job is provided on a computer-compatible tape. Disk serves only as an interim storage facility until data entry for a particular job has been completed. Of course, data for multiple jobs will generally be in various stages of entry and storage at any given time. In some appli-

Figure 4–5
Key-to-Disk Configuration

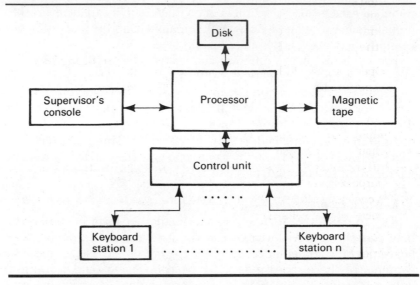

cations some of the keyboard stations may be located at sites remote from the processor and connected over telephone lines.

Because of the processor capabilities, extensive error checking and editing may be employed in a key-to-disk system. An operator may enter data from a source document in a sequential fashion and then rearrange those data into another order in the processor.

Various statistics on operator error rates, keyboard station usage, etc. can also be provided. These are made available at a supervisor's console. In addition, the supervisor may determine the status of any data entry job through the console.

Terminals

A **terminal** is a device that provides data as input to a central processing unit and accepts output from that unit. It is usually located at a site remote from the central processor and connected by a telecommunications link to the processor.

Operations at a terminal may involve only retrieving data from a file or updating (i.e. changing) the contents of the file itself. Clearly errors occurring in an updating application are of greater concern than those involved in a *read-only* operation. The problem of cumulative errors is a real one in a batch environment; it is an especially serious one in an on-line environment. Cumulative errors result in a continually deteriorating file status. As a result, extensive error checking is required.

In addition to error checking that is applicable in a batch environment, the following rules may be of value:

1. Operators should be notified immediately after an error has been committed.
2. Data entered should be displayed for operator verification before any further action is taken.
3. Alphabetic descriptors for identification codes entered or selected should be displayed, if possible.
4. All transactions should be numbered for later identification and for purposes of error recovery.
5. A check should be made that all data required for a transaction have been entered before further processing is attempted.

The two most commonly used types of terminals are teleprinters and cathode ray tube (CRT) display units. CRT terminals are also called video display terminals (VDTs). A teleprinter uses a keyboard for input and prints its output in hard copy form. A CRT terminal usually has a keyboard for input (although other input devices, e.g. a light pen, may be used) and displays its output on a CRT screen. No hard copy output is directly available. An option to also copy the displayed output on a small printer is, however, available on many devices.

The two major categories of CRT terminals are alphanumeric and graphic terminals. An **alphanumeric CRT terminal** can display only alphabetic, numeric, or special symbol data. **Graphic terminals** may display pictorial data, such as graphs, charts, etc.

An **intelligent terminal** is one that contains some processing capability. As a result, the terminal may carry out some processing that would otherwise have to be carried out by the central computer. Although there is a wide range of capability, the intelligent terminal is most frequently used to validate input data and to check for errors. Microcomputers (see Chapter 5) are also used as intelligent terminals. Nonintelligent terminals are called **dumb terminals.**

Magnetic Ink Character Recognition

Magnetic ink character recognition (MICR) involves directly sensing characters recorded in magnetic ink on a document and is a form of source data recording. To date, MICR has been used almost exclusively in the banking industry. The American Banking Association has standardized on a print font known as **E–13B.** This font uses 14 standard characters: the 10 numeric digits and 4 special symbols.

The characters are preprinted on checks, and the checks serve directly as the input medium. The amount of the check must be entered on the check manually using a keyboard device known as a **proof-inscriber.** Thus a limited data capture function is still required. The checks are read and sorted by a **MICR reader-sorter,** which both physically sorts the checks and accepts as input to a computer based system the data read from the checks.

An advantage of a MICR system is that the characters are both human-readable and machine-readable. Disadvantages include the lack of alphabetic and other special characters, and the requirement to enter the amount of each check manually.

Optical Character Recognition

Optical character recognition (OCR) equipment senses characters or coded representations of characters directly by their shape and is another form of source data recording. The contents of the source documents are read directly by the OCR equipment. The read operation is accomplished by recognizing a difference between light reflection from a dark character and from its light surrounding area. Since a white surface reflects a greater amount of light than a black surface, a character or its coded representation is read by shining light on the area under investigation and sensing the amount of light reflected. OCR equipment covers a wide range of input capabilities, although any one piece of equipment may have limitations and constraints on its operation. Tight printing controls on forms is common, and limitations of input to specialized print fonts are usually required. OCR devices fall into two broad categories: code readers and character readers.

Code Readers

A **code reader** reads a character by sensing a code representation for the character. Code readers are less complex than character readers. They require preprinted forms. The two main classes of code readers are mark sense readers and bar code readers.

Mark Sense

Mark sense devices read characters by sensing marks entered on a source document by hand. These marks are placed in specific locations on the documents. Standard punched cards are sometimes used. Spaces printed on the card are filled in by the user with a pencil. This provides a great deal of flexibility, since data can be entered on the card wherever the user happens to be. A disadvantage is that the space required to enter a mark is greater than the space required to directly punch the same data into the card. The capacity of a mark sense card is usually limited to 27 mark sense characters. A piece of unit record equipment called the **reproducer** has the capability (among other capabilities) of reading the mark sense entries and then punching the sensed characters into the card. As a result, mark sense cards can involve a two-step process: the manual data capture and the reproducer punching.

Documents other than punched cards are also used. Mark sense equipment, in this case, generally reads the characters entered on the document and writes them on a magnetic tape.

Bar Codes

Bar codes cover a wide range. Individual code formats are highly dependent on the specific field of application. They tend to be limited to the representation of numeric characters only. A character is represented in such a code by a combination of light and dark lines or bars. The thickness of the lines may also vary.

Probably the most familiar bar code is the **Universal Product Code (UPC),** which has been accepted as a standard in the grocery industry. It is an all numeric code. Figure 4–6 illustrates the main components of the UPC. The code is printed on the product by the manufacturer. It is divided into left and right halves. The left half is a code for the product manufacturer; the right half is a code for the specific product. Each character consists of a seven-bit code. A *1* is represented by a bar and a *0* by the lack of a bar (or of a space). The code on the left side is the complement of the code on the right side for each digit.

The numeral 5, for example, has the bar representations shown in Figure 4–7. The right side code in this figure consists from left to right of a bar of one standard width, followed by a space of double width, followed by a bar of triple width, followed by a space of single width. This code represents the bit string 1001110. All codes contain two bars and two spaces. The left side code in the figure can be seen to be the complement of the right side code. Figure 4–8 gives both the left and the right side codes for all 10 digits. The left side codes use odd parity, that is, the number of 1s must be odd; the right side codes use even parity. The code for each digit begins with the first

Figure 4–6
Universal Product Code

bar toward the center. The code may be successfully read either from left to right or from right to left. A single width bar, space, and bar delineate both sides of the left side and right side codes. The center combination is shared by both sides.

In addition, a special code, specifying one of five allowable variations of the UPC code in use, appears as the first digit in the left side code, and a check digit (discussed below) appears as the last character in the right side code. The Figure 4–6 layout assumes the 0 variation. This is the most commonly encountered variation. UPC codes are human-readable, readable by fixed scanners, or by hand wands.

Character Readers

A **character reader** identifies a character by its shape. Some devices are limited to input data printed in one or more special fonts. Other devices accept standard typed characters, and some accept hand-printed characters. Devices accepting hand-printed input require strict constraints on the formation of the characters. For example, characters must be kept within well-defined areas on the document, must fill most of the area, must be simple, and must have no irrelevant gaps or extensions. Figure 4–9 illustrates these constraints. There are two main classes of character readers: document readers and page readers.

Figure 4–7
UPC Code for the Digit 5

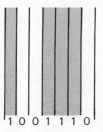

(a) Right side code

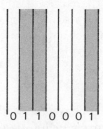

(b) Left side code

Figure 4–8
Left and Right Side UPC Codes

	Left							Right						
0	0	0	0	1	1	0	1	1	1	1	0	0	1	0
1	0	0	1	1	0	0	1	1	1	0	0	1	1	0
2	0	0	1	0	0	1	1	1	1	0	1	1	0	0
3	0	1	1	1	1	0	1	1	0	0	0	0	1	0
4	0	1	0	0	0	1	1	1	0	1	1	1	0	0
5	0	1	1	0	0	0	1	1	0	0	1	1	1	0
6	0	1	0	1	1	1	1	1	0	1	0	0	0	0
7	0	1	1	1	0	1	1	1	0	0	0	1	0	0
8	0	1	1	0	1	1	1	1	0	0	1	0	0	0
9	0	0	0	1	0	1	1	1	1	1	0	1	0	0

Figure 4–9
OCR Character Reader Constraints on Handwritten Data

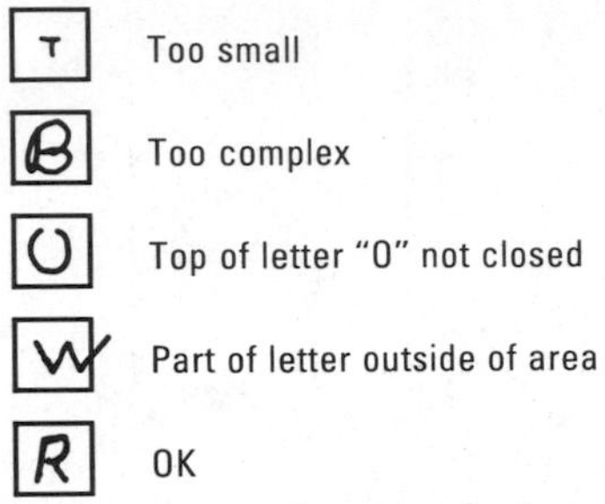

T	Too small
B	Too complex
O	Top of letter "O" not closed
W	Part of letter outside of area
R	OK

Document Readers

Document readers are OCR character readers that accept as input documents smaller than a standard 8.5″ by 11″ page. These are frequently used in applications involving credit card charge slips or airline tickets. The amount of data read on each input document is relatively low and, consequently, higher document handling speeds are possible.

Page Readers

Page readers are OCR character readers that accept as input a wide range of document sizes, including those exceeding a standard 8.5″ by 11″ page. The amount of data read on each document will tend to be more than that read with a document reader. As a result, document handling speeds will tend to be lower. Exact handling speeds depend on the amount of data to be read from each document.

Point-of-Sale Terminals

Point-of-sale (POS) terminals are devices that are placed at remote retail sales locations and do not require relatively specialized training to operate. The terminal serves both as a remote entry terminal to a computer system and as a cash register at the remote site. Sales data entered not only produce a dollar sales total at the terminal but are also used to update various inventory and sales files at the central computer site. Entries are made by a cash register type keyboard, by a wand reading of an optical bar code or a magnetic stripe on a sales ticket, or by other means. Customer credit may also be checked in some POS-based systems. Advantages of POS systems include:

1. Tighter inventory control
2. Better sales analyses
3. Greater accuracy in data entry

POS terminals may operate either on-line or off-line. If the terminal operates on-line, data are transmitted to the central site with each transaction. If the terminal operates off-line, data are stored at the terminal and, when requested by the computer, are transmitted to the central site. This may be done automatically each evening at the close of the day's sales activity.

Data Validation

Data validation is concerned with testing input data to determine whether or not they are legitimate before further processing of the data is allowed. Data verification checks that data have been entered from a source document correctly; data validation attempts to check that the data on the source document itself were correct. Data validation is also called **data editing.** Data validation is frequently carried out in a batch environment by means of a special run called an **edit run.** The output of an edit run is a report of invalid data items, which must then be corrected, and a set of validated data. If a separate edit run is not made, then the validation checks must be included in the processing run. Data that are rejected are reviewed by a data clerk and corrected.

A more general term for the edit run is **preprocessing run.** This implies that in addition to editing, that is, making data validation checks, other functions are carried out in the same run. These functions may include reformatting, merging, sorting, or writing the valid data on a secondary storage device.

In an on-line environment, validation is accomplished after the input of each data transaction. If intelligent terminals are being used, validation is usually done at the terminal. If dumb terminals are being used, validation is done by the central computer. Data that are rejected as invalid are corrected by the data entry operator. In some cases, a supervisory terminal may be used to override validation decisions. However, most corrections are expected to be made by the operator. As a result, data entry training in an on-line environment is more complex than that required in a batch environment.

Sometimes redundancy is deliberately built into the transaction so that data can be cross-checked. For example, both store number and state may be entered in a sales transaction, even though store number implies state. This does violate the general principle of minimizing data input, and it should be used sparingly.

Data may be entered and validated on-line but processed at a later time in a batch mode against other permanently stored data. As a result, some invalid data may not be caught until the batch run. In this situation an invalid data report is produced, and provision must be made for the correction of the data on that report.

The following are commonly used data validation checks. These may be used in either a batch or an on-line environment.

Sequence Check

A **sequence check** determines if the data being read are in some given order. For example, time card data may be required to be in employee number order so that they can be efficiently processed against an employee master file stored on magnetic tape. This test may also check for any missing data if no gaps are expected in the input sequence. A check may also be made for duplicate data if duplication is not allowed. For example, only one set of time card data per employee might be expected in a payroll system, but more than one set of credit charges might be expected in a credit card application.

Character Check

A **character check** determines that only legitimate characters have been entered in a given field. For example, some fields may be purely numeric and, therefore, entry of alphabetic characters or special symbols in these fields is invalid.

Combination Check

A **combination check** tests one or more interrelationships among data items, that is, instead of testing the contents of data fields independently, it tests fields as a group. It is possible that, although the contents of several data fields individually are valid, the fields taken together form an invalid combination. For example, a valid salesperson number may be recorded in combination with a valid product number. This may still be an invalid transaction if the salesperson does not handle that product. Another example might involve accounting transaction data. Although individual accounts might be valid, the account combination in an individual transaction might not be valid.

Limit (or Reasonableness) Check

A **limit (or reasonableness) check** tests to determine if a particular piece of data does not exceed some prespecified limit. For example, the hours worked by an employee in a single week might not be allowed to exceed 60. Some data items should never be less than zero. Limit checks may also be included after processing has been completed. For example, the maximum amount for a monthly payroll check may be specified as 3,000 dollars.

A **range test** is simply a limit check that tests whether a particular data item falls between a specified minimum and maximum. If the range of valid data includes gaps, then any invalid data falling into such a gap will pass this test.

Authorized Code Check

If only a limited number of valid codes may be entered in a particular data field, then an **authorized code check** may be used to test such entries for validity. The valid codes may be contained either within the applications program or in a table previously read into primary memory. For example, a file updating application may allow adding a record to the file, deleting a record, or changing the contents of a record already in the file. These alternatives might be encoded as 1, 2, or 3 respectively. An authorized code check would test that the code entered was one of these three possibilities. In this example, the valid code could easily be incorporated within the application program. As another example, a national retailer might use zip codes to identify its sales outlets (assuming that no more than one outlet may be located in one zip code area). A table containing all valid zip codes could be used in this case.

Self-Checking Digits

An identification code may include a **self-checking digit.** This is an additional digit added to the original code. After reading, an algorithm is applied to the code. If the code passes this test, it is accepted as valid; if the code does not pass the test, it is rejected as invalid.

A study by Beckley[1] indicates that data entry errors fall into the following distribution:

Transcription	86%
Transposition	9
Other	5

A **transcription error** occurs when one character is substituted for another, e.g. 12345 is entered as 12845. A **transposition error** occurs when two characters are interchanged, e.g. 12345 is entered as 12435.

Check digit systems involve calculating the modulus of a number. A number **modulus N** is the remainder of the number after it has been divided by N. For example, 32 modulus 10 is 2.

Check digits are incorporated directly into the identification code. Users of the code may not even be aware of the function of the extra digit. Although the check digit may appear anywhere in the code, it is usually placed in the far right position.

A discussion of some of the more commonly used self-checking digit techniques follows. All methods use either a modulus 10 or a modulus 11 scheme.

Modulus 10 Simple Sum Method

This is the simplest of the check digit techniques. The individual digits in the identification code are summed. The sum modulus 10 is subtracted from 10. The difference is the check digit. As an example, assume that the basic identification code is 82419.

(a) $8 + 2 + 4 + 1 + 9 = 24$

(b)   24 mod 10 = 4

(c) $10 - 4 = 6 =$ check digit

The complete identification code becomes 824196. The six-digit number modulus 10 is now 0.

This method should catch all single transcription errors and non-compensating multiple transcription errors. As examples, assume that the following codes are entered instead of the valid identification code 824196:

Case I—Single Transcription: 8 2 5 1 9 6

(a) $8 + 2 + 5 + 1 + 9 + 6 = 31$

(b)   31 mod 10 = 1

(c)   1 does not equal 0

—number is determined to be invalid

Case II—Noncompensating Multiple Transcription: 8 2 5 1 9 7

(a) $8 + 2 + 5 + 1 + 9 + 7 = 32$

(b) $32 \bmod 10 = 2$

(c)   2 does not equal 0

—number is determined to be invalid

Case III—Compensating Multiple Transcription: 8 2 5 1 8 6

(a) $8 + 2 + 5 + 1 + 8 + 6 = 30$

(b) $30 \bmod 10 = 0$

(c)   0 does equal 0

—number is incorrectly accepted as valid

Modulus 10 Alternate Weights Method

The simple sum method assumes an equal weight for each digit in the code. This method uses alternate weights on the digits. As an example, using a 2–1–2 weighting scheme and a basic code of 82419:

	Basic Code:	8	2	4	1	9
(a)	Weight:	2	1	2	1	2

$$16 + 2 + 8 + 1 + 18 = 45$$

(b) $45 \bmod 10 = 5$

(c) $10 - 5 = 5 = $ check digit

Another weighting scheme used is 3–1–3. This is the check digit method used in the Universal Product Code. As an example:

	Basic Code:	8	2	4	1	9
(a)	Weight:	3	1	3	1	3

$$24 + 2 + 12 + 1 + 27 = 66$$

(b) $66 \bmod 10 = 6$

(c) $10 - 6 = 4 = $ check digit

This method will catch single transposition errors, and noncompensating multiple transcription and transposition errors. Whether this method will also catch all single transcription errors depends on the weighting scheme. If the transcription error results in a weighted change that contributes an even multiple of 10, the error will not be detected. As an example, assume that the identification code 824195 is entered incorrectly as 824145 and that a modulus 10 alternate 2–

1–2 weighting scheme is in use. The following illustrates the validity check:

	Code:	8	2	4	1	4	5
(a)	Weight:	$\underline{2}$	$\underline{1}$	$\underline{2}$	$\underline{1}$	$\underline{2}$	$\underline{1}$
		$16 + 2 + 8 + 1 + 8 + 5 = 40$					

(b)   40 mod 10 = 0

(c)   0 does equal 0

—number is incorrectly accepted as valid

If the weights used are limited to those that are relatively prime to 10, that is, there are no common divisors of that weight and 10 except 1, then all single transcription errors will be caught. There are only four numbers less than, and relatively prime to, 10: 1, 3, 7, and 9. Thus identification codes of a maximum of four digits can be checked for single transcription errors with certainty using a modulus 10 method. Modulus 11 systems do not have this restriction, since all numbers less than 11 are relatively prime to 11.

Modulus 11 Arithmetic Method

This method uses an arithmetic progression in the weighting scheme and calculates the check digit using modulus 11. For example:

	Basic Code:	8	2	4	1	9
(a)	Weight:	$\underline{6}$	$\underline{5}$	$\underline{4}$	$\underline{3}$	$\underline{2}$
		$48 + 10 + 16 + 3 + 18 = 95$				

(b)   95 mod 11 = 7

(c)   11 − 7 = 4 = check digit

This scheme will catch all single transcription errors, any transposition error, e.g. 824194 entered as 424198, and noncompensating multiple transcription or transposition errors.

A problem that does arise in any modulus 11 system is the calculation of a check digit of 10. This is, of course, two digits. For example:

	Basic Code:	1	2	1	1	0
(a)	Weight:	$\underline{6}$	$\underline{5}$	$\underline{4}$	$\underline{3}$	$\underline{2}$
		$6 + 10 + 4 + 3 + 0 = 23$				

(b)   23 mod 11 = 1

(c)   11 − 1 = 10 = check digit

A number of different approaches can be used:

1. Reject as unusable any candidate identification codes that would result in a check digit of 10. In the above example, 12110____ would not be used as a code.
2. Place the check digit on the left of the basic code. This approach loses the fixed length characteristic of the code and, as a result, is not often used.
3. Use an alphabetic character, e.g. the letter A or X (Roman numeral 10), as a check digit to represent 10.
4. If the weighting scheme results in a check digit of 10, use an alternate weighting scheme and recalculate the check digit. If the new check digit is not 10, use it; if the new check digit is also 10, reject as unusable the basic identification code. This method was introduced by Campbell[2].

Additional Comments on Check Digits

There is never any reason to use a weight in a check digit scheme that is greater than the modulus used. For example, assuming a modulus of 10:

	Basic Code Digit:	4	4
(a)	Weight:	13	3
		52	12

(b) $\qquad$ 52 mod 10 − 2 $\quad$ 12 mod 10 = 2

Any weight modulus 10 produces the same result as the original weight.

Wild[3] has set down the following criteria for a good modulus N check digit system:

1. N must be greater than 9.
2. All weights must be less than N.
3. The sum of two or more consecutive weights is not equal to N or to any integer multiple of N.
4. No two weights are the same.
5. N is a prime number.

Batch Control Totals

Control totals are values calculated outside of the computer system for a batch of data and entered into the processing phase as another type of validation check. The total is recalculated in the computer and compared against the entered total. If they do not agree, an error or omission has occurred.

Batches of data for which the control total is calculated should be kept reasonably small, yet should form some natural grouping. If a mismatch between the submitted control total and calculated control total exists, then the smaller the batch of data the quicker the error can be found. Of course, if batches are too small much time will be spent calculating the control totals. By dividing batches of data into natural groupings, e.g. time cards by department, responsibility for the individual batch will be more clearly defined.

Sometimes larger batches may be created from smaller batches. In this case, a control total is associated with each smaller batch and a grand control total is associated with the large batch.

There are three major types of control totals: financial totals, hash totals, and document, or record, counts. In addition, a batch number check as a control is discussed.

Financial Control Totals

A **financial control total** is a total that may be normally calculated anyway as part of the processing. It is a total that in itself has meaning. This control total is frequently used with financial data but is not limited to financial data. Examples of possible control totals are sales amounts, hours worked, units ordered, expenses incurred, etc. In a batch environment a card may be punched containing one or more control totals and be followed in the data deck by the individual data cards.

Hash Control Totals

A **hash control total** is a total that is not normally calculated as part of the processing but serves the same purpose as a financial control total. The total itself may be meaningless. Examples of such control totals are the sum of individual employee identification numbers, the sum of individual customer numbers, and the sum of accounting system transaction numbers. The total has meaning only in terms of its control function.

Document (or Record) Count

A **document (or record) count** is simply a count of the number of records entered in the batch. Thus, in a card-oriented system, if the batch contains 45 data cards the control total is 45. As with the other types of control totals, the records are counted as they are read in and the totals are compared. This is primarily a safeguard against the loss of some records from the batch after data entry and before the data are read into the computer.

Batch Number Check

Each batch may be numbered, and every record within the batch contains this batch number. A check will then reveal if any records from another batch have been included in this batch.

Error Correction

After errors are discovered, steps must be taken to correct them. As previously pointed out, the earlier an error is discovered the less expensive it is to correct. It is better to discover and correct an error at the data capture point in the data input process than later. Verification after data capture frequently is used not only for error checking but also for control purposes. For example, a time card filled out by an employee may be verified and signed by that employee's supervisor so as to ensure not only accuracy but also honesty.

On-line data entry should be designed around real time data verification. The data entry operator should be allowed to verify the correctness of the data immediately. Off-line verification is generally performed in the same organizational unit as the original data entry operation (e.g. a keypunch and verify operation).

Failure of one or more data validation checks must result in the prevention of further processing of the invalid data. The reason for the rejection of the data as invalid must be clearly presented. This is done after entry of each invalid item in an on-line system or in an invalid data report for all data items on a batch system. It is essential that the person who must make the correction receives a clear indication of the cause of each rejected data item. An error report should be returned to the department responsible for preparing the data. There are two main reasons for this:

1. The preparing department should be most familiar with the data and, therefore, in the best position to correct the errors.
2. Without feedback on errors, training gaps may not be recognized and closed.

All corrected data must be reentered in the data input system and undergo complete verification and validation checking again. This is important since some *corrected* data may contain new errors.

In so far as possible, the finding and rejection of invalid data should not stop further processing of valid data. Data input to processing should result in two broad output classes:

1. Output resulting from the processing of all successfully validated data.

2. Error reports precisely identifying the cause of rejection for all un-
    successfully validated data.

After successful entry of all data and successful processing of it,
concern with and correction of errors cannot be assumed to be finished. Review of the output by its users will locate additional errors.
For example, an incorrect bill to a customer will result in a com-
plaint. Action must be initiated to correct the bill if, in fact, it is
determined to be in error. It should be mentioned that there may be
an inherent bias in the types of errors reported by users. The customer who is overbilled may report the error with high probability;
the customer who is underbilled may report the error with a lower
probability. Such bias may exist in many practical situations. It is
imperative that a means of taking corrective action on errors discovered after processing has occurred be built into the entire system.

Conclusions

Data input and the control of errors is of great importance to the
designers and users of a computer based information system. Upon
this depends every other function.

The problem of cumulative errors in a system that continuously
updates secondary storage files is of great concern. These files may
represent the current status of some components of an organization's
operations. Even though only a very small percentage of erroneous
data may slip through the verification and validation checks on any
updating, the cumulative effect of these errors will eventually seriously degrade a file and the information system using this file.
Means of confirming and correcting data in the file on a regular
basis must be provided. Manual systems also face this problem—
although obviously incorrect data may be caught by a visual inspection in a manual system. A manual inventory system requires a physical inventory on a regularly scheduled basis to bring the inventory
file into accord with the actual physical inventory status. Analogous
means must be used on many continuously updated files.

Some errors may be tolerated in a processing run. The misspelling
of a product description, for example, may not have any serious implications if the product description is still clear to users. It is obvious that the alphabetics: LARGE WALNUT BOOKCOSE describe
a particular bookcase in a furniture manufacturing environment.

All errors cannot be eliminated. A good system will detect and
eliminate the vast majority. It must be flexible enough to take correc-

tive action when some are identified at a later time, and it must strive to reconcile the picture of reality presented by the data with the actual status determined independently of the computer based system.

References

1. Beckley, D. F. "An Optimum System with 'Modulus 11.'" *Computer Bulletin* 11, No. 3 (December 1967), pp. 213–15.
2. Campbell, D. V. A. "A Modulus 11 Check Digit System for a Given System of Codes." *Computer Bulletin* 14, No. 1 (January 1970), pp.12–13.
3. Wild, W. G. "The Theory of Modulus N Check Digit Systems." *Computer Bulletin* 12, No. 8 (December 1968), pp. 309–11.

Additional Readings

Anderson, L. K., et al. "Self-Checking Digit Concepts." *Journal of Systems Management* 25, No. 9 (September 1974), pp. 36–42.

Aronson, R. L. "New Encoding Methods Spark New Card, Badge, Ticket Uses." *Control Engineering* 16, No. 10 (October 1969), pp. 88–94.

Eisdorfer, A. "A System of Optical Character Recognition." *Journal of Systems Management* 21, No. 11 (November 1970), pp. 19–22.

Gilb, T., and G. M. Weinberg. *Humanized Input: Techniques for Reliable Keyed Input.* Cambridge, Mass.: Winthrop Publishers, 1977.

Jancura, E. G., and A. H. Berger. *Computers: Auditing and Control.* Philadelphia: Auerbach Publishers, Inc., 1973.

Martin, J. *Design of Man-Computer Dialogues.* Englewood Cliffs, N.J.: Prentice-Hall, 1973.

————. *Security, Accuracy, and Privacy in Computer Systems.* Englewood Cliffs, N.J.: Prentice-Hall, 1973.

On Optical Character Recognition. Princeton, N.J.: Auerbach Publishers, Inc., 1971.

Porter, T. W. *EDP Controls and Auditing.* Belmont, Calif.: Wadsworth, 1974.

Savir, D., and G. J. Laurer. "The Characteristics and Decodability of the Universal Product Code Symbol." *IBM Systems Journal* 14, No. 1 (1975), pp.16–34.

Shneiderman, B. *Software Psychology.* Cambridge, Mass.: Winthrop Publishers, Inc., 1980.

Review

1. Differentiate between data capture and data entry.
2. Give two examples of desirable identification code characteristics that may be somewhat incompatible.
3. Give the Soundex code for each of the following names:

    a ANTHONY

    b BIRD

    c CHANCELLOR

4. Differentiate between data verification and data validation.
5. What is a buffered keypunch?
6. Differentiate between a key-to-tape system and a key-to-disk system. On what medium are the output data written in each system?
7. What is a POS terminal?
8. What is an intelligent terminal?
9. What is a turnaround document?
10. What is E–13B?
11. Differentiate between a document reader and a page reader.
12. Differentiate between an OCR code reader and an OCR character reader.
13. Differentiate between an edit run and a preprocessing run.
14. Describe each of the following data validation checks.

    a sequence check

    b character check

    c combination check

    d limit check

    e range test

    f authorized code check

15. Given the following basic identification code: 51102___, calculate the check digit using each of the indicated methods:

    a Modulus 10 2–1–2 alternate weighting

    b Modulus 11 arithmetic method

16. Differentiate between a financial control total and a hash control total.

Chapter 5

Hardware

Introduction

Hardware refers to the physical components of a computer system and any supporting equipment, such as unit record equipment, etc. Figure 5–1 shows a generalized computer system and its many components. The heart of any computer system is the **central processing unit,** or **CPU.** It is sometimes simply called the **processor.**

Figure 5–1
Generalized Computer System

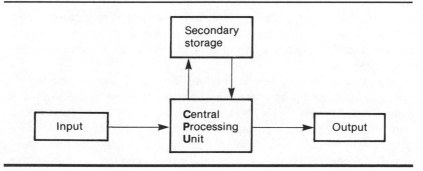

An input device is required to provide a means to enter data and programs in the processor, and an output device is required to receive at least some of the results of the processing. In summary, data are entered into the processor, manipulated in accordance with the instructions contained in a program, and some output is provided to the user.

Data and programs that are to be reused may be stored on special input/output devices called **secondary storage devices.** The term "secondary storage" is used to differentiate this form of memory from primary storage, that is, memory contained within the CPU. Secondary storage devices have a relatively large capacity, and retrieval time is relatively short. In addition, these devices are under the direct control of the CPU and may be accessed without human intervention. The two most commonly used classes of secondary storage devices, magnetic tape and magnetic disk, are discussed in some detail in Chapter 7.

Computers fall into two main groups: digital computers and analog computers. In some applications a hybrid configuration involving both digital and analog components is used.

Digital computers manipulate discrete values represented by digital pulses or states. **Analog computers** manipulate continuous values represented by either physical or electrical magnitudes. An analog variable may theoretically take on any value (at least within a range). A digital variable may take on only one of a finite number of possible values. As an example, watches are of both types. The traditional watch with sweep hands is analog in nature and can represent any time. The newer digital watch, however, can only represent time to the nearest second (or fraction of a second).

Precision is a measure of the number of significant decimal places that can be represented for a value. Digital computers have greater precision than analog computers. Analog computers are usually limited to representation within 1 percent. Digital computers far exceed this precision value. The exact precision possible in any digital computer is dependent upon the hardware and software.

Analog computers are used in scientific or engineering applications and in process control. Digital computers are also used in these areas. Business applications and information systems use digital computers almost exclusively.

Digital computers may be categorized as either general purpose or special purpose computers. A **general purpose computer** is one designed in such a way that it may process a wide range of possible applications. A **special purpose computer** is one designed to carry out efficiently a relatively narrow range of tasks. Special purpose computers are used in areas such as navigation and process control. Because of their nature, general purpose computers support a myriad of applications. They may be oriented around either scientific or business applications, or both.

The most commonly encountered computer is a general purpose digital computer that uses stored programs. In unit record (or punched card) equipment and in the very earliest computer systems, instructions were provided to the machine by making wiring connections on a panel. To change instructions, rewiring was necessary. Programs existed as panels of wiring connections. The **stored program concept** means that instructions are represented internally either magnetically or electrically and may be changed or replaced at electronic speeds. Stored programs allow an enormous amount of flexibility in a computer.

Table 5–1
Common Prefixes

| Prefix | Meaning | |
	English	Mathematical
Pico-	one trillionth	10^{-12}
Nano-	one billionth	10^{-9}
Micro-	one millionth	10^{-6}
Milli-	one thousandth	10^{-3}
Kilo-	one thousand	10^{3}
Mega-	one million	10^{6}
Giga-	one billion	10^{9}
Tera-	one trillion	10^{12}

Table 5–1 presents a number of common prefixes used in computer technology and their meanings. For example, a nano-second is one billionth of a second. Kilo- and mega- are frequently abbreviated as K and M respectively.

Computer Generations

Digital computers are generally considered to have evolved through three generations. A computer generation is usually defined in terms of its most basic hardware component.

First generation computers had as their basic component the vacuum tube. The first commercially available computer was the UNIVAC I, which was introduced in 1951.

The **second generation** was introduced in the late 1950s and replaced the vacuum tube with the transistor. The advantages obtained by this change were:

1. A reduction in the physical size of the processing equipment.
2. An increase in reliability.
3. A reduction in power requirements.
4. A reduction in air conditioning requirements.
5. A reduction in cost.
6. An increase in processing speed.

The **third generation** was introduced in 1965 and replaced the discrete transistors of the second generation with integrated circuits. An **integrated circuit** is a piece of semiconductor material containing the equivalent of transistors, various other devices, and their interconnections. This circuitry is fabricated on a chip. The advantages obtained by this change were continuations of all of those obtained in the shift to the second generation. In addition to this hardware advance, third-generation computers introduced a number of new software developments, e.g. multiprogramming (see Chapter 6).

If the introduction of the second and third generations can be called revolutionary, development since then can be called evolutionary. The density of circuitry on a chip has continuously increased, and the technology and materials used to create these chips have also changed many times.

A **microprocessor** is a chip that contains all of the circuitry necessary to carry out the functions of a central processing unit. Microprocessors are used both for specialized, dedicated applications and as the basis for microcomputers. The microcomputer has found application in small businesses and as intelligent terminals, and can no longer be considered just a sophisticated source of games.

With increasing density and higher yields, the cost of a chip has decreased spectacularly over the years. The technology of chip design and production is such that there is a relatively high fixed cost and a relatively low variable cost. As a result, the per unit cost drops sharply with volume. This effect has been widely noticed in the price charged for hand-held calculators. It has decreased significantly year after year.

There is no generally accepted definition of a hardware fourth generation. There are, however, fourth generation languages (see Chapter 6). The Japanese government and industry have announced plans to develop fifth-generation computers. While requiring a number of hardware advances, this project is primarily dependent on software development and is also discussed in Chapter 6.

Central Processing Unit

The central processing unit is the heart of any computer system. It is in the central processing unit that programs are executed. All data that are operated on by a program must be copied into the CPU (although not necessarily at the same time).

The CPU can be viewed as consisting of three main components. These are:

1. The control unit.
2. The arithmetic and logic unit.
3. The storage unit.

It should be pointed out that sometimes the storage unit is viewed as outside the central processing unit. The memory chips are physically separate from the CPU chip.

The **control unit** consists of hardware that controls and monitors the operation of the CPU itself. It initiates and controls the flow of data and instructions within the CPU. It interprets those instructions to be executed and then physically implements whatever actions are necessary to carry out the execution of those instructions.

The **arithmetic and logic unit** carries out the arithmetic operations determined by the control unit. It also can make comparisons betweeen data to determine if they are equal or unequal, or if one piece of data is greater than, or less than, another piece of data.

The **storage unit** consists of memory locations. It is also called **primary memory** (to differentiate it from secondary storage). It is also frequently called **core.** This term relates to a no longer used memory technology that used tiny ferrite cores as the basic memory unit.

Primary memory is divided into a series of memory locations, each of which may store a piece of data. The capacity of primary memory is defined in terms of bytes or words. A **byte** is a unit of memory that can hold one character. For example, a CPU with a primary memory of four megabytes can hold up to 4 million characters. This is only approximately true, since a nominal 1K (or 1,000) is equal to 1,024. Four megabytes is 4,000 K, or 4,096,000 bytes. A word is made up of bytes. The makeup of a byte or word varies. For example, in IBM machines a byte consists of eight bits and 4 bytes make up a word, whereas in CDC machines a byte consists of six bits and 10 bytes make up a word. A byte or word can be individually addressed, but a bit cannot be.

Primary memory holds not only the instructions necessary to carry out a task, but also the data needed for that task. Primary memory locations are **random access,** that is, the same time is required to access any given location.

Each location in primary memory has an **address** associated with it, i.e. a number that uniquely identifies that location. Machine language instructions referencing memory locations refer to them by their addresses.

Registers

Registers are special storage locations contained within the CPU. They are not considered part of primary memory. Registers are used for temporary storage of data during the execution of an instruction. They are usually built using memory devices that provide very fast access. Registers of different lengths may exist in the same CPU.

Registers are either general purpose, that is, available to the programmer, or reserved for specific purposes by the CPU and not directly available to the programmer. A register used for a specific purpose is usually named for that purpose.

On many systems the contents of specific registers are indicated on a control panel by a series of lights. In the event of a failure, the contents of these registers at the time of the failure are, as a result, available to maintenance personnel.

The following are examples of registers used for specific purposes. The **instruction register** holds a single instruction for decoding by the control unit after that instruction has been retrieved from primary memory. The instruction is broken into components consisting of an **operation code** (signifying, for example, addition) and one or more data addresses. An **operation code register** holds the operation code, and an **address register** holds the address of a required data item. The **storage register** holds data being transferred into or out of primary memory. An **accumulator** is a register that accumulates computational results. The use of **base registers** is discussed in Chapter 6.

Machine Cycles

The amount of time required by the CPU to carry out one elementary machine operation is called a **machine cycle.** Machine cycles occur in a regular, fixed increment of time that is determined by an internal electronic clock.

A program instruction usually contains both an operation code and one or more data addresses. The **operation code** is a bit sequence that specifies the basic operation, e.g. addition, which is to be executed. The data addresses specify the locations of the data to be used in the execution of the instruction.

The number of machine cycles required to execute an instruction depends on the instruction. Some instructions require more than one elementary machine operation and, therefore, use more than one machine cycle.

The total set of elementary machine instructions is called the **instruction set.** Those instructions reserved to the operating system, that is, the complex of programs that operate the computer system, are called **privileged instructions.**

Executing an instruction consists of two parts: copying the instruction from primary memory into the appropriate register for interpretation, and execution of the instruction.

The first phase is called an **instruction fetch,** and the time for this phase is called **instruction time** (or **I-time**). I-time is the same for all instructions. The second phase is called the **instruction execute,** and the time required for it is called the **execution time** (or **E-time**). This phase may take more than one machine cycle. Although the cycle time is frequently given for a CPU, two or more cycles are required to execute a single elementary instruction.

Memory Technology

Memory is commonly divided into two broad categories: primary memory and secondary storage. **Primary memory** is memory within the CPU; **secondary storage** is memory physically separate from the CPU but under the control of the CPU. Secondary storage has been, and continues to be, dominated by electromechanical storage devices.

Primary memory is transient, that is, at the end of a program run any data involved in that program remaining in primary memory are lost. No permanent record remains unless a copy of the data (or program) has been placed on secondary storage. Secondary storage devices are *permanent* repositories of data and programs. They may be accessed and copies of the stored data or program placed in primary memory as needed. Although intended to be permanent, secondary storage can be accidentally erased or destroyed. Procedures for making backup copies and restoring critical data and programs must be established.

Some types of memory are **volatile** (i.e. when power is removed from the memory the contents are lost). Other memories are **non-**

volatile or **retentive** (i.e. the contents are not lost when power is removed). Obviously secondary storage devices must be nonvolatile.

Primary Memory

For many years, primary memory consisted of interconnected planes of small cores. These cores, resembling tiny doughnuts, were made from a ferrite (i.e. iron oxide) material and, as such, were capable of magnetization. Core storage is nonvolatile. Although core storage dominated primary memory technology for many years, it is no longer used. The term **core,** however, lingers on as a synonym for primary memory.

Integrated circuits (ICs) now dominate primary memory technology. These circuits are fabricated on a tiny piece of semiconductor material called a **chip.** Various components and their interconnections all exist on the same chip. When this complete integration has occurred, the chip is called a **monolithic integrated circuit.**

Integrated circuit chips are used not only for primary memory but also for the various logic circuits used throughout the central processing unit. A **microprocessor** is a chip that contains the logic circuitry required for a CPU.

As integrated circuit technology progressed, the density of circuits obtained on a chip increased dramatically. Originally production chips contained less than 10 active elements. **Medium scale integration** expanded this into the hundreds. **Large scale integration (LSI)** refers to chip densities ranging from 1,000 to 50,000 active elements. **Very large scale integration (VLSI)** has now also been achieved. VLSI refers to densities of over 50,000 active elements per chip. **Ultra large scale integration (ULSI)** is now being mentioned. This will extend chip density even further.

RAMs, ROMs, PROMs, and EPROMs

New types of memory on chips have been introduced in recent years. **RAM** is an acronym for random access memory. In fact, all primary memory is random access, that is, the time to access any data in the memory is the same for all data locations. More accurately, RAM implies that the data may be stored in the memory (write) and/or retrieved from the memory (read). Traditionally, primary memory has been read-write memory.

ROM stands for read only memory. Data may be retrieved from the memory, but the memory may not be written on. ROM is random access. The contents of the ROM are entered onto the chip at the factory. Program instructions cannot alter these contents at a later time. ROM is often used to store small, special purpose programs that are frequently needed. These programs are called **microprograms.** Access to these programs is very fast.

A **PROM** is a programmable read only memory. Whereas a ROM is manufactured and then incorporated into a piece of hardware, a PROM chip is produced; a particular bit pattern as required for a particular application is *burned* into the chip, and then incorporated into the hardware. Thus the same basic chip may be used with different *burnings* for a number of different applications. Because permanent physical changes are made in the chip, it can only be programmed once. The program placed in the chip is permanent. PROMs are sometimes used to store BASIC interpreters (see Chapter 6).

An **EPROM** is an erasable programmable read only memory. This memory can be restored by means of ultraviolet light to its original unprogrammed state, and then a new bit pattern may be impressed on it. This, as with the standard PROM, involves changes in the physical state of the memory that cannot be modified with software.

Cache Memory

Cache memory is a very high-speed semiconductor memory that is interposed between primary memory and the arithmetic and logic component of the processor. Cache memory is transparent to the user, that is, the user does not have to take into account the existence of this memory. Cache memory is utilized directly by the system and not by the user.

The underlying philosophy behind the use of cache memory is that data or instructions that are required next in a job are, with high probability, the data or instructions that are contiguous with those currently in use. As a result, a reference to a location in primary memory results in the transfer not only of the contents of that location to cache memory, but also the contents of a number of contiguous locations. If requirements are sequential, then the next contents needed are already available in cache memory, and access is very fast.

Data Representation

Data are represented within a computer system by means of an internal code. Externally, individual alphabetics (A through Z), numerics (0 through 9), and special symbols (e.g. +, -, [,],.) are used separately or in combination to represent data. In fact, these are the symbols that human users find most familiar and with which they are most comfortable.

Within the computer system, direct representation of these characters cannot be done. Primarily due to engineering constraints, the internal circuitry and storage media of the system are designed to handle only two representations. These two internal representations are termed *0* and *1*. They are implemented as either magnetic states of storage media, e.g. magnetization in one of two possible directions, or electrical states of various circuit devices, e.g. off or on. An analogy with a common light bulb might be instructive. If the bulb is on, it can represent a *1;* if the bulb is off, it can represent a *0.* It is arbitrary which state represents the *1* and which state represents the *0.* It is essential, however, that the representation be standardized.

A number system based on only two digits, that is, *0* and *1,* is called the **binary number system.** All digital computers employ components that take on either of two states. As a result, the binary number system is inherent in the design of all digital computers.

Binary Number System

The binary number system is a base 2 number system in the same way that the decimal number system is a base 10 system. Any base system uses a weighting of the digits in each position. A number system using base n uses powers of n as the weights. Figure 5–2 shows an example in the decimal (base 10) system. The number 1,234 is the sum of 1 weighted by 1,000, 2 weighted by 100, 3

Figure 5–2
Decimal Weighting

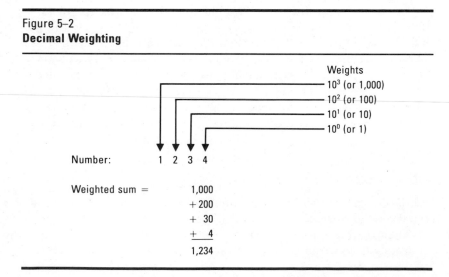

	Weights
	10^3 (or 1,000)
	10^2 (or 100)
	10^1 (or 10)
	10^0 (or 1)

Number: 1 2 3 4

Weighted sum =   1,000
   + 200
   + 30
   + 4
   1,234

weighted by 10, and 4 weighted by 1. The highest digit in the base 10 system is 9. The next number after 9 involves a shift of one position to the left, that is, to the next highest weight, and 10 results.

Similarly, a number in the base 2 system involves a positional weighting of powers of 2. Figure 5–3 shows an example in the binary system. The binary number 1011101 is equivalent to the decimal number 93.

Figure 5–3
Binary Weighting

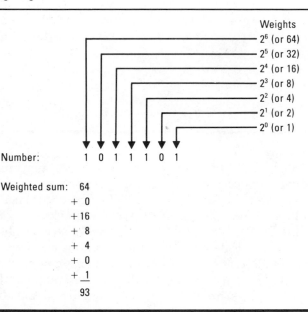

Each digit in a binary number is called a **bit** (i.e. the contraction of binary digit). The term "bit" obviously also has parallels with the bit of information theory.

If there are n bits in a bit string, then the number of combinations available for the data representation is 2^n. For the representation of integers, the values: 0, 1, 2, . . ., $2^n - 1$ can be represented. Figure 5–4 shows the integer values that can be represented by a four-bit string.

Binary Coded Decimal
Binary coded decimal or (**BCD**) is a four-bit code that has sometimes been used to represent numeric digits. The code consists of

Figure 5–4
Four-Bit Binary Representation

Decimal	Binary
0	0000
1	0001
2	0010
3	0011
4	0100
5	0101
6	0110
7	0111
8	1000
9	1001
10	1010
11	1011
12	1100
13	1101
14	1110
15	1111

the first 10 bit combinations in Figure 5–4. The remaining six bit combinations, that is, those representing 10 through 15, are not valid in BCD. In effect, the full potential of a four-bit code is not used and, as a result, the code is not as efficient as it could be.

A **six-bit BCD** is also used. The number of code combinations is 64, i.e. 2^6. In this code the two left bit positions carry zone bits and the four right bit positions carry numeric bits. For numerics the zone bits are 00 followed by the four-bit BCD representation. Alphabetics and special symbols are represented by zone bit combinations other than 00. Figure 5–5 lists the standard six-bit BCD code. The code for the letter *K* is 10 0010. The code for the numeric 0 is 00 1010—not, as would be expected, 00 0000. This last code represents a blank. Only upper case alphabetics are represented in six-bit BCD.

ASCII

The **American Standard Code for Information Interchange (ASCII)** is a seven-bit code that is used mostly in telecommunications applications. ASCII is more properly pronounced *Ask E Two* . ASCII provides 128 code combinations. An eight-bit version of this code called ASCII–8 has also been produced. Figure 5–6 lists the ASCII code. The code includes both upper and lower case alphabetics. ASCII–8 is a popular internal representation in microcomputers.

Figure 5–5
Six-Bit BCD Code

Numeric Bits	Zone Bits			
	00	11	10	01
0000	blank	&	—	b̸
0001	1	A	J	/
0010	2	B	K	S
0011	3	C	L	T
0100	4	D	M	U
0101	5	E	N	V
0110	6	F	O	W
0111	7	G	P	X
1000	8	H	Q	Y
1001	9	I	R	Z
1010	0	?	!	≠
1011	#	.	$	,
1100	@	□	*	%
1101	:	[	]	—
1110	>	<	;	\
1111	√	≢	△	⧻

Figure 5–6
Seven-Bit ASCII Code

Right 4 Bits	Left 3 Bits							
	000	001	010	011	100	101	110	111
0000	NUL	DLE	blank	0	@	P	`	p
0001	SOH	DC1	!	1	A	Q	a	q
0010	STX	DC2	"	2	B	R	b	r
0011	ETX	DC3	#	3	C	S	c	s
0100	EOT	DC4	$	4	D	T	d	t
0101	ENQ	NAK	%	5	E	U	e	u
0110	ACK	SYN	&	6	F	V	f	v
0111	BEL	ETB	'	7	G	W	g	w
1000	BS	CAN	(	8	H	X	h	x
1001	HT	EM	)	9	I	Y	i	y
1010	LF	SUB	*	:	J	Z	j	z
1011	VT	ESC	+	;	K	[	k	{
1100	FF	FS	,	<	L	\	l	|
1101	CR	GS	−	=	M	]	m	}
1110	SO	RS	.	>	N	∧	n	~
1111	SI	US	/	?	O	_	o	DEL (delete)

Special control characters

EBCDIC

The **Extended Binary Coded Decimal Interchange Code (EBCDIC)** is an eight-bit code that provides 256 code combinations. This is a code that was developed by IBM for use on its System/360 series of computers. It continues to be used on its successors. Other computer manufacturers have also standardized on this code. In addition to numerics and special symbols, both upper case and lower case alphabetics are represented in EBCDIC. A number of the code combinations are unassigned. These combinations and some others do not have a corresponding print symbol. As a result they cannot be printed out and are called **unprintable characters.** In EBCDIC the four left bit positions hold zone bits and the four right bit positions hold numeric bits. Figure 5–7 lists the EBCDIC code combinations.

Hexadecimal Notation

Hexadecimal notation uses a number system based on 16. It is frequently used to represent a four-bit combination in more compact form. Figure 5–8 shows the hexadecimal representation for all four-bit combinations. Numeric digits are used up to and including 9. For bit combinations representing 10 through 15, alphabetics are used. Hexadecimal notation is convenient for representing EBCDIC codes, since these codes consist of two sets of four bits. An EBCDIC code can be represented either as eight bits or as two hexadecimal characters. For example, the numeric digit *1* is represented in EBCDIC as 1111 0001. This bit representation can be abbreviated in hexadecimal notation as *F1*, where F is the hexadecimal equivalent of the bit string 1111 and 1 is the hexadecimal equivalent of the bit string 0001. Similarly, the EBCDIC code for the upper case alphabetic *L* is 1101 0011. This can be represented in hexadecimal as D3. Output can be obtained in hexadecimal from a computer system. The conversion to the bit representation is relatively simple. Hexadecimal notation is most frequently used in debugging, that is, finding the cause of an error in a program.

Parity Checking

Parity checking is a technique used to detect errors. An extra bit is appended to a bit string, usually to a bit string representing a single character. Parity is either even or odd. In an **even parity scheme** the number of *1s* in the string is even; in an **odd parity scheme** the number of *1s* in the string is odd. The parity bit is

Figure 5–7
EBCDIC

		Left 4 Bits														
Right 4 Bits	0000	0001	0010	0011	0100	0101	0110	0111	1000	1001	1010	1011	1100	1101	1110	1111
0000	NUL		DS		blank	&	-									0
0001			SOS				/		a	j			A	J		1
0010			FS						b	k	s		B	K	S	2
0011		TM							c	l	t		C	L	T	3
0100	PF	RES	BYP	PN					d	m	u		D	M	U	4
0101	HT	NL	LF	RS					e	n	v		E	N	V	5
0110	LC	BS	EOB	UC					f	o	w		F	O	W	6
0111	DEL	IDL	PRE	EOT					g	p	x		G	P	X	7
1000	EOM								h	q	y		H	Q	Y	8
1001									i	r	z		I	R	Z	9
1010		CC	SM		¢	!	¦	:								
1011					.	$	,	#								
1100					<	*	%	@								
1101					(	)	_	'								
1110					+	;	>	=								
1111					|	¬	?	"								

Special control characters

Figure 5–8
Hexadecimal Notation

Bit Combination	Decimal	Hexadecimal
0000	0	0
0001	1	1
0010	2	2
0011	3	3
0100	4	4
0101	5	5
0110	6	6
0111	7	7
1000	8	8
1001	9	9
1010	10	A
1011	11	B
1100	12	C
1101	13	D
1110	14	E
1111	15	F

calculated and added to the bit string automatically. Parity checks are carried out by hardware. If the correct parity is not found during a check, an error is assumed to have occurred. For example, in Figure 5–9 bit string 1 would pass an even parity check, whereas bit string 2 would fail the same check.

Figure 5–9
Parity Checks

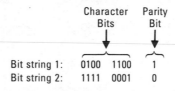

	Character Bits	Parity Bit
Bit string 1:	0100 1100	1
Bit string 2:	1111 0001	0

The use of a parity bit will allow the detection of a single (or any odd number) bit error. It cannot, however, detect two (or any even number) erroneous bit changes that will compensate. It, of course, cannot correct any errors—it can only detect them. More complex error correcting codes do exist.

Input/Output Devices

Input/output (or **I/O**) devices are the hardware devices that interface directly with the CPU and the user. These devices cover a wide range of capabilities and characteristics. Terminals and miscellaneous other I/O equipment were introduced in Chapter 4. Secondary storage devices are a type of high-speed input/output device that is under the direct control of the CPU. These are discussed in Chapter 7. Input/output devices are also called **peripherals**.

Card Devices

The punched card as a basic input medium forms a shrinking part of the total input market. On-line processing with the use of terminals has replaced many batch processing applications using punched cards. However, punched cards remain as the basic input medium for some applications. The input device for punched cards is the **punched card reader** or, as it is more simply known, the **card reader.** The output device producing punched cards is the **card punch.**

Card Reader

The **card reader** converts data that have been represented physically (by means of holes in the card) into data that are represented electrically. As a result of this conversion, the data can be accepted by the processor.

A card to be read is fed into the reader from a card hopper. It is then read at two read stations and the results compared as a check. The card is then placed into an output card stacker. A vacuum arrangement is frequently used to speed up the physical movement of the card through the reader. There are two general techniques used to read the card: a mechanical brush technique and a photoelectric method.

In the **mechanical method** the card is passed between a roller and a set of brushes. If a hole is punched in the card at a position, contact is made between a brush and the roller. The contact closes a circuit and allows current to flow. As a result, the punched holes are converted into electrical pulses as the card passes through the read station.

In the **photoelectric reader** light is reflected onto the surface of the card. The card passes over a series of photocells. If a hole has been punched in the card at some position, light passes through the hole and impinges on the photocell. A photocell generates a pulse when light shines on it.

Cards may be read either row by row or column by column. A card reader that reads column by column (i.e. column 1, column 2, etc.) is called a **serial card reader.** A card reader that reads row by row is called a **parallel card reader.**

Card readers operate at speeds up to about 1,200 cards per minute. The higher-speed readers are photoelectric readers.

Card Punch

A **card punch** accepts as input a deck of blank cards from an input hopper and punches data into the cards (one card at a time) at a punch station within the device. The card is usually checked at a second station for accuracy. The card is read at that station, and the data punched in it are compared to the data that were provided.

As with card readers, card punches may be either serial punches or parallel punches. Card punches operate at speeds up to about 500 cards per minute.

Card punches may produce as output either interpreted or uninterpreted cards. Cards that contain punched data and the printed character equivalents are said to be **interpreted.** Cards produced by a punch that does not have a printing capability are said to be **uninterpreted.** Uninterpreted cards may be interpreted by use of an **interpreter,** which is a piece of unit record equipment.

Some devices contain both a card reader and a card punch capability. These are called **card read-punches.**

Printers

The printer provides the most direct and most convenient human-readable output from a computer system. As a result, one or more printers are associated with virtually every general purpose computer system installed. Printers cover a very wide range of speeds, print quality, and print technologies. One classification divides all printers into either impact or nonimpact printers.

An **impact printer** uses one element of the printer to physically strike another element. There are two ways that this may occur. In the first, a raised character is struck through a carbon ribbon against the paper. This leaves an imprint of the character on the paper. This is similar to the operation of a typewriter. In the second, a hammer strikes a ribbon and the paper against a raised character. An imprint of the character is also left in this case on the paper.

A **nonimpact printer** is one using any of a number of printing technologies that do not involve impact. Nonimpact printers generally operate at low print speeds and at high print speeds.

Another classification divides printers into serial, line, and page printers. This refers to the number of characters printed at a time.

A **serial** (or **character**) **printer** prints one character at a time. These printers tend to be low speed. Some serial printers offer a bidirectional printing capability. In a printer without this capability, a line is printed left to right, a carriage return is made, and the next line is printed from left to right. A printer with a bidirectional printing capability prints a line from left to right, shifts down to the next line, and prints it from right to left. Every other line is printed in the opposite direction. This capability can save time, since a significant amount of time is required to carry out a carriage return at the end of each print line.

A **line printer** is oriented around printing one line at a time. This does not imply that the entire line is necessarily printed at the same time, but only that the characters are not printed in a strict sequential order. These printers tend to dominate in the medium-speed range and are usually impact printers.

A **page printer** prints a page at a time. These printers are the highest speed printers and are nonimpact.

The following discusses a number of printers that provide examples of these classifications.

Thermal Printer

A **thermal printer** uses special heat-sensitive paper. Selected wires in a matrix are electrically heated to form a character that is then imprinted on the paper. The heat results in a color change in the paper under the matrix-formed character. Thermal printers are serial printers. They operate generally in the range of 30 characters per second (cps) to 120 cps. The special paper has a tendency to fade over time and is expensive. Print quality also tends not to be high. (Figure 5–11 shows a matrix arrangement.)

Daisy Wheel Printer

A **daisy wheel printer** uses a printing mechanism in which spokes radiate from a central hub. At the end of each spoke is a raised character. Figure 5–10 illustrates this. The hub rotates until the correct character is adjacent to the print line. A hammer strikes the character, leaving an imprint of it on the paper. The daisy wheel printer is a serial impact printer. The top printing speed is approximately 75 cps.

Figure 5–10
Daisy Wheel Printer

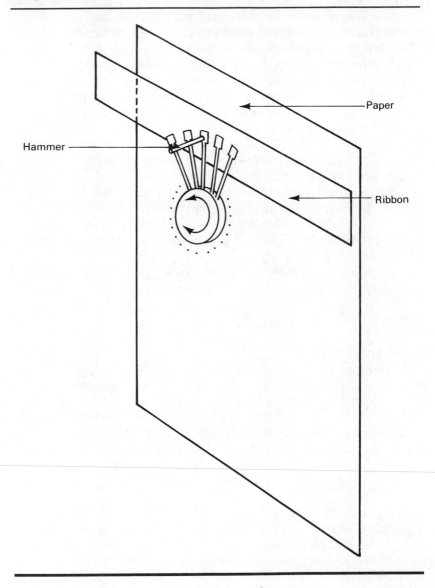

Electrosensitive Printer

An **electrosensitive printer** uses a special black paper covered with a metallic coating. The paper is sensitive to voltage differences. Voltages are applied to a print matrix. These voltages burn off the metallic coating from the paper, leaving the shape of the character exposed in black. These printers are serial and operate in a range of 160 to 6,600 cps. The paper is subject to damage during handling and the print quality is not high.

Ink Jet Printer

An **ink jet printer** uses a stream of ink droplets to form the desired character on the paper. These printers may be either continuous flow or ink on-demand printers. In either case the ink droplets, which are electrically charged, are shifted horizontally and vertically by deflection plates. In a **continuous flow printer** the ink droplet stream flows continuously and is deflected to the paper when a character is to be printed. Ink not used is recycled through a reservoir. In an **ink on-demand printer** the ink droplet stream is produced only when a character is to be printed. Print quality and print speed vary greatly.

Dot Matrix Printer

The **dot matrix** concept is used in a number of printers, including thermal printers, electrosensitive printers, and some ink jet printers. However, some dot matrix printers use an impact approach. A character is formed using a matrix of small hammers that are selectively fired against the paper. Figure 5–11 shows a matrix arrangement. These matrices are commonly 7 × 5 or 9 × 7. The character is formed by an arrangement of dots on the paper. In the example the hammers represented by the darkened circles would strike to form the character *H*, leaving the hammer pattern on the paper. Without looking too closely at the print, the character appears continuous. The character matrix arrangements are sometimes stored in a ROM built into the printer. Impact dot matrix printers may be either serial or line printers. The print speed on a serial printer is in the range of 30 cps to 330 cps. Line printer speeds are up to 500 lines per minute (lpm).

Cylinder and Golf Ball Printers

A **cylinder printer** contains a small metallic cylinder that has the full character set raised on its surface. The cylinder rotates to the correct column and then moves up or down to place the correct

Figure 5–11
Dot Matrix Arrangement

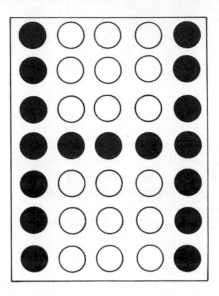

character in position. A hammer then strikes, leaving an imprint of
the character on the paper.

A **golf ball printer** contains a small spherical (or golf ball) surface containing a raised character set. The sphere rotates to the
correct character and the entire sphere then strikes the surface of
the paper, leaving an imprint. This concept is used in the IBM Selec-
tric typewriter also.

Both of these printers are serial printers and are slow (i.e. up to
15 cps). An advantage of the golf ball printer is that the spheres may
be changed easily to obtain a different print font.

Drum Printer

A **drum printer** uses metal cylinders (or drums) mounted on a
central shaft that runs the width of the printer. The drums have
raised characters on their surfaces. These printers are impact line
printers. Figure 5–12 shows the physical arrangement of the drum
printer. Around the circumference of the drum all print characters
are formed. One complete circle of characters exists for each print
position. The drums are mounted on the same central axis and spin.
A hammer exists for each print position. As the required character

Figure 5–12
Drum Printer

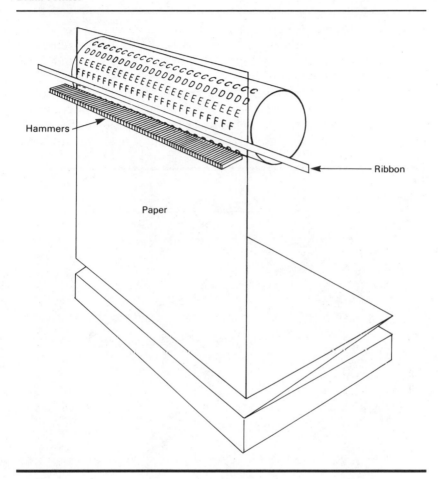

comes into alignment at a print position, the hammer at that position
fires. The impact of the hammer through the ribbon leaves an imprint of the character on the paper. In general, the required character
will come into alignment at more than one print position at the same
time. For example, the letter *E* or the numeric *1* may be printed at
more than one location on the same line. As a result, more than one
hammer may fire at the same time. Since the drums spin continuously, the hammers must strike the drum surface *on the fly.* This
continues until the print line is complete. The paper then advances

and the cycle repeats. Print speeds range from 300 lpm to 1,600 lpm. Print quality is generally good.

Chain Printer

A **chain printer** is one that uses a print chain as its basic mechanism. These printers are impact line printers. A print chain is mounted on two sprocket wheels and is rotated rapidly around these wheels across the width of the paper. Raised characters are located on the surface of the chain. There will be more than one set of characters on a chain. Figure 5–13 shows the basic print chain arrangement. This printer has a number of similarities to the drum printer. As the required character comes into a print position, the

Figure 5–13
Chain Printer

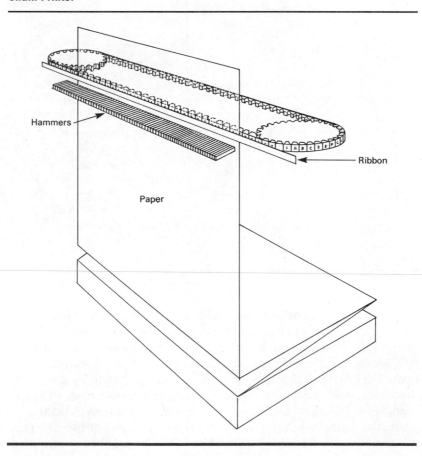

hammer at that print position fires, leaving an imprint of the character on the paper. More than one character will, in general, be printed at the same time.

Print chains may contain the same complete set of print characters repeated a number of times (usually five), or may have characters repeated a number of times depending on their relative frequency. As an example of the latter, more Es appear on the chain since E is the most frequent letter occurring in English, and few Zs appear since it is the least frequently occurring letter. This arrangement will increase the effective speed if, in fact, the printed material does approximate the frequency distribution of the characters on the print chain.

Chain printers operate up to over 2,000 lpm. Print quality is good, and it is possible to change the character set by changing the print chain.

Electrostatic Printer

An **electrostatic printer** is a nonimpact printer that is controlled by a small specialized computer. It is a page printer, and speeds up to 210 pages per minute (ppm) or 18,000 lpm can be achieved. The printer may be run offline, that is, output is written on a magnetic tape that is then processed and printed by the specialized computer based printing system. Because of the computer capability, a high degree of flexibility is available to interleave pages. Preprinted forms are not required, since these can be produced on the printed output as needed. Some ability to switch between print fonts and print sizes both between pages and within pages is available.

A special paper is used that can carry an electrical charge. Characters are formed on the paper by charging a series of spots in the correct shapes. The paper is then passed through a toner bath. The ink particles adhere to the charged spots, and the ink is quick dried.

Laser (or Xerographic) Printer

A **laser** (or **xerographic**) **printer** uses a laser and xerographic process to produce the print. It is a nonimpact page printer that is also controlled by a small computer. A laser is used to create, on a drum surface, an image of the page to be printed. The surface goes through a toner bath that picks up dry ink particles. This is transferred to the paper, and the ink is then fused to its surface.

Speeds as high as 20,000 lpm can be achieved, although laser printers are also used at much lower speeds. Flexibility in changing print fonts and print sizes is high. Forms may also be optically over-layed on the drum and incorporated into the print operation.

Channels

Transferring data between the central processing unit and an I/O device as the result of a read or write command is a complex (and time-consuming) operation. Although the CPU could handle this operation directly, it would be an inefficient use of CPU time. A piece of hardware known as a channel is used to handle I/O operations.

When the CPU encounters an I/O command, it passes responsibility for this data transfer to a channel. The CPU is then free to continue with other processing. The **channel** is a small, highly specialized computer whose only function is to handle data transfers to and from I/O devices. Its instructions are **hardwired,** that is, are contained in hardware and not in software. Because the channel is a separate processor, its operation can be carried on in parallel with the CPU.

A CPU may have associated with it more than one channel. Figure 5–14 illustrates the relationship between the CPU, the channels, and the I/O devices. An I/O device may be accessible to more than one channel. This provides an alternate path to the device if one channel is occupied with another data transfer.

The channel receives instructions from the CPU concerning the location and destination of the data. When the task is complete, the channel then informs the CPU of that fact and of its availability for another I/O assignment. If the I/O operation has failed, the CPU is also notified.

The maximum rate at which the channel can transmit data to, or receive data from, an I/O device is the **channel capacity.** Channel capacity is measured in kilobytes per second or megabytes per second. The capacity must be sufficient to handle the fastest I/O device that can be connected to it.

Channels require the use of I/O buffers in the CPU. **I/O buffers** are storage areas set aside in primary memory to hold data to be transmitted by the channel during a write operation, or to receive data from the channel during a read operation. There are two main types of channels: multiplexor channels and selector channels.

Multiplexor Channels

Multiplexor channels are used to interface with relatively slow I/O devices. A number of low-speed I/O devices are connected to the same channel. Data transmitted between the CPU and the I/O de-

Figure 5–14
Channels

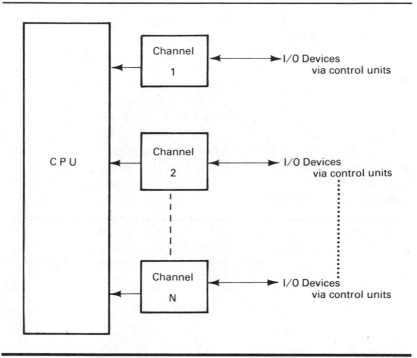

vices are interleaved. In effect, there is a mismatch in speed between the I/O devices and the channel. As a result, the channel can handle a number of relatively slow I/O devices almost *simultaneously.* Card readers and punches, paper tape devices, and printers are typically connected to a multiplexor channel.

Selector Channels
Selector channels are used to connect high-speed devices, such as magnetic tape or magnetic disk, to the CPU. A selector channel transmits data to or from only one I/O device at a time. The channel may provide a path to more than one I/O device, but once data transmission begins between the channel and an I/O device, all other devices connected to the channel are blocked from using it. Of course, an I/O device may be connected to more than one channel. In this case, use of one channel does not block use of another channel.

Minicomputers

The minicomputer was introduced in the late 1960s. At present minicomputers hold a major portion of the market, ranging from those that compete with larger microcomputer systems to those that overlap in capability smaller mainframes.

If a spectrum of computing capability is established, then the microcomputer is at the low end, the minicomputer is in the middle range, and a large computer (called a **mainframe**) is at the high end. Obviously there is not always a clear-cut boundary between these computer types. The term **small business system** has been applied to the large microcomputers and the smaller minicomputers that are designed to support typical business functions. The larger minicomputers are sometimes called **midis.** Very fast, high-capability mainframes are called **supercomputers.** These relationships are illustrated in Figure 5–15.

Figure 5–15
Computer System Spectrum

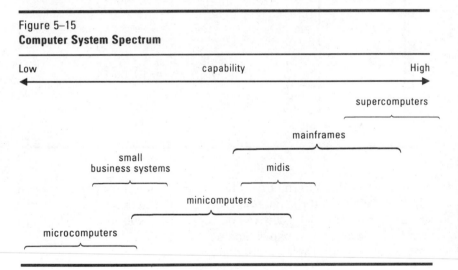

Today numerous manufacturers market minicomputers. Many of these manufacturers specialize solely in producing one or more models. The large mainframe manufacturers, e.g. IBM, Burroughs, Honeywell, NCR, etc., also produce minicomputers. An exact definition of the term *minicomputer* does not exist. In practice, a machine is a minicomputer if its manufacturer calls it a minicomputer. There are some characteristics, though, that tend to be common. These include:

1. The purchase price of a typical configuration is probably under $300,000.
2. The system is generally used for a limited number of applications at any location.
3. Environmental requirements are less rigorous. Most minicomputer systems do not require special air conditioning or humidity controls, but can operate in a normal working environment.
4. The number of I/O devices that can be operated on a minicomputer is more limited than on a mainframe.
5. Minicomputer systems are usually on-line oriented. Input is usually made through a CRT terminal. Output is produced either at the terminal or on a printer. Secondary storage devices are also used.

At the lower end of the spectrum there are some additional characteristics:

1. Primary memory is smaller than in a large processor.
2. A full range of programming languages is not available. Assembly, FORTRAN, BASIC, and RPG are common. COBOL is now available on some systems.
3. These systems assume a less sophisticated user. As a result, applications programs frequently lead the user through a series of decisions. A **menu**, that is, a table of choices, is frequently presented, and the user selects from this menu.
4. In many instances the applications software needed is first selected, and then the hardware on which the software can operate is selected. This is the reverse of the traditional large processor sequence of selecting hardware first and then software.

Some minicomputer systems are sold complete with all of the applications software required for a user's needs. The user, at least theoretically, need only turn on the system and begin using it. These systems are called **turnkey systems.**

Microcomputers

A **microcomputer** is a computer that is based on a microprocessor. In addition to the microprocessor, memory consisting usually of RAM and ROM chips and input/output interfaces are contained within the computer.

Microcomputers are 8-bit, 16-bit, or 32-bit machines. This refers to the number of bits making up a word in the machine. A 32-bit machine offers the greatest capability to the user.

For secondary storage, microcomputers use cassette recorders and floppy disks (see Chapter 7). Hard disks are also becoming popular for these systems, especially for those used as small business systems.

The microcomputer was first used as a personal computer for games and the maintenance of lists and schedules. Since then the personal computer has expanded to include word processing, children's tutorials, environmental control, spreadsheets, and even data base management systems. In addition, they now provide a means of access to various information networks. These networks provide a wide range of computing services and require a fee.

Microcomputers are also increasingly being used as intelligent terminals tied to a mainframe. The availability of these computers has also provided an impetus toward **end user computing,** that is, giving end users a computing capability under their control and management and not under the control and management of a data processing department.

Microcomputers are offered by mainframe and minicomputer vendors. In addition, there are vendors that compete only at the microcomputer level, such as Radio Shack, Apple, and Commodore. IBM entered this market in 1981 and, in a sense, legitimized the microcomputer for business applications. Since then IBM has expanded to become the dominant force in microcomputers. There are a number of IBM compatible systems offered by other vendors.

The BASIC programming language dominates in this market, although other languages such as FORTRAN and PASCAL, are frequently available. The software market has grown dramatically in this area, and a number of packages have been spectacular successes. Microcomputers are also sold as turnkey systems.

Distributed Data Processing

There is no one universally agreed upon definition of distributed data processing (DDP). In general, distributed data processing involves the linking by telecommunications of multiple CPUs. This allows the resources at one CPU to be readily available to users in the network at other CPUs. Network resources may even be transparent to the user, that is, the user may not need to specify or even know which CPU is providing the needed service.

A distributed network provides some of the advantages of decentralized computing without the disadvantages. There has been a trend in the past toward greater processing centralization. The main impetus behind this trend has been an attempt to take advantage of computing economies of scale. Although there is general agreement that these economies have been achieved in the past, it is now less certain that this trend will continue. By using smaller CPUs, especially minicomputers, it is possible to gain greater overall efficiency. There are a number of reasons for this:

1. Smaller computers use simpler and, therefore, more reliable and less costly hardware and software.
2. Smaller computers can be designed for specialized applications.
3. Smaller computers can be placed closer to the users.

The ability to communicate between CPUs allows access by one CPU in the network to the resources of another CPU. In a distributed system, a substantial majority of the resources required by any CPU must be available at the local node. The remaining needs of the CPU require communication with one or more of the other CPUs in the network.

A distributed network also allows control of the local system by its users. Specialized applications and efficient usage of the resources of the local system are the responsibility of the users. Yet compatability and interface standards may be enforced by a central authority. The advantages of local control can be combined with overall system efficiency.

Another advantage of a distributed data processing system over a single centralized processing system is the reduction of the effects of a failure. If a single CPU fails in a distributed system, its capability is lost to the network but the rest of the network can remain operational. If a single large CPU supports all processing, its failure prevents all processing.

If some of the CPUs are subordinate to one or more other CPUs in the network, this is termed **vertical distribution.** On the other hand, if all CPUs are of equal status, this is termed **horizontal distribution.** Of course, a distributed data processing network may contain both horizontal and vertical components.

An example of a network employing vertical distribution might be in a decentralized manufacturing company that operates at multiple locations. Each location has a CPU to meet its local processing needs, that is, it is used to support operational decision making. In addition, a CPU at the company headquarters receives data from each location to support tactical and strategic decision making. An additional characteristic in a vertically distributed network is that the master CPU provides backup to the lower-ranking CPUs as needed.

An example of a horizontally distributed system might be provided by a banking system with geographically scattered branches. An individual customer may have his/her accounts at one branch but wants to be able to carry out transactions at another branch when out of town. In this situation, the out of town branch must have the capability of not only accessing account data for local customers but also retrieving account data for transient customers from a remote CPU.

A major decision in any distributed network concerns the distribution of data. The two extremes on this dimension are:

1. No data are replicated (except in the usual backup and recovery sense) within the network.
2. All data are replicated at all nodes in the network.

Replicated data introduce complications for updating and consistency. For an update all copies of the relevant data in the network may have to be accessed and changed. A failure to successfully accomplish this will result in inconsistency between copies of the same data. An alternative approach that can be used in only some situations involves updating the local data and a central repository copy only, and then rewriting all copies of the data files at intervals from the central repository.

Conclusions

Hardware development has undergone, and is continuing to undergo, a technological revolution. This has been especially pronounced with the central processing unit, where increased chip density and reliability have resulted in a continuous increase in the performance-to-price ratio. Although not as spectacular, there has also been an increase in the storage density and a reduction in the access time for many forms of secondary storage.

There has been a distinct trend to move processing power out from a single central site. Remote processing has expanded dramatically, so that today virtually every computer based information system has such capability. Intelligent terminals have allowed some processing at the terminal location. Distributed processing has spread processing capability throughout a network. Microcomputers have been used in an organizational environment as small local processors. They are now being connected into networks with mainframes.

Hardware costs have been reduced dramatically, whereas software costs have increased. As a result, there has been a shift in recent years from a typical installation dominated by hardware costs to one now dominated by software costs. This tendency will almost certainly continue, since the design and coding of programs is still heavily labor intensive.

Additional Readings

Feigenbaum, E. A., and P. McCorduck. *The Fifth Generation.* Reading, Mass.: Addison-Wesley Publishing, 1983.

Foster, C. C. *Computer Architecture.* New York: Van Nostrand Reinhold, 1976.

Katzan, H. Jr. *An Introduction to Distributed Data Processing.* New York: Petrocelli Books, Inc., 1978.

Martin, J. *Design and Strategy for Distributed Data Processing.* Englewood Cliffs, N.J.: Prentice Hall, 1981.

Scherr, A. L. "Distributed Data Processing."*IBM Systems Journal* 17, No. 4 (1978), pp. 324–43.

Wieselman, I. L. "Non-Impact Printing in the 1980's."*Mini-Micro Systems* 13, No. 1 (January 1980), pp. 93–100.

————. "Printers."*Mini-Micro Systems* 11, No.1 (January 1978), pp. 52–70.

Review

1. Differentiate between digital and analog computers.
2. Define each of the following:
    a nanosecond
    b kilobyte
    c millimeter
    d terabit
3. What is a microprocessor?
4. *a* What is a register?
    b Differentiate between general purpose and special purpose registers.
5. Differentiate between I-time and E-time.
6. What is VLSI?
7. Differentiate between a ROM and a PROM.
8. Give the representation of the numeric 7 in
    a 6-bit BCD
    b ASCII
    c EBCDIC
9. Give the hexadecimal equivalent for the EBCDIC representation of:
    a 7
    b a
    c A

10. Given the EBCDIC represenation: *0100 1100* and assuming odd parity, what is the parity bit that should be attached to this bit string?
11. Differentiate between serial and parallel card readers.
12. Give an example of each of the following:
    a serial, impact printer
    b serial, nonimpact printer
    c line, impact printer
    d line, nonimpact printer
13. What is a channel?
14. Differentiate between multiplexor channels and selector channels.
15. Give five characteristics of minicomputers.
16. What is a turnkey system?
17. What is a microcomputer?
18. What is a mainframe?
19. Differentiate between horizontal and vertical distribution.
20. Give two arguments for distributed processing.

Chapter 6

Software

Introduction

A **program** is a set of instructions for a computer. Programs are also called **software.** This term is used to contrast them with hardware. There are two broad general classes of software: applications programs and systems software. These two categories can be easily differentiated in theory. In practice, classification may be more difficult. Some programs may be clearly systems software, while others may be clearly applications programs. In some contexts, others might be logically considered either.

An **applications program** is a set of computer instructions whose purpose is to carry out a specific user's application. An example of such a program is one which is written to process payroll checks and to produce various management-oriented reports.

Systems software refers to programs consisting of a set of instructions whose purpose is oriented around either efficient handling of an applications program or efficient utilization of the computer system for the benefit of its applications-oriented users. Thus, systems software is of indirect, but critical, benefit to the user, whereas an applications program is of direct benefit to that same user. The term **systems program-**

ming is used to refer to either the creation or maintenance of systems software.

Applications programs primarily manipulate data, whereas systems software programs primarily manipulate applications programs. The available systems software on a computer system defines the limitations within which the applications programmer must operate. In addition, the systems software affects such criteria as throughput and response time.

Throughput is the amount of applications-oriented work processed by the computer system in a given period of time. **Response time** is the time between the entry of a job or request into the system and the first response to that job or request as output. There is somewhat of an inverse relationship between these two criteria, that is, in general it may not be possible to improve one without a degradation in the other, given the same hardware and software. An improvement in both may be achieved with a change in hardware or software.

Systems software programs are, in general, not standard, that is, a particular program on one system may do more or less than a program with a similar name on a different system. The following common software concepts are not all present in the same system, nor is the following discussion meant to describe their implementation on any given system.

Translators

The digital computer uses the binary number system (i.e. a number system that employs only two digits). These digits can be represented by 0 and 1, although in the computer they may be represented by pulses of current, voltage levels, or magnetic states. Within the computer both data and instructions must be represented by bit strings. Viewing the contents of a particular memory location, it would not be evident at all whether the string stored there represented data or an instruction. Under one set of circumstances, a particular string may represent a number; under another set of circumstances, the same string might represent an instruction. In general, there are a number of different codes that may be used internally to represent instructions and/or data. There is only one representation allowed on given hardware for a particular instruction. This internal representation of instructions is said to be in **machine language,** that is, in the language of the machine. A program in this representation is called a machine language program. The computer hardware is capable of executing only machine language. All programs to be executed by the machine must be in machine language. Figure 6–1 illustrates the execution of a program by the computer. A machine language program and the data to be processed by that program are read as input, and the results of the processing are provided as output.

Figure 6–1
Execution of Machine Language Program

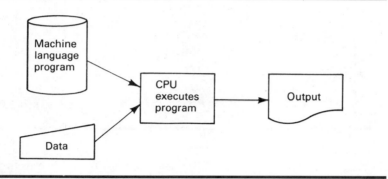

Although the only language executed by the hardware, machine language is difficult to use directly by the programmer. As a result, user-oriented languages have been developed. These languages must then be translated into machine language before an attempted execution by the computer is made.

The set of instructions written in the user-oriented language is called the **source program.** The set of instructions after translation into machine language is called the **object program.** An object program punched out on a deck of cards is called a **binary deck.** Although the creation of a binary deck was common on the earliest computers, the object program is now stored on disk. Figure 6–2 illustrates this process.

Programming in a user-oriented language (i.e. a language other than machine language) involves two distinct phases in the running of the program on a computer: translation of the source program into an object program (machine language) and then the execution of the object program.

Programming in a higher (i.e. user-oriented) language is easier and, therefore, less time-consuming. However, additional processor

Figure 6–2
Translation of a Source Language Program

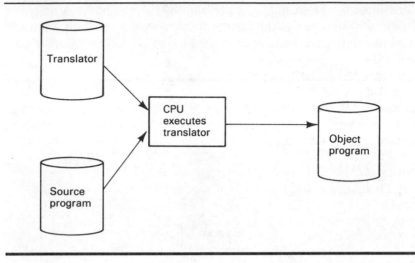

time is required to translate. Thus the tradeoff in the use of higher languages is a decrease in programmer time for an increase in processor time at translation. After translation, the object program is available on disk for repeated use.

Assemblers

An **assembly language** is a user-oriented language that represents a machine language instruction by the use of mnemonic codes. In general, one statement in an assembly language is translated into one statement in machine language. Since machine language is hardware dependent and since an assembly language program is translated mostly on a one-for-one statement basis, an assembly language is unique to a particular computer or to a compatible family of computers.

Memory locations used by the program are referenced not by actual machine addresses but by symbolic addresses or symbolic names. As an example, the following are legitimate assembly language instructions on the IBM family of mainframe computers:

L   6, X
A   6, Y
ST   6, Z

The first instruction loads (or copies) the contents of a memory location in primary memory, symbolically named X, into register 6. **Registers** are memory locations reserved in the computer for special purposes. The second instruction adds the contents of a memory location symbolically named Y to the contents of register 6. The third instruction stores the contents of register 6 into memory location Z. Each of these instructions is translated into a 32-bit long string that forms the machine language instruction.

The translation of an assembly language program is accomplished by a systems software program called an **assembler.** An assembler accepts as input a source program and produces as output an object program. The translation of the program is called **assembling** the program.

An assembler usually makes two passes through the source program. The first pass identifies all of the symbolic names used in the program. The second pass translates the program using the symbolic names collected in the first pass.

Since each computer manufacturer's hardware differs (and differences sometimes exist between computer models offered by the same manufacturer), no universal assembly language exists. An assembly language is machine-dependent.

Macros

Programming some tasks in assembly language may be time-consuming and subject to relatively large inefficiencies in the execution of the code produced. For example, assembly language instructions for input/output operations are of this type. Special commands called macros are utilized. A **macro** is the name for a set of previously defined assembly language instructions. When a macro is encountered by the assembler during translation, the assembler generates a series of instructions tailored to the data values of the program. These instructions are inserted into the object program. In a sense, *the wheel is not reinvented* each time it is needed when the design of the wheel is complex and its efficiency is important.

Compilers

Higher symbolic languages were the next step in the evolution of user-oriented languages. In general, one statement in a higher symbolic language is translated into a number of instructions in machine language. A symbolic language statement can be written in either an English-like or an algebraic-like language. The two most commonly used higher symbolic languages on larger machines are

FORTRAN and COBOL. On microcomputers it is BASIC. Reference to memory locations in these languages is done by means of symbolic addresses, as in assembly language.

As an example, the following is a legal FORTRAN statement:

$$Z = X + Y$$

This instruction results at execution in adding the contents of memory location X to the contents of memory location Y and storing the result in memory location Z. This statement accomplishes the same result as the three instructions used in the assembly language example above.

The translation of a higher symbolic language program is accomplished by a software program called a **compiler.** The translation is termed **compilation.** Thus, to translate a program written in FORTRAN, a FORTRAN compiler must be available. To translate a program written in COBOL, a COBOL compiler must be available.

Fewer source program statements are required with a higher symbolic language than with an assembly language to accomplish the same task. However, more CPU time is required to translate the program and, on the whole, the coding may result in less efficient execution. The main advantages of a higher symbolic language over an assembly language lie in the ease of writing a program on the part of the user, in making modifications to the program, and in debugging the program.

Another important feature of a higher symbolic language is that it is **machine-independent.** A program written in FORTRAN can, in theory, be run on any computer with a FORTRAN compiler. Practice shows that all languages fall short of this ideal to a greater or lesser extent. This means that it is rare for any but a simple program to run unchanged on two different computers. In most cases, at least some statements would have to be modified before a successful run could be made.

A compiler may take several passes through the source program. Symbolic addresses must be identified, statement translation made to machine language, and some degree of code optimization is carried out. In addition, the amount of diagnostic help available and the depth of that help may vary over a wide range. On some compilers an assembly language version of the source program is also available after translation.

A compiler (or an assembler) can only recognize syntax errors in a program. A **syntax error** is one that violates some rule of the language. Translators cannot recognize **logic errors,** that is, those errors which, though not in violation of any language rule, do not accomplish the programmer's goal. For example, in FORTRAN the expression: **X + Y = Z** contains a syntax error, since no arithmetic operation may appear to the left of the equals sign. The expression: **Z = X + Y** is syntactically correct but contains a logic error if, in fact, the programmer should have multiplied the contents of the variables X and Y.

Errors of a syntactical nature are frequently broken by the compiler into two (or more) classes: fatal and nonfatal. A **fatal error** will prevent execution. A **nonfatal error** may result in a warning, the compiler makes a corrective assumption, and execution is attempted.

Compilers tend to be relatively large programs. As a result, in order to conserve space in primary memory the object program produced by the compilation is usually written on a secondary storage device, e.g. disk. This object program is later read back into primary memory for execution.

Load-and-Go Compilers

A **load-and-go compiler** is used for a faster run time. The compiler is kept in primary memory, and the object program produced is placed in another area of primary memory instead of secondary storage. After the translation is complete, control passes to the object program and execution begins. There is a saving in time since the compiler does not have to be loaded into primary memory when needed, and the object program does not have to be retrieved when execution is to begin. The disadvantage is, of course, that space is occupied by both the compiler and the object program at the same time. Load-and-go assemblers are also sometimes encountered.

Interpreters

An **interpreter** is a compiler that translates and executes one source program statement at a time. Because of this one statement translation characteristic, interpreters tend to be simpler than traditional compilers. Due to this simplicity, more extensive debugging and diagnostic aids are frequently available. There are some disadvantages, e.g. if a loop is encountered it must be translated anew on every iteration. As a result, if extensive looping is done, much repeated translation is carried out. Because translation is carried out one statement at a time, code optimization is negligible.

Interpreters are most often used on time-sharing systems and on microcomputers. On smaller systems, they are frequently implemented in ROM. Sometimes an interpreter is used during the debugging and testing phase of a program, but a compiler is used to produce a more efficient object program for production use.

Special Purpose Languages

A number of special purpose languages have been developed. The symbolic languages discussed above are very broad in their range of programming ease in any given special application. As a result, for some widely used applications in specialized areas, special purpose languages have been created. Examples are in the areas of machine tool control, civil engineering, text editing, and simulation. Programming time is saved, but increased time is generally required for both compilation and execution.

Procedural and Nonprocedural Languages

A **procedural language** requires the programmer to define a step-by-step set of instructions to obtain the user's results. A **nonprocedural language** allows the user to specify some results but does not require detailed instructions on how these results are to be obtained. A procedural language is oriented around *how* a result is to be produced; a nonprocedural language is oriented around *what* is required.

Traditionally computer languages have been highly procedural in nature. Nonprocedural languages are becoming available to users. These languages are usually oriented around a narrower range of applications than that covered by a general purpose procedural language such as COBOL. For example, IFPS (Interactive Financial Planning System) by Execucom Systems Corporation provides a financial modelling capability. The main argument for nonprocedural languages is that they may be manipulated by nontechnical users to carry out functional tasks as needed.

Fourth-Generation Languages

A fourth-generation language is usually defined as one that is:

1. Very user friendly.
2. Very high level.
3. Nonprocedural.
4. Capable of making applications changes easily.

An example is Mathematica's RAMIS II. The statement

SUM SALES ACROSS REGION BY PRODUCT

produces a table showing sales in columns by region and rows by product. The data required to respond to this command would, of course, need to have already been stored.

Expert systems

An **expert system** (also called a **knowledge-based system**) is software that incorporates expertise in a specialized area, manipulates this expert knowledge to infer new knowledge, and makes recommendations to its user on the basis of this new knowledge. The system exhibits artificial intelligence within its area of expertise. The primary motivation behind the development of expert systems is that if the rather rare expertise in a field is captured in a computer system, then that expertise is available in many locations at all times. The availability of expertise is multiplied. Practical expert systems have operated, to date, in relatively narrow areas of expertise.

An expert system uses a knowledge base. Whereas the traditional data base contains an inherent structure showing the relationships that exist among data elements, a knowledge base does not. A **knowledge base** consists of a set of symbols and a set of rules with which to infer new symbols. If knowledge can be represented symbolically, then it can also be manipulated to logically produce new knowledge. Programming to manipulate this knowledge base is called **logic programming.** Two leading programming languages used are PROLOG and LISP. These languages provide the ability to create, update, and use the knowledge base.

Expert systems are a growing area of research and form a major component of the planned Japanese fifth-generation project. The concept of knowledge representation and manipulation may be the basis of the next revolution in computer based information systems.

Linkers and Loaders

A compiler (or an assembler) accepts as input a **source module** and produces as output an **object module.** The object module is usually stored on disk. The module is, however, not yet ready for execution. It must be transformed by linking and loading into a **load module.** The load module contains both the machine language instructions and the data locations referenced in the program. It is executable by the CPU. Thus, in fact, a program goes through three major phases as it is handled by the computer system :

1. Compilation (or assembly).
2. Linking/loading.
3. Execution.

A compiler produces as output, in addition to the object code, a **header label** that describes the memory references within the object code and the external references. The header label differentiates between constants, that is, data values which are independent of the location of the object module in primary memory, and values, e.g. addresses, which are dependent on locations in primary memory. **External references** are calls to other independently compiled modules. The compiler does not attempt to reconcile external references.

Linkers (or Binders)

The next step after compilation in preparing a module for execution accepts as input one or more object modules. Each object module contains a header label. This is referred to as **linking** or **binding.** The program that carries out this task is called a **linker** or **binder.**

If the object modules produced by the various translators are compatible, then subprograms originally written in different languages may all be successfully linked into the main program. Compatibility of translator output is a feature that allows significantly greater flexibility at the linking stage.

There are two general types of linkers. These are called the core image builder and the linkage editor.

A **core image builder** is a linker that produces as output a load module that contains absolute addresses. Since the module reflects its appearance in core once loaded, it is said to be a core image. Since the addresses are absolute, the module is not relocatable, that is, its location in core cannot be changed once linking has been accomplished. An advantage of this linker is that the program is relatively simple; a disadvantage is that the module is not relocatable. Core image builders are relatively rare.

The **linkage editor** is a linker that produces as output a relocatable load module. The linkage editor reconciles all external references contained in the header labels. A reference to a subprogram triggers a search for that subprogram. Some of these subprograms may have been entered into the system as part of the source program and were then independently compiled (or assembled) into object form. An alternative source of subprograms is secondary storage, where commonly used subprograms are kept in libraries. In this case, the subprograms are stored in object form. Subprograms from either source must be added to, and reconciled with, the main program.

The linkage editor also prepares a map of the layout of the object modules, including data areas in primary memory, assuming that the entire load module is to be entered starting at location zero.

The output of the core image builder is a module that contains absolute addresses. The output of the linkage editor is a module that contains addresses relative to a zero base point.

Loaders

The **loader** is a program that meshes its operation with the linker. The program copies a complete load module into primary memory. The operating system provides the loader with the address of the first location in primary memory into which the load module is to be placed.

A **binary** or **absolute loader** is a program that loads into primary memory a core image load module. It is loaded into the locations for which the load module was prepared. This loader is relatively simple.

A **relocating loader** is a program that loads into primary memory a relocatable load module. Final addresses within the load module may be handled in two ways: During loading the loader may adjust each address in the module to the absolute address, or during execution the contents of a special register called a **base register** are added to each address in the load module. Figure 6–3 illustrates this concept of **relative addressing.** The load module containing addresses relative to a zero address is loaded starting at absolute 50000. A reference to a relative address of 1200 within the module is converted to an absolute address of 51200 by adding the contents of the base register to the relative address. This is also called **static relocation.** If the module is loaded another time at a different location in primary memory, the relative addresses within the module remain the same, but the contents of the base register change.

Linking

A **linking loader** is a program that performs both linking and loading. In effect, the linking loader is a combination linkage editor and relocating loader. It holds off linking until loading is required. A disadvantage of the linking loader is that, since linking is done at load time, the entire process must be repeated with each execution.

Figure 6–3
Relative Addressing

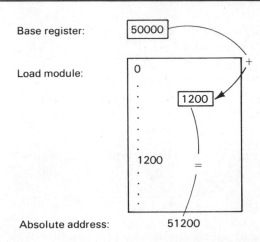

Base register: 50000

Load module: 0

1200

1200

=

Absolute address: 51200

If linking is separated from loading, the same linked module may be reloaded any number of times. In addition, the linking loader will tend to be larger and, therefore, requires more primary memory. If the functions of linking and loading are separated, then the linker and the loader programs will each be smaller than the combined linking loader.

Bootstrap Loader

When primary memory is empty, e.g. after a major failure, shutdown, or initially upon delivery to the user, the CPU can execute no instructions. In order to begin operation, an **initial load sequence** or an **initial program load** must be carried out. This sequence is commonly called **bootstrapping,** since it involves the computer *pulling itself up by its own bootstraps.* The computer operator initiates this load through the use of controls on the system console. A small set of instructions is placed into primary memory by the hardware. This set of instructions makes up the **initial program loader (IPL),** or the **bootstrap loader.** These instructions are loaded into predetermined locations, control is passed to the first instruction, and execution begins. A full loader is usually loaded by the IPL. Once in primary memory, this loader may then load any other program desired from secondary storage.

Operating Systems

An **operating system** is a set of software programs that is designed to operate the computer system in an efficient manner. It consists of a number of interrelated programs that are each designed to perform some necessary function for the system. The operating system runs the computer system; the computer operator monitors the running. The operating system is designed to maximize the amount of useful work the hardware of the computer system accomplishes.

Programs running on the computer system use various resources controlled by the system. Examples of such resources are CPU time, primary memory, input/output devices, etc. The operating system attempts to allocate these resources efficiently.

The operating system provides an interface between the user and the hardware itself. By masking many of the hardware features, the applications programmer is faced with a system that is easier to use.

An increasingly desirable characteristic of operating systems is portability. **Portability** means that the same operating system may be run on different CPUs. Portability has been achieved to some extent at the microcomputer and small minicomputer levels. An example of a portable operating system is AT&T's UNIX system which can run on hardware produced by multiple vendors.

Supervisor

The operating system consists of a set of interacting programs. The total set occupies a relatively large amount of space. As a result, the total operating system is not placed in primary memory. The entire system exists on a secondary storage device (usually disk) frequently called the **system residence device.** Part of the system is **core resident,** that is, it exists in primary memory whenever the computer system is running.

Programs of the noncore resident component of the operating system are placed in an area of primary memory called the **transient area** when they are read from the system residence device. Clearly, if a large portion of the operating system is core resident, there will be little time spent in retrieving those components needed but not in primary memory. However, a large core resident segment will occupy a large amount of space in primary memory. The most frequently used programs of the operating system are those made core resident.

The **supervisor** is that part of the operating system that acts as the overall coordinating program. It is sometimes called the **execu-**

tive. It is always core resident and retrieves from the system residence device any other components of the operating system as they are needed. In addition, it is the supervisor that sees that any compiler or assembler needed for translation of a source program is brought into primary memory.

A **job control language** is a language that allows a user to communicate with the operating system. Commands in a job control language are read by the supervisor (or a subprogram under its control), checked for legality and consistency, and then carried out by the operating system at the right time. Commands in a job control language are usually a type of macro command called a **cataloged procedure.** In effect, one job control command, once read, is replaced by a series of more detailed commands. In addition to specifying any translator required, these commands usually specify such items as location of input data, destination of output data, location of any subprograms needed by the job, input/output devices required, etc. The system is usually designed to provide a default value for many parameters. Frequently defaulted parameters are maximum run time, maximum print line count, maximum number of cards to be punched, etc.

Memory Management

Allocation of memory in an efficient manner is one of the functions of the operating system. Primary memory is treated as a scarce resource. A number of increasingly sophisticated schemes to manage this resource have evolved. The following outlines the steps in this evolution in approximately historical sequence.

Serial Batch

In a **serial batch** system jobs are run in a sequential fashion, that is, one job is run to completion before the next job begins. The inputs to the first job are set up, the job is run, and the output removed at the end of the run. The inputs to the second run are obtained while the first job is running. They are then mounted, and the process is repeated. An obvious problem is that the computer is idle between jobs. This idle time can amount to a significant portion of the total time available. Although efficient human processing and preplanning can reduce this idle time, it still remains a relatively expensive waste. The increase in processing speeds that resulted from the shift from the second to the third generation of computer hardware only exacerbated this problem. The allocation of primary memory in a serial batch system is relatively simple, as illustrated in

Figure 6–4. The applications load module is loaded into contiguous space in the area not occupied by the operating system. Any space not occupied is not utilized. The next applications load module is loaded over the first and may occupy more or less memory space. Of course, any module loaded must completely fit within the unoccupied physical space available.

Figure 6–4
Serial Batch Memory Allocation

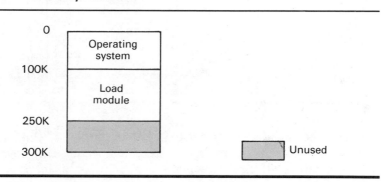

Overlay

Overlay is a technique used to process load modules that are too large to fit into primary memory. The load module is broken into segments, usually by the applications programmer. One segment is the main segment and remains in primary memory during the entire execution. The remaining segments are loaded into memory one at a time. Each segment is placed in the same area as (i.e. overlays) the previous one. A disadvantage is that previous segments are no longer available and, therefore, cannot be referenced. The main segment remains in primary memory at all times and thus serves as the focal point for references. Segments are brought in sequentially until the entire program has been executed. Figure 6–5 illustrates the concept of overlay.

Multiprogramming

In order to increase the throughput of computer systems, **multiprogramming** systems were developed. Two or more applications load modules are placed into core at the same time. The first module is executed until an interruption, e.g. an input request, occurs. The input request for this program is initiated and handled while execu-

Figure 6–5
Overlay

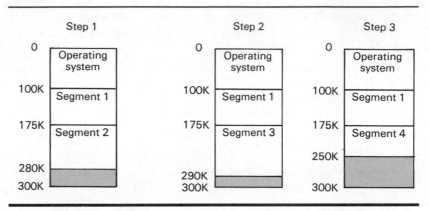

tion of a second module is started. The execution of this second module continues until another interruption occurs, and execution of a third module begins. When the processing of an interrupt has been completed, control may be returned to the program that made the request.

A multiprogrammed system is an extension of a concept inherent in a serial batch (or uniprogrammed) system. In a serial batch system, both the core resident portion of the operating system and an applications load module reside in primary memory at the same time. In a multiprogrammed system, the core resident part of the operating system and more than one applications load module reside in primary memory at the same time. Figure 6–6 illustrates the allocation of memory in such a system.

The concept of multiprogramming should be clearly differentiated from that of **multiprocessing.** In a multiprocessing system, more than one processor is used. Input/output devices may be shared by the processors, although each processor may also control some devices exclusively. In some cases, all processors may share primary memory. As a result, more than one CPU operation may be carried on in parallel, that is, each processor may execute a load module at the same time. In a multiprogramming system, only one load module may execute at any given time, although multiple modules reside in primary memory. Multiprogramming is implemented by software. Multiprocessing is primarily a hardware implementation, although some software is involved.

Figure 6–6
Multiprogrammed Memory Allocation

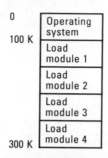

Partitioning

The area in core assigned to a load module in a multiprogrammed environment is called a **partition.** Partitions may be either fixed length or variable length. A system using **fixed length partitioning** assigns to every load module loaded into primary memory the same sized area. A system using **variable length partitioning** assigns various sized areas to load modules loaded into primary memory. Figure 6–7 illustrates a fixed length partition allocation where the partition size is 50K.

In memory allocation, the basic question is: Where in primary memory should a given load module be loaded? With fixed size partitioning the question reduces to that of whether or not a partition is available. On many systems the size of the partition is selected from a limited number of alternatives at IPL time.

In some multiprogrammed systems, one or more partitions may be devoted to batch processing and the remainder to timesharing. In some systems a partition with high priority is called **foreground.** In this case, all jobs ready for execution in foreground partitions are executed before any job in a **background** partition. Foreground partitions may also have priorities relative to each other.

Fixed partitioning results in a relatively inefficient allocation of primary memory. Since it will be rare for any load module to exactly fit into a partition, part of the partition will be unused and wasted. Figure 6–7 also illustrates this problem. Each partition contains both a used and unused portion. This pattern of alternately used and unused areas of primary memory is called **fragmentation, fracturing,** or **checkerboarding.**

Figure 6–7
Fragmentation with Fixed Length Partitioning

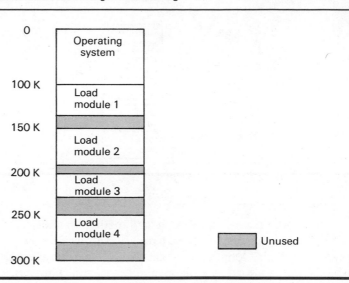

With a variable sized partition scheme, different sized areas of primary memory may be allocated to a load module. Thus, a load module requiring 20K of primary memory need be allocated only 20K, whereas another load module requiring 100K can be allocated 100K. Variable length partitioning is more efficient in the allocation of primary memory but requires a more complex operating system. Figure 6–8 illustrates the allocation of primary memory using a variable length partitioning scheme. In such a system, the assignment of memory is made not to the nearest byte (or word) but to some small increment, e.g. 1K. Thus, a load module requiring 15,768 bytes would be allocated 16K. Some space is still wasted with variable length partitioning, but it is much less, on the average, than with fixed length partitioning.

Relocation
Relocation was discussed previously in connection with linking and loading. The linkage editor prepares the load module so that all addresses within the load module are relative to a starting address of zero. The loader then copies this load module into a partition in primary memory.

Static relocation refers to the ability of the linker/loader pro-

Figure 6–8
Variable Length Partitioning

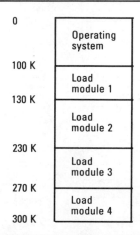

grams to prepare a load module for placement in any part of primary memory just prior to loading. The placement of the load module is not decided until it is absolutely necessary.

With variable length partitioning, fragmentation remains as a problem. When the execution of one program is completed, a new load module replaces it. If the second module is smaller than the first, wasted space results. Figure 6–9 illustrates this after a number of new loadings. In the figure, if a new load module of size 20K is to be loaded, there are two locations where it may fit. If a module of size 40K is to be loaded, no contiguous set of memory locations in primary memory of this size is available—although more than this amount in total is available.

Dynamic relocation is a means of relocating load modules in primary memory after they have been loaded. In effect, dynamic relocation involves *pushing together* the load modules already in memory so that the unused space is made contiguous and thus available for one or more additional load modules. Figure 6–10 shows the space in Figure 6–9 reconfigured after the completion of load module 4. In this example, 80K of primary memory is now available for loading additional load modules.

Dynamic relocation can be implemented because all addresses referenced within a load module are internally consistent (i.e. the first location is at relative address zero, the second location immedi-

Figure 6–9
Fragmentation with Variable Length Partitions

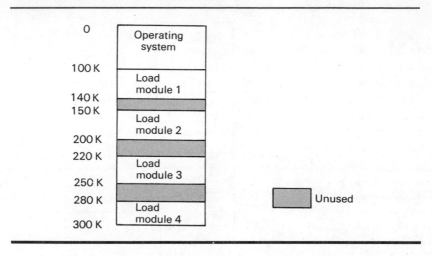

Figure 6–10
Dynamic Relocation

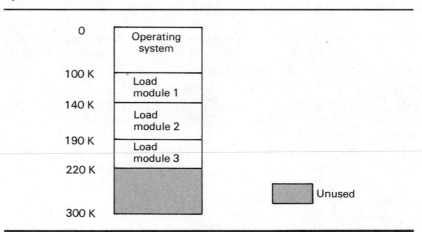

ately follows it, etc.). They are relative addresses and not absolute addresses. To relocate after loading, the load module is copied into its new area of primary memory, and the base register for that module is updated with the new base address.

Deadlock

A problem to be avoided in a multiprogramming environment is deadlock. **Deadlock** occurs when each of two programs requires a nonshareable resource held by the other. Figure 6–11 illustrates a deadlock situation. Program 1 accesses record 1 for update. To complete this update, it requires data from record 2. The program locks out all other users from record 1 until the update is complete. Program 2, however, is updating record 2 and requires data from record 1. It locks out all other users from record 2 until the update is complete. Each program will wait indefinitely for its required record to be freed. Deadlock, if it occurs, must be broken either by the operating system or by the intervention of the computer operator.

Figure 6–11
Example of Deadlock

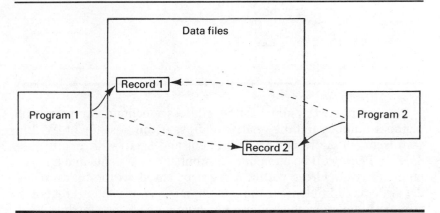

Segmentation

Programs, in general, consist of a main program and a number of independently translated subprograms. **Segmentation** is a means of breaking the module to be loaded into parts (segments) based on this independence, and then loading these segments into primary memory separately. As a result, the entire load module is not loaded into contiguous space. Each segment is loaded contiguously but not necessarily adjacent to its cosegments. This results in a load module being broken into pieces that can be more flexibly loaded into smaller areas of available primary memory. Figure 6–12(a) illustrates this concept. In the example the load module is broken into three segments of 40K, 20K, and 10K.

Figure 6–12 (a)
Segmentation

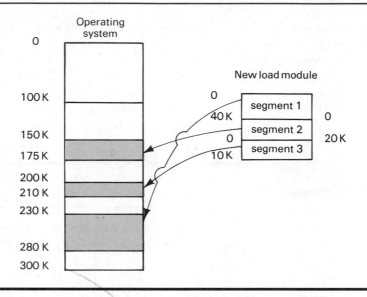

In a segmented system relative addresses contain two parts: the segment number and the relative address within a segment. Within each segment addresses are consistent and begin with relative address 0. There will be a maximum number of segments and a maximum relative address within a segment based on the hardware of the system. To implement the system, a segment table is created in primary memory by the operating system for each load module. This table contains the base address for each segment. A reference to a relative address results in the following: The segment number of that relative address is looked up in the segment table and the base address for that segment is obtained, and the base address is added to the relative address in that segment. Figure 6–12(b) illustrates this for the segmented allocation of Figure 6–12(a). If a segment must be relocated, only the entry for that particular segment in the segment table need be updated.

Paging
In a paged system, the load module is divided up into fixed length parts called **pages.** Each relative address consists of two parts: a page number and the relative address within that page. Primary

Figure 6–12 (b)
Calculation of Absolute Address with Segment Table

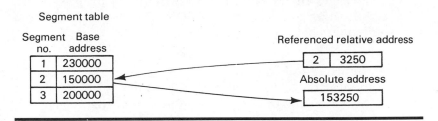

Segment table

Segment no.	Base address
1	230000
2	150000
3	200000

Referenced relative address

2	3250

Absolute address

153250

memory is divided into areas of the same length as the pages. Such an area in primary memory is called a **page frame.** Thus, a page is placed into a page frame. Figure 6–13 illustrates this for a page size of 4K.

The operating system maintains a page frame table that contains the current availability/nonavailability of all page frames. In addi-

Figure 6–13
Paging

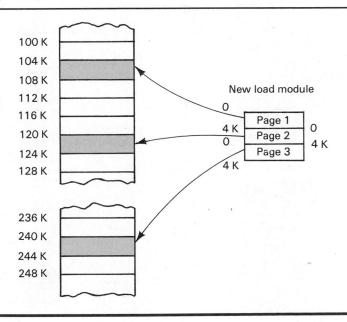

tion, a **page table** is maintained for each load module indicating the locations in primary memory for each page. Absolute addresses are calculated in a manner analogous to that in segmentation systems.

Since all pages are the same size and will fit into any page frame, memory allocation consists merely in determining the availability of the required number of page frames.

Segmentation and Paging

A **segmentation and paging scheme** combines the features of both segmentation and paging. The load module is first segmented, and then each segment is divided into pages. The operating system maintains a segment table and, for each segment, a page table. Addresses consist of three parts: segment number, page number within the segment, and relative address within the page. Figure 6–14 illus-

---

Figure 6–14
Calculation of an Absolute Address in a Segmentation and Paging System

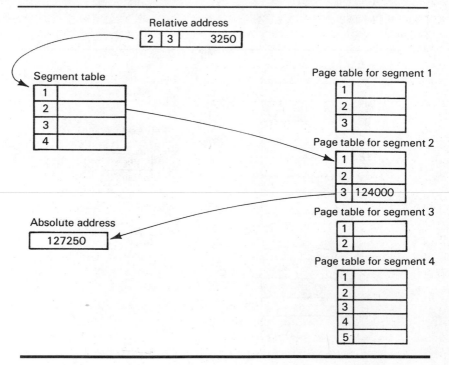

trates the calculation of an absolute address in a segmentation and paging system.

Virtual memory

Virtual memory allows the user to program as if primary memory were larger than it actually is. It is implemented by means of a segmentation and paging system. With virtual memory, all of the pages of a load module need not be loaded into primary memory at the same time. As the program executes, control passes from one page to another. If the succeeding page is already in primary memory, execution continues. If the succeeding page is not in primary memory, a delay is encountered until that page is loaded. In effect, primary memory is extended onto a secondary storage device. This allows the user to work with a pseudo, or virtual, memory that is larger than physical memory. The disadvantage is that some delay will be encountered when pages are unavailable and must be loaded. This is called **demand paging,** that is, pages are brought into primary memory only when needed. A **page table** in such a system contains for each page a bit that indicates whether the page is in primary memory at this time.

A tradeoff exists on the selection of page size. If the page size is large, then poorer utilization of primary memory results, since fewer load modules may have pages residing in primary memory. For an individual load module, however, there may be less loading of pages from secondary storage. If the page size is small, better utilization of primary memory results, but more pages must be described in page tables and a higher paging rate may be required.

A rule must be applied when all page frames are filled and a new page must be brought in or **paged-in.** A page must be selected for replacement. If this page has had any change made in it, then it must be copied onto secondary storage to replace its earlier version. This is called **paging-out.** If no change has occurred, then paging-out is not required, since a copy of this page already exists on secondary storage. One rule for replacing pages is **first in first out (FIFO),** that is, the page that has been in primary memory the longest is replaced. Another more frequently used rule is **least recently used (LRU),** that is, the page that has been least recently referenced is replaced.

A danger with any replacement rule is that the page replaced may need to be loaded back into primary memory again. A situation in which a page is replaced, referenced, reloaded in place of another page, which in turn is referenced, etc., is called **thrashing.**

A paging rate that gets too high will seriously degrade the performance of the system. If this rate becomes unacceptable, the operating system can halt further processing of a job and release the page frames used by that job to the remaining jobs. As a result, the paging rate is reduced. Jobs may continue to be halted until the paging rate is reduced to an acceptable level. The component of the operating system handling paging is usually called the **paging supervisor.**

Time Sharing

Time sharing is really an extension of multiprogramming. In this mode, a number of users operate on-line with the same CPU, and each uses a different input/output terminal. The load module (or part of a load module) of one user is placed into a partition. Execution is carried on for a given period of time called a **time slice,** or until an I/O request is made. As in multiprogramming, other modules of other users have also been placed into primary memory in other partitions. Execution passes to another module at the end of a time slice and rotates among all users. There may be more users than partitions in primary memory. As a result, the module may be swapped out of memory after execution during a time slice, that is, the status of the module may be copied onto a secondary storage device and the partition is filled with the next module in the queue. When a module is swapped out, the contents of any data holding memory locations and the contents of various registers showing the current status of the program are saved. A copy of the original module is already contained on the secondary storage device. The module is loaded back into a partition prior to the time it is again required, and data holding memory locations and registers are restored.

Virtual Machine Operating System

A **virtual machine** is a computer system that appears to a user as real but, in fact, has been created by the operating system. A **virtual machine operating system** makes a real machine appear as multiple machines to its users.

Each user may choose a different operating system for his/her virtual machine. As a result, multiple operating systems may exist in the real machine at the same time. Different versions of the same operating systems may appear in different virtual machines.

The most popular virtual machine operating system is IBM's **VM/SP** (or **VM**). Figure 6–15 illustrates this system with an example. The **Control Program (CP)** supervises the real machine and keeps track of each virtual machine's operation. **MVS** and **DOS** are two

Figure 6–15
VM/SP Operating System Example

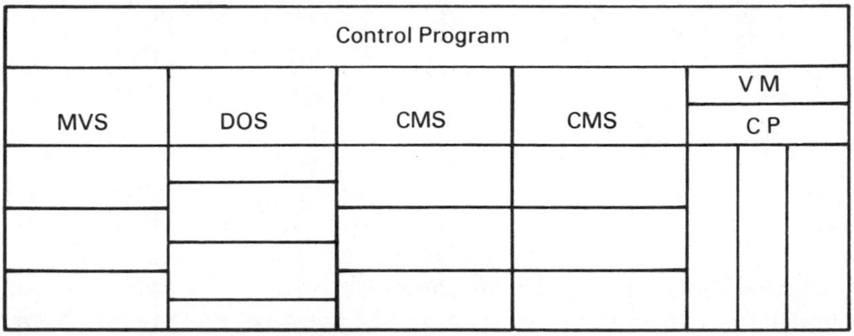

Control Program					
				V M	
MVS	DOS	CMS	CMS	C P	

other IBM operating systems. Each divides primary memory into partitions to hold different jobs. The **Conversational Monitor System (CMS)** is a system that provides the user with a highly interactive environment coupled with easy access to translators, editors, and various debugging aids. **VM** may also be chosen to run in a virtual machine under the CP. **VM** offers great flexibility to its users, and the illusion of a machine dedicated to each user's work.

Job Management

Job management is concerned with the scheduling and monitoring of jobs processed by the computer, in addition to various other administrative tasks. Included on this function is the reading and interpreting of job control language instructions. If inconsistencies or errors exist in the job control instructions, the job is cancelled. If the job control instructions are acceptable, various resources must be allocated to the job before attempted execution of the job is made, e.g. the mounting of a particular tape or disk pack, or the assignment of a particular device to the program on an exclusive nonshareable basis. Some assignments can be made by the operating system; other assignments must be made by the computer operator. If human intervention is required, the operator is informed of the required action by the operating system through the console.

In addition, various performance monitoring statistics may be gathered for later analysis by the job management routines.

Scheduler

The scheduler is a program that may carry out the following functions:

1. Selection of a job for loading into primary memory from a waiting queue.
2. Monitoring of the status of all programs already in primary memory.
3. Selection of a program to which control should be passed when the currently executing program finishes, requires an I/O operation, or reaches the end of its time slice.
4. Selection of the sequence of I/O operations for a device so as to minimize total access time.

A number of job scheduling algorithms are employed. The simplest is the **round-robin** algorithm. All jobs are treated equally, and rotation is made among all jobs in the system. A **compute-bound** job is one that requires a relatively large amount of processing with relatively few I/O operations. An **I/O -bound** job is one that requires a relatively high number of I/O operations with a relatively small amount of processing. Using a round-robin algorithm, responsiveness of the system may drop significantly if one or more compute-bound jobs enter the system.

Other scheduling algorithms use a multiple queue. Jobs are classified into one of several queues. Each queue has a certain priority. Those jobs in the queue with the highest priority are taken first; those in a second priority queue are taken next, etc. Jobs may be given time slices relative to the priority of the queue, that is, low priority jobs are executed infrequently, but once control passes to such a job it is granted a longer period of time in which to execute. It is possible that some jobs of low priority may never be selected, or may be required to wait an extremely long time. To offset this, one approach is to move a low priority job to a higher priority queue after a certain period of waiting time has elapsed. Additional moves up in priority may occur after additional time delays until the job is brought into execution.

Another concept is the replacement of a job of lower priority in the queue. This is sometimes called **roll out-roll in.** As the priority scheme becomes more complex, so too does the scheduler that must implement it.

Accounting

The operating system must determine whether a particular user is authorized access to the computer system. This is usually accomplished by use of an account number and, perhaps, a password associated with that account. A table of authorized account numbers and associated passwords (if any) is maintained. A check is made to insure that a legitimate account number and, if applicable, the correct password associated with that account have been provided by the user.

Costs for processing time, etc., may be charged to the user account by the system. Further access to the system is usually denied to a user once the user account reaches a maximum expenditure level.

Task Management

A job is made up of a number of tasks, e.g. compilation, linkage editing, updating of a file, sort/merging that file, etc. **Task management** is concerned with the handling and monitoring of a task. It handles supervision of those resources that cannot be allocated before the running of a program, e.g. time slices. It also monitors, by means of a timer, the CPU time used. If this exceeds a maximum, intervention is made and the program is interrupted. It is also concerned with error recovery. The means used to carry out the functions of task management are interrupts.

Interrupts

An **interrupt** is a signal generated by hardware or software that notifies the operating system that a condition exists which requires special processing by the operating system. The condition that has generated the interrupt may either be an error (or illegal) condition or a condition that in itself is legal but processing of it is reserved to the operating system.

The following are typical examples of interrupt-generating conditions:

1. Input/output—An instruction from an applications program to either read data from or write data on a peripheral device generates an interrupt. All input/output operations are controlled and initiated by the operating system. An interrupt is also generated whenever a channel that has been occupied becomes available for the next input/output operation.
2. Timer—Expiration of time either allocated to a program in a time slice or as a maximum amount for an execution generates an interrupt. If a time slice has expired, control transfers to another program. If maximum time allocated to a program has expired, an abnormal termination of the program is initiated.

3. External—The operator's console, another CPU, or a terminal may generate an interrupt.
4. Program check—An attempt by a program either to execute instructions reserved to the operating system or to execute instructions that would produce results in error will generate an interrupt. Division by zero is an example of the latter; attempting to change tables reserved to the operating system or reference to an address outside of the program's assigned partition are examples of the former.
5. Machine check—The failure of a parity error check, failed circuitry, a card reader jam, or an out of paper condition on a printer are all examples of this class of interrupt.

The generation of an interrupt produces a transfer of control to an area of the operating system. On some systems, all interrupts result in a transfer of control to the same location within the operating system. With execution starting at that location, a determination of the type of interrupt generated and the appropriate action to be taken is made. On other systems, different types of interrupts result in transfer to different locations in the operating system where the appropriate action is taken.

After some types of interrupts have been processed, it may be necessary to return to the applications program and continue execution of it. In order to successfully continue execution, the contents of various registers and data locations must have been saved. Before returning control to the interrupted applications program, these contents are restored.

There may also be a priority system, that is, some types of interrupts have precedence over others. A higher priority interrupt may suspend the processing of a lower priority interrupt. When processing of the higher priority interrupt is complete, processing may be resumed on the lower priority interrupt. The highest priority may be one generated by a machine error, since such an error may result in meaningless further processing for all programs.

File Management

File management refers to those routines in the operating system devoted to setting up, deleting, or changing files, allocating secondary storage space, handling input/output operations and, usually, controlling the file security system.

These routines also usually handle device assignment and insure that one program does not obtain access to a nonshareable device, e.g. a magnetic tape drive, that has already been allocated to another program. The operating system controls this through a **device assignment table.**

With direct access devices the sequence of input/output requests from different applications programs may be reordered in such a way as to minimize read/write head movement.

Input/Output Control

Input/output operations are complex. As an example, consider reading a block from magnetic tape. Assume that as the block is read, an error is discovered by checking parity bits. The tape must now be backspaced, reread, and rechecked. If successful on this attempt, the operation is complete; if unsuccessful, the operation is repeated a given number of times before failure is accepted.

A number of peripheral devices may be operating simultaneously. The amount of detailed programmed instructions necessary to handle this complex situation is large.

Additionally, if the programmer were required to specify the exact input or output device to be used, his or her program could not be run if the device was temporarily inactive or permanently removed from the system.

The **input/output control system** handles these and other details. The programmer's task is thus made easier. The input/output system takes over from the applications program and handles any input or output requests made. In addition, it handles the special actions demanded when the end of a file is reached or any error conditions occur.

Utility Programs

Utility programs are a miscellaneous set of commonly used programs that perform a variety of maintenance or service tasks. They may include a number of debugging aids. They usually include the following.

Librarian

The **librarian** is a set of programs that maintains the systems library. In addition to systems software, applications programs may be stored on secondary storage devices by users. The librarian keeps track of the programs that have been saved and their locations. Programs may not only be added to, but also deleted from, the library. The librarian updates its records to reflect these changes.

Sort/Merge

A program that can accept a file and sort it on a specified key is contained in a **sort/merge package.** The data file can be accepted from a number of input devices, and the sorted output can be placed on any of a number of output devices. Formatting of the data is usually very flexible. Data files located on a number of input devices may be handled, and the output merged into a single logical output file. A sort/merge program is usually written in a very general manner and requires the specification of a number of parameters before it can be used.

Dumps

Routines are available to provide a **dump,** that is, an output (usually on the printer) of the contents of storage (usually primary memory). The output provided is close to a mirror image of the contents (i.e. little formatting or interpretation is provided). The representation is usually in hexadecimal or octal notation and is used in debugging. A dump is sometimes requested when an abnormal termination (also called an **abend**) is encountered.

Spooling

"Spool" is an acronym for simultaneous peripheral operations on-line. **Spooling** involves reading and writing on devices that are mismatched in speed. The goal of spooling is to increase system throughput by copying data located in a relatively slow input device onto a relatively fast device. When the data are required by an executing program, they are then returned much faster from the second device. As an example, a deck of cards may be read in and placed on disk. The spooling program basically initiates an input operation, and control is transferred to an applications program. At some later time the input operation is completed, an interrupt is generated, and control reverts to the spooling program. An output operation that transfers the results of the previous input operation is begun, and the cycle repeats. At a later time images of the card data are retrieved from disk at a much higher rate. Data intended for a low-speed output device, such as a printer, may also be spooled. Images of the print lines are placed on a fast output device, such as disk. Later the data are spooled from disk to the printer in a manner analogous to spooling input.

Jobs may also be spooled into a system and placed in a queue for further processing. This queue (or queues) may be arranged in any priority order. Similarly, a job may spool printer output to disk independent of the availability of a printer at that time.

Checkpoint/Restart

In the execution of any program there is always the possibility of a program or system failure. If such happens, the program must be rerun from the beginning. This may be a serious problem in very long running programs, where restarting from the beginning may involve a significant loss of processor time. An approach to reducing this loss of processor time is to take a **checkpoint** at one or more points in a program. When such a point is reached in the execution of a program, data in primary memory, the contents of various registers, etc., are saved on a secondary storage device. If the program fails after this checkpoint has been taken, it can be **restarted** from this point instead of from the beginning.

System Generation/System Maintenance

Operating systems offered by a manufacturer consist of a number of mandatory and optional modules. Some parts are not required by some installations. **System generation** refers to the selection, modification (if necessary), and integration of these operating system modules into a system that will meet the requirements of a particular installation. It includes bringing the system up into successful operation.

   System maintenance refers to the updating and modification of an operating system already installed. This may be due to design changes and/or debugging.

Conclusions

Software consists of relatively complex programs that have evolved steadily over the years. The objective of all software is to make the use of computer hardware easier and more flexible for the user.

   Perhaps the most complex software is that contained in an operating system. The basic function of the operating system is the controlling of the computer system in an efficient manner. As an operating system (or any software) is able to more efficiently control operations, it becomes more complex and uses more processing time. As more processing time is used by the operating system, less time is available to the applications programs. Thus there is a point of diminishing returns. In the extreme, most of the available CPU time can be taken by the operating system to optimize system performance, but the amount of processing time remaining available for directly useful processing of applications programs is reduced to a minimal level. The amount of processing time devoted to operating system execution is called **overhead**. Overhead cannot be allowed to dominate the system.

Expert systems are a new thrust in software development. Their manipulation of knowledge rather than simple data is a break with traditional systems. They offer promise in many applications areas.

Reference

1.   Dovovan, J. J. *Systems Programming.* New York: McGraw-Hill, 1972, p. 149.

Additional Readings

Clocksin, W. F., and C. S. Mellish. *Programming in Prolog.* New York: Springer-Verlag, 1981.

Deitel, H. M. *An Introduction to Operating Systems.* Reading, Mass.: Addison-Wesley Publishing, 1983.

Harris, L. R.. "Fifth Generation Foundations." *Datamation* 29, No. 7 (July 1983), pp. 148–56.

Hayes-Roth, F.; D. A. Waterman; and D. B. Lenat, eds. *Building Expert Systems.* Reading, Mass.: Addison-Wesley Publishing, 1983.

"Knowledge Representation" (Special Issue). *Computer* 16, No. 10 (October 1983).

Lee, J. A. N. *The Anatomy of a Compiler.* 2d ed. New York: Van Nostrand Reinhold, 1974.

Madnick, S. E., and J. J. Donovan. *Operating Systems.* New York: McGraw-Hill, 1974.

Martin, J. *Application Development Without Programmers.* Englewood Cliffs, N.J.: Prentice-Hall, 1982.

Presser, L., and J. R. White. "Linkers and Loaders." *Computing Surveys* 4, No. 3 (September 1972), pp. 149–67.

Tsichritzis, D. C., and P. A. Bernstein. *Operating Systems.* New York: Academic Press, 1974.

Yourdon, E. *Design of On-Line Computer Systems.* Englewood Cliffs, N.J.: Prentice-Hall, 1972.

Review

1. Differentiate between applications programs and systems software.
2. Differentiate between an assembler and a compiler.

3. Differentiate between a syntax error and a logic error.
4. Define each of the following:
   a source module
   b object module
   c load module
5. Define each of the following:
   a linkage editor
   b relocating loader
   c linking loader
   d bootstrap loader
6. What is a job control language?
7. Differentiate between multiprogramming and multiprocessing.
8. With respect to primary memory, what is checkerboarding?
9. Differentiate between static relocation and dynamic relocation.
10. Briefly describe the concept of virtual memory.
11. *a* What is thrashing?
    b What is the approach taken to relieve thrashing?
12. What is a virtual machine?
13. Differentiate between a compute-bound and an I/O-bound job.
14. What is an interrupt?
15. What is a utility program?
16. What is a dump?
17. What is spooling?
18. Why is simple checkpoint/restart inadequate for direct access update programs?
19. Briefly differentiate between system generation and system maintenance.
20. What is an expert system?

Chapter 7

Magnetic Tape and Magnetic Disk

Introduction

In the various possible configurations of a computer system, there are some standard input devices and output devices. In a batch environment these may include a card reader and one or more high-speed printers. In an on-line environment these peripheral devices will be primarily terminals, although other devices, such as high-speed printers, may also be included. A wide range of peripheral devices is available in addition to these types.

Where the primary purpose of a peripheral is to store data (or programs) for later (and, perhaps, frequent) reading into a central processing unit, it is called a **secondary storage device.** This is to contrast it with primary memory, where the work of the central processing unit is carried out. Secondary storage devices may be used to both read from (i.e. data stored on the device may be copied into primary memory) and write on (i.e. data stored in an area of primary memory may be copied onto the device).

There are a number of advantages in using secondary storage devices:

1. Data stored in primary memory are transient (i.e. they are available only during the execution of a job). At the job's termination or at a

system failure, these data are lost. Data stored on a secondary storage device are meant to be permanent and available for use until they are changed or erased.

2. Primary memory is relatively expensive. Secondary storage is less expensive and, therefore, is an economical means of supplementing primary memory.

3. Secondary storage can be extended almost indefinitely.

4. On-line secondary storage is under the control of the central processing unit and, as a result, input and output can be carried out rapidly.

5. In virtual memory systems, secondary storage is used to hold the complete load module from which pages are swapped into and out of primary memory.

Secondary Storage Devices

In recent years a number of new technologies for secondary storage have been introduced into the market, while still others have entered a research or development stage. The most common secondary storage approach available today, however, uses a moving surface capable of being magnetized. This surface is moved relative to read and write heads. A **read head** senses the magnetic state on the recording surface of a storage device at a particular location; a **write head** changes the magnetic state on the recording surface of the device at a particular location. The two most commonly used classes of secondary storage are magnetic tape and magnetic disk devices. Probably the most important characteristic of magnetic surface secondary storage devices is reusability.

There are a number of interrelated terms commonly used to describe magnetic tape and magnetic disk operations. The **data transfer rate** refers to the rate at which data are transferred from the storage device to the central processing unit. It is usually measured in bits per second or bytes per second. The **recording density** refers to the number of bits recorded in a given surface length. It is usually measured in bits per inch for magnetic disk devices and bytes per inch (or bits per inch) for magnetic tape devices. The speed at which the recording surface moves under the heads and the recording density determine the transfer rate. **Storage capacity** refers to the total amount of data that can be stored on a particular device. It is usually measured in bytes (and occasionally in bits). A **volume** is a single physical unit of storage, e.g. a reel of tape or a disk pack (discussed below).

Control Units

A piece of hardware called a **control unit** serves as an interface between the channel and the secondary storage devices. Figure 7–1 illustrates this. The control unit accepts and interprets various file-oriented commands originating in the central processing unit and passed by means of the channel to it. The control unit supervises the carrying out of these commands on a storage device.

The control unit is also involved in parity checking data read from a storage device for validity, and it notifies the CPU via the channel when a nonrecoverable error has occurred. In addition, it indicates when data transfer has been successful or when an end-of-file condition has been sensed.

Logical and Physical Concepts

An **elementary data item,** in general, is the smallest, or the most basic, unit dealt with within information systems. It is not logically

Figure 7–1
I/O Path

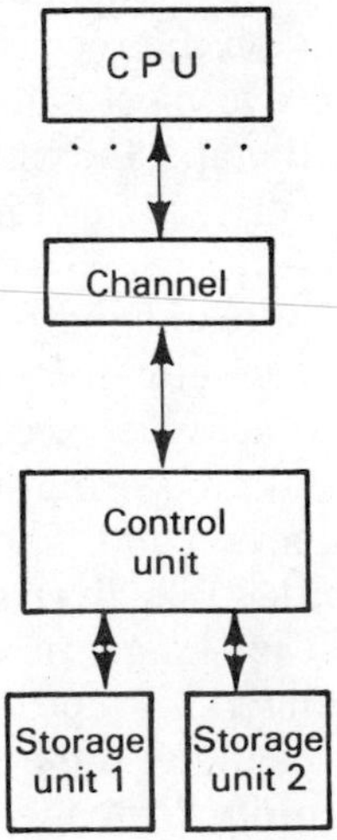

divisible. It is sometimes called a field from punched card terminology. Examples of elementary data items might be employee name, employee number, hourly rate, position, etc.

A **logical record** is a set of elementary data items (or fields) related in some manner. A record is treated as a logical unit. An example is an employee record containing for one employee data on name, number, salary, position, etc.

A **file** is a set of logical records related to each other, e.g. all employee records may form a personnel file.

Thus, elementary data item, logical record, and file are hierarchic in nature. Data items combine to form a record; records combine to form a file. These are the basic logical concepts in information systems and are represented in Figure 7–2.

Figure 7–2
Relationship of Logical Concepts

Elementary Data Items

	Employee Name	Employee Number	Hourly Rate	Position
Record 1	Jones	145	6.60	Clerk
Record 2	Smith	219	5.85	Aide
.	.	.	.	.
.	.	.	.	.
.	.	.	.	.
.	.	.	.	.
.	.	.	.	.
.	.	.	.	.
Record N–1	Lee	607	10.50	Manager
Record N	Brown	712	8.35	Analyst

Personnel File

A **physical record** is a set of data written contiguously on a storage medium. A physical record is not necessarily synonymous with a logical record.

A logical record may encompass more than one physical record. For example, the personnel data for a single employee (a logical record) may be entered on three punched cards, that is, three physical records. Of course, the data in one logical record may be entered in one physical record.

On secondary storage devices, logical records can be combined into a larger physical record before writing. In this case, a physical record is also called a **block.** A block consists of data physically written as a unit on a secondary storage device. Blocking creates a physical record containing one or more logical records. Figure 7–3 illustrates blocking, using the example of Figure 7–2. The **blocking factor** is the number of logical records contained in the block. In the example, the blocking factor is *two.*

Figure 7–3
Blocking

		Logical Record				Logical Record		
Block 1	Jones	145	6.60	Clerk	Smith	219	5.85	Aide
	·	·	·	·	·	·	·	·
	·	·	·	·	·	·	·	·
	·	·	·	·	·	·	·	·
	·	·	·	·	·	·	·	·
	·	·	·	·	·	·	·	·
	·	·	·	·	·	·	·	·
	·	·	·	·	·	·	·	·
Block N/2	Lee	607	10.50	Manager	Brown	712	7.35	Analyst

The applications program reads and writes logical records; the operating system reads and writes physical records, or blocks. A block is physically read and written as a unit. When an applications program encounters a write command during its execution, the data specified in the command are copied as a logical record to a buffer area under the control of the operating system. If the records are to be blocked, no physical write is executed yet. After another write command is encountered, another logical record is transferred to operating system control. After a block has been assembled, the operating system initiates a physical write command and the entire block is transferred to, and stored on, a secondary storage device. The procedure is reversed if a blocked file is to be read. When an applications program encounters a read command, control is transferred to the operating system, which initiates a physical read. A block is copied from the storage device to a storage area in primary memory under control of the operating system. Only the logical record specified by the applications program is then copied into the storage areas specified by the applications program's read command. Other logical records contained in the block are not available to the applications program, but are available to the operating system. If the applications program requests another read operation and the logical record requested is already available to the operating system, it is then copied into the applications program storage area. A request for a logical record not residing in the operating system area of primary memory results in the initiation of a new physical read.

In general, blocking results in two types of savings: Space is saved on the storage device, since gaps are used to separate physical records, and time is saved by not requiring a physical read with every logical read.

It should be noted that blocking results in a time savings only if the logical records are required by the applications program in the same sequence (or at least in approximately the same sequence) as they are physically stored. If they are required randomly, blocking may actually result in a longer retrieval time. This is so since it takes longer to physically transfer a longer physical record, and yet a new physical record is required for each logical read.

Blocking is accomplished by the operating system. It is defined by the file user in job control language, e.g. in FORTRAN, or within the applications program, e.g. in COBOL, at the time the file is created.

Records in a file may also be of fixed length or of variable length. Variable length records will have appended to them an additional set of bits specifying the length of the record.

Magnetic Tape Devices

Magnetic tapes have an iron oxide mixed with a binding agent coated on one side of a mylar strip. Conventional tapes are 0.5 inch wide and mounted on reels. The most common reel diameter is 10.5 inches. Conventional tape systems are also called **reel-to-reel** systems. The most common tape length is 2,400 feet.

The surface of a magnetic tape is divided into tracks across its width. Both seven-track and nine-track tape are standard. The read and write heads have the capability of transferring seven or nine bits in parallel. Figure 7–4 presents a somewhat conventionalized repre-

Figure 7–4
Nine-Track Magnetic Tape

Character
represented

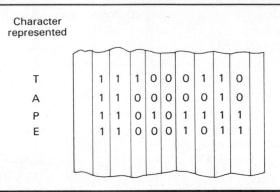

T	1	1	1	0	0	0	1	1	0
A	1	1	0	0	0	0	0	1	0
P	1	1	0	1	0	1	1	1	1
E	1	1	0	0	0	1	0	1	1

sentation of a nine-track tape. Across the width of the tape a nine-bit encoding of a character is recorded. This is the internal representation of the character, e.g. EBCDIC, plus a parity bit. The representation for one character after another is recorded sequentially down the tape. In the example, EBCDIC and odd parity are assumed. Standard recording densities are 200 (rare), 556 (uncommon), 800, 1,600, and 6,250 bits per inch (or bytes per inch).

As recording density increases, the requirement for tape surface smoothness also increases. Roughness in the surface results from dust particles being ground into the medium. In addition, wear of the tape through use results in small specks of material being loosened and then ground into the surface at other points. Small defects in the surface itself may exist. Any defects in the surface result in **dropouts,** that is, areas where magnetic recording is not successful. When a tape's performance has deteriorated so that it cannot be used, it is termed **tape failure.**

The tape reel contains a slot for a **write protection ring** (or **file protection ring**). Writing on the tape may occur only if the ring is in place. If the tape is to be protected from writing, the ring is removed. Reading may occur with or without the ring in place.

In most instances, data are read back automatically immediately after they have been written on the tape. The data read are compared against the data that should have been written. If the comparison is successful, the write operation continues; if the comparison is unsuccessful, the write operation stops, and recovery from the error is attempted. The tape is backed up and a rewrite is attempted. A number of such rewrites are tried before a permanent error condition is accepted.

The device that reads or writes on magnetic tape is called a **magnetic tape drive.** Figure 7–5 is a sketch of such a drive. The supply reel, that is, the reel containing the magnetic tape, is usually mounted on the right side of the drive, and an empty take-up reel is mounted on the left. The tape thus moves from right to left. The read head is to the left of the write head, so that an automatic read may be made after a write. The heads are in direct contact with the tape. A capstan drive and roller physically move the tape. These are frequently supplemented by vacuum columns. The columns contain a loop of tape immediately after the supply reel and another loop of tape immediately before the take-up reel. On each column are two photoelectric circuits. A photoelectric circuit contains a light source and a photocell. If a light shines on the photocell, a current is gen-

Figure 7–5
Magnetic Tape Drive

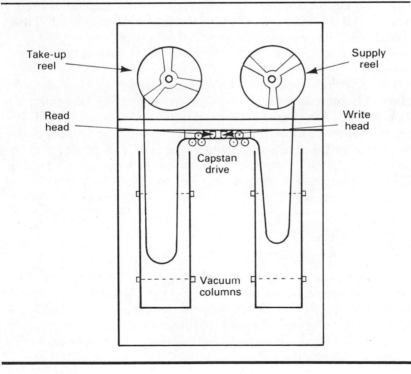

erated, and this current is used to control a vacuum pump. If the tape loop breaks the lower beam of a column, the vacuum is decreased in that column, and the tape is allowed to retract up the column. If the tape loop does not break the upper beam, the vacuum is increased in that column, and the tape loop increases in length. In effect, the two vacuum columns serve as tape reservoirs. The bottom of the tape loop in each column should always stay between the two light beams.

A magnetic tape contains special markers to distinguish the physical beginning and the physical end of the tape. These markers are reflective surfaces that are attached to the reverse (i.e. the nonrecording) side of the tape. They are detected by photocell sensors in the tape drive. The point on the tape containing the **beginning-of-tape (BOT)** mark is called the **load point.** Analogously, the mark at the end of the tape is called the **end-of-tape (EOT)** mark.

Tape files are terminated with an **end-of-file mark.** The mark is usually placed on the tape automatically under the control of the operating system. The mark consists of a special set of characters that, when read, indicates an end-of-file condition.

A file may also contain labels. The labels referred to are **internal labels,** that is, labels recorded on the magnetic tape itself. These should be differentiated from **external labels,** that is, printed identification forms attached to the outside of the tape reel container or tape reel.

There are two types of internal labels: header labels and trailer labels. A **header label** is a set of data recorded at the beginning of a file and containing various file descriptive and security data. These data would probably include file name, retention period, password, etc. A **trailer label** is a set of control data that may be stored at the end of the file.

Blocks written on magnetic tape are separated by a space called an **inter-block gap (IBG).** The standard gap widths are:

Seven-track tape—0.75 inch.
Nine-track tape—0.60 inch.
6,250 bpi tape—0.30 inch.

After a block is read, the tape stops with the read/write heads in the IBG. Thus the sequence is as follows: Read the next block, stop in the IBG, read the next block, stop in the IBG, etc. In addition to physically separating the blocks, the IBG allows time for the tape to decelerate from its operating speed to rest and then to accelerate from rest to operating speed.

As an example, assume that the contents of a standard 80-column punched card are to be read in and written on magnetic tape with one logical record per punched card. As further assumptions, the tape is written at an 800 bpi density, is nine-track, and the records are unblocked. Each record, therefore, occupies 0.1 inch. With a 0.6 inch IBG the tape arrangement appears as in Figure 7–6(a). Obviously, this is a grossly inefficient use of the tape surface. If the recording density were higher, e.g. 1600 bpi, the inefficiency would be even greater. By blocking the records, greater efficiency is achieved. Figure 7–6(b) and (c) show the effect of blocking factors of 10 and 100. As the blocking factor increases, a more efficient use of the tape space is achieved, and fewer physical accesses are required to retrieve all (or most) of the records.

Magnetic tape is inherently a sequential access medium. **Sequential access** means that the average time required to access a given piece of data is dependent upon the location of that piece of data in

Figure 7–6
Effect of Blocking Factors

	0.1″	0.6″	0.1″	0.6″	0.1″
	Data	IBG	Data	IBG	Data

(a) Unblocked

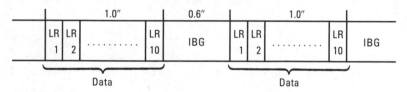

(b) Blocking factor of 10

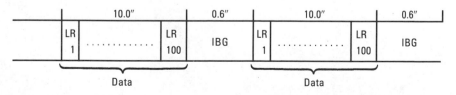

(c) Blocking factor of 100

the file and the current position of the read/write heads. Assuming that the read/write heads are on the tape at the start of a file, then the time required to reach the first logical record will be relatively short, and the time required to reach the last logical record will be relatively long. The last record can be reached only by reading over all of the intervening records.

A magnetic tape may be rewound, that is, the tape is returned to the beginning of the file. After a **rewind,** the next record read is the first one in the file. During a rewind operation the heads are retracted so that contact is not maintained with the surface of the tape. In addition, the rewind is usually made at high speed. **Degaussing** is a process by which the data recorded on the magnetic tape are erased.

Magnetic Tape Cassettes

A **tape cassette** consists of a container enclosing a magnetic tape that remains within the container at all times. Although the tape is completely contained within the cassette, it is exposed on one side, where data may be read or written.

The almost universally used cassette is the Philips cassette, which measures approximately 4 inches by 2.5 inches. The tape has a standard width of 0.15 inch (although it is sometimes referred to as ⅛ inch tape). Cassettes were originally used in audio applications but were adapted and improved for digital recording. Tape lengths commonly encountered are 150, 300, and 450 feet.

Advantages of the tape cassette over a full-size conventional tape are:

1. It is less expensive.
2. It can be easily loaded into, and removed from, a cassette device.
3. It is smaller and, therefore, cassettes can be stored and even mailed easily.
4. It can be moved backward and forward easily.

Disadvantages include:

1. A cassette has a much lower storage capacity than a conventional reel of tape.
2. Its transfer rate is lower.

Magnetic Tape Cartridge

A **tape cartridge** falls between a full-size reel-to-reel tape system and a cassette system. The tape remains within a container at all times. A commonly used tape width is 0.25 inch. The tape may be found on a single reel and consist of an endless loop, but sometimes the cartridge contains two reels in a more conventional arrangement. An opening in the cartridge allows contact between the tape surface and the read/write heads.

In effect, a tape cartridge offers a compromise between a tape cassette and a full size reel-to-reel system. Advantages and disadvantages of this device fall between the larger and smaller systems.

Magnetic Disk Devices

Magnetic disks have an iron oxide compound plated on a light metal surface. Disks are usually mounted in a stacked arrangement where one disk appears directly above another. The disks are mounted on a common central shaft. Figure 7–7 illustrates this. Disk speeds generally lie in the range of 1,800 to 3,600 rpm. The topmost and/or the bottommost disk surfaces are sometimes not used to store data. There are two possible reasons for this nonstorage: These surfaces may be more susceptible to physical damage and, therefore, loss of data, and a surface may be reserved for control and timing purposes.

Each disk surface is divided into concentric **tracks** around the central shaft. Data are recorded in a track bit by bit. Figure 7–8 shows this in a top view of a disk.

Most commonly the read/write heads move in and out as a unit, and one set is assigned per surface. Thus, the heads are simulta-

Figure 7–7
Physical Structure of Disk

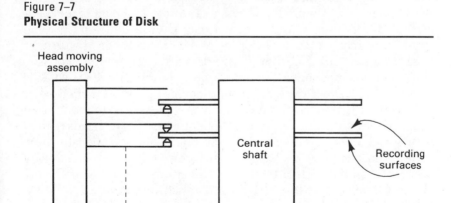

Head moving assembly

Central shaft

Recording surfaces

Figure 7–8
Track Arrangement on Disk Surface

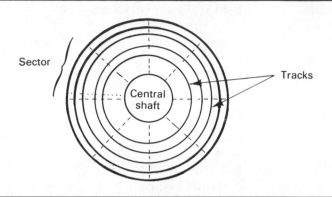

neously all positioned on tracks 1 or all positioned on tracks 2, etc. The set of all tracks on which the heads are positioned at one time is called a **cylinder.** A cylinder, then, consists of track 1 on surface 1, track 1 on surface 2, track 1 on surface 3, etc. There are as many cylinders as there are tracks on a surface. Configurations other than one set of read/write heads per surface are also used. For example, more than one set of read/write heads per track or one set of read/ write heads permanently allocated to each track per surface may be encountered.

A disk unit is a direct access device. **Direct access** means that the average time required to access a given piece of data is independent of the location of that piece of data within the file. The time required to reach a particular piece of data recorded on the disk, or to reach a particular location where data are to be written, consists of two main components: The time required for the read/write heads to reach the correct track from their current position (called **seek time**), and the time required for the data (or location) to rotate from their current position to a position under the read/write heads (called **rotational delay**). The average rotational delay is called **latency time.** If one set of heads exists per surface and the heads are already positioned on the correct track, then the average access time to any piece of data will be the time for a one-half revolution of the disk. Herein lies the significance of the cylinder concept—no head movement is required to reach any piece of data within the cylinder. Thus, the most efficient allocation of tracks to a data file is the assignment of tracks within the same cylinder to the extent possible. If more than one set of heads exists per surface, the average access time is reduced accordingly. Disk units do not use an automatic read after write check, as is done in magnetic tape units.

Some disk systems divide the disk surface into pie-shaped areas called **sectors.** Addressing may then be done to the individual sector. Not all disks, however, use the sector concept.

There are two types of heads used: fixed heads and flying heads. In neither case do the heads actually make contact with the disk surface. A fixed head is set at a fixed distance from the recording surface. A floating head rides aerodynamically on an air cushion created between it and the recording surface. Most disks use floating heads.

There is more area available to record data in an outer track than on a track located adjacent to the central shaft, that is, tracks on the outer periphery of the disk surface have a greater storage capacity than do the innermost tracks. There are basically three recording approaches used:

1. Store the same amount of data on each track. This clearly does not make efficient use of the outer tracks. However, it does involve simplicity in implementation and, in fact, is the most common approach taken.
2. Store the maximum amount of data in each track. Implementation of this approach is rare.
3. Segment the surface of the disk into zones and store the same amount of data per track within each zone. More data are stored in each track in the outer zones than in the inner zones. For example, on a disk with 200 tracks zone 1 may consist of the outermost 50 tracks, zone 2 of the next 50 tracks moving in toward the central shaft, etc.

Bit interleaving is sometimes used. One physical track holds two or more separately addressable tracks. For example, bits 1, 3, 5, etc., may belong to one addressable track and bits 2, 4, 6, etc., may belong to another.

The beginning of a track is indicated by an **index point**. This may either be a physical slot sensed by a photocell or a bit pattern recorded on the disk surface.

The disk is mounted on a **disk drive,** that is, a piece of hardware that serves a purpose analogous to a magnetic tape drive. Disks may be mounted permanently on a disk drive, or separately stored disks (called **disk packs**) may be mounted on a drive as needed. Disk packs are stored in dustproof containers, and the heads are inserted through openings. They offer the same flexibility of magnetic tape reels plus the advantage of direct access.

Disk drives may contain one, two, or four spindles. Some drives offer a combination of permanently mounted and removable (or demountable) disks.

The number of recording surfaces available on a permanently mounted disk or on a demountable disk pack is commonly between 10 and 30. The number of cylinders may be 200 to 555, and storage capacity may run from 20 megabytes to 2½ gigabytes.

Disks used with small business systems tend to be **Winchester** type. This is a design produced originally by IBM that has become almost a *de facto* standard. The disks, access arms, and read/write heads are completely sealed within the module. Storage capacities on this type of disk have increased dramatically and now range from 5 megabytes to over 100 megabytes. Track densities are now approaching 1,000 tracks per inch. Winchester disks come in 14 inch, 8 inch, and 5¼ inch designs. This dimension refers to the disk diameter. The 8 inch and the 5¼ inch disks are the most commonly used.

A **disk control unit** may manage more than one drive and basically carries out the same interface functions as a tape control unit. Some control units may be shared by more than one channel.

Rotational position sensing (RPS) is a feature of some disk systems. It is based on the sector concept. No attempt is made to access a record until the correct sector passes under the heads. The current sector position is determined. In the time before the required sector becomes available, other disk I/O requests may be serviced. Thus the RPS feature allows waiting time on one request to be used to access data on another request. In effect, an interleaving of access requests is accomplished.

Floppy Disks

A **floppy disk** is a small, flexible, mylar-based, iron oxide-coated device that resembles a 45 rpm phonograph record. It is also called a **diskette.** The disks come in 8 inch and 5¼ inch sizes. In addition, there are a number of disk sizes in the 3 to 3½ inch range, including 3 inch, 3¼ inch, 3½ inch, among others. It is probable that a new standard will be established someplace in this range. The disk is permanently contained in a square plastic envelope. When not in use, the envelope is usually placed in a cardboard holder for protection. Figure 7–9 illustrates the physical makeup of a floppy disk. A gap appears in the envelope over the recording surface to allow ac-

Figure 7–9
Floppy Disk

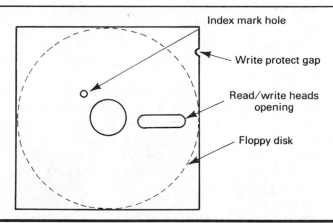

cess to the surface by the read/write heads. A write protect feature is also used. A gap is either punched out or filled on the envelope. A light source and photocell arrangement detects the presence or absence of the gap. An index hole appears in the disk itself, and an index access hole appears in the envelope. A light and photocell arrangement detects the index mark that defines the beginning of the track. Disks other than floppy disks are sometimes called **hard disks.**

Floppy disks are divided into sectors. Two approaches are used: hard sectoring and soft sectoring. **Hard sectoring** defines the sectors by means of equally spaced holes placed on the periphery of a disk. Detection is by photocell. **Soft sectoring** defines the sectors by means of a special bit code recorded at the start of each sector. Soft sectoring offers greater flexibility.

Standards on storage capacity vary. Dual-density drives can read data recorded on a floppy disk at twice a standard density; quad density drives read at four times a standard density. Dual-sided floppy disks record data on both sides of a diskette. Double-track systems double the number of tracks on a disk surface.

The main advantages of the floppy disk are:

1. It is inexpensive.
2. Storage is easy.
3. It offers faster access than magnetic tapes.
4. Changing the diskette is easy.

Conclusions

Peripheral devices cover a wide range of capabilities and characteristics. Those devices primarily used to store a relatively large amount of data with relatively rapid access to those data are called secondary storage devices. Although a number of different types of secondary storage devices are available, the two most commonly used types are magnetic tape and magnetic disk devices.

These two classes also represent two different forms of access capability, that is, sequential access and direct access. Tape devices are inherently of a sequential nature. Data may be retrieved from disk devices in a sequential fashion, but the capability of accessing stored data in other than a sequential fashion also exists. Thus, for those applications requiring a direct access capability, magnetic disk devices have been commonly used.

A wide range of tape and disk devices exist. Magnetic tape drives cover a range from a high-capacity 2,400 foot (or longer) tape recorded at 6,250 bpi to a small-capacity but convenient tape cassette. Similarly, magnetic disks offer a capacity ranging from 2½ gigabytes on a large disk to a quarter of a million bytes on a floppy disk.

Both magnetic tapes and disk packs, and floppy disks offer the advantages of offline storage and a virtually unlimited expansion capability. These demountable media can be mounted on available drives as needed.

A volume, e.g. a tape reel, tape cassette, disk pack, floppy disk, etc., may store more than one file. On the other hand, a large file may require a multi-volume capacity, that is, a particular file may be spread over a number of volumes.

Additional Readings

Bohl, M. *Introduction to IBM Direct Access Storage Devices.* Chicago: Science Research Associates, 1981.

Geller, S. B. "Erasing Myths about Magnetic Media." *Datamation* 22, No. 3 (March 1976), pp.65-70.

Hoagland, A. S. "Mass Storage—Past, Present and Future." *Proceedings of the Fall Joint Computer Conference* 41 (1972), pp.985-91.

Hobbs, L. C. "Low-Cost Rotating Memories: Status and Future." *Computer* 9, No. 3 (March 1976), pp. 21–29.

Kolk, A. J. Jr. "Low-Cost Rotating Memories: Status and Future." *Computer* 9, No. 3 (March 1976), pp. 30–34.

"Mag Tape Systems—Part I—Cassette, Cartridge, and Small Tape Transports." *Modern Data* (July 1971), pp. 32–35.

Zschau, E. V. W. "The IBM Diskette and Its Implications for Minicomputer Systems." *Computer* 6, No. 6 (June 1973), pp. 21–26.

Review

1. What is a secondary storage device?
2. Give three reasons for the use of secondary storage devices.
3. Define the following terms:
   a recording density
   b storage capacity
   c data transfer rate
4. Differentiate between a logical record and a physical record.
5. *a* Explain the concept of blocking.
   b What is a blocking factor?
6. Give two arguments for blocking.
7. What are the standard magnetic tape recording densities?
8. What is a file protection ring?
9. Briefly explain the operation of a vacuum column on a magnetic tape drive.
10. How does a tape drive sense the load point?
11. What is an internal label?
12. What are the functions of an interblock gap?
13. What is degaussing?
14. *a* Give two advantages of a tape cassette system compared to a reel-to-reel system.
    b Give two disadvantages of a tape cassette system compared to a reel-to-reel system.
15. On a magnetic disk, what is a:
    a track?
    b cylinder?
    c sector?
16. Differentiate between sequential access and direct access.
17. What is a Winchester disk?
18. Differentiate between hard sectoring and soft sectoring on a floppy disk.

Chapter 8

Sorting

Introduction

There are a number of applications that may require that the data being entered into a computer system be in a particular order, or that the data produced as output by a computer system be arranged in some order.

If data are to be processed against a file that has been stored on magnetic tape, then it is necessary, for all practical purposes, that the data read in be in the same order as the data on the tape. Since tape is a sequential access medium, records must be read in sequence. To avoid wasteful tape motion and repetitive read operations, the records on the magnetic tape should be retrieved once and used at that time. This is possible if the transaction data are in the same order as the data stored on the magnetic tape.

Reports produced by an information system may provide more information if the data presented are in some order. For example, sales volume, profit or loss, personnel turnover, scrap volume, etc., may be more meaningful if the data are presented in order from highest to lowest. This requires that the data be sorted before the report is output.

Basically, **sorting** is the arranging of data into sequence in accordance with some rule. In numeric sorting, the rule is the arithmetic order of the numbers themselves. In alphanumeric sorting, the rule for sequencing is usually called the **collating sequence.** For alphabetics, the sequence is clear: A precedes B, which precedes C, etc. The collating sequence with respect to special symbols (i.e. characters that are not numeric and not alphabetic) is not, however, standard. The collating sequence is a function of the internal representation of the characters. For example, in EBCDIC the codes for the alphabetics are less than the codes for the numeric digits, whereas in ASCII the codes for the numeric digits are less than the codes for the alphabetics. In EBCDIC a + is less than an *, but in ASCII an * is less than a +.

Sorting can be done in either an ascending or descending sequence. A sort in ascending order sequences the data from lowest value first to highest value last; a sort in descending order sequences the data from highest value first to lowest value last.

The **sort key** is the data item on which the sort is based. Sorts can involve moving entire sets of data, e.g. logical records, or just the locations (or pointers) of the data. Figure 8–1 shows an original table of data

---

Figure 8–1
Complete Sort and Pointer Sort

	Employee Number	Employee Name	Hourly Rate
1	014	JONES	8.20
2	031	SMITH	7.35
3	067	BROWN	7.65
4	084	DAVIS	9.50
5	101	ADAMS	8.60

Original Data   SORT KEY

084	DAVIS	9.50
101	ADAMS	8.60
014	JONES	8.20
067	BROWN	7.65
031	SMITH	7.35

Complete Sort

4
5
1
3
2

Pointer Sort

and the resulting complete descending sort, using the hourly rate data as the sort key. It also shows the same sort using pointers only.

Sorting can be divided into two categories: internal sorting, in which all of the data to be sorted can be placed into primary memory at the same time, and external sorting, in which all of the data to be sorted cannot be placed into primary memory at the same time.

Internal Sorting

An **internal sort** is the sequencing of data that can all be placed into primary memory at the same time. The entire set of data to be sorted is available simultaneously for sequencing. More than one data item may be involved in the sort. For example, sets of data for each employee containing employee number, employee name, and rate of pay may be available. If the data are to be sorted into employee number order, all of the employee data must be moved when employee number is moved in the sort. The alternative is to use pointers and then use the sorted pointers as a path through the data.

All of the methods described below assume that the sort keys are stored in an array A of length N and are numeric. It is also assumed that the data are to be sorted into descending order. In all cases, analogous procedures can be used to sort the array into ascending order. It is also assumed that only the sort keys are involved in the sort.

Linear Selection Sort

An additional array B is used for this sort. The array A is searched for the largest element. This is copied into the first cell of array B. The largest number in A is then replaced by a small number (perhaps a large negative number). This new number placed in A to *destroy* the previous number must be smaller than any other number in the array. Array A is again searched for the largest number, and this is placed into the second cell of array B. It is replaced in A again by a small number. This is repeated until array B is full. Figure 8–2 provides an example showing the changes made in arrays A and B with each pass. The number −99 is an arbitrary number used to replace the values in array A in the example. If it is desired to sort the data into ascending order, then the approach is to select the smallest number and to replace it in array A with a large number.

The number of passes through the data required to complete the sort is N. This is so since one number is moved into array B on each pass.

Figure 8–2
Linear Selection Sort

A	B		A	B		A	B	....	A	B
49	0		49	70		49	70		− 99	70
28	0		28	0		28	57		− 99	57
57	0		57	0		− 99	0	....	− 99	49
12	0		12	0		12	0		− 99	41
41	0		41	0		41	0		− 99	28
70	0		− 99	0		− 99	0	....	− 99	12
Original arrays			After pass 1			After pass 2			After pass 6	

The number of memory locations required is 2N + 1. This includes the two arrays and one additional memory location needed to store the location in A from which the most recent data transfer into B has occurred. At the end of a pass this location provides the data location in A into which the arbitrary small number, e.g. − 99, is placed.

There are N passes and each pass requires (N − 1) comparisons. Thus, the total number of comparisons required is always N(N − 1).

Linear Selection with Interchange Sort

In this sort the largest element of A is found and interchanged with the first element of A. Then the largest element of A in the N − 1 last cells is found and interchanged with the second element of A. This is repeated for the N − 2 last cells, etc., until the array is sorted. Usually an interchange is not made until the end of the pass. As an example, Figure 8–3 illustrates this sort with the same data that were used in Figure 8–2.

Figure 8–3
Linear Selection with Interchange Sort

A	A	A	A	A	A
49	70*	70	70	70	70
28	28	57*	57	57	57
57	57	28*	49*	49	49
12	12	12	12	41*	41
41	41	41	41	12*	28*
70	49*	49	28*	28	12*
Original array	After pass 1	After pass 2	After pass 3	After pass 4	After pass 5

* Elements interchanged

The number of passes required to complete the sort is $(N-1)$, since when the next to the last element is placed into its correct position it results in the last element also being placed in its correct position. Notice also that the passes get progressively shorter.

If interchange is postponed until the end of the pass, $N+2$ memory locations are required. These hold the array A, a location to hold the highest number found so far in a pass, and the location of that number in the array. If interchange is done throughout the pass, $N+1$ memory locations are required. These hold the array A and a temporary location for use in the interchange.

The total number of comparisons is:

$$(N-1) + (N-2) + \ldots + 2+1 = N(N-1)/2$$

This reflects the progressively shorter nature of each pass.

Exchange (or Bubble) Sort

In this sort, data which are below their correct positions tend to *bubble up* to their proper positions. On each pass the first element of A is compared with the second element, and the larger assumes the first position. The second element is then compared with the third and the larger assumes the second position, and so on through the array. This process is repeated on each pass through the array until no exchanges take place in a pass. In effect, at least one element is placed into its correct position on each pass. Thus, after pass 1 the smallest element is in the last position, after pass 2 the next smallest is in the next to last position, etc. As an example, Figure 8–4 illustrates two passes of this sort.

The number of passes required depends on the initial degree of

---

Figure 8–4
Exchange (or Bubble) Sort

A	A	A	A	A	A		A	A	A	A	A. . . .
49	*49	49	49	49	49		*57	57	57	57	57
28	*28	*57	57	57	57		*49	*49	49	49	49
57	57	*28	*28	28	28		28	*28	*41	41	41. . .
12	12	12	*12	*41	41		41	41	*28	*70	70
41	41	41	41	*12	*70		70	70	70	*28	*28
70	70	70	70	70	*12		12	12	12	12	*12. . .
Original array		Pass 1						Pass 2			

*Elements compared
Elements interchanged

order of the data. If M is the largest number of positions that an element is out of its proper position, then the number of passes required is M + 1. The only way to be certain that the sort is complete is to continue until a pass occurs with no exchanges. If the data are already in order, then 1 pass is required. If the largest piece of data is in the last position, then $N - 1$ passes are required.

The number of memory locations required is $N + 2$. These hold the array A, a temporary location for the exchange, and a switch to indicate whether or not an exchange has occurred on a particular pass.

The number of comparisons depends on the number of passes required. There are $N - 1$ on the first pass, $N - 2$ on the second pass, etc., for $M + 1$ passes. Since at least one element is placed into its correct position starting from the end of the array on each pass, one fewer comparison is required on each pass. The minimum number of comparisons is $N - 1$ and the maximum number is $N(N - 1)/2$. The expected number is approximately $(N^2/2) - (3N/4)^3$.

Sifting (or Shuttlesort) Sort

Sifting, which is also called the **shuttlesort,** begins in the same manner as an exchange (or bubble) sort. The first element is compared to the second element, the second element is compared to the third, etc., until an exchange is called for. These comparisons are called **primary comparisons.** The larger element at this point is then compared backward up the list until either a larger element appears or the first position is reached. These are called **secondary comparisons.** When the secondary comparisons are complete, the primary comparisons restart at the position from which the first exchange was made. Thus, in general, a primary comparison may give rise to more than one secondary comparison. The sort is complete when the end of the list is reached. Figure 8–5 illustrates this sort.

There is only one primary pass made through the data. Since each comparison on the primary pass may trigger secondary comparisons, this is a more complicated pass than exists in other sorts.

The number of memory locations required is $N + 2$. These hold the array A, a temporary location used for the interchange, and a location to hold the current position of the primary comparison.

The minimum number of comparisons is $N - 1$ (when the data are already in correct order). If the data are in reverse order, then each primary comparison triggers a set of secondary comparisons that runs back to the beginning of the list. There will be $N - 1$ pri-

Figure 8–5
Sifting (or Shuttlesort)

A	A	A	A	A	A	A	A	A	A	A	A
49	*49	49	*57	57	57	57	57	57	57	57	*70
28	*28	*57	*49	49	49	49	49	49	49	*70	*57
57	57	*28	28	*28	28	*41	41	41	*70	*49	49
12	12	12	12	*12	*41	*28	28	*70	*41	41	41
41	41	41	41	41	*12	12	*70	*28	28	28	28
70	70	70	70	70	70	70	*12	12	12	12	12
Original array											End of sort

*Elements compared
Elements interchanged

mary comparisons. For each primary comparison there will be an average of $(N-1)/2$ secondary comparisons. The total number of secondary comparisons will be $(N-1)^2/2$. Thus, the maximum number of primary and secondary comparisons will be $(N-1) + (N-1)^2/2$. In calculating the expected number, the number of primary comparisons remains at $N-1$. Assuming that each string of secondary comparisons backtracks on the list halfway to the beginning, the expected number of secondary comparisons is $(N-1)^2/4$. The total number of expected comparisons is, therefore, $(N-1) + (N-1)^2/4$.

Insertion Sort

The **insertion sort** is analogous to the procedure a card player follows in arranging a hand of cards. Data are taken one at a time and inserted into their correct positions. In effect, the array A is divided into two partitions: one containing data already sorted and the other containing the remaining unsorted data. The partition boundary moves from the top to the bottom of the array, eventually expanding the first partition to include all of the array. Figure 8–6 illustrates this sort.

In general, the array contains two subsets of data: the sorted data in the first cells and the unsorted data in the last cells. A pointer must be maintained to locate the bottom element of the sorted data. In general, the bottom element must be shifted down, then the next to the bottom element is shifted into its place until the proper position for insertion is found.

Figure 8–6
Insertion Sort

A	A	A	A	A	A	A
49	49	49	57	57	57	70
28	28	28	49	49	49	57
57	57	57	28	28	41	49
12	12	12	12	12	28	41
41	41	41	41	41	12	28
70	70	70	70	70	70	12
Original array						End of sort

— Boundary

The number of passes required to complete the sort is N − 1. Each pass becomes potentially longer as the sort progresses.

The number of memory locations required is N + 2. These locations hold the array A, a temporary location used in the exchange, and a pointer to locate the bottom element of the sorted data.

The minimum number of comparisons in N − 1, which will occur when the data are in order. The maximum number of comparisons will occur when the data are in reverse order. On each of N − 1 insertions all of the previously inserted data must be compared and shifted. The average length of the shift/comparisons is N/2. Thus, the maximum number of comparisons is N(N − 1)/2. In general, an insertion will require a shift of half the previously inserted data, thus giving an expected number of comparisons of N(N − 1)/4.

Shellsort

The **Shellsort** is a variation of sifting. Comparisons are made between elements a given distance apart. This distance is reduced on each pass until a distance of 1 is achieved and adjacent elements are compared. If a primary exchange takes place, then a series of secondary exchanges within the same partition may occur. Using this method, elements far from their final position will move closer faster by taking long jumps in the early passes.

In this sort the contents of the array are conceptually divided into a series of partitions. Elements within the same partition are compared and placed into correct order with the partition.

Shell,[2] the inventor of the sort, suggested using an initial distance of N/2 for an even number of elements and (N − 1)/2 for an odd number of elements. Thus, the initial partitions each contain two elements (or the first partition contains three elements if the length of the array A is odd). The distance on each succeeding pass is halved (truncated, if necessary), and the number of elements in each partition is doubled until, in the final pass, a distance of 1 is used.

Figure 8–7
Shellsort

A	A	A	A	A
*49	49	49	49	49
28	*28	70	70	70
57	57	*57	57	57
12	12	12	*12	19
*41	41	41	41	41
70	*70	28	28	28
27	27	*27	27	27
19	19	19	*19	12

Original array   End of pass 1

A	A	A	A	A	A	A	A
*49	57	57	57	57	57	57	57
70	*70	70	70	*70	70	70	70
*57	49	*49	49	49	49	49	49
19	*19	19	*19	*28	28	28	28
41	41	*41	41	41	*41	41	41
28	28	28	*28	19	19	*19	19
27	27	27	27	27	*27	27	27
12	12	12	12	12	12	*12	12

End of pass 2

A	A	A	A	A	A	A	A	A	A
*57	70	70	70	70	70	70	70	70	70
*70	*57	57	57	57	57	57	57	57	57
49	*49	*49	49	*49	49	49	49	49	49
28	28	*28	*28	*41	41	41	41	41	41
41	41	41	*41	28	*28	28	*28	28	28
19	19	19	19	19	*19	*19	*27	27	27
27	27	27	27	27	27	*27	19	*19	19
12	12	12	12	12	12	12	12	*12	12

End of pass 3

*Elements compared
Elements interchanged

Figure 8–7 illustrates the Shellsort, using an initial distance of 4 between elements in the same partition. This distance is halved on each pass until a distance of 1 on the third pass is achieved.

If the number of elements in the array is odd, then there will be three elements in the first partition. Figure 8–8 shows the sequence of comparisons needed to insure that the first partition is in correct order.

Figure 8–8
Shellsort with Odd Number of Elements

A	A	A	A
*27	41	41	*57
•	•	•	•
•	•	•	•
•	•	•	•
•	•	•	•
*41	*27	*57	*41
•	•	•	•
•	•	•	•
•	•	•	•
•	•	•	•
57	*57	*27	27
Original array			End of partition 1 sort

Some alternative methods for calculating the initial distance have been suggested. There is an advantage if the initial distance is odd. If the initial distance is even, all subsequent distances are even and, as a result, odd elements are not compared until the last pass.

The number of passes required using Shell's distance method is $\lceil \log_2 N \rceil$ where $\lceil \log_2 N \rceil$ indicates the smallest integer value greater than, or equal to, $\log_2 N$. The number of memory locations required is $N + 2$. These locations hold the array A, a temporary location used in exchange, and a location to hold the current distance.

The minimum number of comparisons required is $N \log_2 N$. The expected number of comparisons has not been calculated.

Quicksort
This method divides the array to be sorted into two partitions. An element of the array called the **bound** forms the dividing line between the two partitions. One partition contains elements that are

less than the bound, and the other contains elements that are greater than the bound. Each of these partitions is, in turn, divided into two partitions on the basis of a new bound. The procedure continues until each partition contains only one element and the entire array is in the correct order.

In detail, this sort involves placing all elements greater than the bound at the start of the array and all elements less than the bound at the end of the array. All elements are compared against the bound. A pass consists of breaking the array into two partitions. At the end of a pass, the bound is placed into the one remaining slot in the array that is its correct position. The goal is to select a bound at the start of each pass as close to the median of the data as possible. If the median is selected, then both partitions will be of equal length. The farther the bound is from the median, the more unbalanced the partitions will be.

If the data are in completely random order, then any element may be selected as the bound, since there is an equal probability of it being the median as any other. If the list is partially ordered, then the middle element is the most reasonable selection.

Another approach is to select a sample of data from the list and then select the bound from the sample. The median value of this sample could be taken as the bound. A sample of larger size would result in greater confidence that the bound selected is closer to the actual median.

After completion of the first pass, the smaller partition is used in the second pass. The boundaries of the larger partition are placed in a stack. (A stack is a storage structure based on the principle of last in first out. See Chapter 10 for more detail.) The procedure described in the first pass is repeated. The boundaries of the larger partition generated are placed on the stack, and the smaller partition enters pass three. This procedure continues until a one-element partition results. The partitions in the stack are removed and processed similarly in order.

A beginning and an ending pointer are used in the list of data. For pass one these specify the start and the end of the data array. For later passes these pointers specify the beginning and the end of the partitions to be processed. The length of the partition is determined by subtracting the beginning pointer from the ending pointer. A partition to be processed must have at least two elements. If the beginning pointer equals the ending pointer, the length of the partition is one. In this case, the next partition defined in the stack is processed. If none are available on the stack, the sort is complete. The original algorithm (developed by Hoare[1]) compares the beginning and the ending pointers with the limits for the pass for each change of the pointer. This check is made at each comparison so that the limits of the partition are not exceeded. The two pointers are compared with each other only when an exchange is to take place. If the beginning pointer is not above the ending pointer on the list, the end of the pass has been reached.

Another approach to determining the end of a pass is used in a variation of the sort called **Quickersort.** In this method the algorithm moves down the list. If an element smaller than the bound is found, then the procedure shifts to the bottom of the list. A search is made progressing up the list seeking an element larger than the bound so that an exchange can be made. The search in both directions is constrained by the pointer values. When the pointers are equal, the element in the position above the point of their meeting is moved to the free position, and the bound replaces it.

Figure 8–9 illustrates the Quickersort. The bound for the first pass has been selected (perhaps randomly) as 28. The piece of data in the first location (i.e. 49) is interchanged with the location of the bound. The beginning pointer is set to 1 and the ending pointer to 8. Starting at the end of the array, each element is compared to the bound until an element greater than the bound is located. This element is moved to the beginning location. In the example, 70 is moved to location 1. The location of the bound and the ending pointer are moved to 6. The beginning pointer is moved to 2. Continuing at the beginning pointer, each element is compared to the bound until an element less than the bound is located. This element is interchanged with the location of the bound. In the example, 12 is moved to location 6. This procedure continues until the beginning and ending pointers are equal. The bound is inserted at this point in the array. In this example, pass 2 starts with a selection of a new bound from the partition 12–27–19 and the assignment of the location holding 12 to the beginning pointer and the location holding 19 to the ending pointer. Pointers specifying the boundaries of the 70–49–57–41 partition are placed on the stack to await processing in a later pass.

The number of passes required or partitions processed depends on the selection of the bounds. The number of memory locations required is $N + 4 + 2\log_2 N$. These locations hold the array A, the bound, and the beginning and ending pointers during a pass. In addition, if the shorter partition is always processed first, the stack will never require more than $\log_2 N$ locations. The location of the beginning and end of each of these partitions will require $2\log_2 N$

Figure 8–9
Quicksort

A	A	A	A	A	A	A
49	49	– ←B	– ←B	– ←B	70	70
28	–	49	49	49	49←B	49
57	57	57	57	57	57	57←B
12	12	12	12	12	12	12
41	41	41	41	41	41	41
70	70	70	70	70←E	– ←E	– ←E
27	27	27	27←E	27	27	27
19	19	19←E	19	19	19	19
Original array		Start of pass 1				

A	A	A	A
70	70	70	70
49	49	49	49
57	57	57	57
12←B	– ←B	41	41
41	41←E	– ←B, E	28
– ←E	12	12	12
27	27	27	27
19	19	19	19
			End of pass 1

←B = beginning pointer
←E = ending pointer

locations. An additional location will hold the current location of the processing in the stack.

The minimum number of comparisons occurs when the median is selected for the bound each time. This is approximately $N \lceil \log_2 N \rceil$. The maximum number of comparisons occurs when either the smallest or the largest element is selected for the bound each time. This results in $N(N-1)/2$ comparisons. The expected number of comparisons is dependent on selection of the bound and lies between $1.1N \lceil \log_2 N \rceil$ and $1.4N \lceil \log_2 N \rceil$[4].

Table 8–1 provides a summary comparison of the internal sort methods discussed. Although the amount of memory required is important, a usually more important criterion in the selection of an appropriate internal sort method is the expected number of comparisons. The approximate amount of time required for an internal sort is a function of this number. In general, the sorts reviewed fall into

Table 8–1
Comparison of Internal Sort Methods

Method	Passes	Memory Locations	Comparisons		
			Minimum	Expected	Maximum
Linear selection	N	$2N+1$	$N(N-1)$	$N(N-1)$	$N(N-1)$
Linear selection with interchange	$N-1$	$N+2$*	$N(N-1)/2$	$N(N-1)/2$	$N(N-1)/2$
Exchange (or bubble)	$M+1$†	$N+2$	$N-1$	$(N^2/2)-(3N/4)$	$N(N-1)/2$
Sifting (or shuttlesort)	1‡	$N+2$	$N-1$	$(N-1)+(N-1)^2/4$	$(N-1)+(N-1)^2/2$
Insertion	$N-1$§	$N+2$	$N-1$	$N(N-1)/4$	$N(N-1)/2$
Shellsort	$\lceil \log_2 N \rceil$	$N+2$	$N\log_2 N$	Unknown	Unknown
Quicksort	‖	$N+4+2\log_2 N$	$\text{Approx.}N\lceil \log_2 N \rceil$	$1.1N\lceil \log_2 N \rceil \rightarrow$ $1.4N\lceil \log_2 N \rceil$‖	$N(N-1)/2$

*$N+1$ if interchange is not postponed until the end of the pass.
†M is the largest number of positions that a piece of data is out of position.
‡Backtracking involved.
§Number of comparisions, etc., not constant during each pass.
‖Depends on selection of bounds.

those in which the sort time is a function of N^2 and those in which the sort time is a function of $N \log_2 N$. There can be a dramatic difference in sort times between sorts falling into these two categories. For example, a sort of 1,000 elements requires in the order of 1 million comparisons in the first case and approximately 10,000 comparisons in the second case. For a large N, sorts requiring N^2 comparisons may be infeasible; for a small or moderate N, they're quite feasible and easy to implement.

External Sorting

An **external sort** is used when the list of data is too long to be fit into primary memory at the same time. External sorting consists of two phases. First, the original file is divided into parts called strings. A **string** is a set of data that can fit into primary memory. These strings are sorted and written on secondary storage. This is called the **sort phase.** Second, these sorted strings are merged into progressively longer strings until the complete list of data is sorted. This is called the **merge phase.** The sort phase uses an internal sort. The difference between various external sorting methods lies in the merge phase. The number of strings merged together at one time during the merge phase of an external sort is called the **order of merge.**

Many external sorts have been developed around the use of magnetic tape. All of these sorts can also be applied to magnetic disk. The use of magnetic disk allows additional flexibility in the sort (discussed below). The following merge techniques assume magnetic tape in the examples.

Balanced Merge

If there are k tape units available for the merge and the sorted strings are initially written onto k/2 tape units and the merged strings alternate between these k/2 units and the remaining k/2 units, then this is called a **balanced merge** or a **k/2-way merge.** For example, if four tape units are available and the progressively lengthening strings alternate between tape units 1 and 2 and tape units 3 and 4, this is a two-way merge. It is balanced in the sense that the merged strings at the end of each pass always alternate between the first two tape units and the second two tape units (except for the final merge pass when the entire data file is merged onto one tape unit). k/2 is the order of merge.

The number of passes required on the merge is $\lceil \log_{k/2} n \rceil$ where n is the number of strings. As an example, if there are 25 strings and a two-way merge is used, there will be $\lceil \log_2 25 \rceil$ or five passes required. The number of strings after a two-way pass is ½ the number going into the pass, after a three-way pass ⅓, etc. The length of the strings after a two-way pass is doubled, after a three-way pass is tripled, etc.

Figure 8–10(a) and (b) illustrate a balanced merge. The example is that of a two-way merge, since four tape drives are used. Figure 8–10(a) shows the status at the beginning of the sort phase. These tape drives are numbered 1 through 4. The file to be sorted is located on tape drive 3.

Figure 8–10 (a)
Start of a Balanced Merge Sort

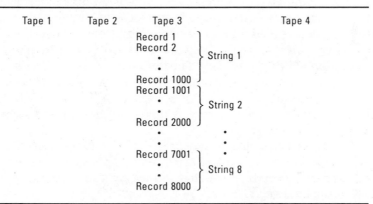

Figure 8–10 (b)
Merge Phase of a Balanced Merge

	Tape 1	Tape 2	Tape 3	Tape 4
Start of Merge Phase:				
	Sorted String 1	Sorted String 2		
	Sorted String 3	Sorted String 4		
	Sorted String 5	Sorted String 6		
	Sorted String 7	Sorted String 8		
Pass 1:				
			Strings 1–2	Strings 3–4
			Strings 5–6	Strings 7–8
Pass 2:				
	Strings 1–4	Strings 5–8		
Pass 3:				
			Strings 1–8	

A string length of 1,000 records is used. The first string is read into primary memory. These records are sorted using an internal sorting technique, and the sorted string is written on Tape 1.

A second string is read from Tape 3 into primary memory, sorted, and written on Tape 2. Strings continue to be read from Tape 3, sorted, and alternately written on Tape 1 and Tape 2 until the entire file has been processed. Tape 1 and Tape 2 now each contain four strings, and within each string the data are sorted. As a precaution the original file contained on a tape reel mounted on tape drive 3 is usually removed and a blank tape is mounted.

Figure 8–10(b) shows the progression of the sort through the merge phase. The first step is to merge Tapes 1 and 2. Tapes 1, 2, and 3 (if a blank tape has not already replaced the original tape) are rewound, that is, they are set back to the beginning of the tape reels. One record from string 1 (on Tape 1) and one record from string 2 (on Tape 2) are read into primary memory. The record with the larger key is written onto Tape 3, and a new record is read from whichever tape supplied the larger key. The keys are again compared, and the record with the larger key is again written on Tape 3. The procedure is repeated until all the records from strings 1 and 2 have been written on Tape 3. These records from the two merged strings will be sorted in order on Tape 3.

The records, of course, may be blocked. In that case, a block from both Tape 1 and Tape 2 is read in, internally sorted, and written out blocked on Tape 3. Blocking may significantly improve the time taken by the sort/merge.

The procedure is repeated with strings 3 and 4, and the sorted records are written on Tape 4. Strings are merged two at a time and alternatively written on Tapes 3 and 4 until the entire file has been written.

The tapes are rewound. The roles of Tapes 1 and 2 and Tapes 3 and 4 are reversed, that is, Tapes 3 and 4 are read record by record into primary memory and the sorted records are written on Tapes 1 and 2.

The tapes are rewound, and the final merged and sorted file is written on Tape 3.

Figure 8–11 shows a highly simplified numerical example.

It should be noted that rewinding is necessary after each merge pass. This may involve a significant amount of time. There are a number of factors that individually affect the time to rewind. These include the following—each of which is discussed assuming all other factors remain constant.

Figure 8–11
Numerical Example of Balanced Merge

	Tape 1	Tape 2	Tape 3	Tape 4
Sort Phase:				
			49 ⎫ String 1	
			28 ⎭	
			57 ⎫ String 2	
			12 ⎭	
			41 ⎫ String 3	
			70 ⎭	
			27 ⎫ String 4	
			19 ⎭	
Merge Phase:				
Start:				
	49	57		
	28	12		
	70	27		
	41	19		
Pass 1:				
			57	70
			49	41
			28	27
			12	19
Pass 2:				
	70			
	57			
	49			
	41			
	28			
	27			
	19			
	12			

1. Amount of data—The more data written on the tape, the more tape length required and the longer the time needed to rewind over that tape length.
2. Recording density—The denser the data, the less tape length required and the shorter the time needed to rewind over that tape length.
3. Rewind speed—Some tape units rewind at a higher speed than the speed at which they read/write.

4. Blocking—The greater the blocking factor, the fewer the inter-block gaps, the shorter the tape length, and the less time needed to rewind over that tape length.
5. Parallel rewind—There may be a limit on the number of tape units that can be rewound simultaneously. If this limit is less than the number required to be rewound, then the total rewind time may double or triple.

Backward Balanced Merge

Some tape units can be read backward. If this capability exists, then the rewinds at the end of each merge pass can be eliminated, and a **backward balanced merge** results.

Figure 8–12 shows the progression of the merge phase in a backward balanced merge. It is assumed that the original data are the same as those shown in Figure 8–10(a). The sort phase is the same as that used in the balanced merge.

Figure 8–12
Backward Balanced Merge

	Tape 1	Tape 2	Tape 3	Tape 4
Start:				
	Sorted string 1	Sorted string 2		
	Sorted string 3	Sorted string 4		
	Sorted string 5	Sorted string 6		
	Sorted string 7	Sorted string 8		
	(Descending Order)			
Pass 1:				
			Strings 7–8	Strings 5–6
			Strings 3–4	Strings 1–2
			(Ascending order)	
Pass 2:				
	Strings 5–8	Strings 1–4		
	(Descending order)			
Pass 3:			Strings 1–8	
			(Ascending order)	

At the start of the merge phase, Tape 4 is at the beginning of the tape and Tapes 1, 2, and 3 are further down. The first merge pass will write the expanded strings on Tapes 3 and 4. There is an inconsistency: Tape 4 is at the beginning of the tape and Tape 3 is further down. The problem disappears, however, if Tape 3 has to be removed anyway. It is rewound and saved. In that usual case it is replaced with a new tape at its start. If the tape is not saved, one rewind is necessary at this time. It should also be noted that the sorted strings on Tapes 1 and 2 are in order from high key value to low key value, that is, in descending order.

Sorted string 7 on Tape 1 and sorted string 8 on Tape 2 are merged and placed on Tape 3. This pass continues until the strings have been merged alternately on Tape 3 and Tape 4. Since the strings were backward read, they are now in ascending order.

This procedure repeats as in the balanced merge, but with alternating ascending and descending sequences. In this example, the final merge pass has created a sorted file in ascending order when descending order is desired. One more pass is required to copy the contents of Tape 3 onto another tape in descending order.

If the number of merge passes is even, the order is correct at the end of the final merge pass; if the number of merge passes is odd, the order is incorrect at the end of the final merge pass, and an additional reversing pass is required.

It is possible for the sort/merge program to calculate how many passes will be required. If the number of passes is even, the sort/merge continues as described above. If the number of passes is odd, the sort phase creates ascending strings (instead of the usual descending) that will result in a descending string at the end of the final merge pass.

Imperfect Balanced Merge

An **imperfect balanced merge** occurs when a balanced merge is run on a number of strings that is not an even power of the order of merge. For example, if a two-way merge is run on 12 strings, an imperfect balanced merge results. Since in this example $\lceil \log_2 12 \rceil = 4$, four passes are required. Although the number of passes cannot be reduced, it is possible to shorten one or more of the passes. An imperfect balanced merge saves time by reducing the total number of strings copied from one tape to another.

Figure 8–13 illustrates this. The sort phase and the first two passes of the merge phase are identical to the usual balanced merge. With the third merge pass the first merged string on Tape 1 is merged with the first merged string on Tape 2 and written on Tape 3. Because of the imperfect nature of the merge, no string exists to merge with the next string on Tape 1. If the general rule that merge passes alternate between Tapes 1 and 2 and Tapes 3 and 4 holds, then the remaining string on Tape 1 is simply copied onto Tape 4. If the merge algorithm is flexible, a time saving can be made by allowing the last string on Tape 1 to remain there and, on the final merge

Figure 8–13
Imperfect Balanced Merge

Tape 1	Tape 2	Tape 3	Tape 4
Start of merge phase:			
Sorted string 1	Sorted string 2		
Sorted string 3	Sorted string 4		
Sorted string 5	Sorted string 6		
Sorted string 7	Sorted string 8		
Sorted string 9	Sorted string 10		
Sorted string 11	Sorted string 12		
Pass 1:			
		Strings 1–2	Strings 3–4
		Strings 5–6	Strings 7–8
		Strings 9–10	Strings 11–12
Pass 2:			
Strings 1–4	Strings 5–8		
Strings 9–12			
Pass 3:			
Strings 9–12		Strings 1–8	
Pass 4:			
	Strings 1–12		

pass, merging it with the string on Tape 3. These two strings are of different lengths, but the basic merge rule is still valid.

On the fourth and final pass, the two strings are merged onto Tape 2. Thus, in an imperfect balanced sort, the final merge pass may begin once the number of strings remaining to be merged becomes equal to, or less than, the order of merge.

This approach may be complicated or even found infeasible if an imperfect backward balanced merge is involved. Thus, some strings may be descending and others ascending when the final merge pass becomes practical.

Another approach is to adjust the strings at the start in such a way as to produce an even power of the order of merge. In this case, a balanced merge results.

Imbalanced Merge

An **imbalanced merge** uses an odd number of tape units. The tape units are divided into two groups—one group having one more unit than the other. The sort phase distributes the strings onto the larger group of tape units. These are then merged onto the smaller group in the first merge pass, merged onto the larger group in the second pass, etc.; as a result, a higher order of merge is achieved on every other pass in the merge phase.

Figure 8–14
Imbalanced Merge

Tape 1	Tape 2	Tape 3	Tape 4	Tape 5
Start of merge phase:				
		String 1	String 2	String 3
		String 4	String 5	String 6
		String 7	String 8	String 9
		String 10	String 11	String 12
		String 13	String 14	String 15
		String 16	String 17	String 18
Pass 1:				
Strings 1–3	Strings 4–6			
Strings 7–9	Strings 10–12			
Strings 13–15	Strings 16–18			
Pass 2:				
		Strings 1–6	Strings 7–12	Strings 13–18
Pass 3:				
Strings 1–18				

Figure 8–14 illustrates the merge phase for this merge. In the example, 18 strings are used.

Polyphase Merge

The polyphase merge attempts to make greater utilization of the tape units. In a balanced merge using k tape units, $(k/2) - 1$ are not in use at any given time, since only 1 tape unit is being written on while $k/2$ are being read. A **polyphase merge** attempts to use $k - 1$ tape units for reading and 1 tape unit for writing. The sort phase places an uneven number of strings on the output tapes. Once an input tape has been completely read and its strings merged, it can then be used as an output tape. For optimum performance, the number of strings placed on the output tapes by the sort pass must be a function of a Fibonacci series.* After a merge pass the number of strings is reduced in accordance with the series.

The sort phase assigns strings to the output tapes in accordance with the following rules:

1. Assign the first string to one tape unit.
2. Viewing the tape units, select the maximum number of strings on any output unit and assign that number of additional strings to all output tape units except the unit holding the present maximum number.
3. Repeat step 2 until all of the strings have been allocated.

* A **Fibonacci series** consists of a set of numbers in which each number in the series consists of the sum of its immediate predecessors.

Figure 8–15(a) shows the allocation of 17 strings in preparation for a polyphase merge involving four tape units. The allocation of the first string is arbitrary. If two tapes hold the same number of strings, as in allocation step 3, it is also arbitrary which tape unit is selected as holding the maximum.

In general, for N tape units, the Fibonacci series is made up of the immediately preceding N values. Since the strings in the example of Figure 8-15(a) are being allocated to three tape units, the total number of strings allocated at the end of each step will be the sum of the total number of strings allocated in the previous three steps. The total number at the end of step 4 in the example is 9 (i.e. the sum of 1, 3, and 5). The total number at the end of step 5 is 17 (i.e. the sum of 3, 5, and 9).

Figure 8–15 (a)
Allocation of Strings for a Polyphase Merge

	Tape 1	Tape 2	Tape 3	Tape 4	Number of Strings Allocated
String 1					
•					
•					
•					
String 17					
Allocation Step:					
1				String 1	1
2		String 3	String 2		3
3		String 5	String 4		5
4		String 8			String 6	
		String 9		String 7	9
5			String 14	String 10	
			String 15	String 11	
			String 16	String 12	
			String 17	String 13	17

Figure 8–15(b) shows the successive passes of the merge phase for the strings allocated in Figure 8–15(a). All tapes must be rewound before the merge phase begins. The first four strings on Tapes 2, 3, and 4 are merged onto Tape 1. Tape 2 is now empty and rewound. Tape 2 now becomes the output tape for the next pass. Tape 1 is also rewound. After merging the first two strings on Tapes 1, 3, and 4, Tape 3 becomes empty. Tapes 2 and 3 are rewound, and Tape 3 becomes the output tape for the next pass. The first string on Tapes

Figure 8–15 (b)
Polyphase Merge

Tape 1	Tape 2	Tape 3	Tape 4	Number of Strings Remaining
Start of merge phase:				
	String 3	String 2	String 1	
	String 5	String 4	String 6	
	String 8	String 14	String 7	
	String 9	String 15	String 10	
		String 16	String 11	
		String 17	String 12	
			String 13	17
Pass 1:				
Strings 1–3				
Strings 4–6				
Strings 7–8, 14				
Strings 9–10, 15				
		String 16	String 11	
		String 17	String 12	
			String 13	9
Pass 2:				
	Strings 1–3, 11, 16			
	Strings 4–6, 12, 17			
Strings 7–8, 14			String 13	
Strings 9–10, 15				5
Pass 3:				
		Strings 1–3, 7–8, 11, 13–14, 16		
	Strings 4–6, 12, 17			
Strings 9–10, 15				3
Pass 4:				
			Strings 1–17	1

1, 2, and 4 is merged onto Tape 3, and Tape 4 becomes empty. For the final pass, Tapes 3 and 4 are rewound and the entire file is merged onto Tape 4. At the end of each pass the total number of strings remaining is the reverse of the Fibonacci series established in the original allocation.

Multireel Sort

If the data to be sorted do not all fit onto one tape, a multireel situation exists. When the first reel has been read, processing stops, the tape is rewound and removed, the second data reel is mounted, and processing resumes. An alternative approach is to use two tape units for input and have the system switch over automatically to the second unit when the reading of the first tape has been completed.

An analogous reverse operation must be performed during the final merge pass, when all the data must come together again on multiple reels.

Direct Access Merge

With a direct access storage device, access to all data or strings is equally convenient. All of the tape merges described above can be implemented with direct access storage. However, simpler types of sort/merges can be implemented by taking advantage of the direct access characteristics of the storage device.

Figure 8–16 illustrates a direct access merge using three files and 32 strings.

Figure 8–16
Direct Access Merge

File 1	File 2	File 3
Start of sort phase:		
String 1		
•		
•		
•		
String 32		
Start of merge phase:		
	String 1	String 17
	•	•
	•	•
	•	•
	•	•
	String 16	String 32
Pass 1:		
Strings 1–4		String 17
Strings 5–8		•
Strings 9–12		•
Strings 13–16		String 32
Pass 2:		
Strings 1–4	Strings 17–20	
Strings 5–8	Strings 21–24	
Strings 9–12	Strings 25–28	
Strings 13–16	Strings 29–32	
Pass 3:		
	Strings 17–20	Strings 1–16
	Strings 21–24	
	Strings 25–28	
	Strings 29–32	
Pass 4:		
Strings 17–32		Strings 1–16
Pass 5:		
	Strings 1–32	

In the example given, more than four strings could have been merged together at the same time. The more strings merged on one pass, the fewer merge passes are required. With tape units the constraint on the order of merge is provided by the number of tape drives available. This constraint does not exist with direct access storage, since many files may be located on the same storage device and accessed, or multiple accesses to the same file can be accomplished with the same average access time.

The order of merge can be increased by increasing the number of strings merged on one pass. If the order of merge is increased, then the number of merge passes required is decreased. Thus, the total amount of data transferred within the sort/merge is decreased.

The order of merge on a direct access device, however, cannot be increased indefinitely. There is a tradeoff between total transfer time and total seek time.

Transfer time (i.e., the amount of time necessary to move data from a secondary storage device to primary memory) is determined by the number of characters of data moved. Therefore, if the effective order of merge is increased, the total transfer time is decreased.

Total seek time (i.e., the time to locate the blocks, including the time to move the read/write heads to the proper track) is determined by the number of blocks accessed. If the file to be sorted is long and many strings exist, then as the order of merge increases, seek time increases, since the read/write heads will have to be moved to access additional blocks. Thus, as the order of merge (i.e., the number of strings merged at one time) increases, transfer time decreases but seek time increases. There is a point at which the increase in total seek time exceeds the decrease in total transfer time. Thus, a constantly increasing order of merge in a direct access environment is not the best policy. There is an optimum order of merge that depends on the characteristics of the hardware used.

Conclusions

Sorting is a technique that can be implemented in a number of ways, depending on the requirements of the particular application. If all of the data to be sorted can be handled in primary memory at the same time, an internal sort technique can carry out the sequencing. If the volume of data is too large, then an external sort is required. An external sort requires the sorting of the data in parts called strings. These strings are merged into progressively longer strings until one string encompasses the entire set of data.

Sorting can be a very time-consuming procedure. This is especially so for external sorts, since a large number of I/O accesses are made. The selection of a sort technique (either internal or external) for a particular application is not a trivial decision.

There is a wide range of internal sorting techniques. In addition to each of the basic methods, a number of variations and improvements exist around some of them.

External sorting techniques have been designed primarily around magnetic tape as the storage medium. The rather widespread use of magnetic disk as a storage medium has offered new opportunities and flexibility in designing sort techniques. This is a field, however, that has not yet developed a well-established set of techniques independent of magnetic tape technology.

References

1.   Hoare, C. A. R. "Quicksort." *Computer Journal* 5 (1962), pp. 10-15.
2.   Shell, D. L. "A High-Speed Sorting Procedure." *Communications of the ACM* 2, No. 7 (July 1959), pp. 30-33.
3.   Lorin, H. *Sorting and Sort Systems.* Reading, Mass: Addison-Wesley Publishing, 1975, p. 29.
4.   *Ibid.,* p. 106–7.

Review

1. What is a collating sequence?
2. Clearly differentiate between internal sorting and external sorting.
3. If a linear selection sort is to be made on data in the range 0 through 100,000 and the sort is to be ascending, give a number that can be used to replace data in the original array.
4. Given the following internal sorts:
   Linear selection
   Linear selection with interchange
   Bubble
   Quicksort
   which of these
   a Can require the fewest memory locations?
   b Requires the smallest expected number of comparisons?
5. Which internal sorts involve both primary and secondary comparisons?
6. Why should the initial distance in a Shellsort be odd?
7. What is an order of merge?

8. On a balanced merge using six tape units and 30 strings, how many merge passes are required?

9. Give four factors that affect rewind time on tape. What is the effect of each of these factors?

10. If the number of merge passes on a backward balanced merge is five and the initial pass produced strings in descending order, in what order will the final data be?

11. What is the main advantage of an imbalanced merge?

12. If the number of strings created for a polyphase merge can be anywhere from 20 to 30 and three tape units (including that holding the original data) are available, show the original allocation of strings in preparation for the merge.

13. Why cannot the order of merge increase indefinitely in a direct access sort?

Chapter 9

Search Techniques and File Organization

Introduction

In general, the search problem is concerned with locating a particular piece of data or set of data within a larger grouping of data. The object of the search is to locate such data within a data storage area contained within primary memory, or within a data file stored on a secondary storage device. A search within primary memory is a simpler problem; a search on a secondary storage device is complicated by considerations of the physical characteristics of the device itself. Since searching of a secondary storage device involves a more complicated environment, the discussion of search techniques is oriented around such devices, that is, around file search techniques.

Searching is concerned with the following four possibilities. The search may look for:

1. A unique set of data satisfying certain criteria.
2. All sets of data satisfying certain criteria.
3. Some sets of data satisfying certain criteria.
4. Establishing that no sets of data satisfy certain criteria.

The general file search problem is to search for data contained in a logical record within a file under one of the above four conditions. The file that contains the desired data (if they exist) is known and is located on a secondary storage device. The objective is to find that logical record (or those logical records) within the file which meets the search criteria. The search for multiple logical records may be exhaustive (i.e. require a complete identification of all logical records meeting the search criteria), or be limited (i.e. require the identification of some—one or more—logical records that meet the search criteria). When the data are brought into primary memory from secondary storage, the individual data items may be utilized as needed. If no logical records meet the search criteria, this also provides information to the user.

The search is organized on a particular data item called the **search key.** For example, a simplified personnel file may contain for each employee a record holding his or her employee number, name, and hourly salary as data items. Given a particular employee number, it may be desired to find the name (or hourly salary) of that employee. The search will then utilize this employee number as the search key. When the logical record identified by this key is found, the name (and hourly salary) will also be found in data items within this record. This example assumes key uniqueness.

A file may, of course, be searched on more than one key. For example, it is necessary to have the capability of searching a file of checking accounts in a bank on at least two keys. The normal search would be on account number. Customers do, however, forget their account numbers, and an ability to search on customer name would be necessary. The search techniques used on different keys may not be the same.

Eight different file search techniques and their relationships to file organization are reviewed, in addition to some basic concepts and definitions. Advantages and disadvantages of each technique are also presented.

Logical and Physical Access

The access of a file by a program can be viewed as a two-step process: the logical access and the physical access. The applications program makes a **logical access;** the operating system makes the **physical access.** In effect, the applications programmer is blocked from making a physical access directly. When an input or output statement in the applications program is encountered, that is, a READ or WRITE, an interrupt is generated and control is passed to the operating system. After evaluation by the operating system as an input or an output command, a set of commands in the operating system is executed. A channel handles all of the details necessary to locate the correct data in the correct file on the correct secondary storage device for a READ, or to transfer the correct data to the correct location in a file on the correct secondary storage device for a WRITE. Extensive error checking may be involved. When the operating system has successfully processed the interrupt, control is transferred back to the applications program. With a READ statement, this means that the data copied from a secondary storage device are available in primary memory for further processing.

Thus, the applications program selects the record to be read or to be written on by means of a logical access. The selection of the record will involve a file search technique. After selection and passing to the operating system, a physical access is made. The selection of the record to be accessed will involve a file search technique by the operating system. The software instructions within the operating system that are used for physical access are called **access methods.** A file search is inherently two-level: logical access followed by physical access.

In the following discussion, it is assumed that one physical record is the same as one logical record, and that the file search techniques are employed by applications programs as logical access techniques. Blocking would, of course, reduce the number of physical accesses required by some techniques. Physical considerations and access methods are discussed later.

Sequential Search

If the file is located on a sequential access device (e.g., a file residing on magnetic tape), this is the only type of search possible. If the file is located on a direct access device, then all of the discussed search techniques are possible, including a sequential search.

Using sequential search, the first record in the file is read. A check is then made to see if that record meets the search criteria. To do this, the search key is matched against the appropriate data item. If a match results and key uniqueness is assumed, the record has been found and the search is complete. If multiple records may meet the search criteria and a match is found, the record is available and the search continues for additional records. If there is no match, the next record is read and an attempt to match is made again. This procedure continues until either a match is made or the end of the file is reached.

For example, assume that the highly simplified personnel file shown in Figure 9–1 exists on secondary storage. Each record consists of three fields: employee number, employee name, and hourly salary. The search key, employee number, is unique.

Figure 9–1
Sequential Search

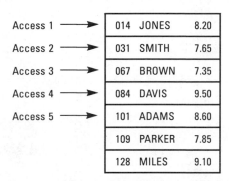

It may be possible to copy the entire file into primary memory and then search in primary memory for the required record. For large files, this is impractical. The alternative is to bring into primary memory a record at a time as the search progresses. (Of course, a physical record or a block may contain more than one logical record.)

As an example, consider a requirement to obtain the name of employee number 101 using the above personnel file. The first record (i.e. the JONES record) is read, and the first data field containing 014 is matched against the key 101. There is no match, and the second record is read. This continues until a match is made on the fifth record. The second field in this record contains the name of the employee having number 101. This name may then be further processed as appropriate.

To reach the record for employee number 101, five logical accesses were necessary. The number of logical accesses required clearly depends on the required record's location in the file.

What is the expected number of logical accesses needed? Assume each record has an equal probability of being requested. From this assumption it is implied that in N requests for data each record is requested once, on the average, for a file of length N.

Therefore, N requests will require the following number of logical accesses:

$$1 + 2 + 3 + \ldots + N = \sum_{i=1}^{N} i = \frac{N(N+1)}{2}$$

On the average, $\dfrac{\dfrac{N(N+1)}{2}}{N} = \dfrac{N+1}{2}$ logical accesses per request.

For example, in a file of length 7, $\dfrac{N+1}{2} = 4$, that is, on the average we would expect to search halfway through the file before a match is achieved. Sometimes 1 logical access is all that is required, sometimes N logical accesses are required, but on the average $\dfrac{N+1}{2}$ logical accesses are required.

If there is not an equal probability of any record being requested, the logical approach is to sequence the file in order of highest probability to lowest, that is, the most probable record is first, the second most probable next, etc.

The expected number of comparisons required, then, depends on the actual probabilities. The expected value can be calculated using these probabilities in the formula:

$$\bar{x} = \sum_{i=1}^{N} p_i x_i$$

where p_i is the probability of record i being required and x_i is the number of logical accesses (or the relative position in the file) required to reach record i sequentially.

The expectation, of course, assumes stable probabilities. If the probabilities are not stable, then the approach becomes less clear. The simplest solution is to ignore the lack of probability stability and assume equal probabilities. The alternative may be to update probabilities with each search. After a certain increment of time or of number of searches, the file could be resorted in order of probability (highest to lowest). A modification of this approach might be to exchange records in the file after they have surpassed some threshold of being out of probability order.

Figure 9–2 shows a flow chart for this sequential search, assuming that the file is not necessarily in order on the search key. It also assumes that the search key identifies only one record.

A sequential search does not require that the records of the file be in any order. However, if they are in order on the search key, then a search for a nonexistent record may be terminated earlier than the

Figure 9–2
Flow Chart for Sequential Search

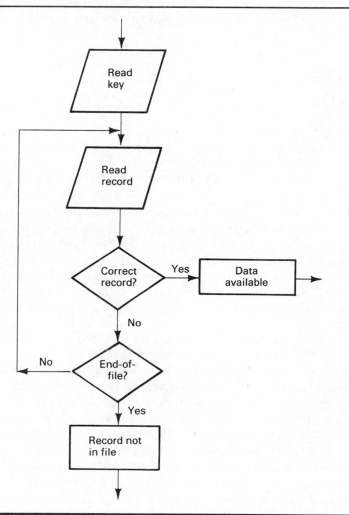

end of the file. Assuming that the file is in ascending order on the search key, then once the search algorithm encounters a record identified by a key higher in value than the sought-after key, it can be concluded that the required record does not exist in the file.

Activity refers to the percentage of records in a file processed in a single run. For a very active file, e.g. a payroll file, in which almost every logical record must be accessed, then a sequential search of blocked records is the most efficient approach. The expected number of logical accesses to the next record required decreases as file activity increases. As a result, high activity files that are not required to be on-line are usually stored on magnetic tape and searched sequentially.

Binary Search

A **binary search** requires that the file be located on a direct access device, that it be in order on the search key, and that the search key be unique. This technique is based on the strategy of maximizing information obtained from each logical access. A maximum of $\lceil \log_2 (N + 1) \rceil$ logical accesses would be needed, where N is the length of the file. The basic approach is to halve the file under investigation with each logical access.

The search is started by reading the middle record in the file. If it is the correct one, the search is complete; if it is not, then it can be determined if the record is before or after the required one, that is, are the data in the key field read greater than or less than the sought-after data? If the key is higher, then the next record to be read is in the middle of the high remaining subset. If the key is lower, then the next record to be read is in the middle of the low remaining subset. The process is repeated until either the correct record is found or $\lceil \log_2 (N + 1) \rceil$ comparisons have been made. If the latter occurs, then the sought-after record is not contained in the file.

As an example, consider a requirement to obtain the name of employee number 101 using the already referenced personnel file shown in Figure 9–3. First the middle record (i.e. 084 Davis 9.50) is read and a match is attempted. Since 084 is less than 101, all records from the beginning of the file up to and including 084 may be eliminated from further consideration. Next the middle record from the remainder of the file is checked (i.e. the record containing 109 Parker 7.85). Since 109 is higher than 101, all records from 109 up can be eliminated. Access is once again made to the middle record of the remaining subset. In this example, the only record (and the correct one) is 101 Adams 7.60.

To summarize, the strategy is to halve the remaining records with each logical access. In information theory terms, each logical access results in the gaining of maximum information (approximately). Since any record in the file can be reached with the same average access time, it is feasible to *jump around* in the file.

Table 9–1 compares the number of logical accesses required in a sequential search and in a binary search for a given file length of N

Figure 9–3
Binary Search

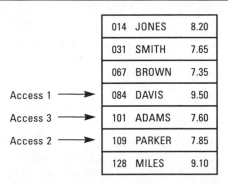

014	JONES	8.20
031	SMITH	7.65
067	BROWN	7.35
084	DAVIS	9.50
101	ADAMS	7.60
109	PARKER	7.85
128	MILES	9.10

Access 1 ⟶ 084 DAVIS
Access 3 ⟶ 101 ADAMS
Access 2 ⟶ 109 PARKER

and a unique search key. The comparison is for the *expected* number of logical accesses required by a sequential search and the *maximum* number required in the binary search. For a value of N greater than 100, the expected number of logical accesses required in a binary search may be approximated by the maximum number minus 1.

An assumption has been made in the above discussion that there is an equal probability of any record being required. If there is not such an equal probability in a binary search, then there should be as close to an even split in probability as possible with each logical access. With other than equal probability, less information is obtained on each access. The implementation of an effective search technique in this case is difficult.

Table 9–1
Comparison of Sequential and Binary Searches

	Logical Accesses	
N Length of File	Sequential (Expected)	Binary (Maximum)
1	1	1
3	2	2
7	4	3
15	8	4
31	16	5
1,023	512	10
8,191	4,096	13
65,535	32,768	16

Figure 9–4 shows a flow chart for a binary search that assumes an equal probability that any record will be required. In all cases, a binary search requires that the file be sorted on the key field. The logic of this flow chart assumes that the file is in ascending order on the key, that is, the first logical record is identified by the lowest key

Figure 9–4
Flow Chart for Binary Search

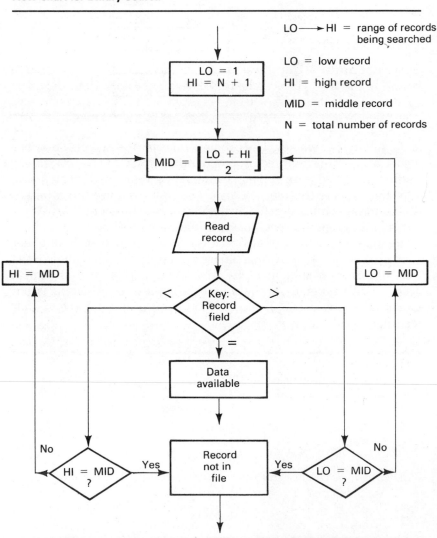

and the last logical record is identified by the highest key. It also assumes that the search key identifies a unique record. The symbol ⌊argument⌋ indicates the floor of the argument enclosed, that is, the minimum integer value closest to, or equal to, the argument.

If the length of the file changes, a simple approach is to store the current length in a given location, e.g. in the first record. Any addition or deletion to the file will then involve an update of this record also.

Direct Addressing

In **direct addressing** the address (i.e. the location) of the desired record in the file to be searched is known by the user. In the simplest case, the key is the address itself. For example, a search for the record identified by a search key of 101 goes directly to address (or record) 101.

Direct addressing is impractical if the file changes rapidly, the key has a meaning outside of the computer, or the range of the search key would result in an inefficient utilization of file space. Another complication is that if variable length records are used and the space allocated for one record is exceeded, then there must be a capability to link to another area to store the remaining data.

Figure 9–5 presents a flow chart for direct addressing. A variation of this method obtains the address after a transformation of the key, using some algebraic manipulation. As a simple example, a file might contain marketing data by telephone area code (100 through 999). If one logical record were created for each area code and they were filed in order, then the address for any area code could be obtained by subtracting 99 from the area code key. Thus, area code 100 data would be in record 1, area code 101 in record 2, etc. A special symbol at a record location could indicate that this number represents an invalid area code. Figure 9–6 presents a flow chart for direct addressing involving an arithmetic manipulation.

Hashing (or Randomizing)

Hashing uses the key to calculate the address of the required record as in the case above, but in a manner that deliberately randomizes the calculated address. A drawback is that the calculated address may not be unique. As an example, suppose that the key is divided by 100 and the remainder is taken as the address. In this case, 205 and 105

Figure 9–5
Flow Chart for Direct Addressing

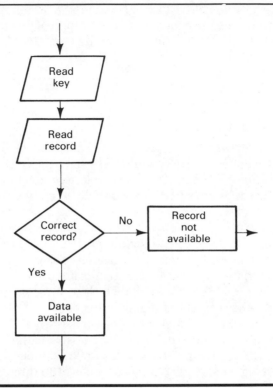

will be divided, and a remainder of 5 will result from both. This is an **overflow** condition. Only one record may be stored at 5. There must be a link at record 5 to an overflow area. Thus, the data for 105 may be filed at address 5, and a link (either implicit or explicit) to a record in the overflow area for 205 exists. Records 105 and 205 are sometimes also called **synonyms.**

In general, the hashing algorithm maps the search keys identifying the logical records onto the relative record addresses across the file. Ideally, the calculated addresses should be evenly spread over the length of the file without grouping or bunching of the records, that is, the algorithm should distribute the records in accordance with a uniform distribution. Hence, the term "randomizing" is used. Practically, a good algorithm will result in some synonyms, but there should be few. The specific algorithm used in any application is

Figure 9–6
Flow Chart for Direct Addressing with Transformation

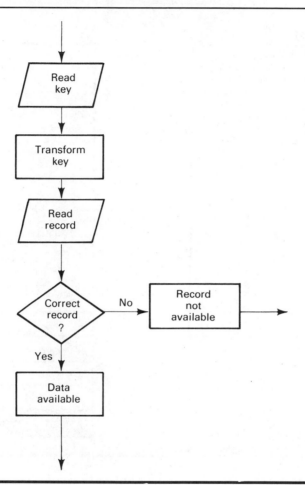

dependent on the characteristics of the search keys to be used. For example, truncating all of the digits of the key but the last few would not be efficient if a significant majority of the keys were odd (or even).

There will be, in general, gaps in the file. When combined with an overflow area, experience shows that a well-designed file for a hash search generally requires approximately 120 percent of the space required in a fully packed file. This is illustrated in Figure 9–7.

Figure 9–7
Hashed File

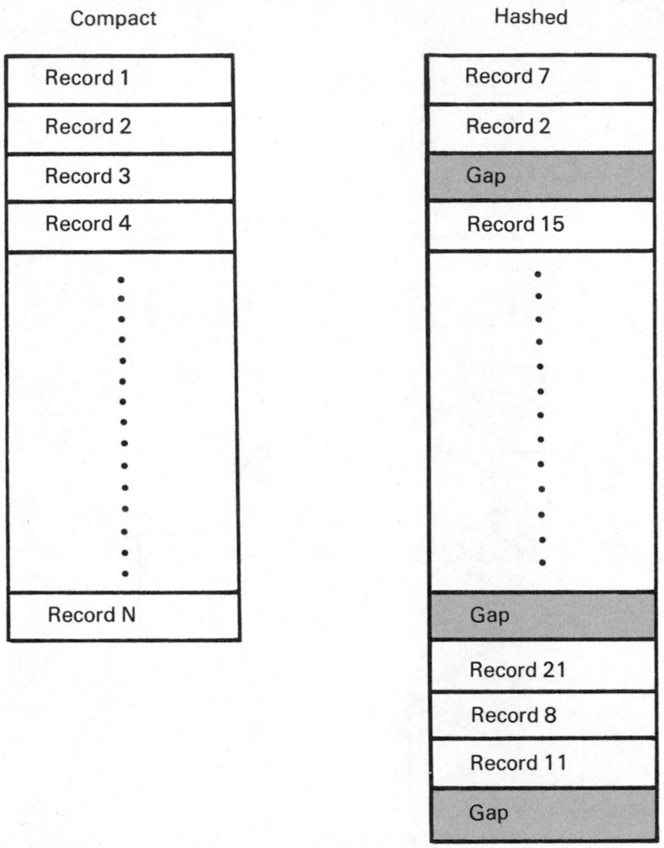

Compact		Hashed
Record 1		Record 7
Record 2		Record 2
Record 3		Gap
Record 4		Record 15
Record N		Gap
		Record 21
		Record 8
		Record 11
		Gap

The file must have been designed with randomizing in mind. Many different methods are used to randomize. Five typical basic methods are as follows:

1. Divide the key by the number of records in the file and take the remainder.
2. Divide the key by the greatest prime number less than the number of records in the file and take the remainder. (Note: A prime number is an integer that can be divided evenly only by itself and 1.)

3. Truncation of the key, that is, *chopping off* the high, low, or middle digits. The digits saved should clearly be those that are most uniformly random.
4. *Folding* (i.e. splitting the key into several equal-sized portions and adding them together). For example, a key of 123456 could be divided three ways into 12, 34, 56, and after adding an address of 102 is obtained.
5. *Squaring* (i.e mutiplying the key by itself and taking the appropriate number of digits from the middle of the result). This method was an early one used for random number generation in computers.

Again, note that it is probable that at least some of the keys will produce the same address. For example, assuming method 3 above and *chopping off* all but the last four digits in social security numbers, then 085-30-1036 and 417-45-1036 will produce the same address: 1036.

As a second example, assuming method 4 above and dividing the key into three parts of two digits each, then 122436 and 242424 will produce the same address: 72.

Figure 9–8 presents a flow chart for hashing. The search key is read in, hashed, and the record at that calculated location is retrieved. In most searches this first access is successful. In a few cases, that is, those involving synonyms, a second logical access is required. In a very few cases, three or more accesses may be needed. The expected number of accesses required, though, should be between one and two.

The simplest (but not only) method for handling overflow is to have set aside an area of the file called the **overflow area.** It is frequently reserved at the end of the file. The hashing algorithm calculates an address in the first part (or primary area) of the file, that is, in locations 1 to N. Any overflow records are stored starting in location N + 1. An unsuccessful access in the primary area results in a sequential search of the overflow area. More efficient linkages between the primary and overflow areas are discussed in Chapter 10.

Directory Lookup

Another search technique for a unique key is a **directory lookup.** This technique uses a table to store the address for each record in the file to be searched. It is also called a **table lookup** or **index**

Figure 9–8
Flow Chart for Hashed File Search

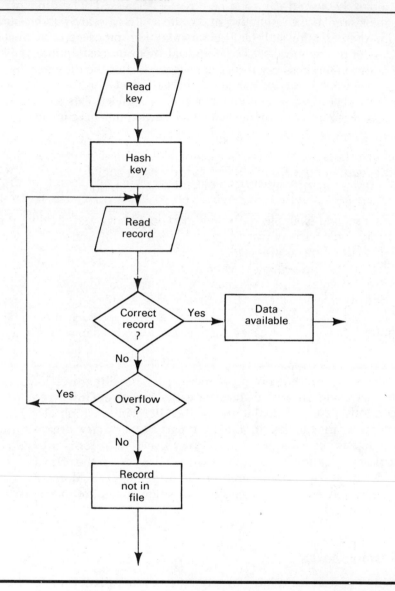

lookup. The address for a required record is found by using the key to search the table (called a **directory**). Using the address found in the table, the record can then be directly addressed. The directory may be stored at the beginning of the file so that a search of the file begins with an access to the directory and then proceeds to a direct address of the required record. If multiple records are required, only one additional access per record is necessary after the directory has been copied into primary memory.

No space is lost in the primary file as a result of gaps (as in hashing techniques), and no space is used up for overflows. On the other hand, the directory itself takes up space.

In one sense, the problem of the search has merely been placed back one step, that is, the question of how to search the directory now arises. It might appear on the surface that the search of the directory now required plus one access to the primary file has resulted in a net loss. This is generally not true. The directory is smaller, usually very much smaller, than the primary file. As a result, the directory may be paged into primary memory—a search in primary memory is very much faster than a search of secondary storage. Records can be relocated within a file, and all that needs to be done is to change an entry in the appropriate directory.

Figure 9–9 illustrates a directory search utilizing the personnel file example previously employed and assumes a search is required for employee number 101. The directory (or table) is searched for a

Figure 9–9
Directory Lookup

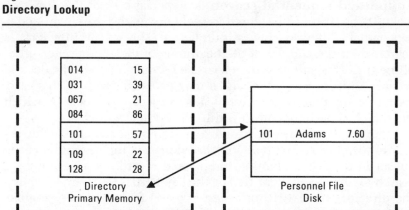

match on the search key (i.e. 101). Associated with the key in the table is the address of the logical record in the primary file. At address 57 is the logical record containing data on employee number 101. If there is no match of the key in the directory, then no record exists in the primary file for that key.

It is possible to arrange the directories in a hierarchy. The first directory selects one directory from a number of second-level directories. This second directory is then searched for either a third-level directory or for the direct address.

Multiple keys can be used to access into the same file, that is, a separate directory could be maintained for each key. For example, a personnel file could be accessed through either of two directories. The first directory might be keyed on social security numbers; the second directory might be keyed on employee number.

Different search techniques may be used on each of several directories. For example, the system could be designed such that the file can be accessed after a binary search on the key in one directory, or after a hashing technique has been applied on another.

In general, there is no reason for the records to be in any particular order in the file. The exception would occur if, in addition to using a directory approach on one or more keys, a binary search directly on the file using another key is desired. In that case, of course, the file must be sorted in order on the binary search key.

Indexed Sequential

An **indexed sequential search** is a special case of the directory lookup. The file must be stored in sequence on the search key and is conceptually divided into a number of subsets. A directory is searched for the address of the beginning of the appropriate subset of the file. This subset is then searched sequentially for the desired record. A hierarchy of directories may be established. In this case, the address in the first directory leads to a second directory in which the search is narrowed down within the original subset.

Figure 9–10 illustrates an indexed sequential search. The directory is searched sequentially for the address of the beginning of the subset in the file containing the desired record. As an example, a search for the record identified by the key 1010 is found by searching the directory until 1010 or a larger key is found. In the example, 1036 is the first key exceeding 1010. The subset of the main file starting at address 74 is then searched for the record.

Figure 9–10
Indexed Sequential Search

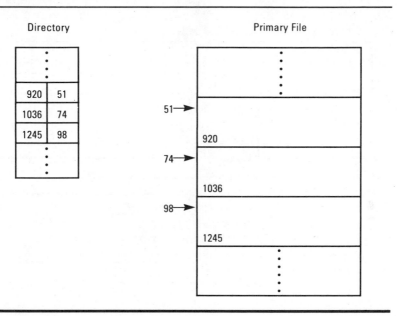

Directory   Primary File

Inverted Files

In some applications, more than one record may be required in a search on one key. In an **inverted file** two levels are maintained, as in the indexed sequential structure. As an example, consider Figure 9–11. Entry to a personnel file is required by department number, and records on all employees of that department are required. The directory is searched on the department number, e.g. 7172. The addresses of the records of all employees in that department are read. The primary file is then directly addressed for each of these records.

Inverted files also provide ease in determining records that meet multiple criteria. For example, Figure 9–12 shows a file with inverted lists. If it is required to find all those employees who are salaried and members of the retirement plan, most search techniques will be very time-consuming. If the file can be searched as an inverted list, improvement is possible. For example, if the inverted list provides the locations for salaried employees, then only those records need be checked for participation in the retirement plan. If

Figure 9–11
Inverted File

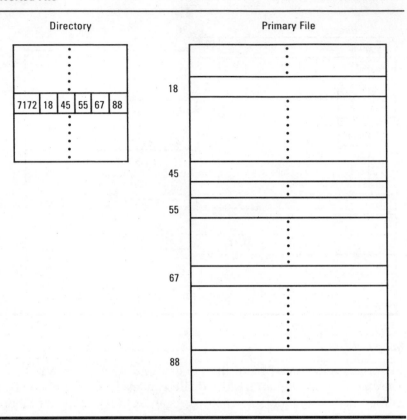

entry to the file by means of two inverted lists (i.e. a salaried/hourly list and a retirement plan list) is possible, then only those locations common to both lists need be retrieved. In the example, the entries common to the salaried list and the retirement plan list are 1 and 4. The records describing personnel who are both salaried and members of the retirement plan are located at addresses 1 and 4 in the primary file. A requirement to locate records meeting one criterion or another criterion can be met by retrieving both relevant lists, combining them, and eliminating duplicates. For example, using Figure 9–12 again, a requirement to find those employees who are either salaried or members of the retirement plan produces a list of locations of 1, 3, 4, 5, 6, and 7.

Figure 9–12
Multiple Criteria Example with an Inverted File

Inverted Lists

Salaried	1	4	5	6
Hourly	2	3	7	
Retirement Plan	1	3	4	7
No Plan	2	5	6	

Primary File

Employee Number	Employee Name	Salaried/ Hourly*	Retirement Plan‡
014	JONES	S	P
031	SMITH	H	N
067	BROWN	H	P
084	DAVIS	S	P
101	ADAMS	S	N
109	PARKER	S	N
128	MILES	H	P

*S = salaried, H = hourly
‡P = participant, N = nonparticipant

Bit Indexes

The contents of a record may be described by various characteristics, and it is frequently a combination of these descriptive characteristics that is the basis for file search. Inverted files are one means to provide this capability. **Bit indexes** provide another more compact approach to this problem. A string of bits is kept for each possible search characteristic. One bit position exists for each record location. If the characteristic represented by the bit index is present in the record at location n, then bit n is set to *1;* if that characteristic is absent, it is set to *0.* Figure 9–13 provides an example using bit indexes. The indexes were created as follows:

Index	Position						
	7	6	5	4	3	2	1
Salaried	0	1	1	1	0	0	1
Medical	1	0	1	1	0	1	1
Retirement	1	0	0	1	1	0	1

If it is required to find all those employees who are salaried and members of the retirement plan, the two relevant bit indexes can be combined with a *logical AND* operation.

A **logical AND** operation is defined as follows:

A	B	A·B
0	0	0
1	0	0
0	1	0
1	1	1

Figure 9–13
Bit Index Example

Bit Indexes

Salaried	0 1 1 1 0 0 1
Medical	1 0 1 1 0 1 1
Retirement	1 0 0 1 1 0 1

Number	Name	Salaried/ Hourly*	Medical Plan‡	Retirement Plan‡
014	JONES	S	P	P
031	SMITH	H	P	N
067	BROWN	H	N	P
084	DAVIS	S	P	P
101	ADAMS	S	P	N
109	PARKER	S	N	N
128	MILES	H	P	P

*S = salaried, H = hourly
‡P = participant, N = nonparticipant

That is, the output of a logical AND operation is 1 if, and only if, both inputs are *1*.

Combining the salaried index and the retirement index results in an "index" indicating the relevant records:

$$\begin{bmatrix}1\\0\\0\\1\\1\\1\\0\end{bmatrix} \cdot \begin{bmatrix}1\\0\\1\\1\\0\\0\\1\end{bmatrix} = \begin{bmatrix}1\\0\\0\\1\\0\\0\\0\end{bmatrix}$$

Thus, only records 1 and 4 meet the requirements.

Logical OR operations may also be used. A **logical OR** operation is defined as follows:

A	B	AUB
0	0	0
1	0	1
0	1	1
1	1	1

That is, the output of a logical OR operation is 1 if either one input or the other input or both inputs are 1.

As another example, if it is required to find all those employees who are salaried and not members of the retirement plan, the following approach can be taken. Negate (or take the *complement* of) the retirement index:

$$\begin{bmatrix}1\\0\\1\\1\\0\\0\\1\end{bmatrix} \Rightarrow \begin{bmatrix}0\\1\\0\\0\\1\\1\\0\end{bmatrix}$$

Negation changes every 1 to a 0 and every 0 to a 1 in the index. This new index represents nonmembers of the retirement plan. Combining this index with the salaried index by means of a logical AND operation answers the question:

$$
\begin{bmatrix} 0 \\ 1 \\ 0 \\ 0 \\ 1 \\ 1 \\ 0 \end{bmatrix} \cdot \begin{bmatrix} 1 \\ 0 \\ 0 \\ 1 \\ 1 \\ 1 \\ 0 \end{bmatrix} = \begin{bmatrix} 0 \\ 0 \\ 0 \\ 0 \\ 1 \\ 1 \\ 0 \end{bmatrix}
$$

Records 5 and 6 refer to salaried employees who are not members of the retirement plan. Several logical ANDs, ORs, or negations may be used to answer compound questions.

Table 9–2 summarizes some of the characteristics of the various file search techniques. The number of logical accesses required and the effectiveness of blocking (in some cases) are the two most important determinants of response time. Those search techniques using close to one logical access will be the most effective for rapid response. For retrieval of multiple records meeting the search criteria, the inverted file and the use of bit indexes may be the most effective techniques.

Table 9–2
Comparison of File Search Techniques

Search Technique	Max Logical Accesses	File Sorted	Percent Storage Space	Primary Memory Space	Muliple Record Search	Blocking Helpful
Sequential	N	No (but helpful)	100	Same	—	Very
Binary	$\log_2(N+1)$	Yes	100	Same	—	Little
Direct Address	1	No	100	Same	—	No
Hashing	1+	No	>= 120	Same	—	Overflow if sequentially searched
Directory	1†	No	Increase*	Increase*	—	No
Indexed Sequential	‡	Yes	Increase*	Increase*	—	Very
Inverted File	1†	No	Increase*	Increase*	Good	Little
Bit Index	1†	No	Increase*	Increase*	Good	Little

N = length of file
*to store directory or index
†after directory search or index manipulation
‡depends on the size of the final subset

Volatility refers to the addition and deletion of records from a file. A volatile file is one in which records are added and deleted at a high rate. Such a file requires a file organization that allows not only efficient searching of the file, but also efficient incorporation of new records and deletion of old records from the file. High volatility requires much time to be spent not only in updating the primary file but also in updating any directory used, e.g. with inverted files, bit indexes, etc.

Another consideration is space required for the file on secondary storage. Because of gaps, hashing requires a significant (equal to or greater than 20 percent) increase in space over a fully compacted version of the same file. Direct addressing is practical only if the search keys fall in a relatively narrow range, that is, leave few gaps in the file. Any technique using a directory requires additional space to store the directory.

Physical Considerations

The above discussion has dealt with logical searches and has ignored physical considerations. Physical considerations may impact the practicality of using any one of these search techniques to a greater or lesser extent.

Physical considerations take on greater importance as the size of the file to be searched becomes large. It has been assumed that the access time to any given record is the same on the average. In large files this can no longer be assumed. For example, if a file spans multiple cylinders on disk the time for read/write head movement may be significant. A search technique that involves multiple head movements may be very time-consuming.

Although a binary search may be an effective search technique in many applications, a large file on disk drastically reduces this effectiveness. Since a binary search makes relatively large jumps within the file, shifts between cylinders are involved, and movement of the heads will absorb a relatively large amount of time.

An indexed sequential search is frequently used to physically access a file stored on disk. In this case, the directory gives the physical address of the track, and a sequential search of the track ensues.

An overflow area used in a hashed organization should reside in the same cylinder as the primary area. For a multicylinder file an overflow area may exist in each cylinder. As a result, synonyms appear in the same cylinder, and access time is minimized.

Physical Access

There is no industry standard for data formatting on disk. Vendors differ in their approach to the layout of a track. As an example, Figure

Figure 9–14
IBM Disk Track Format

9–14 illustrates the data formatting used on an IBM disk track. Each track consists of both data and nondata groups of characters separated by gaps.

The start of each track is indicated by an **index point.** This may be either a particular bit pattern or a physical hole or slot.

The **home address** identifies the particular track. This address consists of the cylinder number and the head number. This combination uniquely identifies the track. A flag indicates whether the track is operational or damaged. If damaged, the contents of the home address area and the track descriptor record are used to identify the alternate track to be used.

The **track descriptor record** is the first record after the index point and the home address. There is one track descriptor record on each track. In addition to cross-referencing for defective tracks, this record is also used in a direct access file organization.

One or more **data records** are stored on the track following the track descriptor record. These records store the data provided by a program. Figure 9–15 shows the makeup of a data record. Data records are either in a key data format or in a nonkey data format. The records consist of three components in the nonkey data format and four components in the key data format:

1. The address marker.
2. The count area.
3. The key area (in key data format only).
4. The data area.

The **address marker** locates the beginning of the data record and is provided by, and used by, the control unit. The **count area** identifies the cylinder number, head number, and record number on the track, the data length, and the key length (if it is in key data format).

Figure 9–15
Data Record

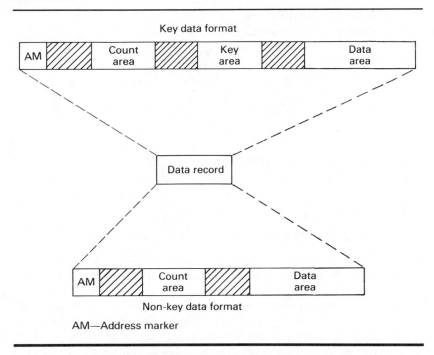

AM—Address marker

The **key area** contains the value of the key that identifies the record. It should be noted that not every higher symbolic language allows a key data format. For example, such a capability does not usually exist in FORTRAN but does in COBOL. For a data record in key data format, the contents of the record itself may contain the same key if the applications program constructs the logical record in that manner. A physical access using the key may be carried out by the system. The data area contains the data stored as a physical record. This may be blocked or unblocked.

File Organization
Physically, files can be organized on only three bases:

1. Sequential.
2. Indexed sequential.
3. Direct.

All access methods are oriented around one or the other of these three basic organizations.

Sequential Organization

In a **sequentially organized** file records are written one after another, usually in sequence on a key. The file is expected to be accessed sequentially and, as a result, the key data format is rarely used. High activity is the main argument for sequential processing. Payroll is the best example of a sequential application. Almost every record in a payroll file will be needed in a payroll run. Payroll is almost always a sequential application.

Indexed Sequential Organization

An **indexed sequential** organization uses three file areas:

1. The primary area.
2. The overflow area.
3. The index or directory.

An indexed sequential organization is not available in every language. For example, it is used in COBOL but does not exist in FORTRAN.

Records in the primary area are key formatted and stored in sequence on the key. Indexes are created and updated by the operating system (not by the applications programmer). An indexed sequential file is also called an **ISAM** file. ISAM is an acronym for an access method used with this organization: **indexed sequential access method.** There are three (or more) levels of indexes used with an ISAM file. these are:

1. The track index.
2. The cylinder index.
3. The master index.

These indexes are hierarchically related to each other.

The **track index** is a directory for a cylinder. It contains the home address for each track and the highest keys stored on that track. There is also an entry for the overflow location for each track.

The **cylinder index** is a directory for each cylinder in the file. Each entry provides the home address for the track index for the required cylinder and the highest key value stored in that cylinder.

The **master index** is optional and is a higher level index that provides entry to a cylinder index. Some systems allow more than one level of master index.

Figure 9–16 illustrates the relationships among these three levels of indexes. A single master index (if it exists) points to one of a number of cylinder indexes. A master index would be used in the case of a file spanning many cylinders. If no master index exists, entry is made into a single cylinder index. The cylinder index points to a track index. One track index exists for each cylinder, and an entry appears for each track in the cylinder. The range of possible locations for the record identified by a particular search key is narrowed down to a cylinder, and then to a track within that cylinder. A physical sequential search is then made in that track.

Using the indexes, a record in the file may be direct accessed. The file may also be sequentially searched based on the physical arrangement of the records.

Figure 9–16
Indexed Sequential Organization

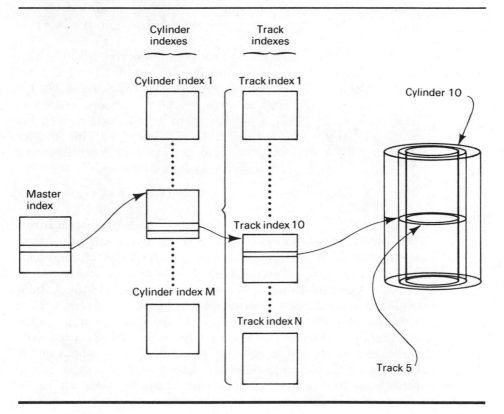

There are two access methods used to implement an indexed sequential file organization on IBM systems. These are ISAM (Indexed Sequential Access Method) and VSAM (Virtual Storage Access Method).

ISAM

Figure 9–17 illustrates ISAM. The storage area consists of a prime area and an overflow area. Each of these areas consists of tracks. An ISAM file is loaded into the prime area in sequential order on the search key. The keys are shown associated with the records loaded in the example of Figure 9–17(a). A load usually fills only a certain percentage of each track in the prime area.

With additions to the file, prime area tracks are eventually filled, and additional records added result in storage in the overflow area. Figure 9–17(b) shows the results of adding records identified by keys 26 and 29. Since sequential order must be maintained, the logical record identified by key 31 is shifted to the overflow area. Additions on other tracks also result in shifts to other tracks in the overflow area.

Deletions in the prime area do not result, however, in shifts back from the overflow area to the prime area. Figure 9–17(c) illustrates this with deletions of the records identified by keys 26 and 28, that is, the deletion of a record does not result in a physical savings in space. As a result, ISAM is an inefficient organization for a highly volatile file. At intervals the file must be reorganized. This involves reloading the file into the prime area and leaving the overflow area empty again. A utility is usually available to do this.

VSAM

Figure 9–18 illustrates VSAM. Storage consists of **control intervals,** which are contiguous but not necessarily related to the physical structure of the storage device. The control interval is analogous to a track in ISAM. A **control area** consists of a number of control intervals. A control area is analogous to a cylinder in ISAM. A file is divided into a number of control areas. A hierachy of indexes (as in ISAM) provide entry to the file. All of the space in a control area not occupied by records at load time is allocated to **distributed free space,** that is, space available for storage of records to be added to the file after the initial load. Distributed free space may be set up within each control interval, in whole control intervals within the

Figure 9–17
ISAM

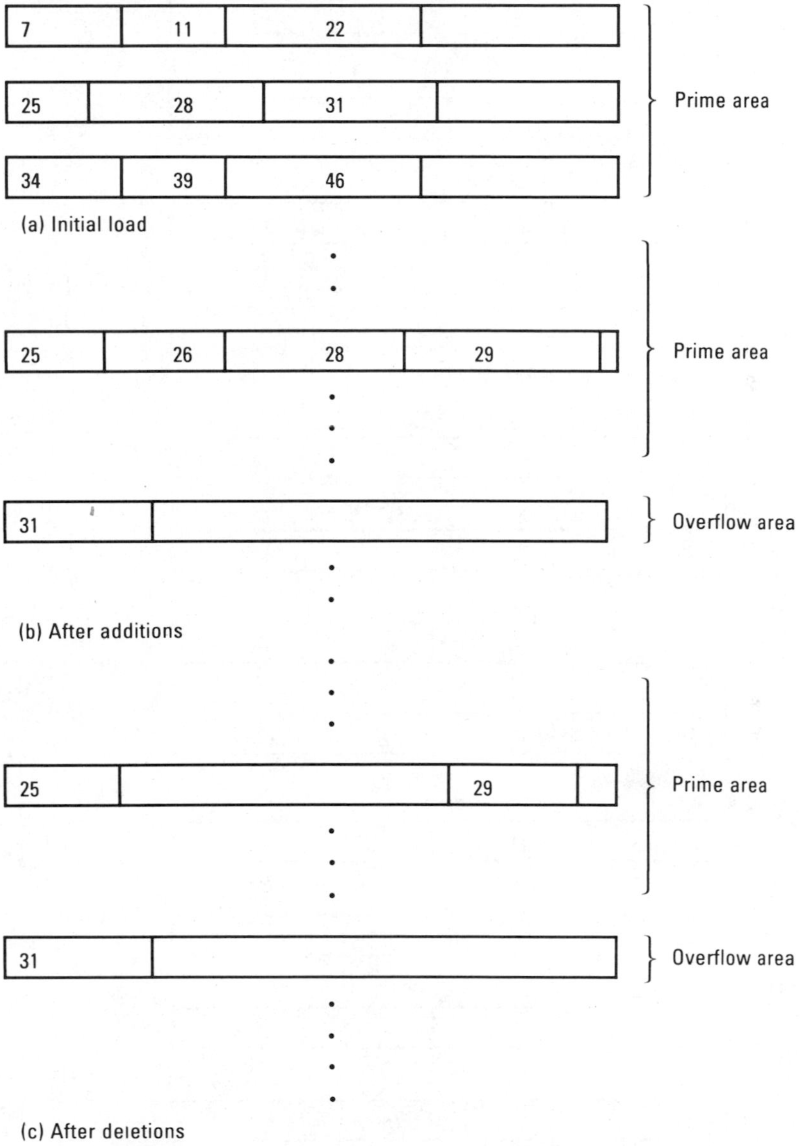

7	11	22	

25	28	31	

34	39	46	

(a) Initial load

Prime area

| 25 | 26 | 28 | 29 | |

Prime area

| 31 | |

Overflow area

(b) After additions

| 25 | | 29 | |

Prime area

| 31 | |

Overflow area

(c) After deletions

Figure 9–18
VSAM

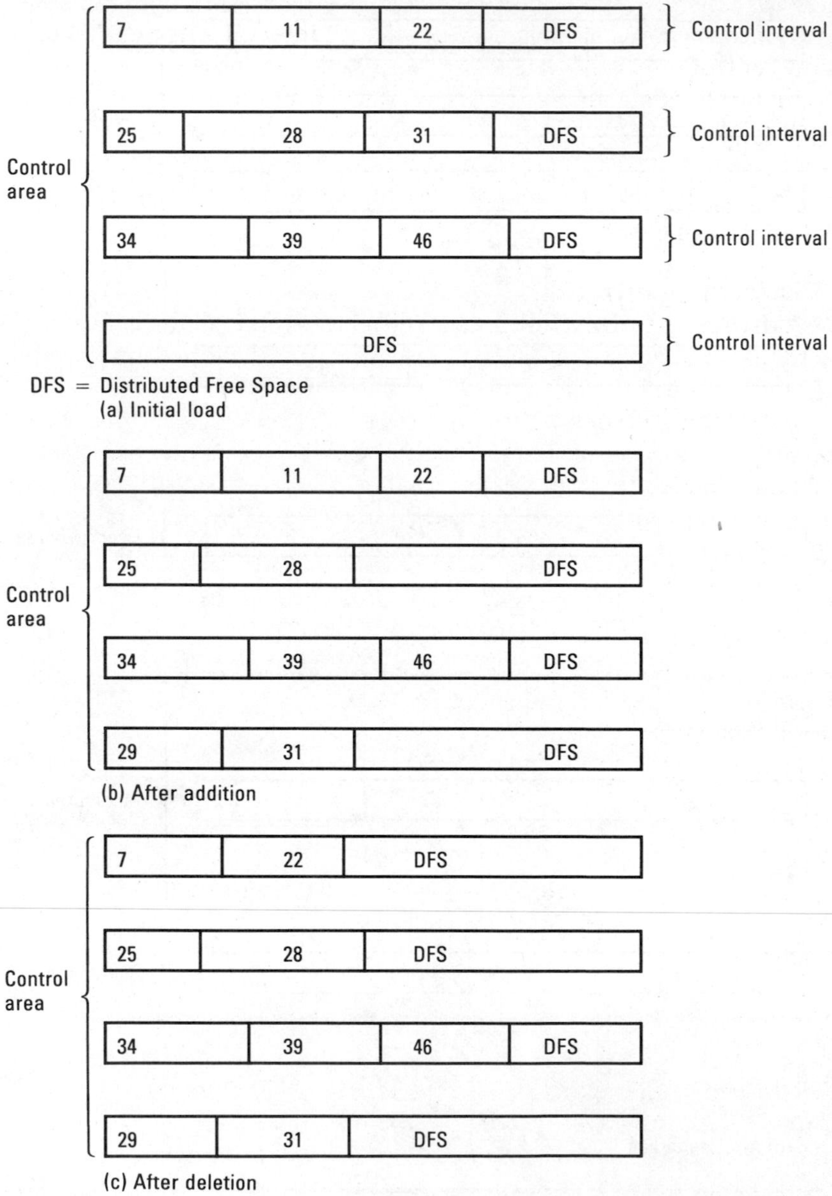

DFS = Distributed Free Space
(a) Initial load

(b) After addition

(c) After deletion

control areas or both. Figure 9–18(a) shows an example with distributed free space after initial load of the file.

Figure 9–18(b) shows the effect of adding a record identified by key 29. This results in a **control area split** by VSAM. Approximately half of the records associated with control interval 2 are moved to a new control interval filled with distributed free space.

Figure 9–18(c) shows the effect of deleting the record identified by key 11. Space freed up in the control interval is returned to distributed free space, and all records after the deleted record are shifted toward the beginning of the control interval. Thus deletions result in usable space.

Direct Organization

A **direct organization** uses a key conversion to determine a record address. This may be done either by direct addressing or indirect addressing.

In **direct addressing** the key is required to be numeric and the records fixed length. The algorithm used to calculate the record address divides the key by the number of records stored per track. The quotient is the relative track address. The remainder plus one (to compensate for the track descriptor record) is the relative record address within the track. An example of this calculation is provided in Figure 9–19.

Figure 9–19
Direct Addressing Calculation

Key =	1234	
Number of records per track =	70	
Direct addressing =	1234/70	
Quotient =	17	= Relative track address
Remainder =	44	
	+ 1	
	45	= Relative record address

Indirect addressing uses a hashing algorithm to determine either the relative track address alone or the relative track address and the relative record address within the track. Both methods are used. Nonnumeric keys can be used. Provision for overflow is required in this organization.

Conclusions

Searching a file can be viewed as a two-step process: the logical access and the physical access. The logical access is the mechanism of the applications program to accomplish I/O. The physical access is the mechanism of the operating system to accomplish I/O. Physical access is handled by the access methods of the operating system.

There are a number of different file search techniques that can be implemented at the logical access level. These are sequential search, binary search, direct addressing, hashing (or randomizing), directory lookup, indexed sequential search, an inverted file, and bit indexes.

The physical implementation of a file can be done on the basis of three file organizations: sequential, indexed sequential, and direct. A sequential organization restricts access to a sequential search. A direct organization allows direct access. A sequential processing of a direct organization file can be extremely inefficient. An indexed sequential organization is a compromise, which allows both sequential and direct processing of the same file. As a compromise, it is less efficient at either form of processing than the sequential or direct organization. ISAM requires frequent reorganizations in a high volatility environment. VSAM is a better choice in such an environment.

In general, each file search technique and file organization offers both advantages and disadvantages. It should be the goal of the system designer to select those search techniques and that file organization which, under a given set of physical and logical constraints, can successfully trade off those advantages and disadvantages.

Additional Readings

Claybrook, B. G. *File Management Techniques.* New York: John Wiley and Sons, 1983.

Dodd, G. S. "Elements of Data Management Systems." *ACM Computing Surveys* 1, No. 2 (June 1969), pp. 117-33.

Hanson, O. *Design of Computer Data Files.* Rockville: Computer Science Press, Inc., 1982.

Loomis, M. E. S. *Data Management and File Processing.* Englewood Cliffs, N.J.: Prentice-Hall, 1983.

Martin, James. *Computer Data-Base Organization.* 2d ed. Englewood Cliffs, N.J.: Prentice-Hall, 1977.

Yourdon, E. *Design of On-Line Computer Systems.* Englewood Cliffs, N.J.: Prentice-Hall, 1975.

Review

1. What is a file search technique?
2. Differentiate between logical access and physical access.
3. Why is a sequential search the only type of search technique practical on magnetic tape?
4. Explain how a binary search is an application of information theory.
5. Why is a direct addressing scheme difficult to maintain in a highly volatile file?
6. Devise a hashing algorithm not discussed in the chapter. What type of key would not work well with this algorithm?
7. Is the directory used in a directory lookup or the directory used in an indexed sequential search shorter, given the same length primary file? Explain.
8. Comparing an inverted file technique with a bit index technique:
   a Which requires more file space?
   b Which requires more primary memory?
9. Which search techniques require a file arranged in the order of the search key?
10. The following products are in the inventory of the Worldwide Widget Company:
    Large red widget
    Large red gadget
    Small blue widget
    Large blue widget
    Large blue gadget
    Small white trinket
    Small red widget
    Large white trinket
    Small red trinket
    Large white gadget
    Small white gadget
    Small blue gadget
    Large white widget
    Small red gadget
    Small white widget
    a Set up a set of eight bit indexes that will be used to search this inventory file. These indexes will identify the locations of widgets, gadgets, trinkets, red, white, blue, large and small items.
    b Test the system with the following search criteria:
       (1) Small red trinkets

(2) Large blue or red gadgets

(3) Nonred widgets

11. Clearly differentiate between activity and volatility of a file.

12. Describe how additions and deletions are made in:

a An ISAM file.

b A VSAM file.

Chapter 10

Data Structures

Introduction

The nature of data processing applications may dictate that certain relationships be maintained among data elements. These relationships are
based on various requirements to manipulate these data. A data structure
allows these logical relationships among data elements to be implemented. This structure may exist among data elements contained in primary memory, or among records contained in a data file on secondary
storage. This relationship, or linking, of one data element to another is
implemented by storing additional data with each set of data. In primary
memory these links are addresses (perhaps locations in an array); in data
files they can be logical record numbers, that is, relative record addresses.

If data structures are used to facilitate the searching of a file, the file
must be stored on a direct access secondary storage device. Primary
memory is, of course, random access. The following discussion will be
oriented toward data files.

In general, a file search technique is used to retrieve one or more records from a file or to determine that no records in the file meet the search
criteria. If the search has been successful, the record sought has been
copied into primary memory, and whatever processing required for its

data elements is carried out. The cycle of finding the desired record through means of a search procedure and copying it into primary memory for further processing may, of course, be repeated any number of times. In addition, a search may be carried out for a number of records, and processing may be performed on this set of records as a whole. There are a number of circumstances that may complicate this rather straight-forward procedure, however.

It may be desirable, even necessary, to maintain a file in some order, although there are frequent additions and deletions of records made on a random basis. If a record is deleted, an entry may be made in the record to indicate that this particular record, whenever encountered, is to be ignored for all further processing. For example, a particular field in the record may have a special character, e.g. a *1,* entered for deletion. When the record is READ by a user's program and the character is found, no further processing is allowed on the contents of that record. At either fixed or variable intervals of time, all such records may be physically de-leted from the file and the remaining records compacted in one program run. This is frequently called **garbage collection.** Additions at the end of the file can be routinely handled, but additions within the file present a problem. They employ a major reshuffling of the records in the file with each such addition or set of additions. If there is an equal probability that a record may be inserted at any point in the file, and insertions are han-dled one at a time, then half of the file must be shifted, on the average, each time a change is made. If the file is long and additions are common, then the total time used for insertion becomes prohibitive.

Under some conditions, the user may want to access a set of records related to each other, or the user may want to access a set of records all identified by the same search key. One approach to this problem is the use of an inverted file.

In the use of a hashing technique, the problem of overflow arises. If a key producing a calculated address proves to be a synonym, then the search must shift to the file overflow area. Figure 10–1 illustrates this for a file of primary area length N. Thus, if the search at a calculated address in the primary area is unsuccessful because of overflow, a shift to the overflow area starting at location $N+1$ is made. A search of the overflow area is then made—usually a sequential search until either the correct record is found or the end of the file is reached. In a large file, a sequen-tial search of the overflow area may be very time-consuming. This is es-pecially wasteful if, in fact, a record identified by the search key does not exist.

In certain applications, it may be important to build into a file certain relationships among the individual records. These relationships may not

Figure 10–1
Hashed Search

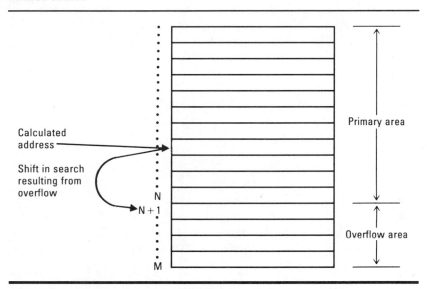

be best represented in a sequential manner. For example, a file containing data on the parts used in an assembly operation may contain much redundancy if organized in a straight sequential fashion. This is illustrated in Figure 10–2. In the example, the final assembly consists of assembly 1, assembly 2, assembly 3 and part 5. Assembly 1 consists of subassembly 1, subassembly 2, and part 5, etc. There is much repetition, e.g part 2 is repeated three times.

The same file may be used for a number of different purposes. For example, a personnel file may be arranged in order on employee number. This order may be useful for some applications. However, if the personnel data are needed in alphabetical order, they may have to be sorted for this second use. Sorting a large file is very time-consuming.

All of the above problems can be effectively handled with the use of pointers. A **pointer** is an elementary data item contained in a record that *points* to another location in the file. In a file organized on a sequential basis, the next logical record is also the next record in sequential order. An additional data item that contains a pointer to the next logical record is incorporated into each record in a file. This allows the logical and physical arrangement of the file to be different. Furthermore, it is possible to maintain a file in a particular sequential order while maintaining a number of other logical relationships within the file at the same time.

Figure 10–2
Bill of Materials Example

```
                    FINAL ASSEMBLY
                     ASSEMBLY 1
                      SUBASSEMBLY 1
                       PART 1
                       PART 2
                      SUBASSEMBLY 2
                       PART 3
                       PART 4
                      PART 5
                     ASSEMBLY 2
                      SUBASSEMBLY 2
                       PART 3
                       PART 4
                      PART 6
                     ASSEMBLY 3
                      SUBASSEMBLY 1
                       PART 1
                       PART 2
                      SUBASSEMBLY 3
                       PART 7
                       PART 8
                       PART 9
                      PART 2
                      PART 4
                      PART 8          .
                     PART 5
```

These logical relationships (which may be different from the relationship existing in the sequential order) among records (or sets of data) in a
file are called **data structures.** This chapter will introduce three different
general data structures. These are:

1. The list structure.
2. The tree structure.
3. The network structure.

In summary, with the use of data structures, one or more connections
(or relationships) are established among different records in a file. The
contents of one record will contain, along with other elementary data
items, the direct address (or the location) of the next record or records as
an additional data item or items. Since the records so linked may be lo-

cated anywhere within the file, a direct access secondary storage device is required.

List Structures

In some applications, it may be desirable to link together in a chain records that are related. Such a chain of records linked sequentially is called a **list,** or a **linked list.** The first record in the list is accessed by means of a key, using some file search technique. The other records in the list can then be accessed directly in sequence. As an example, an accounts receivable file may be sequenced in order by date, but the invoices for each customer may be linked together. Once the first invoice is retrieved (perhaps through a directory), all other invoices outstanding for a given customer are available by means of the list. As a second example, a personnel file may link together in a list all employees with a certain specialized skill. A pointer to the first record is called the **head.** The end of a list (or the **tail**) is indicated by the use of a special symbol. This special symbol may be an impossible address, such as a negative number.

Figure 10–3 illustrates a part of a list structure. The record located at address 17 points to another record located at address 5, etc.

As a more detailed example, assume that the following highly simplified personnel file exists on a direct access device.

Address					
1	•	014	Jones	7.20	7
2	•	031	Smith	6.65	− 99
3	•	067	Brown	6.35	4
4	•	084	Davis	8.50	1
5	•	101	Adams	7.60	3
6	•	109	Parker	6.85	2
7	•	128	Miles	8.10	6

The numbers in the address column on the left are not part of the file, but are provided for ease of understanding. Each record contains four data items. This file is arranged in sequential order on employee number (the first data item).

Assume that it is required to obtain an alphabetical listing of all employees from the file. A search for the first item could be made, then a search for the second item, etc.—clearly a grossly inefficient

Figure 10–3
List Structure

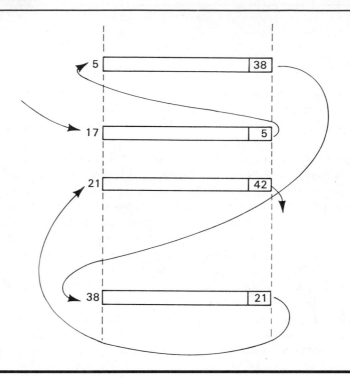

approach. An alternative is to sort the file into order on the employee name field. If the file is large, the sorting may have to be done in parts and then the parts merged. Sorting of a large file is time-consuming. If the requirement for an alphabetical listing is a recurring one, then a significant amount of processing time may be devoted to meeting this requirement. This requirement is met easily, however, by using a list structure.

The first record, i.e. ADAMS, must be found using a search technique, e.g. a directory lookup. The fourth field in this record contains the address of the next record. Thus address 3 is the location of the record to follow ADAMS. After retrieving the record at address 3, i.e. BROWN, the address of the next record is 4. This procedure is repeated until a special piece of data signifying the end of the list is found. In this example − *99* is used as such a device.

The list structure makes it relatively easy to add and delete records in the list. All that is required is to change a pointer. As an example, consider the personnel file above. Assume that employee JAMES joins the organization. He is issued employee number 141 and receives a rate of pay of 8.20. Thus, a new record must be added to the file:

141 JAMES   8.20   _____

The record is physically placed at the end of the file. This maintains the employee number order of the file. It is also at the end of the file that space is available to store the new record. Alphabetically, JAMES falls between DAVIS and JONES. The DAVIS pointer must be changed to 8. The pointer in the JAMES record must be set to point to JONES, i.e. 1. After updating, the file should appear as:

1	•	014	Jones	7.20	7
2	•	031	Smith	6.65	− 99
3	•	067	Brown	6.35	4
4	•	084	Davis	8.50	8
5	•	101	Adams	7.60	3
6	•	109	Parker	6.85	2
7	•	128	Miles	8.10	6
8	•	141	James	8.20	1

Again, considering the same personnel file, assume that employee PARKER resigns from the organization. To update, only a pointer need be changed. The record preceding PARKER in the list is MILES. The pointer in the MILES record can simply be changed from 6 to 2, thus *cutting out* the PARKER record from the list. The record, of course, physically remains in the file temporarily. As a result, an indication must be provided to user programs that this particular record, when accessed, must be ignored. This could be done, in the example, by providing a fifth data item in each record. If this data item is set equal to a particular value, it has been *deleted*. An alternative method would be to set the pointer equal to another special value, e.g. − 9. At certain intervals the file can be compacted, that is, have these indicated records physically deleted.

It might be desirable to keep the location of the end of a list in storage. For example, if a directory lookup is used for obtaining the location of the beginning of the list, then the end of the list might be just as easily provided. This extra pointer in the directory would make it easy to add a record to the end of the list.

Stacks and Queues

A **stack** is a list structure used on a LIFO (last-in, first-out) basis. Additions to the list are made at one end, and deletions are also made at the same end. It is sometimes also called a **push down stack** or a **push down store** in analogy to devices used in restaurants to hold dishes. Dishes are added to the top of the stack, which is pushed down, and dishes are removed from the top as needed.

A stack is used by a compiler in interpreting arithmetic statements. It is also sometimes used to store return addresses in primary memory when subprograms are called. When a return is made from a subprogram to its calling program, the last return address is needed. Thus, as a nest of subprograms is called, return addresses are saved in the order of the calls and are retrieved and used on a last-in, first-out basis by the sequence of returns. Adding an element to a stack is called **putting** or **pushing.** Deletion of an element from a stack is called **popping** or **pulling.**

A **queue** is a list structure used on a FIFO (first-in, first-out) basis. Additions to the list are made at one end, and deletions are made at the other end. A **dequeue** is a queue that allows addition and deletion of elements at both ends of the list.

Figure 10–4
Doubly-Linked List

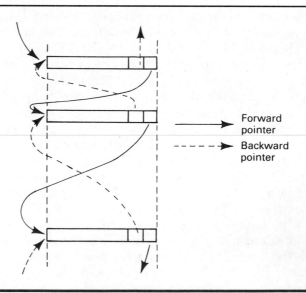

Forward pointer

Backward pointer

Provision is needed with both the stack and the queue for indicating either an empty list or a full list (when a limited number of elements may be included). Overflow or underflow can result in lost data.

Two-Way Pointers

Although the list structure as described above makes it easy to determine the next element in a list, there is no way to directly determine the preceding element in the list. In order to overcome this difficulty, two pointers may be maintained in each record—one pointing forward in the list and the other pointing backward. Greater flexibility is obtained, but at the cost of increased storage space. Such lists are sometimes called **doubly linked lists.** Figure 10–4 illustrates such a structure. The advantage of lists with two-way pointers is that the user may start from any element in the list and move forward or backward with ease.

Adding or deleting a record from a list with two-way pointers, however, becomes a little more complicated than with one-way pointers only. Assume that the file segment shown in Figure 10–5 exists in a longer list. Using this figure as an example, consider deleting

Figure 10–5
Two-Way Pointer Example

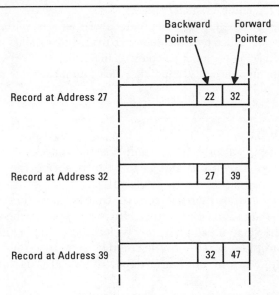

the record at address 32 from the list. The following steps are now required:

1. Record 32 must be read into primary memory to determine its predecessor and its successor records.
2. Record 27 must be accessed and read into primary memory. Its forward pointer must be changed to 39 (thus, *cutting out* record 32).
3. The updated record 27 must then be written back into the file.
4. Record 39 must be accessed and read into primary memory. Its backward pointer must be changed to 27.
5. The updated record 39 must then be written back into the file.

As a second example, consider the original record arrangement in the same figure. A new record is to be inserted into the list between record 32 and record 39. The new record will be located at address 85. The following steps are required:

1. Record 85 must be arranged in primary memory with a backward pointer to 32 and a forward pointer to 39. (The determination of these pointers may have required a search.)
2. Record 85 must be written in the file.
3. Record 32 must be accessed and written into primary memory. Its forward pointer must be changed to 85.
4. The updated record 32 must then be written back into the file.
5. Record 39 must be accessed and read into primary memory. Its backward pointer must be changed to 85.
6. The updated record 39 must then be written back into the file.

Threaded Lists

In some applications, more than one list may be contained in a file. The term **threaded list** is used to describe the situation in which multiple lists weave through a file.

If the lists are mutually exclusive, that is, have no common records, then a data item containing a single pointer may be used to link the lists. The start of each list may be located at the beginning of the file. For example, a personnel file could be structured so as to provide lists of employees in the same department. This is illustrated as follows:

1	•	15	4		25	3	
2	•	014		JONES	7.20		6
3	•	031		SMITH	6.65		2
4	•	067		BROWN	6.35		7
5	•	084		DAVIS	8.50		− 99
6	•	101		ADAMS	7.60		8
7	•	109		PARKER	6.85		9
8	•	128		MILES	8.10		− 99
9	•	141		JAMES	8.20		5

Record 1 contains a directory that shows that the list containing data on employees in department 15 begins at location 4. This list contains, in order of ascending salary, the records of employees in department 15. It continues until the special end of list entry (-99) is encountered at record 5. A second list of employees in department 25 begins at location 3 and continues to record 8. This structure assumes that one employee cannot be in two departments at the same time.

In other applications more than one list may be required, and these lists may not be mutually exclusive. For example, a personnel file could be structured to provide data on employees possessing certain skills. This is illustrated as follows:

1	•	1	3		2	2	3	4	
2	•	014		JONES	7.20	0		3	0
3	•	031		SMITH	6.65	4		6	0
4	•	067		BROWN	6.35	7		0	6
5	•	084		DAVIS	8.50	0		0	0
6	•	101		ADAMS	7.60	0		7	7
7	•	109		PARKER	6.85	8		9	8
8	•	128		MILES	8.10	− 99		0	− 99
9	•	141		JAMES	8.20	0		− 99	0

Record 1 again contains a directory that provides the starting points in the file for lists of employees having three different skills. An individual employee may possess none, one, two, or all three skills. Notice that with this structure, questions such as: *Which employees possess both skill 1 and skill 3?* can be answered by retrieving the lists for skill 1 and skill 3 and finding the common elements. In this example, employees BROWN, PARKER, and MILES meet these criteria. Questions such as: *Which employees possess either skill 1 or skill 3 or both?* can be answered by retrieving both lists, merging them, and eliminating duplicates. In the example, employees SMITH, BROWN, ADAMS, PARKER, and MILES meet these criteria. These questions could also be answered by means of inverted lists or bit indexes.

The use of pointers allows greater ease of retrieval in some cases. However, they take up additional storage space and must be maintained by more complicated programs.

Ring Structures

A **ring structure** is a list structure that closes on itself, that is, the last element points forward to the first element. Thus, the user may enter the ring at any point and still be able to reach any or all other records. Figure 10–6 illustrates such a structure.

Figure 10–6
Ring Structure

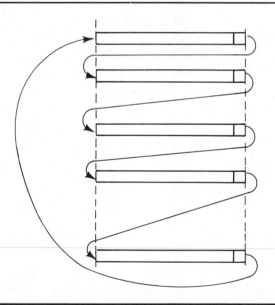

In a ring structure, pointers may link the elements in only one direction (forward) or in two directions (forward and backward). Other than having no *end* to the list, the ring structure is, in all respects, similar to the list structure. It is a circular list.

As an example, such a structure might be used in a billing system using two files—a customer file and an invoice file. The customer file is organized in order on customer number; the invoice file is in sequence on date of order.

Customer file:

1	•	17	JONES CO	2
2	•	29	SMITH CO	1
3	•	35	BROWN CO	5

Invoice file:

1	•	27	 3
2	•	28	 4
3	•	30	102
4	•	33	 7
5	•	34	 6
6	•	36	103
7	•	37	101

Retrieval of all invoices outstanding for a given customer is relatively simple. For example, the JONES CO ring may be followed from the customer file to address 2 in the invoice file. This holds invoice 28, which points to address 4 and invoice 33. The record holding invoice 33 points to address 7 which holds invoice 37. This completes the ring. It is assumed in this example that all pointers over 100 refer to the customer file, and that the address referenced in that file is found by subtracting 100 from the pointer. Clearly, many other methods could be used. Two other rings are also found for the SMITH CO and the BROWN CO. With this structure, data may be obtained on any or all invoices outstanding with a customer; or, knowing an invoice number, data can be obtained on the customer by following the ring from the invoice file into the customer file.

Tree Structures

In some applications, a hierarchical relationship may exist between the individual elements. A tree structure can reflect this relationship. In a list structure, one element points forward to only one other element. In a **tree structure,** one element may generally point forward to more than one other element, that is, one element may have more than one other subordinate element. In addition, every element (except the first) must be subordinate to only one other element.

Each element in the structure is called a **node.** The node at the top of the tree structure is called the **root.** A node superior to other nodes is called a **parent,** and the subordinate nodes are called the **children.** The term "children" is used to include all nodes subordinate to a parent, even multiple levels below the parent's level. Nodes are connected by **branches.**

A **balanced tree** is one in which each mode can have the same number of branches and the difference between the highest level terminal node, that is, the lowest node on the path, and the lowest level terminal node is no more than 1. Sometimes an additional restriction is added to the definition: Branches must be added from left to right as nodes are added to the tree. Figure 10–7 illustrates some of these concepts.

Figure 10–7
Tree Structure

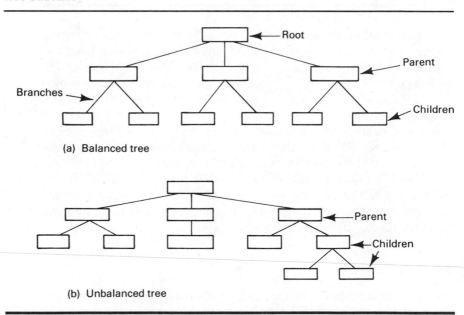

(a) Balanced tree

(b) Unbalanced tree

As an example, consider part of the academic structure of a university illustrated in Figure 10–8. A file containing data organized in this manner (e.g. course and enrollment data) is sketched as follows:

· 10	UNIVERSITY	22	27	31	35	− 99
22	ARTS & SCIENCES					
27	BUSINESS	37	43	49	54	55
31	ENGINEERING					
35	MEDICINE					
37	ACCOUNTING					
43	MANAGEMENT					
49	QUANT. & INFO. SYSTEMS	62	67	71	− 99	− 99
54	FINANCE					
55	MARKETING					
62	MANAGEMENT SCIENCE	− 99	− 99	− 99	− 99	− 99
67	INFORMATION SYSTEMS	− 99	− 99	− 99	− 99	− 99
71	BUSINESS STATISTICS	− 99	− 99	− 99	− 99	− 99

In this example, a maximum of five records may be subordinate to any other record. A dummy pointer (− 99) is used to signify that no other subordinate record exists.

A difficulty may arise if the tree structure is not very balanced, that is, the number of pointers used at each node in the structure varies from none to some maximum number. In this case, an arrangement similar to that used in the university example will result in many null pointers. Null pointers accomplish nothing, yet occupy space. An approach to this problem is to allow each node to have a different number of links, and to store along with the pointers the number of pointers. Ending nodes have no links. Such an approach produces variable length records.

Figure 10–8
Academic Structure in a University

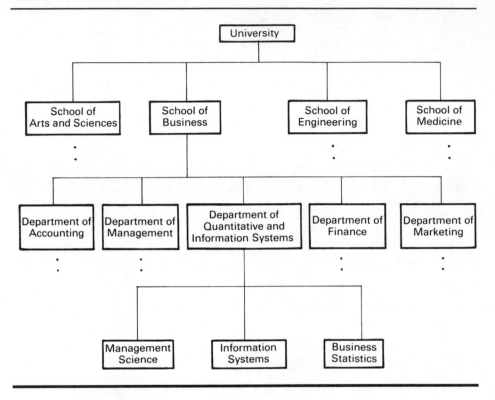

Binary Trees

A **binary tree** is a tree structure that has, at most, two nodes directly subordinate to any other node. It is organized on a search key such that one link of a node points toward nodes having smaller values of the key, and the other link points toward nodes having larger values of the key. Figure 10–9 illustrates such a structure. Note that the pointers are not the keys, but the addresses for records identified by search keys. For example, a pointer with the value 100 *points* to address 100, where the record identified by search key 23 is stored.

If there are frequent additions and deletions to a tree structure, it may become relatively unbalanced, that is, some paths through the tree from the starting record to an ending record may become significantly longer than other paths. This may become a major problem, and rebalancing algorithms may become quite complex. If the tree is

Figure 10–9
Binary Tree

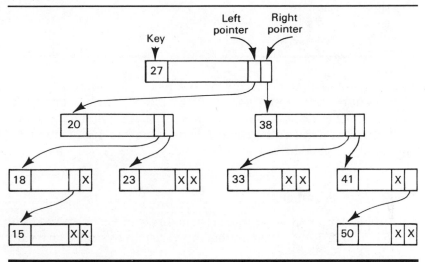

used in a search and it is relatively unbalanced, the search can become time-consuming.

Network Structures

A **network structure** is a more generalized structure in which one node may own more than one other node and, in turn, may be owned by more than one node (except for a root). A network structure is also sometimes called a **plex structure.**

As an example, consider the following organization of the components of a final product. The relationship of the components is also presented in the Introduction of this chapter.

1	•	FINAL ASSEMBLY	2	3	4	12	−99
2	•	ASSEMBLY 1	5	6	12	−99	−99
3	•	ASSEMBLY 2	6	13	−99	−99	−99
4	•	ASSEMBLY 3	5	7	9	11	15
5	•	SUBASSEMBLY 1	8	9	−99	−99	−99
6	•	SUBASSEMBLY 2	10	11	−99	−99	−99
7	•	SUBASSEMBLY 3	14	15	16	−99	−99
8	•	PART 1					
9	•	PART 2					
10	•	PART 3					

11	•	PART 4
12	•	PART 5
13	•	PART 6
14	•	PART 7
15	•	PART 8
16	•	PART 9

Notice that PART 4 (described by the record at location 11) is a component of both ASSEMBLY 3 and SUBASSEMBLY 2, and SUB-ASSEMBLY 2 is a component of both ASSEMBLY 1 and ASSEMBLY 2. This can be a difficult structure both to implement and to maintain for frequent additions and deletions.

Physical Considerations

The implementation of any data structure cannot be carried out without taking into consideration the various physical constraints imposed by the devices used.

If the entire structure can exist among data contained in primary memory, little or few complications result. This is so since primary memory is a true random access medium, and any data element may be accessed in the same time as any other.

If the data structure has been implemented within a data file written on a secondary storage device, physical characteristics of the device must be considered. The storage device holding the structured data must, of course, be a direct access device.

If a list structure is used on a magnetic disk device, then, in so far as possible, all records stored in the same cylinder should be adjacent in the list, and sublists for each cylinder should be sequenced so as to minimize head movement. For example, if a list structure runs through a file spanning three cylinders, then ideally all records in one cylinder are followed by all records in the nearer cylinder, and in turn are followed by all records in the remaining cylinder. Threaded lists may complicate this. It is more difficult to accomplish the same goal with a tree structure, and the problem becomes very difficult to even make an approximate minimization of head movement with a network structure.

In general, a good rule is: *In so far as possible, store records that are frequently required together near each other.* It should also be noted that pointers need not be embedded in the records (as illustrated in the examples of this chapter), but may be stored separately.

Conclusions

The most general type of data structure is the network. A tree results when the network is constrained so that any record may be owned by only one record. A list results when the tree is constrained so that any record may own only one record.

Although it is true that a file can be arranged sequentially in order on only one key at a time, different sequences may be maintained in the entire file or in parts of the file by use of pointers. Thus, a personnel file may be in order on employee number and, at the same time, records of personnel in the same department may be chained together by the use of pointers.

The use of various data structures involves a trade-off in which processing time is reduced but storage space is increased. Access to multiple records that meet search criteria is made easier. Storage space is increased to store the pointers establishing the data structures. There is additional processing time required to manipulate and update the pointers.

Additional Readings

Berztiss, A. T. *Data Structures Theory and Practice*. New York: Academic Press, 1971.

Claybrook, B. G. *File Management Techniques*. New York: John Wiley & Sons, 1983.

Elson, M. *Data Structures*. Chicago: Science Research Associates, 1975.

Harrison, M. C. *Data Structures and Programming*. Glenview, Ill.: Scott, Foresman, 1973.

Kroenke, D. *Database Processing*, Chapter 4. 2d ed., Chicago: Science Research Associates, 1983.

Lewis, T. G., and M. Z. Smith. *Applying Data Structures*. Boston: Houghton Mifflin, 1976.

Loomis, M. E. S. *Data Management and File Processing*. Englewood Cliffs, N.J.: Prentice-Hall, 1983.

Martin, J. *Computer Data-Base Organization*. 2d. ed. Englewood Cliffs, N.J.: Prentice-Hall, 1977.

Review

1. Why can a data structure (other than the physical sequence) not be implemented within a file stored on magnetic tape?
2. What is garbage collection?
3. Define the following terms:
   a head (of a list)

    b threaded list

    c root

    d parent node

4. Differentiate between a stack and a queue.
5. *a* What is the main advantage of a doubly linked list?

    b What is the main disadvantage of a doubly linked list?
6. What is a ring structure?
7. Differentiate between a tree structure and a network (or plex) structure.
8. Show how a binary tree structure is related to a binary search.

Chapter 11

Data Base Management Systems

Introduction

The amount of data stored and the number of applications using these data have increased dramatically over the years in which computer based systems have been in use. Due to the increasing costs of hardware and the increasing sophistication of users, these trends will continue.

Traditionally, a new application has been developed by coding, debugging, and testing the applications programs needed and collecting and loading the data files required to support this application. Each application is supported by its own programs and their associated data files. This is illustrated in Figure 11–1. As a result of this compartmentalized development of applications, a number of problems and complications have developed in the use of these systems. The following discusses some of these issues.

When applications are developed independently, redundancy in the data files is inevitable. The same data used in different applications are entered in multiple files. This results in increased data entry costs for both initial file loads and file updates. As an example, a payroll application, a skills inventory application, and a personnel education/training application developed independently may all contain employee name, employee number, and possibly other common data elements.

Figure 11–1
Traditional Data Processing Applications

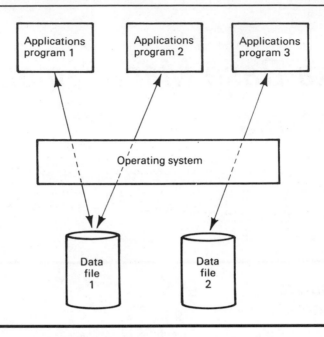

When the same data appear in more than one data file, there is the problem of **inconsistency,** that is, the data in one file may be updated, but the same data contained in other files may not be updated at the same time. As a result, reports based on the data in different files are not compatible.

This data redundancy also makes an inefficient use of storage space. The same data stored in multiple locations obviously require more space than a single occurrence of the data.

An additional problem occurs if a change in content or format in any data file is required. Changing a stored zip code from five numeric digits to nine numeric digits or adding a 12th data element to a file having 11 data elements in a record are examples of such changes. These changes in files trigger changes in the applications programs using these files. To successfully carry out input/output operations, the using programs must now *see* the new form of the files, e.g. a zip code now contains nine numeric digits and not five, or each record now contains 12 data elements and not 11. Changes to existing applications programs are called **maintenance programming.** In a large, complex data processing operation, maintenance programming can come to dominate all programming activity. As a result, developmental work may be postponed. Continuing postponement of new projects leads to a growing backlog and increasing user dissatisfaction.

One-time (or **ad hoc**) information requests are also difficult to handle with the traditional data processing approach. An applications program must be written, debugged, and run. Any modification to the request results in a modification to the applications program that must then be debugged and run again. Obviously, any heuristic data search becomes

Figure 11–2
Data Base Management System Processing

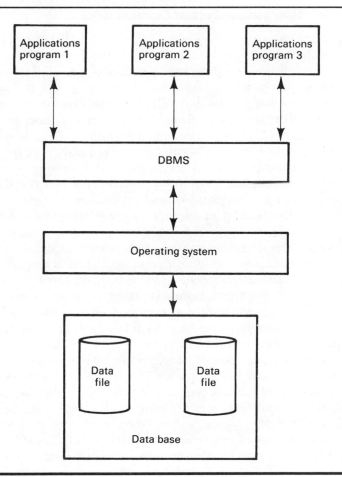

difficult for the user. A search is **heuristic** if it is iterative and the user modifies the search based on the response received from each inquiry. The user narrows down the search as more is learned with successive inquiries.

A **data base management system (DBMS)** is a software package that interfaces between the applications programs and the operating system. It is a tool meant to ease both the problems outlined above and others. A DBMS serves as a buffer between the user and data storage. This is illustrated in Figure 11–2.

Data Base Management System Characteristics

Probably the most significant characteristic of a DBMS is the separation of the logical view of the data from the physical view of the same data. This is called **data independence.** The objective of data independence is to make data storage independent of the applications programs using those data. **Physical data independence** refers to the ability to change physical data storage without having to make changes in the applications programs using those data. Changes in data format or structure are isolated from the using applications programs and do not require corresponding changes in those programs. **Logical data independence** refers to the ability to change the data requirements of one applications program without having to make changes in another program using the same data. Changes may be made in the applications program's view of the stored data without a corresponding change in the physical representation of the data. As a result, different applications programs may *see* the same data in different ways, e.g. in different order or in different format. For example, one applications program may read a nine-digit zip code and another applications program may read a five-digit zip code from the same data. As another example, one applications program may read a file containing 12 data elements in a record and another applications program may read the same file with 11 data elements in a different order. The DBMS acts as the interface between each applications program and the operating system, and translates the requirements of the applications programs to meet the specifications of the physically stored data.

Data redundancy can be reduced with the use of a DBMS, since it is possible to store data physically in one form and provide those data to different applications programs in different forms. With nonreplicated data in the **data base,** that is, the repository of data controlled by the DBMS, data entry is reduced, storage space may be saved, and data inconsistency is reduced. Redundancy may not be completely eliminated in the data base. Some redundancy may be allowed in data base design if it allows faster or easier access to data in some applications.

A data base will, in general, consist of multiple data files located on direct access storage devices. The data base is physically structured by means of a **data definition language (DDL).** When first created the data base is designed by this specialized language, which lays out the relationships that will exist within the data base. The responsibility for the design and ongoing maintenance of the data base resides in a specialist (either an individual or a group) usually called the **data base administrator (DBA).** The DBA must modify the data base physical structure as the needs of the users of the data base change. In addition, the DBA must adjust the data base to improve the performance of the users' applications programs. This is called **tuning** the data base.

A **schema** is the logical view of the entire data base. A **subschema** is an applications program's logical view of the data base. Although only one schema will be associated with any data base, there can be multiple subschemas associated with that data base. A DBMS may also support multiple data bases. Figure 11–3 illustrates this. It also shows that more than one applications program may use the same subschema, as with applications programs 2 and 3.

The language used to interact with the DBMS is called the **data manipulation language (DML).** The DML may be either host language-based or self-contained.

A **host language-based DML** is a set of instructions that can be included within a standard programming language. When executed, these instructions transfer control out of the applications program and into the DBMS. Data may also be transferred. The DBMS interacts with the data base to carry out the requested service. When the DBMS has completed its part, control is transferred back to the applications program. Any data requested (if available) and a status indicator are also returned. The indicator provides data to the applications program on the outcome of the requested service by the DBMS. As examples, the status indicator may show a successful read of a requested record, a rejected record insert into the data base because the key was not unique and was required to be, etc. Figure 11–4 illustrates this sequence of DML-initiated actions. The DBMS

Figure 11–3
Schema/Subschema Relationships

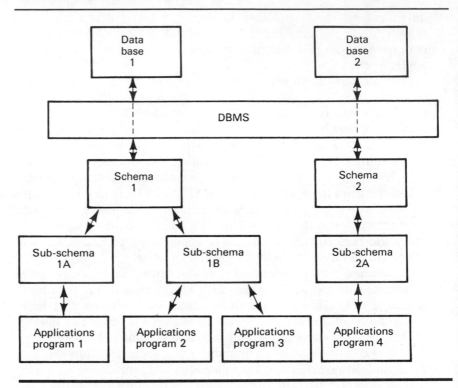

uses the subschema associated with the applications programs and
the schema of the data base to authorize and accomplish the requested service. The host language might be COBOL, FORTRAN,
PL/1, or an assembly language. All major DBMSs can operate out of
several host languages. In effect, additional commands are allowed
in the host language program. When encountered during execution,
they are recognized as DML commands and passed to the DBMS.

A **self-contained DML** is one which is complete in itself, that is,
it contains all of the elements of a language necessary to access and
process data. The self-contained DML offers a query language capability to data base users. The language is very high level, English-
like, and nonprocedural. This means that powerful commands similar to English language specify what is wanted by the user, and the
DBMS query facility determines how the commands are to be ac-

Figure 11–4
Host Language-Based DML

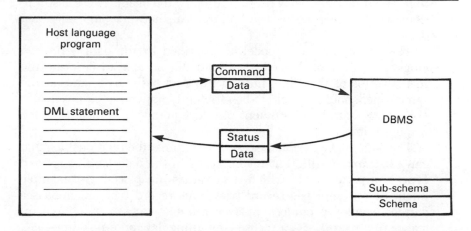

complished. A query language is a tool to respond to ad hoc inquiries (i.e. requests for data by a user that is one-time) or inquiries that are heuristic in nature. The query language is interactive and allows the user to easily modify requests. For example, using the SQL query language (used with IBM's SQL/DS and Relational Software, Inc.'s ORACLE DBMSs), the command:

> SELECT NAME
> FROM PERSONNEL
> WHERE SALARY > 30000

will display from a table (analogous to a file) called PERSONNEL all values in NAME (a column in the table), where the corresponding values in SALARY (another column in the same table) are greater than 30,000. This one command will result in the execution of all the logic necessary to produce the required display. If the table also contains employee numbers, and a display is required of the NAMEs and NUMBERs of all entries in the table with a value greater than 40,000 in SALARY, then the command:

> SELECT NAME, NUMBER
> FROM PERSONNEL
> WHERE SALARY > 40000

will produce the required display.

Data Models

Any data base management system makes one of three basic assumptions about how data may be structured by the users. These assumptions are represented by the hierarchical, network, and relational data models.

The conceptual data model is described by the data definition language. The model used ideally should be able to describe the relationships of the data entering the data base easily and, at the same time, should be able to be efficiently implemented physically. For a large data base, efficient physical storage is critical for good response time.

The data model establishes (and constrains) the relationships that can exist among different record types in the data base. A **record type** is a pattern into which data values are placed. An example might be an employee record type. This record type encompasses data on employee name, employee number, etc. An individual instance of a record, e.g. a record containing data on employee *JOHN SMITH,* number *12345,* is a **record occurrence.**

Hierarchical Data Model

A DBMS using a **hierarchical model** describes data in terms of tree structures. The data base may consist of a number of disjoint (i.e. not connected) trees. The structure and the relationships within the structure are defined by the data definition language. Searchers of the data base are constrained by the structure.

Figure 11–5 illustrates a tree structure. There are three record types: **EMPLOYEE, EXPERIENCE,** and **EDUCATION.** A single arrowhead indicates that the relationship in that direction can be to one record occurrence only; a double arrowhead indicates that the relationship in that direction can be to many record occurrences. In the example, there is a one-to-many relationship between **EMPLOYEE** and **EXPERIENCE** and another one-to-many relationship between **EMPLOYEE** and **EDUCATION.** Employee *SMITH* (a record occurrence) may be related to three experience occurrences (previous jobs) and two education occurrences (high school graduate and B.S. degree). A record occurrence of either **EDUCATION** or **EXPERIENCE** can be related back to only one occurrence of **EMPLOYEE.** This implies that if 100 employees hold a B.S. degree in electrical engineering from a particular university (i.e. the record occurrences are identical), then there will exist 100 identical record occurrences of **EDUCATION** in the data base.

Figure 11–5
Tree Structure

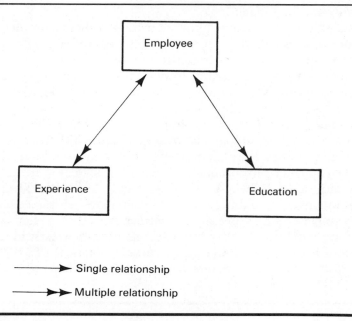

Single relationship
Multiple relationship

The tree may have many levels. Entry to the tree is normally made through the root (**EMPLOYEE** in the example). A tree consisting of many levels may require a long search path to obtain a record occurrence at a lower level. If searches must be carried out starting from a lower level, then alternative entry points may be established to aid in these searches. In the example above, if data on the education of employee *SMITH* are required, entry is made to the root, a search is made through **EMPLOYEE** for the record occurrence of *SMITH,* and it is related to the relevant **EDUCATION** record occurrences. However, in the same example, if the names of all employees with a B.S. degree in electrical engineering from a particular university are required, an exhausting (and time-consuming) search would be needed. The establishment of alternative entry points to a data base to solve this type of problem is common. They would be established for commonly required searches, whereas a more time-consuming search could be tolerated for the less common (or rare) inquiry. One approach is the setting up of a directory (or index) that allows access into a nonroot record type. The disadvantages are that the directory requires additional space and must also be maintained as the data base changes. The advantage is a savings in search time.

Network Data Model

A data base management system using a **network** (or **plex**) **data model** allows multiple superior and subordinate relationships among records. Martin[1] distinguishes between a simple network and a complex network. In a **simple network** the mapping of relationships between one record type and another is one-to-many (in general) in one direction, but the reverse mapping can be only one-to-one. Figure 11–6 illustrates a simple network. The **DEPARTMENT** record type has a multiple relationship with the **EMPLOYEE** record type, that is, each department has multiple employees, but each employee can belong to only one department. A similar structure exists between the **CONTRACT** record type and the **EMPLOYEE** record type, that is, each contract has multiple employees assigned to it, and each employee works on a single contract. Figure 11–7 shows a **complex network.** In this case, multiple relationships exist in both directions between the **CONTRACT** record type and the **EMPLOYEE** record type. In general, more than one employee may work on more

---

Figure 11–6
Simple Network

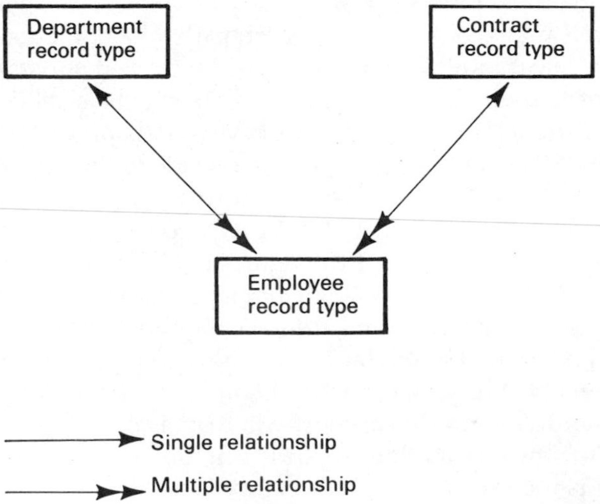

Figure 11–7
Complex Network

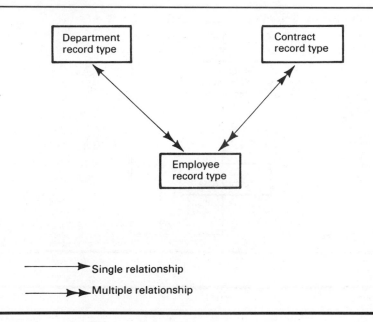

Single relationship

Multiple relationship

than one contract. For example, there are two employees: *JOHN SMITH* and *JANE DOE,* and there are two contracts: *RUBBER WIDGET* and the *GIANT WIDGET.* The *RUBBER WIDGET* contract uses both employees, and *JOHN SMITH* also works on the *GIANT WIDGET* contract.

The distinction between simple and complex networks is important, because many network-based DBMSs can handle only simple networks. Other complications result from the existence of cycles and loops. A **cycle** exists when a circular path among record types is contained within the network. For example, Figure 11–8 shows a network in which students are related to courses, which are related to students having passing grades in these courses. A **loop** is a cycle that contains only one record type. Figure 11–9 shows a loop in which students are related to other students, e.g. those with the same major. Some DBMSs can handle cycles and some cannot. Generally, DBMSs cannot handle loops.

The decision to use a DBMS based on a tree structure versus one based on a network structure should be made only after a study of

Figure 11–8
Cycle

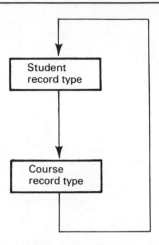

Figure 11–9
Loop

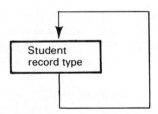

the actual data relationships in the *real world*. If the data to be used in the data base are related as a network, then the DBMS selected must also allow this; if a tree structure is more natural, then the DBMS must reflect this. The DBMS should be fitted to the data. The data should not be force-fitted to the DBMS.

Relational Data Model

A **relational data base** is constructed around relations. A **relation** is a table of two dimensions that has the following characteristics:

1. Each entry has only one value (i.e. there are no repeating groups).
2. Each column holds data of the same kind.
3. The order of the columns and the rows is irrelevant.
4. No two rows are the same.

Operations are carried out on the relations, that is, on the tables.

An **attribute** is a column of the relation, and a **tuple** is a row of the relation. If there are n attributes in the relation, then the row is said to be **n-tuple.** Figure 11–10 illustrates these definitions. An attribute has a **domain,** that is, a set of values that may appear in that attribute.

A relation can be viewed as a conceptual file, that is, it is not necessarily a physical file but is analogous to one. Using this analogy, an attribute corresponds to a field, and a tuple corresponds to a record.

Figure 11–10
Four-Tuple Relation

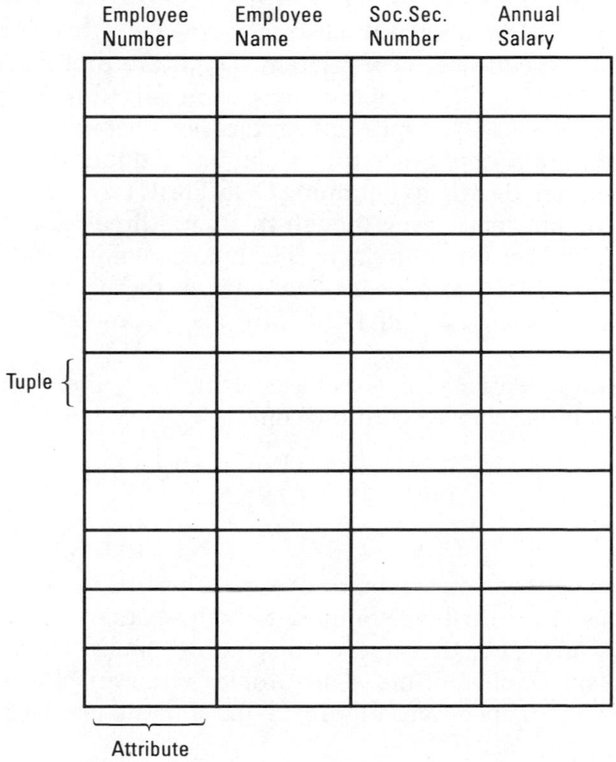

	Employee Number	Employee Name	Soc.Sec. Number	Annual Salary
Tuple {				

Attribute

There are two main user-oriented approaches taken to manipulating a relational data base. These are the relational calculus and the relational algebra approaches.

A **relational calculus** data manipulation language is a nonprocedural language that allows users to specify what data are needed instead of specifying the steps necessary to obtain the data. The DBMS carries out the steps needed to produce the required data. The relational calculus approach has not been implemented to date in any commercial DBMSs.

A **relational algebra** data manipulation language is a procedural language consisting of operators that are used in a step-by-step fashion by the user to produce the required data. The most common relational algebra operations are:

1. Projection.
2. Join.
3. Composition.

Projection

The **projection operator** abstracts selected attributes from a relation and produces a new relation. Duplicate tuples are not allowed. In addition, the attributes may be arranged in a new order. The symbol π is used to represent a projection operation. Figure 11–11 shows a projection. Since tuples cannot be duplicated in the resultant relation, the tuple containing CONTRACT 27–429 and DEPT 102 appears only once, even though there are three relevant entries in the original relation. Similarly, the tuple containing CONTRACT 22–104 and DEPT 107 appears only once in the new relation. The attributes CONTRACT and DEPT are also reordered in the new relation.

In SQL (a relational algebra-based language), the projection of Figure 11–11 is achieved with the command:

SELECT CONTRACT, DEPT
FROM PERSONNEL

Join

The **join operation** combines two relations into one new relation. The values of an attribute common to both relations are compared. If there is a match, then the corresponding tuples of the original relations are combined into a new tuple. The symbol * is used to represent a join operation. Figure 11–12 shows a join based on the attribute: *CONTRACT.*

Figure 11–11
Projection Operation

PERSONNEL

NUMBER	NAME	SALARY	DEPT	CONTRACT
127	SMITH	18000	102	27–429
422	JONES	24000	107	22–104
470	BROWN	20500	102	27–429
513	WORKER	16000	105	27–429
549	DOE	31000	102	23–652
564	DAVIS	28500	107	22–104
601	WALKER	23200	102	27–429
640	KIRK	19800	107	28–120

Original Relation

CONTRACTS

CONTRACT	DEPT
27–429	102
22–104	107
27–429	105
23–652	102
28–120	107

New Relation

CONTRACTS = π PERSONNEL (CONTRACT, DEPT)

In SQL, the join of Figure 11–12 would be carried out with the command:

SELECT NUMBER, NAME, CONTRACT, DESCRIPTION
  FROM EMPLOYEES, CONTRACTS
  WHERE EMPLOYEES. CONTRACT = CONTRACTS. CONTRACT

The WHERE clause identifies the attribute from each relation that is to be used as the basis of the join. The period between a relation

Figure 11–12
Join Operation

EMPLOYEES

NUMBER	NAME	CONTRACT
127	SMITH	27–429
422	JONES	22–104
470	BROWN	27–429
513	WORKER	27–429
549	DOE	23–652
564	DAVIS	22–104
601	WALKER	27–429
640	KIRK	28–120

CONTRACTS

CONTRACT	DESCRIPTION
27–429	WIDGET RESEARCH
27–600	GIANT WIDGET
23–652	RUBBER WIDGET
24–771	MARKETING STUDY
26–333	EXPENSE CONTROL

Original Relations

WORK

NUMBER	NAME	CONTRACT	DESCRIPTION
127	SMITH	27–429	WIDGET RESEARCH
470	BROWN	27–429	WIDGET RESEARCH
513	WORKER	27–429	WIDGET RESEARCH
549	DOE	23–652	RUBBER WIDGET
601	WALKER	27–429	WIDGET RESEARCH

New Relation

WORK = EMPLOYEES * CONTRACTS (NUMBER, NAME, CONTRACT, DESCRIPTION) name and an attribute name qualifies those attribute names that are not unique. The WHERE clause in the above command states that the contents of CONTRACT in EMPLOYEES is to be matched against CONTRACT in CONTRACTS.

Composition

The **composition operation** combines two relations with a join and then deletes the common attribute of this join operation with a projection. A composition operation on the two original relations of Figure 11–12 would result in the relation shown in Figure 11–13. The contract number has been deleted from the new relation of Figure 11–12 to produce that of Figure 11–13.

Figure 11–13
Composition Operation

NUMBER	NAME	DESCRIPTION
127	SMITH	WIDGET RESEARCH
470	BROWN	WIDGET RESEARCH
513	WORKER	WIDGET RESEARCH
549	DOE	RUBBER WIDGET
601	WALKER	WIDGET RESEARCH

In SQL, the composition of Figure 11–13 would be obtained with a single deletion from the SELECT command to obtain the join:

SELECT NUMBER, NAME, DESCRIPTION
  FROM EMPLOYEES, CONTRACTS
  WHERE EMPLOYEES.CONTRACT = CONTRACTS.CONTRACT

CODASYL/DBTG

The **Conference on Data Systems Languages (CODASYL)** is a volunteer (but influential) group representing both computer industry and user organizations. Founded in 1958 to standardize a common programming language, CODASYL developed a new language, COBOL. The conference maintains control over, and publishes approved changes to, the COBOL specifications. Within the CODASYL organizational structure, there is a Data Base Task Group (DBTG) that has studied and published specifications for a data base management language. It is not surprising to find that COBOL-like statements are employed in the data language specifications. CODASYL specifications cover both the DDL and the DML.

The CODASYL model can handle simple networks, but it cannot directly handle complex networks. A complex network must be converted to a simpler structure.

There have been a number of CODASYL/DBTG implementations. Examples include Sperry UNIVAC's DMS 90, Burroughs' DMSII, and Cullinet's IDMS. IDMS is discussed below.

The most basic concept is that of set. A **set** is a relationship between an owner record type and one or more member record types. The set creates a two-level tree. The owner record type must be a different record type from any member since, if owner and member record types are the same, a loop is created. A **set occurrence** relates a particular owner record occurrence with its particular member record occurrences.

An owner record type in one set may be a member of another set. In addition, any record type may be a member or an owner of more

---

Figure 11–14
CODASYL/DBTG Representation of a Network

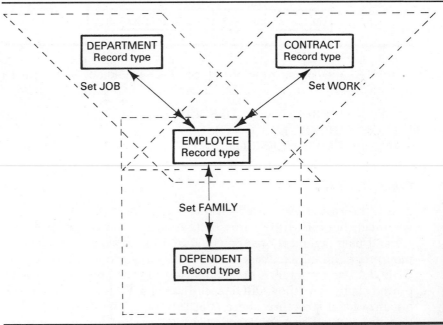

than one set. It is in this manner that networks are built up by linking together sets. Figure 11–14 illustrates such a construction. There are three sets in the example. Set *JOB* has as an owner record type **DEPARTMENT** and as a member record type **EMPLOYEE.** Note that even though **EMPLOYEE** is a member of set *JOB*, it is also the owner of set *FAMILY.* The sets to be implemented are defined in the schema.

The representation of a many-to-many relationship (i.e. a complex network) in the CODASYL/DBTG model cannot be made directly. It can, however, be implemented by transforming the many-to-many relationship between two record types into two one-to-many relationships. Figure 11–15 illustrates such a transformation. An intersection record type is created. This is **CONTRACT-EMPLOYEE** in the example. This record type is a member of both set *WORK* and set *ASSIGN.* Note that the relationship between **CONTRACT** and **CONTRACT-EMPLOYEE** is one-to-many, and each of the many occurrences of **CONTRACT-EMPLOYEE** is related to one occurrence of **EMPLOYEE.** Similarly, the relationship between **EMPLOYEE** and **CONTRACT-EMPLOYEE** is one-to-many, and each of the many

Figure 11–15
Many-to-Many Relationship in the CODASYL/DBTG Model

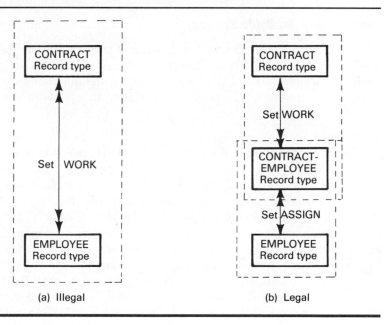

(a) Illegal   (b) Legal

occurrences of **CONTRACT-EMPLOYEE** is related to one occurrence of **CONTRACT.** Thus, a many-to-many relationship effectively exists between **CONTRACT** and **EMPLOYEE.**

Cycles are allowed in the model. In the most recent specifications of the CODASYL/DBTG model, loops are also permitted, that is, a record type may be both an owner and a member of the same set. Individual implementations may still lack this capability, however.

The latest CODASYL/DBTG specifications allow three levels of schema. These are the subschema, the schema, and the data structure description. The subschema and schema are as previously defined. The data structure description maps the schema onto physical storage. The schema contains no physical specifications. The data structure description is the only source of information on physical storage of the data base and, as a result, any physical changes impact only this description.

The CODASYL/DBTG model has undergone evolution over the years of the task group's efforts. The model is a complicated one, and it has been criticized on this basis. It is an important model because of its introduction of concepts and terminology that are used selectively in non-CODASYL/DBTG model implementations. It is also the basis for a number of commercial implementations.

Commercially Available Systems

The following very briefly describes some of the commercially available DBMS packages. There are other packages available, and more are being announced. Table 11-1 summarizes the major characteristics of these packages. The packages are listed in alphabetical order.

ADABAS

The **Adaptable Data Base System (ADABAS)** is marketed by Software AG of North America. The parent company is Software AG of West Germany. Although ADABAS literature refers to it as a relational data base, it is, in fact, based on a network data model. ADABAS is called from a host language. COBOL, FORTRAN, PL/1, APL, and assembly language may be used as hosts. A data dictionary forms an integral component of the system. The definitions of data in the data base are contained in the **data dictionary.**

ADABAS uses an inverted file structure based on each field in a file designated as a descriptor. The inverted lists provide internal sequence numbers (ISNs) that are converted by ADABAS into ad-

Table 11–1
Some Commercially Available DBMS Packages

NAME	SUPPLIER	MODEL	HOST LANGUAGES	QUERY LANGUAGE
ADABAS	Software AG	Network	COBOL FORTRAN PL/1 APL Assembly	YES
DMSII	Burroughs Corp.	Network (CODASYL/DBTG)	COBOL PL/1 ALGOL RPG	NO
IDMS	Cullinet Software, Inc.	Network (CODASYL/DBTG)	COBOL FORTRAN PL/1 Assembly	YES
IMS	IBM Corp.	Hierarchical	COBOL PL/1 RPG Assembly	NO
MAGNUM	TYMSHARE	Relational	None	YES
SQL/DS	IBM Corp.	Relational	COBOL PL/1 Assembly	YES
SYSTEM 2000	Intel Systems Corp.	Hierarchical	COBOL FORTRAN PL/1 Assembly	YES
TOTAL	CINCOM Systems	Network	COBOL FORTRAN PL/1 RPG II Assembly	YES

dresses. The ISN is unique for each record in the file, and the inverted lists are maintained in sequence for each descriptor. The first entry in each list is a count of the number of entries in the primary file described by the descriptor value. This is followed by the ISNs of that value. Figure 11–16 provides an example. A personnel file has entries in the directory for the descriptor *JOB*. There is an entry for the job *DBA*. There are two records for this position, and these records are identified by ISNs 3 and 6. It should be observed that questions such as: *How many DBAs work in the organization?* may be answered by reference to the inverted list alone. No retrieval in the primary file is required. ADABAS allows multiple criteria entries using the operations *AND* and *OR*. A single list meeting these criteria is created from the ISNs before any retrieval is attempted.

Figure 11–16
ADABAS Search Procedure

Inverted Lists

	Count	ISNs			
DBA	2	3	6		
Programmer	5	1	2	5	7	9
Systs. Analysts	3	4	8	10		

ADABAS also automatically carries out data compression on stored data. Leading zeros, trailing blanks, and empty fields are compressed. Numeric data are packed. This results in a savings in storage space. (Data compression is discussed in Chapter 12.)

ADABAS offers data protection at the file level by means of passwords and encryption. When a file within the data base is opened, a password must be supplied if password protection is used. Individual files within the data base may also be encrypted as an additional security measure. (Data encryption is discussed in Chapter 14.)

There is a query language and a **report writer,** that is, a package that produces reports as needed and handles most or all of the required formatting. ADABAS also offers a direct access capability, which bypasses the inverted lists and uses an algorithm to calculate the physical location of the required record.

DMSII

Data Management System II (DMSII) is a DBMS marketed by the Burroughs Corporation. It is an implementation of the CODASYL/DBTG model and is, therefore, a network-based DBMS. DMSII is a host language DBMS that can be called from COBOL, PL/1, ALGOL, or RPG host programs. COBOL, PL/1, and ALGOL capability is not available on all systems, however.

The data base is made up of data sets (or files). Retrieval from a data set is made by means of an indexed sequential search. This search may use a hierarchy of directories for a large data set. Data may be retrieved from a data set on more than one key, that is, an indexed sequential capability exists for each search key.

IDMS

The **Integrated Database Management System (IDMS)** is a DBMS marketed by Cullinet Software. It uses a network data model based on the CODASYL/DBTG specifications. IDMS is a host language system that can be called from COBOL, FORTRAN, PL/1, or assembly language. Two different on-line query systems and a report generator exist.

The data base is made up of **pages.** A page contains record occurrences. The physical location of a record occurrence may be set in four ways:

1. By hashing to a page.
2. By placing a member record occurrence as physically near its owner as possible.
3. By specifying the page in which the record occurrence is to be stored.
4. By placing record occurrences in a physical sequential order based on a key value.

Because of the existence of these options, the DBA may choose the best one for any particular search requirement.

IDMS offers only limited password protection. This protection essentially limits actions allowable to a particular subschema. The system does not provide an encryption capability, but does allow the data base administrator to provide his/her own encryption/decryption routines. Data compression routines may also be provided by the data base administrator.

IMS

The **Information Management System (IMS)** is marketed by IBM and is based on a hierarchical data model. IMS is a host language system that may be called from COBOL, PL/1, or assembly language programs. Some systems also have an RPG host language capability. Records in the data base are called **segments.**

The data can be organized in two different ways: hierarchical sequential and hierarchical direct. In the **hierarchical sequential organization,** the segments are physically consecutive (i.e. sequentially related to each other). In the **hierarchical direct organization,** the segments are not necessarily physically contiguous but are related by pointers.

IMS access methods are not true access methods, but are mechanisms that interface with the access methods of the operating system. Physical access is (as always) carried out by the operating system.

There are two access methods used with the hierarchical sequential organization, **hierarchical sequential access method (HSAM)** and **hierarchical indexed sequential access method (HISAM).** These access methods provide sequential and indexed sequential physical access, respectively. An indexed sequential access to root segments in a tree is provided by HISAM. Nodes under the root are then accessed sequentially.

There are also two access methods used with the hierarchical direct organization: **hierarchical direct access method (HDAM)** and **hierarchical indexed direct access method (HIDAM).** These methods provide a hashed and an index- (or table) based physical access, respectively. HDAM allows direct access to root segments, which are in turn linked to subordinate nodes by pointers. Synonym root segments are connected together in a list structure. HIDAM indexes to root segments, which in turn are also linked to subordinate nodes by pointers.

Indexes to a segment type below the root segment in the tree may also be established. A separate data base called a secondary index is set up, based on a field of the segment type. Retrieval involves a directory lookup in this data base. The directory entry points to the requested segment occurrence.

External (to IMS) encryption/decryption routines may be called. Password protection is also part of the system. A user's processing options, e.g. get, insert, delete, or replace a segment occurrence, are contained in the subschema. In addition, the subschema identifies those segments sensitive to a user. Nonsensitive segments are not available to that user.

MAGNUM

MAGNUM is a DBMS provided by TYMSHARE as part of its time-sharing service. The package is self-contained. It can carry out computations and does not require a host language. It is based on the relational data model. The data base in MAGNUM is made up of relations that consist of data fields. The DML has been designed around the relational algebra approach. The relations in MAGNUM are implemented on an indexed sequential basis. MAGNUM has no security features beyond those required to gain access to the TYM-SHARE system.

SQL/DS

The **Structured Query Language/Data System (SQL/DS)** is a DBMS marketed by IBM. It is also sometimes called SEQUEL. It is based on a relational data model.

The SQL commands may be used either in a query mode or embedded in a COBOL, PL/1, or assembly language host program. It is essentially based on the relational algebra approach.

Multiple criteria using ANDs and ORs may be created. In addition, there are built-in functions that can calculate the average value in a column, the total of the values in a column, the minimum and maximum in a column, and a count of the number of values. Relations displayed may also be sorted.

Security is provided by passwords. A user may be limited to what operations, e.g. add, delete, etc., can be carried out at the relation, tuple, or attribute level.

SYSTEM 2000

SYSTEM 2000 is a DBMS marketed by Intel Systems Corporation. It is based on a hierarchical data model. A data dictionary is an integral part of the system.

The system uses a host language and can be called from COBOL, FORTRAN, PL/1, and assembly language programs. There are two terminal-oriented modes of operation that provide a query language/ update capability. One is interactive but is run as a batch job; the other is fully interactive. There is also a report writer capability.

Access to the data base is through an inverted file structure. Embedded pointers are also used. Passwords can be used, and access authorization, e.g read only, update, etc., can be implemented down to the data element level.

TOTAL

TOTAL is a DBMS marketed by CINCOM Systems. It is based on a network data model. A data dictionary is available as an option. TOTAL is a host language system that can be called from COBOL, FORTRAN, PL/1, RPGII, or assembly language programs. It has a query language capability.

There are two types of data sets in TOTAL: **single entry** (or **master**) **data sets** and **variable entry** (or **detail**) **data sets.** A single entry data set can have multiple variable entry data sets as dependents. Each data record in a single entry data set is identified by a unique key. The relationship between the two types of data sets is called a **linkage path** and is implemented by means of pointers.

Figure 11–17 illustrates these concepts. Access is made to a data record in a single entry data set by hashing the key value. Pointers link this record to the variable entry data set. Within this data set a list structure containing both forward and backward pointers exists. A network may be constructed by means of these linkage paths.

Figure 11–17
Data Sets in TOTAL

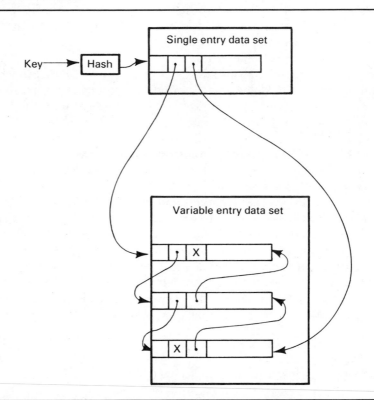

Conclusions

The DBMS concept seems to be one whose time has come. The use of these packages is increasing. As with the use of most generalized software, there is a trade-off. The user is able to more easily interface with the collection of data (i.e. the data base) available on his/her system. This can be done without regard to what may be relatively complicated relationships among these data. At the same time, there is increased overhead on the system. The package itself handles almost all of the details necessary to retrieve the data required by the user.

In addition, there is the requirement for the function of data base administration. By its very nature, a data base must be centrally controlled. The data base administrator (whether a single individual or a group) must lay out a physical arrangement for the contents of the data base that will provide to all users a reasonable response time with a reasonable storage space requirement. The use of a DBMS implies that the needs and priorities of its users must be balanced.

One of the unfortunate aspects of the DBMS field is the nonstandardization of terminology. The same term is sometimes used to represent two different concepts, and essentially the same concept is called by two or more different descriptive names. This lack of standardized definitions makes it more difficult to compare the underlying philosophy and the performance of different DBMS packages.

The use of a DBMS is not a *one shot* design effort but is, in fact, an ongoing effort. Performance monitoring must be carried on, and the data base must be tuned as needed to improve user performance.

Reference

1. Martin, J. *Computer Data-Base Organization.* Englewood Cliffs, N.J.: Prentice Hall, 1977, pp. 91-93.

Additional Readings

Cardenas, A. F. *Data Base Management Systems.* Boston: Allyn & Bacon, 1979.

Chen, P. "The Entity-Relationship Model: Toward a Unified View of Data." *ACM Transactions on Database Systems* 1, No. 1 (March 1976), pp. 9–36.

Curtice, R. M., and P. E. Jones. *Logical Data Base Design.* New York: Van Nostrand Reinhold, 1982.

Date, C. J. *An Introduction to Database Systems, Volume 1.* 3d ed. Reading, Mass.: Addison-Wesley Publishing, 1981.

————. *An Introduction to Database Systems, Volume 2.* Reading, Mass.: Addison-Wesley Publishing, 1983.

————. *A Guide to DB2.* Reading, Mass.: Addison-Wesley Publishing, 1984.

Fernandez, E. B.; R. C. Summers; and C. Wood. *Database Security and Integrity.* Reading, Mass.: Addison-Wesley Publishing, 1981.

Hammer, M., and D. McLeod. "Database Description with SDM: A Semantic Database Model." *ACM Transactions on Database Systems* 6, No. 3 (September 1981), pp. 351–86.

Howe, D. R. *Data Analysis for Data Base Design*. London, U.K.: Edward Arnold Publishers Ltd., 1983.

Kroenke, D. *Database Processing*. 2d ed. Chicago: Science Research Associates, 1983.

Martin, J. *Principles of Data-Base Management*. Englewood Cliffs, N.J.: Prentice-Hall, 1976.

_____. *An End-User's Guide to Data Base*. Englewood Cliffs, N.J.: Prentice-Hall, 1981.

_____. *Managing the Data-Base Environment*. Englewood Cliffs, N.J.: Prentice-Hall, 1983.

Merrett, T. H. *Relational Informational Systems*. Reston, Va.: Reston Publishing, 1984.

Sandberg, G. "A Primer on Relational Data Base Concepts." *IBM Systems Journal* 20, No. 1 (1981), pp. 23-40.

Tsichritzis, D. C., and F. H. Lochovsky. *Data Base Management Systems*. New York: Academic Press, 1977.

Wiederhold, G. *Database Design*. New York: McGraw-Hill, 1977.

Review

1. Give five arguments for the use of a data base management system.
2. What is the function of the data base administrator?
3. Describe each of the three DBMS data models.
4. Differentiate between each of the following pairs of terms:
    a logical and physical data independence
    b data definition language and data manipulation language
    c schema and subschema
    d simple and complex network
    e relational calculus and relational algebra
5. Describe each of the following relational operators:
    a projection
    b join
    c composition
6. Name a DBMS that is based on the:
    a hierarchical data model
    b network data model
    c relational data model
    d CODASYL/DBTG specifications
7. What is a report writer?

Chapter 12

Data Compression

Introduction

Data compression is concerned with more efficiently representing the
data stored on a secondary storage device or transmitted over telecommunications lines. When the amount of data stored on secondary storage
devices approaches storage capacity, an additional investment is required
to add one or more such devices to the system. An alternative approach
is to consider storing the current data on these devices more compactly
and, thus, free up space for additional data. Similarly, telecommunications
lines have an inherent capacity (or limit on the amount of data transmitted
per unit of time within an acceptable error rate). If approached, this limit
requires the adding of more lines at additional cost. By more efficiently
coding the data before transmission, more data may be sent in a given
period of time. Data compression is concerned with transforming data
representations in such a way that either storage space or transmission
time is reduced.

In this chapter, the discussion centers on compression of data on secondary storage devices. Nevertheless, the extrapolation to telecommunications should be straightforward.

In general, a trade-off between storage space and processing time is
made. Space on secondary storage devices is saved, but CPU time is

used to compress the data before storage and then to decompress the data upon retrieval from storage.

The measure of effectiveness of a compression technique is the **compression ratio,** which is defined as:

$$1 - \frac{\text{(length of compressed data)}}{\text{(length of original data)}}$$

Data compression techniques attempt to represent data in such a way that no information (in an information theory sense) is lost. In effect, they attempt to reduce the number of bits used to represent the data to a number closer to the number of bits required to represent the theoretical information content of the data. The compression algorithm must be completely reversible in the decompression algorithm.

This chapter discusses both pure data compression techniques and preliminary techniques. Preliminary techniques are herein defined as storage saving methods that are, strictly speaking, not data compression techniques but, nevertheless, achieve the same objective.

Preliminary Techniques

Preliminary techniques achieve a level of data compression without using the more formal techniques of data compression. In fact, some of these preliminary techniques are simply good practice in systems design. The preliminary techniques discussed should be considered for incorporation in the system design before any of the more formal data compression methods are used.

Elimination of Redundant Data Items

The same data items should not be entered in more than one location in the same file, or in locations in different files. As an example, two files might exist: The first contains personnel data and the second contains payroll data. Redundancies of employee name, employee number, etc., might exist. The elimination of such redundancies and the concomitant release of secondary storage space is one of the goals of data base management systems. (This goal is sometimes, in practice, compromised in order to speed up retrieval time.)

Even without the use of a DBMS, the elimination of all unnecessary redundancy is desirable. When the same data are stored in multiple locations, problems of inconsistency can arise. For example, if the data in one location have been updated, reports based on these two separate data items will not reconcile. Synchronization of updates and use of these data become critical and must be taken into account in the systems design. This adds complexity, whereas simplicity should be the objective of design.

Recognition of Cases of Mutual Exclusion

Two data items may be mutually exclusive, that is, they cannot both exist (or be relevant) at the same time. As an example, a part-time or temporary employee may not be eligible for company insurance or medical benefits. Thus, allocating space for the details of such benefits for these employees would be wasteful. As another example, an employee may not be both hourly and salaried at the same time.

Calculation of Data Values

Some data values can be easily calculated from other data values. If this is so, it may not be necessary to store the derived data values. As an example, overtime may be easily calculated as those hours worked by an employee in a week exceeding 40. There may not be a need to store both hours worked and overtime hours. In this case, the saving in storage space does cost a very small increment in processing time. Storage space and processing time are scarce resources, and the use of one is balanced against the use of the other.

Use of Coded Values

If the number of possible alternative values is limited, then the data values may be able to be encoded in a shorter form. As an example, in a personnel record sex might be entered as *MALE* or *FEMALE* requiring six bytes or as *1* or *2* requiring one byte. For output, conversion from the coded values to their expanded equivalents may be done by lookup in a table, or by substitution in the applications program itself. Conversion by means of a table is preferred if there are more than a few values, or if these values are changeable. Embedding the conversion within the applications program should be done only if the values are few in number and permanent. (Experience clearly demonstrates that few data values are permanent.)

Compact Notation

Related data that are normally stored as two or more data elements may be compacted into one stored piece of data. As an example, the use of Julian dates, instead of storing month, day, and year as three separate data items, saves space. As another example, consider a personnel file in which three data items (among others) are included in each record: sex, participation in retirement plan, and participation in group insurance plan. Possible entries are:

Sex	Retirement	Insurance
M	Yes	Yes
F	No	No

More efficiently, the retirement and insurance data fields could contain a *1* or a *2*. An even more space efficient scheme would be to combine all three data entries into one field as follows:

1—male, retirement, insurance
2—male, retirement, no insurance
3—male, no retirement, insurance
4—male, no retirement, no insurance
5—female, retirement, insurance
6—female, retirement, no insurance
7—female, no retirement, insurance
8—female, no retirement, no insurance

A single digit ranging from 1 to 8 now contains all of the information contained previously in three data fields. Conversion back into individual data must be carried out as needed.

Packed Fields

Several data may be combined into one data element by **packing.** Unpacking reverses the process. As an example, consider four single-digit numbers stored in an array:

1	2	3	4

All four may be stored in one data field using the following algorithm:

(a) Copy the leftmost digit in the array into a new data location.

(b) Shift the number in the new data location one position to the left (i.e. multiply by 10).

(c) Add the next digit (moving to the right) in the array to the number already in the new data location.

(d) If this is not the last digit in the array, go back to step (b).

(e) Stop.

Using the example:

Step	New data location
(a)	1
(b)	10
(c)	12
(b)	120
(c)	123
(b)	1230
(c)	1234
(e) stop	

To unpack the digits, the procedure is reversed with the following algorithm:

(a′) Save the digit resulting from taking the packed number modulo 10 and place it in the next available location in a new array starting on the right.

(b′) Divide the number by 10 and truncate.

(c′) If this is not the last digit in the primary location, go back to step (a).

(d′) Stop.

Using the example:

Step	Packed data	New array
(a′)	1234	4
(b′)	123	
(a′)	123	3 4
(b′)	12	
(a′)	12	2 3 4
(b′)	1	
(a′)	1	1 2 3 4
(d′) stop		

For two-digit numbers, the shift should be two positions to the left on each pass of the packing algorithm. A modulus of 100 and division by 100 should be used in the unpacking algorithm for two-digit numbers. Extension to three- or four-digit numbers should be clear. There is a limit, however, on how many digits can be placed in one data location on any given machine. This may be approached very rapidly with three- or four-digit numbers. Packing can be an effective means of storing large arrays of data.

Suppression Techniques

Suppression techniques are concerned with the elimination of repeating characters in a data record or with the elimination of characters that, though not repeating within the record, can be re-created by comparison with some standard. Decompression reverses the process by restoring the missing characters to their proper positions. Suppression of zeros and nulls (blanks) in data is the most elementary form of these techniques.

Front Compression

In front compression the leading or front bits or characters of data in a record that are the same as the leading bits or characters of data in the preceding record are suppressed. The rationale is that if a front string of bits or characters is the same as a front string of bits or characters already available, there is no need to repeat it. For a front string of bits the next bit is also included, since if the first n bits of a string are the same, then the n + 1st bit must be different and, therefore, is also determined. A number specifying the length of the front string is substituted. As an example, consider the following two simplified personnel records:

ADAMS, CAROL E	145	8.50
ADAMS, CHARLES T	217	8.15

The first eight characters in the second record duplicate the first eight characters in the first record. The second record may be compressed to:

*8HARLES T   217   8.15

If the third record is:

ADAMSON, PAUL K   170   6.65

the first five characters in this record are the same as the first five characters in the second record. As a result the third record may be compressed to:

*5ON, PAUL K   170   6.65

*is used in the example as a special symbol to signify front compression. The number following this special symbol indicates the number of characters replicated. Clearly, this technique's effectiveness is limited to sorted data and files that will be accessed sequentially.

Differencing

With **differencing** the data contents of a record are compared to a *standard* record. Only the differences found between the two are saved. This technique is really a variation, or a more general form, of front compression. Identical strings anywhere within the records are compressed, whereas in front compression identical strings only at the front of the record are compressed. As an example, consider the following two records:

ADAMS,△CAROL△E△△△145△SENIOR△CLERK△8.50
ADAMS,△CHARLES△T△217△SENIOR△CLERK△8.15

where △ signifies a blank. Assuming that the first record is the standard record, the second record might be compressed to:

*8HARLES△T△217△*12△8.15

where *8 indicates that the first 8 characters are identical to the first 8 characters in the standard record, the next characters are unique, the next 12 characters are identical to the corresponding 12 characters in the standard record, and the last 5 characters are unique.

Null suppression may be considered a special case of differencing in which the pattern record is all nulls. **Zero suppression** may similarly be considered as involving a comparison with a standard record containing all zeros.

For most applications, the data vary too widely to allow only one standard record for the entire file. One approach is to always use the immediately preceding record in the file as the standard record. This is similar to the front compression method described above and, as in that method, assumes sequential retrieval.

For blocked direct access files, the standard record may be the first logical record in the block, and all other logical records in the block are compared with it. The effectiveness of the comparison, that is, the compression ratio, depends on the data similarity of the logical records within the block. If many data in each logical record are identical, then a large blocking factor can be helpful.

Run Length Coding

In **run length coding** a *run* or a series of identical data characters is replaced by a special symbol and a number. The special symbol represents that a run has been compressed, and the succeeding number represents the length of the original run.

If the internal character representation includes unused code combinations, e.g. EBCDIC, then one or more of the combinations may be used as run symbols. If an internal representation does not contain unallocated code combinations, the most infrequently used symbols may be used. (Special arrangements must be made, then, to recognize these infrequent characters when they occur as part of the data.) As an example, consider the following data record:

ADAMS,△C△△△△△△△△△H△217△0000CLERK

This might be compressed to:

ADAMS,△C*9H△217△#4CLERK

In this example, * is used as a special symbol to represent a run of blanks and # is used as a special symbol to represent a run of zeros. The blanks run is of length 9 and the zeros run is of length 4. Of course, if unused code combinations in an internal representation like EBCDIC were used, then these symbols would be unprintable.

Pattern Substitution

Pattern substitution compresses data by substituting a coded entry for a data pattern. The data patterns selected are those expected to occur most frequently within the data to be compressed. Null suppression and zero suppression may also be viewed as particular versions of this technique in which patterns of nulls and zeros are replaced, respectively. As an example, consider the following data record:

ADAMS,△C△△△△△△△△△H△217△0000CLERK△△

where △ again signifies a blank.

This might be compressed to:

ADAMS,△C##△H△217*0+

In this example, # is used as a code for the pattern △△△△, * is used as a code for the pattern △000, and + is used as a code for the pattern CLERK△△. It is assumed that these patterns occur relatively frequently within the data to be compressed.

Bit Maps

In some applications, a data record may contain a variable number of fields. It is possible that some fields do not apply, or are unknown. If these fields are filled with zeros or blanks, a significant amount of space may be wasted. In this case, a field may be used to store a **bit**

map. Each bit position in the map corresponds to one of the variable set of fields. A *1* in a particular position of the bit map indicates the presence of a field in the corresponding field position; a *0* indicates the absence of a field. As an example, consider the following compressed data record:

01011001	27	42	29	8
Bit Map	Field 1	Field 4	Field 5	Field 7

There are eight possible fields in this example. The bit map (in a ninth field) indicates that data exist only in the first, fourth, fifth, and seventh fields (counting from the right), since only those positions in the bit map contain a *1*. There are no data (or the data are zeros or blanks) for the second, third, sixth, and eighth fields.

Coding Techniques

Coding techniques involve the substitution of a shorter representation of a piece of data for the original data item. The techniques discussed in this section are more general applications of the *Use of Coded Values* discussed under *Preliminary Techniques* above.

Bigram Coding

In **bigram coding,** two characters (i.e. a bigram) that appear together in the data with high probability are replaced by one special character. In EBCDIC, a large number of the code combinations are not used. With this internal representation, these unused special characters can be conveniently used as replacements for the bigrams. One such application is described by Snyderman and Hunt[1] and criticized by Dumey[2]. The most efficient approach, that is, the one that results in the highest compression ratio, replaces the most frequently occurring bigrams.

Figure 12–1 illustrates the algorithm that is used for compression in bigram coding. The data can be visualized as a string. The following is a review of the main logic of the algorithm. The first character is checked. If it is not the first half of a compressible bigram, it is stored. If the first character may be the start of a compressible bigram, the next character is checked. If it completes a compressible bigram, a single character is substituted and stored; if it does not

Figure 12–1
General Flow Chart for Bigram Coding

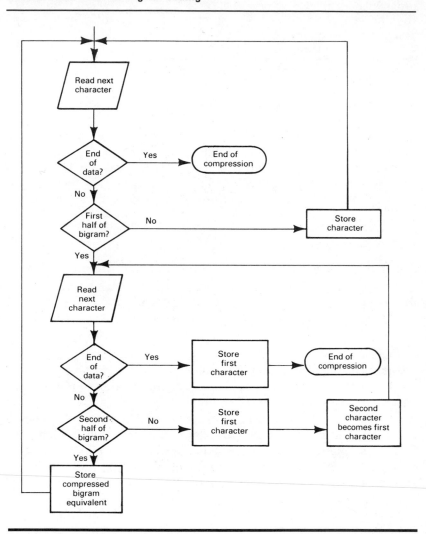

complete a compressible bigram, the first character is stored, the second character becomes the first, and the algorithm repeats. As an example, assume that the character string INFORMATION △SYSTEMS is to undergo compression. Assume further that the compressible bigrams and their equivalents are:

Bigram	Equivalent
ER	*
IN	&
MA	#
N△	@
S△	¢
ST	$
TH	↑
TI	+

In this example, the data are compressed to:

&FOR# + O@SY$EMS

Blanks are normally considered legitimate characters and legitimate components of bigrams.

The technique can be extended to include trigrams and higher order character combinations. However, the coding and decoding algorithms become complex and, as a result, are rarely used.

Dictionary Coding

With **dictionary coding** a set of characters (usually a word but, in general, any set) is replaced by a code. The codes used are contained in a table, and a table lookup is required both in the encoding and the decoding. This technique may be very effective if the vocabulary of the data undergoing compression is limited. If the entire table can be brought into primary memory at the same time, search time will be reduced. In addition, if the table is organized so that the entries range from the most frequent first to the least frequent last, search time is minimized for a sequential search of the table. Dictionary coding is most often used to compress textual data.

Zipf's[3] law relates the frequency of occurrence of words to their rank of occurrence. It implies that half of the different words in a set of textual data occur only once, and that a rapidly decreasing percentage of these words occurs more frequently. Thus, only the most frequently occurring words may be encoded, yet a reasonable compression ratio may be obtained.

Statistical Techniques

Statistical techniques attempt to encode data in such a way that the more frequently occurring characters are encoded with a shorter bit string and the less frequently occurring characters are encoded with a longer bit string. The average information content per character produced by a source is:

$$H = \sum_{i=1}^{n} p_i \log_2 p_i \text{ bits} \tag{12-1}$$

where p_i is the probability of character i and there are n characters produced by the source. This value also defines the minimum average number of bits per character required to encode the output of the source. Using a variable length encoding scheme, it is possible to approach this limit. In general, the closer to this limit the average number of bits per character comes, the more complex the encoding/ decoding scheme also becomes. Thus, a trade-off is made between efficiency and complexity.

One of the requirements for a statistical code is the prefix property. In a continuous bit stream of variable length codes, it must be possible to unambiguously determine the end of one code and the start of the next code. The **prefix property** requires that no shorter code may be a subset that begins a longer code. For example, if code 1 is 10 and code 2 is 101, then the prefix property is not met. There is no way to determine if the bit string 10 represents code 1 or the start of code 2.

Huffman Code

The Huffman[4] code possesses the prefix property and, in addition, is a minimum redundancy code. A **minimum redundancy code** has the minimum average length, that is, the minimum average number of bits, for a given set of data. This finite set of data cannot be expressed in fewer bits. Huffman coding assumes that the probability of any character occurring is independent of the probability that any character has previously occurred. This is not strictly true in practice. (Bigram coding, for example, assumes the opposite.)

For Huffman coding to remain optimal, character probabilities cannot change. In practice, they cannot change too drastically.

To develop the Huffman code for a set of characters, they are arranged in order from most probable (first) to least probable (last). As an example, assume that the possible characters and their associated probabilities are as follows:

Character	Probability
A	0.45
B	0.25
C	0.20
D	0.10
	$\overline{1.00}$

The two least probable characters are combined, the probabilities of these characters are added, and the sum reinserted into the list in proper order. This procedure is repeated until a probability of 1 is achieved. Using the above example:

	Characters	Probability
Step 1:	A	0.45
	CD	0.30
	B	0.25
Step 2:	BCD	0.55
	A	0.45
Step 3:	ABCD	1.00

In the event of a tie in the selection of the two least probable combinations, either alternative will suffice. Assign a *0* or a *1* to each of the two character combinations selected at each pass. Thus:

		Step	
Characters	1	2	3
A			1
B		1	01
C	1	01	001
D	0	00	000

The weighted average of this code is calculated as:

Characters	Code	
A	1	0.45
B	01	0.50
C	001	0.60
D	000	0.30
Weighted Average		$\overline{1.85}$

There are 1.85 bits on the average per character required in this code. The average information content of this set of characters requires an absolute minimum of 1.815 bits per character. This minimum can be easily calculated using Equation 12–1.

It should be noted that the Huffman code for a particular set of characters and their associated probabilities is not unique, since the assignment of each *0* and *1* may be reversed and the selection of a tie is arbitrary.

Huffman codes are usually implemented in hardware for rapid coding/decoding. They are most often applied in telecommunications applications. The compression ratio will be greatest when there are wide differences in probabilities among the set of characters encountered. In information theory terms, a highly skewed distribution means that there is significant redundancy, which can be reduced by efficient coding.

Conclusions

In all of the true data compression techniques and in some of the preliminary techniques, a trade-off is made between storage space and processing time. To save space on a secondary storage device, the data are compressed when stored and decompressed when retrieved. This compression/decompression uses CPU time. The remaining preliminary techniques require, perhaps, additional systems design time on the part of the human designer to save storage space.

There is no one best compression technique. The effectiveness of a technique depends on the characteristics of the data to be stored. It may be worthwhile to analyze the data to be compressed (if they are available) as to characters, frequency distribution of these characters, etc. A reasonable sized sample of the same data may be less costly and almost as good as a full analysis.

Shifts in the data characteristics may result in a decrease in the compression ratio. Thus, any technique is more effective if the data file remains stable in content or in the characteristics of new data added. Two or more techniques may be combined for improved compression.

Since, in general, all data compression techniques (except some of the preliminary techniques) result in variable length records, this capability must be available on the system in use.

References

1.   Snyderman, M., and B. Hunt. "The Myriad Virtues of Text Compaction." *Datamation* 16, No. 16 (December 1970), pp. 36–40.

2. Dumey, A. I. "Of Vice and Virtue." *Datamation* 17, No. 10 (May 1971), pp. 147–48.
3. Zipf, G. K. *Human Behavior and the Principle of Least Effort,* Chapter 2. Cambridge, Mass.: Addison-Wesley Publishing, 1949.
4. Huffman, D. A. "A Method for Construction of Minimum Redundancy Codes." *Proceedings of the IRE* 40, No. 9 (September 1952), pp. 1098–1101.

Additional Readings

Gottlieb, D.; S. A. Hagerth; P. G. H. Lehot; and H. S. Rabinowitz. "A Classification of Compression Methods and Their Usefulness for a Large Data Processing Center." *Proceedings of the NCC* 44 (1975), pp. 453–58.

Hahn, B. "A New Technique for Compression and Storage of Data." *Communications of the ACM* 17, No. 8 (August 1974), pp. 434–36.

Held, G. *Data Compression.* New York: John Wiley & Sons, 1983.

Martin, J. *Computer Data-Base Organization,* Chapter 31. Englewood Cliffs, N.J.: Prentice-Hall, 1975.

Ruth, S. S., and P. J. Kreutzer. "Data Compression for Large Business Files." *Datamation* 18, No. 9 (September 1972), pp. 62–66.

Schieber, W. D., and G. W. Thomas. "An Algorithm for Compaction of Alphanumeric Data." *Journal of Library Automation* 4, No. 4 (December 1971), pp. 198–206.

Shannon, C. E. "Prediction and Entropy of Printed English." *Bell System Technical Journal* 50, No. 1 (January 1951), pp. 50–64.

Turner, L. F. "The On-Ground Compression of Satellite Data." *Computer Journal* 18, No. 3 (August 1975), pp. 243–47.

Review

1. Show how bit maps and bit indexes are similar.
2. Show how packing can be used to create a bit index.
3. Briefly describe each of the following compression techniques:
    a Front compression.
    b Differencing.
    c Null compression.
4. Why is an internal code with unassigned code combinations, such as EBCDIC, convenient for compression?
5. Why is the prefix property necessary in a code used over a telecommunications line?
6. Which compression would probably be used in a library storage of abstracts? Justify.
7. All compression techniques assume that the characteristics of the data remain the same. Why is this important?

Chapter 13

Telecommunications

Introduction

Telecommunications is concerned with the communications links and
facilities available for transmission of information from one location to
another. More precisely, it is concerned with communications based on
electrical, electronic, or optical techniques. Although the same communications links may carry either voice or data, this chapter deals with data
communication. Telecommunications links allow the exchange of data between a central processing unit and its terminals located at remote sites,
or with another central processing unit.

Some computer based systems inherently require geographic dispersion of on-line terminals, e.g. airline reservations systems. Other systems, while not requiring such a capability, use on-line terminals to
maintain tighter control or to improve efficiency in operations, e.g. point-
of-sale terminal systems in retail food chain operations, or the use of
terminals for credit authorization or check approval. Other retail operations forward end-of-day sales data to a central location.

The marriage of computers and communications facilities results in
both a more complex operating environment and one with more potential
for providing better and faster information to those needing it. The use of
telecommunications capabilities within a computer based information

system must be justified ultimately in an economic sense. Essentially the question is: Is the increased cost for such capability offset by the increased value of the processing provided?

Telecommunication-oriented computer systems consist of:

1. The central processing unit(s).
2. The remote terminals and other devices.
3. The communications lines linking the CPU(s) either to terminals or to other CPU(s).
4. The interface equipment between the CPU(s) and the communications lines.
5. The interface equipment between the remote terminals and the communications lines.

A telecommunications capability has become common in computer based information systems. The systems designer and the knowledgeable user require familiarity with the basic concepts and definitions of the telecommunications field. This chapter will introduce some of those basic concepts and definitions involving communications links and interface equipment.

Digital and Analog Lines

The telecommunications links that connect two points can be engineered to transmit in two different modes. Although the transmission media may be physically the same, the termination and relay equipment for the links differ. The two types of telecommunications links transmit data in different forms: digital and analog. Data may be transmitted in either mode, but a link engineered to handle one or the other mode can transmit data only in that mode.

Digital data can take on only discrete values, whereas analog data can take on any value within a given range. Digital data are exemplified by digital computer data where values are represented by the binary digits 0 and 1. Analog data can be illustrated by a slide rule. The values set on and read off the slide rule can theoretically take on any value.

On a communications line engineered for digital transmission, data are sent over the line in the form of a stream of pulses. As a pulse passes over a line, it is weakened (or degraded) and eventually becomes too weak to be sensed. Hardware devices called repeaters are used. A **repeater** accepts as input a weak train of pulses and produces as output a clean, full-strength train of pulses. This is illustrated in Figure 13–1. Repeaters are spaced on the line at distances sufficiently close to recognize the pulses and regenerate them before they completely disappear. As the pulse rate increases, the repeaters must be spaced closer together, since the pulses degenerate more rapidly at higher transmission rates.

Figure 13–1
Effect of a Repeater on a Train of Pulses

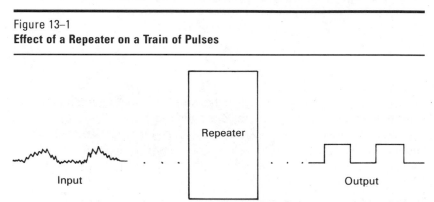

On a communications line engineered for analog transmission, data are sent over the line in the form of continuously varying signals. The line does not use repeaters. Instead it uses amplifiers, which strengthen the signal but do not regenerate it.

The signals transmitted over an analog line differ significantly from those transmitted over a digital line. It should be mentioned that data of any kind may be passed over either a digital or an analog line, but the form of the data will be different.

The number of oscillations in signal strength per second is called the **frequency.** Frequency is measured in **hertz** (abbreviated as hz), where one hertz equals one cycle per second.

Public telephone lines were designed for analog transmission, since they were engineered to carry the human voice (analog by nature). The voice produces output over a range of frequencies. The higher frequencies are heard as higher pitch; the lower frequencies as lower pitch. A violin produces higher frequencies; a kettle drum produces lower frequencies. The human voice is a sound consisting of a mix of many frequencies.

The human ear is sensitive to frequencies in the approximate range of 50 hz to 18,000 hz. Individuals may be sensitive to a somewhat broader or narrower range than this. Dogs can hear higher frequencies than humans. Dog whistles producing a signal at a frequency over 20,000 hz cannot be heard by humans but are clear to dogs.

Experimentally, it has been found that the bulk of the energy in the human voice lies in a range narrower than 50 to 18,000 hz. The telephone system has been designed to transmit frequencies from approximately 300 to 3,300 hz. Thus, those frequencies below 300 and above 3,300 hz in the human voice are cut off. Yet the voice is clearly recognizable.

Computers use digital data. The public telephone network has been engineered to transmit data in analog form. This presents a problem if this network is to be used to connect data processing equipment, that is, processors and remote terminal equipment. There is a mismatch between the equipment and the communications lines. In order to send digital data over an analog line, the data must be carried by an analog signal. This is done with a device called a modem.

Modulation/Demodulation

The device that serves as the interface between digital devices and an analog line is called a **modem.** Modem is an abbreviation for modulation/demodulation. Modulation is the encoding of digital data on an analog signal, and demodulation is the reverse. The modem performs both functions. The telephone companies refer to modems by the term **"data sets."** IBM calls them **"line adaptors."**

The simplest possibility for data transmission is to use direct wiring. This is practical only if the distance is relatively short and the transmission speed is relatively slow. This is sometimes referred to as **baseband signaling.** Because of the distance constraints and the amplifiers used on analog lines, baseband signaling cannot be used over the public telephone network.

Another possibility is to use an **acoustic coupler.** This is a device that performs the same function as a modem but without direct electrical connection between the terminal and the telephone line. The digital pulses are converted into audible tones (as is done in a Touchtone telephone). These tones all fall within the telephone line frequency range. The process is reversed at the receiving end of the line. Acoustic couplers are less expensive than modems and are used with relatively slow terminals. They are commonly used in conjunction with teletypes, and are frequently built into the terminal itself.

The third possibility is to use a modem. A sine wave is transmitted over the line, and the digital data input to the modem is used to modify or modulate it. The equation of a sine wave is:

$$a = A \sin (2 \pi ft + \theta)$$

a = amplitude at time t
A = maximum amplitude
f = frequency
θ = phase angle

Thus, for a given value of A, f, and θ the value of the wave at any time t is known. In order to modulate the wave, then, one of these three values must be modified. In fact, there are three general forms of modulation used:

Value Modified	Modulation Type
A	amplitude modulation (AM)
f	frequency modulation (FM)
θ	phase modulation (PM)

Both AM and FM are also used in radio transmission.

Modems also frequently offer a dialing capability. A connection is made by voice, and then the modem is manually switched into a data mode. Unattended answering is another feature that may be found. Modems also limit signal levels sent over the line so as to minimize interference with signals on other lines.

Equipment connected to the telephone network may be supplied by any vendor. The equipment must, however, be registered (or certified) by the FCC, that is, approved for direct connection to the public telephone network. This requirement includes modems.

Modems operate either at a fixed data transmission rate or at any speed up to a maximum rate. Some offer the capability of operating at more than one fixed speed.

Amplitude Modulation

In **amplitude modulation** the value of A in the sine wave equation takes on two values: one value for a *1* and another value for a *0*. The most common form of such modulation is called **continuous wave (CW)** modulation. In this case, a signal of some set frequency is transmitted for a *1*, and no signal (or a signal of zero amplitude) is transmitted for a *0*. Figure 13–2 illustrates this.

Figure 13–2
Continuous Wave (CW) Modulation

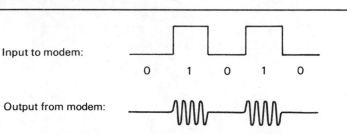

Input to modem:

0   1   0   1   0

Output from modem:

Frequency Modulation

In **frequency modulation** the value of f in the sine wave equation changes. The simplest form of frequency modulation is called **frequency-shift keying (FSK)** modulation. In FSK one frequency is transmitted for a *1* and another frequency is transmitted for a *0*. Figure 13–3 illustrates this.

Figure 13–3
Frequency-Shift Keyed (FSK) Modulation

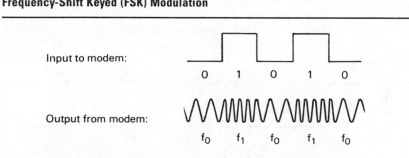

Input to modem:

0   1   0   1   0

Output from modem:

f_0 f_1 f_0 f_1 f_0

Phase Modulation

In **phase modulation** the value of θ in the sine wave equation changes. In the simplest case, θ takes on values 180° apart, that is, the sine wave reverses phase. Figure 13–4 illustrates this.

Pulse Modulation

In **pulse modulation** an analog signal is sampled and converted into digital data. This is modulation in a direction opposite to previ-

Figure 13–4
Phase Modulation

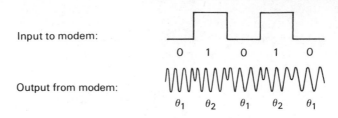

Input to modem:

0   1   0   1   0

Output from modem:

θ_1 θ_2 θ_1 θ_2 θ_1

ously discussed forms. This is a broadening of the traditional definition. Pulse modulation is used on digital lines. The interface
device is frequently called a **codec.** This is an abbreviation for coder/
decoder. The sampling must occur at least twice in each cycle of the
highest frequency of the analog signal. For example, if the analog
signal contains frequencies in the range of 1,000 to 3,000 hz, then
the sampling rate must be at least 6,000 times per second (i.e. the
highest frequency 3,000 hz times two). The sampling determines
the instantaneous value of the analog signal at that time. The instantaneous value is represented by a single pulse. In the simplest case,
the amplitude of this pulse is proportional to the analog signal amplitude. This is called **pulse amplitude modulation (PAM).** Figure
13–5 illustrates this.

Figure 13–5
Pulse Amplitude Modulation

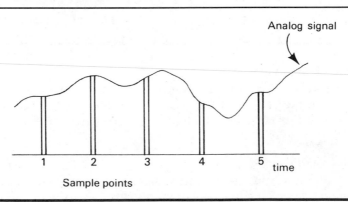

Analog signal

1   2   3   4   5
time

Sample points

In pulse amplitude modulation, the amplitude of the pulses may theoretically take on an infinite number of values. It is more practical to create a pulse with an amplitude that is one of a finite number of possible values. Of course, the greater the number of possible values, the greater the precision in the pulse representation of the analog signal. Commonly 128 pulse amplitudes are used. These amplitudes can be represented by seven bits or by seven possible *0–1* pulses. In **pulse code modulation,** an analog signal is sampled; its amplitude is then conceptually represented by a pulse that takes on one of a larger number of possible values, e.g. 128, which is then represented as a train of two valued pulses. Figure 13–6 illustrates this. For purposes of simplification, it assumes only four possible amplitude values, which can then be represented by two bits.

Figure 13–6
Pulse Code Modulation

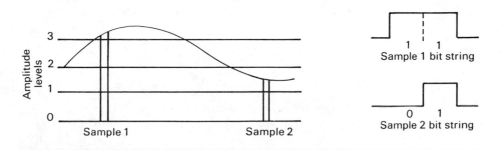

Other forms of modulation and demodulation are used. There also exists analog-to-analog modulation. Remote sensing applications may produce analog data outside the frequency range of a telephone line that are sent over analog telephone lines to a central site, e.g. process control or medical sensing applications. Facsimile can transmit documents, photographs, or even handwriting over telephone lines. In all these cases, an interface between the analog data source and an analog line is required.

Channel Capacity and Bandwidth

The data transmission rate of a communications line is measured in either bits per second (bps) or baud. **Baud** refers to the number of discrete pulses that can be transmitted over a line without unacceptable error. A bit is a unit of information; **bits per second** measures the amount of information that can be transmitted over the line per second. In most systems, the transmission rate measured in baud is the same as the transmission rate measured in bits per second. These terms are often used interchangeably. If the pulse transmitted can take on more than two values, then more than one bit of information will be transmitted per pulse, and the baud and the bps rates will not be the same. For example, if each pulse can take on one of four possible values with equal probability, then each pulse carries two bits of information. In this case, if 1,000 pulses can be carried per second, then the line can be rated as either a 1,000 baud or a 2,000 bps line.

Shannon[1] showed that the capacity of a channel (or line) in bits per second is:

$$C = W \log_2 \left(1 + \frac{S}{N}\right)$$

where

W = the bandwidth of the channel
S = the power of the signal
N = the power of white noise on the channel

The ratio S/N is called the **signal-to-noise ratio.** Thus, only three possibilities exist for increasing the capacity of a communications line:

1. Increase the bandwidth.
2. Increase the power of the signal.
3. Decrease the thermal noise.

The thermal noise may be decreased only by reducing the temperature. Practically, this cannot be done across the whole communications channel. Some specialized radio/radar systems may reduce the temperature of the receiving equipment.

The power of the signal can be increased. On private lines, this is one feasible approach. Increasing signal strength on lines of a public network, however, may result in interference. Maximum signal strength is, as a result, limited on these networks.

The most effective and practical approach is to increase the bandwidth of the channel. The **bandwidth** is the difference between the highest frequency and the lowest frequency that can be transmitted over the channel. This difference is measured in hertz. If a channel can transmit a wide range of frequencies, then it has a high bandwidth. Bandwidth is a function of the physical characteristics of the channel. If signal strength is increased or thermal noise is decreased, capacity increases only as the logarithm of one plus the signal-to-noise ratio. On the other hand, there is a linear increase in capacity with an increase in bandwidth. An additional complication is that the power of the thermal noise increases somewhat with bandwidth. As a result, the capacity increases somewhat less than expected with increased bandwidth. Nevertheless, increased bandwidth is the most practical approach to increased capacity. The higher the bandwidth that a communications line possesses, the higher the rate of data transmission possible over that line.

It should be noted that the capacity of Shannon's formula is a theoretical one. All practical equipment falls short of this ideal.

The bandwidth of a line has nothing to do with the frequency of transmission. For example, a line operating between 100,000 and 103,000 hz has a bandwidth of 3,000 hz. A line of 6,000 hz bandwidth can carry approximately twice the data that a line of 3,000 hz can carry in a given period of time. Some applications require large bandwidths. For example, a television channel requires a 6 million hz bandwidth, whereas a telephone voice channel requires a 3,000 hz bandwidth.

Signal Degradation

As a signal is sent over a communications line, a number of negative factors come into play. These factors cause the quality of the signal to deteriorate. If the deterioration is too great, the signal is lost and cannot be recovered. There are three types of signal degradation that occur on a communications line. These are distortion, attenuation, and noise.

Distortion

As a signal is transmitted over a communications line, its shape is changed. This is the simplest type of **distortion.** Figure 13–7 illustrates this on a simple train of digital pulses on a communications line. Distortion is caused by electrical qualities of the communications line itself.

Attenuation

As a signal is transmitted over a communications line, its signal strength decreases with line distance. This is called **attenuation.**

Figure 13–7
Signal Distortion

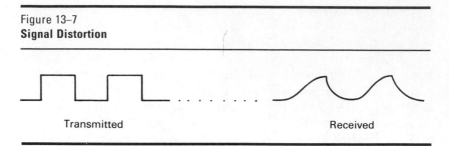

Transmitted   Received

Figure 13–8 illustrates attenuation and distortion of a train of pulses on a communications line.

Attenuation is caused by the electrical resistance of the line. Since the resistance of the line increases with distance, attenuation increases as line length increases.

A problem also arises if there is an attempt to transmit too rapidly over a communications line. Greater attenuation occurs, and the signal disappears into the noise level more rapidly.

Figure 13–8
Signal Attenuation and Distortion

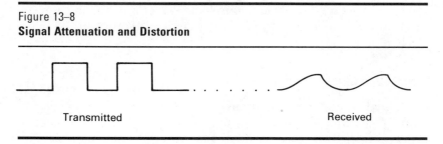

Transmitted   Received

Noise

Noise consists of random variations introduced on the signal. Since these variations are random, they are not predictable except in a probabilistic sense. There are two broad categories of noise: white noise and impulse noise.

White noise is also called **Gaussian noise.** It is a relatively steady background noise on communications lines. It is primarily composed of **thermal noise.** This is noise caused by the motion of atoms. Thus, if all other sources of noise could be eliminated from a communications line, there would still exist thermal noise. Absolute zero (approximately $-459.7°F$) is that point at which all atomic motion ceases. In practice, of course, this temperature cannot be achieved. At any temperature above absolute zero, thermal noise exists. As temperature increases, thermal noise increases.

For some extremely sensitive applications, reduction in the temperature of the receiver may be a necessity. One advantage of communications satellites is that equipment on these satellites operates in space at very low temperatures. As a result, background noise is reduced.

Impulse noise is noise of relatively high strength that occurs for relatively short periods of time. Lightning in the vicinity of a cable on a pole line is a source of impulse noise. The use of welding equipment in the neighborhood of communications lines may also introduce impulse noise. Electromechanical switching gear can also be a noise source.

Figure 13–9 illustrates both white and impulse noise combined with attenuation and distortion of a pulse train on a communications line. It should be clear that impulse noise especially may lead to an error in interpreting the received signal.

Figure 13–9
Noise on a Communications Line

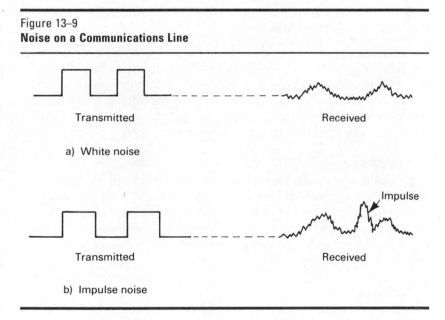

a) White noise

b) Impulse noise

Essentially, once a signal is attenuated too much it becomes mixed with background noise and cannot be separated out. The signal is lost.

Crosstalk and Echo

Crosstalk and echo may also be considered as forms of noise. However, they are usually identified separately. **Crosstalk** involves signals on one line affecting signals on another line. On a telephone voice connection it may be heard as faint conversation in the background. Crosstalk can occur between two lines physically adjacent to each other, e.g. lines next to each other in the same cable, and will increase with increased signal strength and with increased distance over which the lines run together.

Echo involves the reflection of part of the signal back to the transmitter. It is caused by an electrical mismatch in the line. On a telephone voice connection one's own voice may be heard as a faint echo. Circuits known as **echo suppressors** are used. On a voice circuit one user's voice triggers a relay that switches the echo suppressor into the return path. When the user stops speaking, the relay switches the circuit out of the return path so that the other party's voice may be carried. Echo suppressors must be disabled for data transmission, or the initial data in a transmission will be cut off.

Physical Transmission Media

Communications lines may consist of a series of links connecting one point to another. These links may not always utilize the same physical transmission medium. This is especially true with the public networks. Although either data or voice communications may be sent over any of these media, various characteristics, such as bandwidth and susceptibility to various types of error, may differ.

Open Wire Pair

An **open wire pair** consists of two wires mounted on a pole line. This was the earliest transmission link used and is now found generally only in rural areas of the United States. Open wire pairs are particularly susceptible to weather conditions. Wet conditions—rain or snow—increase attenuation and electrical storms are a source of noise.

Cable Pair

Cables containing multiple pairs of wires are found both mounted on poles and buried. They are usually lead sheathed.

Submarine Cable

The first transatlantic cable was laid in 1858. It was a telegraph cable. The first voice or telephone grade transatlantic cable was laid in 1956. In general, the upper frequency limit of **submarine cables** is less than that of land-based cables. Because of significant increases in telecommunications, transatlantic submarine cables are now inadequate in capacity and are supplemented by satellite links. In other parts of the world it is impractical to lay submarine cable, and high frequency radio, tropospheric scatter systems, or satellite systems must be used.

Coaxial Cable

Coaxial cable has a much wider bandwidth than the previously described physical media. Figure 13–10 illustrates a cross section of a coaxial cable. At higher frequencies the current in a conductor flows mostly on the outside of the conductor. This is called the **skin effect.** This effect increases electrical resistance and energy lost through radiation from the conductor. However, crosstalk is minimized, and some distortion is reduced. Its greatest advantage is the cable's ability to carry higher frequencies with a wider bandwidth. This increased bandwidth can be used to obtain a higher data transmission rate.

Figure 13–10
Coaxial Cable Cross Section

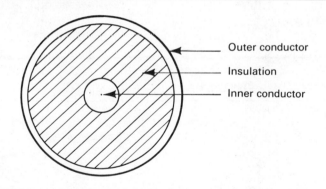

Outer conductor

Insulation

Inner conductor

Radio Systems

There are two main classes of radio systems in use: high frequency radio and tropospheric scatter systems. Table 13–1 lists the various frequency bands.

High frequency radio links bounce radio waves off the ionosphere. The **ionosphere** is the outer layer of the atmosphere. There are actually a number of layers located between approximately 70 and 200 miles high. These layers consist of ionized particles that can

Table 13–1
Frequency Bands

Band		Range
VLF	Very Low Frequency	3– 30 Khz
LF	Low Frequency	30– 300 Khz
MF	Medium Frequency	300–3,000 Khz
HF	High Frequency	3– 30 Mhz
VHF	Very High Frequency	30– 300 Mhz
UHF	Ultra High Frquency	300–3,000 Mhz
SHF	Super High Frequency	3– 30 Ghz
EHF	Extremely High Frequency	30– 300 Ghz

K = kilo-
M = mega-
G = giga-

reflect high frequency radio waves. The high frequency radio band is in the range of 3 to 30 megahertz. Figure 13–11 illustrates this. Such systems are designed for long distance and are inherently over-the-horizon systems. Because the ionosphere changes and shifts, high frequency radio circuits are subject to a relatively high error rate. Fading and distortion occur. During times of high solar flare activity, they may be completely blacked out. As a result, they tend to be used only when no alternative system is practical.

Figure 13–11
High Frequency Radio Signal

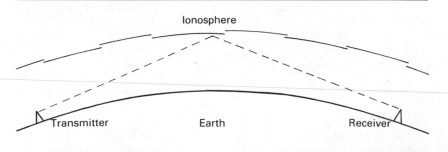

Tropospheric scatter systems use the troposphere to reflect the signal beyond the horizon. The **troposphere** is the lower part of the atmosphere. The signal is scattered, and multiple reflections occur. The receiving equipment must sort out one intelligible signal from these multiple reflections. Tropospheric scatter systems operate in the range of 400 to 10,000 megahertz, that is, in the UHF and SHF bands. Such systems tend to be more reliable than high frequency radio systems. However, they tend to be used when no practical alternatives are available, e.g. establishing a communications link over very rugged terrain.

Microwave Systems

Microwave systems allow line of sight transmission, that is, the transmitting antenna must be visually aligned with the receiving antenna. In practice, antennas are mounted on towers or tall buildings that may be from 20 to 30 miles apart. Microwave links consist of a series of relay stations that receive the signal, either amplify or regenerate it, and retransmit it to the next relay station. Microwave is in the super high frequency band of 3 to 30 gigahertz. Microwave offers a wide bandwidth but can sometimes be affected by atmospheric conditions, such as temperature layering, or by temporary blocking, such as that caused by a helicopter breaking the beam. An additional problem of congestion in metropolitan areas exists. Nevertheless, it is a very commonly used wideband link in the public networks.

Satellites

Communications satellites are now in regular, commercial use. Most such satellites are placed in **synchronous orbit.** This occurs at approximately 22,300 miles above the earth. At this altitude the satellite orbits the earth once in 24 hours. As a result, the satellite appears stationary in the sky to an observer on the earth.

The **Communications Satellite Corporation (COMSAT)** operates an international satellite network. It has placed in orbit a progressively more sophisticated series of satellites called **INTELSAT.** The first domestic satellite to serve North America was the Canadian **ANIK** in 1972. The first U.S. domestic satellite was **WESTAR,** which began operation for Western Union in 1974. **Satellite Business Systems (SBS)** is an organization set up by IBM, COMSAT, and Aetna to offer communications channels within the United States. Its original objective was to serve users having large data transmission requirements. SBS has since expanded its market downward to small users.

A satellite receives signals in one frequency band from an earth station transmitter, shifts to another frequency band and amplifies those signals, and retransmits them back to one or more earth station receivers. The transmission to the satellite is called the **up-link,** and the transmission from the satellite is called the **down-link.** This is shown in Figure 13–12. The up-link and the down-link must be carried out in different frequency bands, or the much more powerful down-link signal will wipe out the weak up-link signal. The frequencies used are compactly represented in a form such as 4/6 Ghz. The 4 Ghz represents the down-link frequency band, and the 6 Ghz represents the up-link frequency band. In fact, these numbers are only approximations; on both links they represent a 0.5 Ghz bandwidth. The up-link is usually 5.925 to 6.425 Ghz, and the down-link is 3.7 to 4.2 Ghz. Other links coming into use are 12/14 Ghz. Allocation of frequency bands is carried out internationally by the **International Telecommunications Union.**

Figure 13–12
Communications Satellite Operation

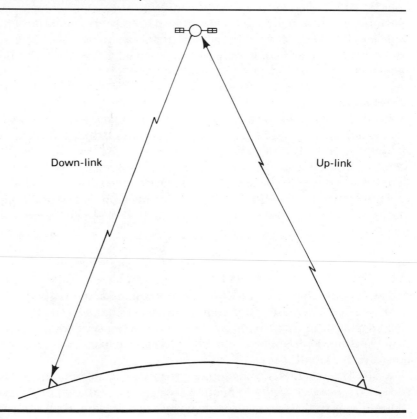

Down-link   Up-link

Transmission from a satellite may be aimed at that portion of the earth *facing* the satellite, at a wide geographic area such as the United States, or at a relatively small geographic area such as New England. Transmission to a relatively small area is carried out by a **spot beam,** that is, a narrow directional transmission by the satellite antenna. A number of spot beams may be transmitted to different geographic areas simultaneously from a satellite.

A consideration with the use of a communications satellite in a link is the time for the signal to travel from the transmitter to the satellite to the receiver. This is approximately ¼ second. For a return signal to be received at the original transmitting station, therefore, requires approximately ½ second if satellite links are used in both directions.

Optical Links

An **optical fibre** is a very thin, flexible fibre made of very pure glass. Light can be modulated and transmitted through the fibre. As light passes down the fibre, it is completely reflected from the fibre surface. This is illustrated in Figure 13–13. Lasers serve as the light source. The optical fibres are combined into an **optical cable,** that is, many fibres are contained in parallel within the cable structure. Because the cable is reasonably flexible, it can be installed in a manner similar to wire pair cable. Optical links offer a very high bandwidth and are now being installed in some high traffic areas.

Figure 13–13
Optical Fibre

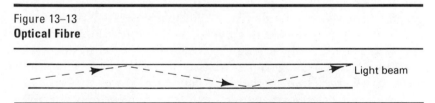

Light beam

Communications Common Carriers

A **common carrier** is a company that offers services to all persons impartially and is subject to either federal and/or state regulation. Companies offering communications services on an interstate basis are subject to regulations by the Federal Communications Commission (FCC). The authority of the FCC is outlined in The Communications Act of 1934. Those offering services intrastate are subject to similar state regulatory agencies. In some locations, e.g. Texas, local or city regulatory agencies may also exist.

A **tariff** is a document filed with, and approved by, a regulatory agency. It specifies the services provided by a communications common carrier and the costs for these services. Tariffs are available for public inspection.

American Telephone and Telegraph Company

In early 1982 the **American Telephone and Telegraph Company,** also known as the **Bell System,** legally agreed to divest itself of its operating companies. Prior to this corporate split the Bell System was by far the largest domestic communications common carrier. It had approximately 83 percent of the installed telephones in the United States. The telephone facilities of the former AT&T operating companies and other communications common carriers are integrated into one nationwide public network. With this agreement, the Bell operating companies became independent. AT&T, as a result of the agreement, became free to enter a number of data processing and telecommunications markets from which it had previously been prohibited.

There were 22 Bell operating companies (telephone companies). With divestiture, these 22 companies have been reorganized into 7 regional companies. For example, New York Telephone Company and New England Telephone Company have formed the NYNEX Corporation. A telephone company's geographic area is divided into **Local Access and Transport Areas** (**LATA**s). Calls made within a LATA are handled completely by the local telephone company. Calls between LATAs require the services of a long distance company. Thus, the local telephone company provides access to the public network and local services only. A long distance call initiated in one LATA goes through the local network, is passed to a long distance network, and is passed back into another local network at its destination.

The public telephone network may be used not only for voice communication but also for data communication. The most significant advantage of using the public telephone network for data transmission is that telephones are located almost everywhere, and a terminal may be easily connected for greater flexibility.

Long Distance Companies

Although the local telephone company holds a monopoly within its area (and is regulated), competition exists among long distance companies. These companies include AT&T Communications (a product of the AT&T divestiture), MCI Communications Corporation, and GTE's SPRINT network.

Wide Area Telephone Service

Wide Area Telephone Service (WATS) is a service offered on the public telephone network. Both Outward WATS and Inward WATS are available. Outward WATS allows unlimited outgoing calls, and Inward WATS allows unlimited incoming calls. A fixed monthly fee is charged for either.

The United States is divided into five geographical zones outside of the subscriber's state within the continental United States. Two additional zones outside of the continental United States include Alaska and Hawaii (zone 6) and Puerto Rico and the Virgin Islands (zone 7). The zones spread out from the subscriber's state somewhat concentrically: zone 2 includes zone 1, zone 3 includes zones 2 and 1, etc. WATS service is selected for a zone, and up to 240 hours of call time per month are allowed. Any type of call involving special handling, e.g. person-to-person, collect, conference, etc., is not included in the WATS service. Figure 13–14 shows the WATS zones as defined from Missouri.

A limited WATS service is available with **Measured Time WATS.** This is similar to full WATS service except that only 10 hours of call time per month are allowed. All time used beyond that limit incurs an additional charge.

For illustrative purposes only (and subject to change), the following rates apply for WATS service centered in Missouri:

Zone	MONTHLY SERVICE CHARGE	
	Full Service	Measured Time
1	$1,400	$224
2	1,500	226
3	1,610	234
4	1,640	238
5	1,660	242
6	3,474	351
7	7,858	700

Dataphone Digital Service

Dataphone Digital Service (DDS) is a data network completely independent of the public voice network operated by the Bell System. It is available in only a limited number of cities and offers data transmission rates of 2,400, 4,800, 9,600 and 56,000 bps. The interface between the network and the customer's data equipment is carried out by a piece of equipment called a **service unit.**

Figure 13–14
WATS Zones Centered on Missouri

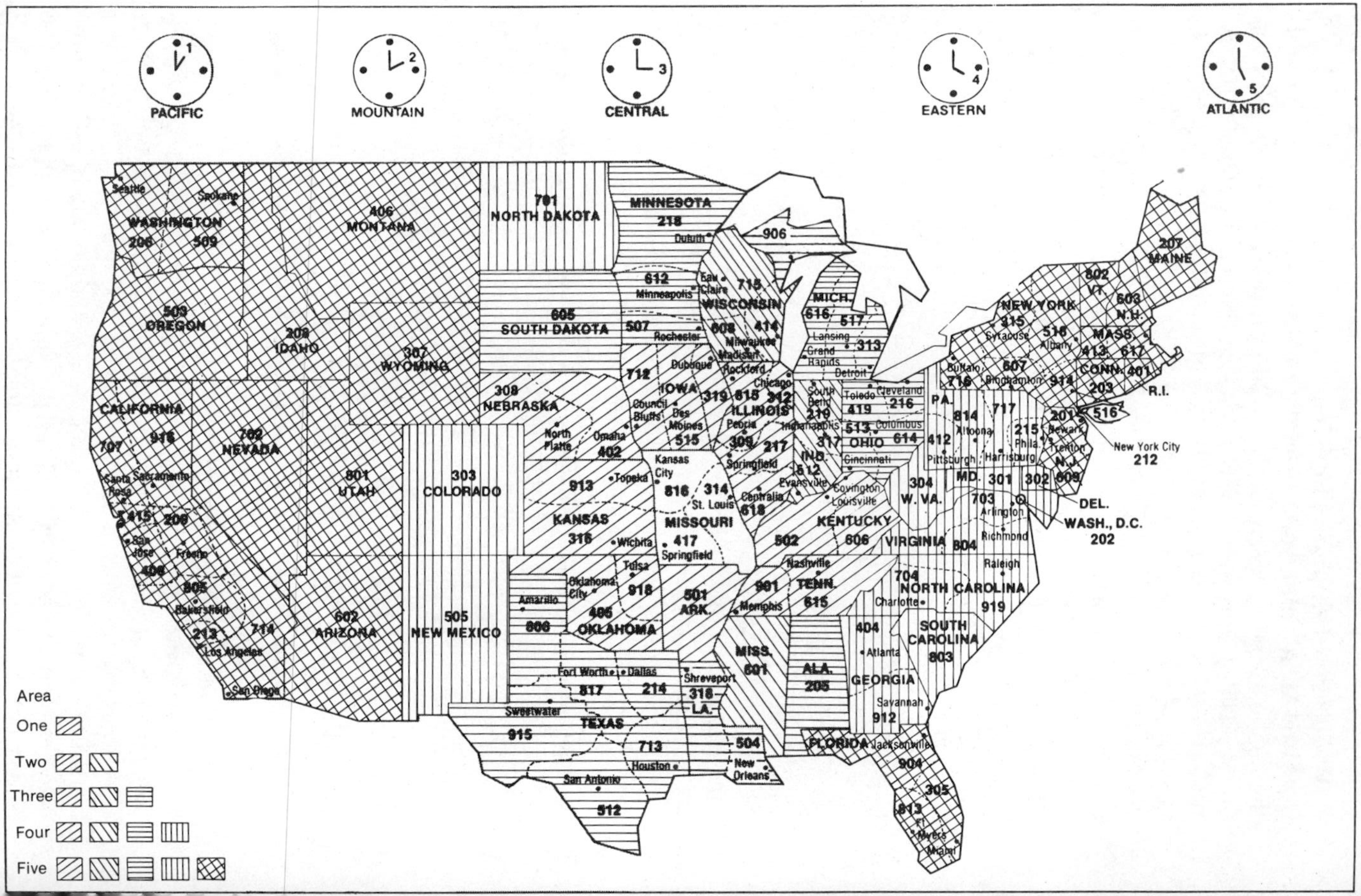

Western Union

Western Union Telegraph Company offers nationwide telegraph grade services in the United States, along with miscellaneous other services. Western Union operates two public telegraph grade networks. These are the telex network and the Teletypewriter Exchange network. In addition, it also offers a data transmission service called Western Union Private Wire.

Telex

The U.S. **Telex** network is a switched public network that uses teleprinter terminals. It can connect to a worldwide Telex network. Any terminal may dial directly any other terminal in the same country. Terminals located in Canada and Mexico may also be dialed directly from terminals in the United States. Connections to other countries from the United States must be made by an operator. Transmission speed on the Telex network is 50 bps. Paper tape capability is optional. In addition, the teleprinter may be unattended, that is, the terminal switches itself off upon completion of the message.

Teletypewriter Exchange

The **Teletypewriter Exchange (TWX)** network was originally operated by AT&T but was sold to Western Union in 1971. There are three types of access:

1. TTY–TWX: Access to the network is made by a teletypewriter provided by Western Union.
2. CPT–TWX: Access to the network is made by a user-owned terminal that is either a teletypewriter or a device that appears to the line as a teletypewriter.
3. CE–TWX: Access to the network is made through any customer equipment. A terminal with CE–TWX access can communicate only with a terminal having the same access.

TWX directories similar to telephone directories are published listing subscribers having TTY–TWX or CPT–TWX service. CE–TWX subscribers are not listed, since subscriber equipment may not be compatible.

Interconnection with the Telex network is possible. In addition, the capability to switch a teleprinter from the TWX network to the public telephone network is available. The TWX network operates at speeds up to 150 bps.

Western Union Private Wire

Western Union Private Wire offers transmission speeds of 75, 150, 300, and 600/1,200 bps. The three lower-speed services are available in many U.S. cities. The 600/1,200 bps service is currently available in a fewer number of cities. Extensions may be made to the service from nondirect access cities for an additional charge.

International Common Carriers

The United States has three **communications gateway cities:** New York, Washington, and San Francisco. At these cities connections can be made from the domestic networks to the international networks.

AT&T serves as the international carrier for telephone communications. For record traffic the largest of the international common carriers are: RCA Global Communications (a subsidiary of RCA), ITT World Communications (a subsidiary of ITT), and Western Union International (not associated with the domestic Western Union Telegraph Company).

Specialized Common Carriers

The term **specialized common carrier** covers a variety of relatively new communications companies that offer telecommunications services in a competitive environment.

Carriers owning and operating networks in competition with communication services of AT&T Communications and Western Union include MCI Communications Corporation, General Telephone and Electronics (GTE), and United States Transmission System, Inc. (a subsidiary of ITT).

MCI was the first specialized common carrier. It was authorized by the FCC in 1969 to provide specialized common carrier services in competition with AT&T and Western Union. This decision was broadened in 1971 to allow general competition in private line services. MCI operates a coast-to-coast microwave network. It offers both leased line and other services. Connection to the MCI long distance network can be made through the local telephone company.

GTE also operates a coast-to-coast microwave network. Connection to GTE's SPRINT network can also be made through the local telephone company system.

Another group of carriers operate **value-added networks.** These carriers do not own communications networks but lease lines from other common carriers, add some additional features and services, and then re-lease the lines to users. These companies include Graphnet (a subsidiary of Graphic Scanning), Tymnet (a subsidiary of Tyme Share), and Telenet.

Many of the carriers sell services and capacity to other carriers. Western Tele-Communications, Inc., for example, operates as a carrier's carrier. It operates a microwave network in 16 western states and leases out capacity to other carriers, including MCI and Western Union. It also serves the radio and television networks.

Other Networks

Railroads have their own lines along their tracks. Some companies have their own lines using microwave, infrared, or optical transmission systems. Optical systems use a narrow beam of light through the air. Microwave links require a license. Infrared and optical systems do not require a license but may suffer interference from snow, heavy rain, fog, etc. These links also transmit only over a relatively short distance.

Line Categories

Telecommunications lines are categorized on the basis of a number of criteria. The following are commonly used.

Leased and Public Lines

Communications lines may be either leased or public lines. A connection between two telephones is made most often by means of public exchanges, or switching centers. A connection made over a public network for the purposes of transmitting data is also switched.

A leased line is connected between two terminals *permanently*. Although it may pass through a switching center, it does not involve use of the switching equipment itself. Switching equipment, particularly the older nonelectronic systems, are a source of electrical noise on the circuits. An additional consideration is that connections made between two points on a switched network may be over different routes on different occasions.

Leased lines avoid the noise caused by the switching equipment and always have the same route each time they are used. Because the route remains the same, the lines may be conditioned. **Conditioning** is a means of compensating for distortion on lines and involves an additional charge. Conditioning adjusts for two types of distortion.

In one type, the attenuation of the signal is different at different frequencies, that is, a signal encompassing a frequency range is attenuated differently at different points within that range. This is called **attenuation distortion.** In the other type, the signal takes a different amount of time to travel a given distance at different frequencies. This is called **delay distortion.** Conditioning adjusts the circuit in such a way that both types of distortion are equalized over the frequency range. As a result, a higher transmission rate of data is possible, or a lowering of the error rate is achieved. Additionally, if the line is to be used for more than a certain number of hours per day (depending on the appropriate tariff), it will be less expensive to lease the line.

Simplex, Half-Duplex, and Duplex Lines

Another categorization of communications lines deals with directions of transmission. There are three categories.

A **simplex** line can carry transmission in only one direction. An example might be encountered in an application involving remote sensors sending data one way to a central processor. In practice, simplex lines are rare.

A **half-duplex** line can carry transmission in both directions but not at the same time. There will be a delay whenever the direction of transmission is reversed. This is called the **line turnaround time.** In most cases half-duplex lines are used even when data are transmitted in only one direction, since control signals will be transmitted back from the receiver.

A **duplex** (or **full-duplex**) line can carry transmission in both directions at the same time. Clearly, more efficient use of the line can be made. The increase in cost for a full-duplex over a half-duplex line is relatively small, but the additional cost for equipment to handle two-way transmission may be significant.

Subvoice, Voice, and Wideband Lines

A third categorization of communications lines is by transmission speed. There are three general types of lines.

A **voice grade** line is a telephone quality line. It can carry up to 9,600 bps. Attempts to transmit at a rate much higher result in an increased error rate. More frequently they are used at lower rates, such as 1,200, 2,400, or 4,800 bps.

A **subvoice grade** (or **telegraph grade**) line is capable of handling a transmission rate less than that of a voice grade line. It may operate up to approximately 300 bps.

A **wideband** (or **broadband**) line is capable of carrying at a rate greater than that of a voice grade line. This type of line has the greatest bandwidth of the three, since an increased bandwidth is needed for an increased transmission rate.

Multidrop Lines

A **multidrop line** has multiple terminals (or other devices) connected to the line. Although multiple terminals may be connected at one end of the line, only one may transmit at a time over the line. Two or more transmissions at the same time will simply produce a garbled flow of data. Therefore, a line discipline must be imposed. The essential question is: How is the next terminal to transmit selected? There are two disciplines used: polling and contention.

Polling

With **polling,** the central site controls transmission over the line. A terminal is queried whether it has data to transmit. The terminal then transmits the data or responds negatively. No terminal transmits unless requested. The simplest discipline is round robin, that is, each terminal is called in turn and requested to transmit any data that it has at that time. After polling each terminal, the procedure is repeated. Priorities may be introduced—certain terminals may be called more often than others.

Contention

With **contention,** each terminal competes for the line. If a terminal has data to transmit, it checks to see if the line is available. If the line is free, the terminal obtains use of it and transmits. If the line is not free, the terminal waits for a period of time and tries again. Contention is analogous to the use of a party line on the telephone. Once a terminal obtains the line, it has full use of that line. If the line is committed, then any other terminal seeking access to the line is denied it until the line becomes available again.

Multiplexing

Multiplexing is a technique for combining the data transmission from more than one source onto one communications line. Its purpose is to save on the number of lines used and, therefore, on the total cost of the communications lines. Figure 13–15(a) and (b) illustrate this concept.

In the configuration shown in Figure 13–15(a), three communications lines are used to connect three remote terminals to a central processor. If the distances involved are relatively long, the line costs

Figure 13–15
Multiplexing

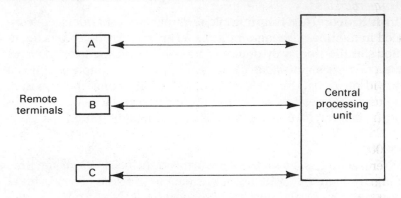

(a) Non-multiplexed configuration

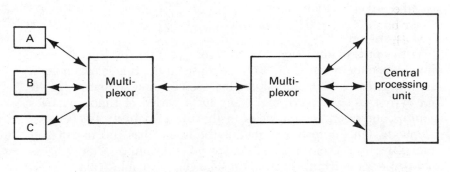

(b) Multiplexed configuration

can be high. In the configuration shown in Figure 13–15(b), the data transmitted between all three terminals and the central processor are multiplexed onto one line. This assumes that the terminals are located much nearer to each other than to the processor, e.g. all three terminals are in the same city, but the processor is in a distant city. This configuration results in a savings in line costs but incurs additional costs for the multiplexing equipment itself. Voice channels are multiplexed onto wideband lines by the long distance telephone companies for intercity connections. There are two types of multiplexing used: frequency division and time division.

Frequency Division Multiplexing

In **frequency division multiplexing,** each channel's data are placed in a different frequency band. All frequency bands are transmitted simultaneously over a common line. The data for each channel are at different frequencies on the common line. For example, if the bandwidth required for each channel was 3,000 hz and five channels were used, then the data for channel 1 might be transmitted in the band from 100,000 hz to 103,000 hz; channel 2 in the band from 104,000 hz to 107,000 hz, etc. Thus, a total band from 100,000 hz to 120,000 hz would be used. The data transmitted in one band do not interfere with those transmitted in the other bands. This is similar to radio or television broadcasting. Many radio or TV stations broadcast at different frequencies. They do not interfere with each other, and any desired station may be selected out by a receiver. A gap called a **guard band** is left between bands in a multiplexed system to prevent any overlap between bands. At the other end of the communications line, each band is filtered out separately and the data are recovered. In summary, in frequency division multiplexing a wider band of frequencies is subdivided into narrower bands, and each channel is assigned to one of these narrower bands.

Time Division Multiplexing

In **time division multiplexing** a time increment is divided into smaller increments, and each of the smaller increments is assigned to a channel. It can be considered as analogous to the sharing of time in the central processor of a time-sharing system. Data are transmitted over a small increment of time for one channel, then another channel, and so on until all channels have transmitted. The procedure then repeats. A **guard time** is needed between the time slices allocated to each channel. Interleaving of data from the various sources may be done bit by bit or character by character.

Concentrators

A **concentrator** is an intelligent multiplexor. The concentrator interfaces low-speed terminal equipment with a communications line (as a multiplexor does), but can adjust to the actual data transmission requirements. Allocation of time or frequency bands can be made on an as-needed basis. Those terminals requiring a greater allocation of line capacity can be assigned more, and those terminals requiring less can be assigned less. As an intelligent device, a concentrator has processing capability. It can, therefore, also carry out other functions, such as compression, error checking, and polling on multidrop lines.

Switching

If equipment located at two different sites must carry on frequent communication, then the simplest (though not necessarily the least expensive) approach is to *permanently* connect them, e.g. by means of a leased line. If a number of stations must all communicate with each other, then permanent connections may be established among all of them. Figure 13–16 illustrates this for five such stations.

Figure 13–16
Five Stations Interconnected

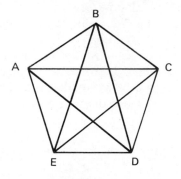

In general, if there are N stations, then there are $N(N-1)/2$ such interconnections. As N gets large, the number of interconnections becomes very large. For example, for $N = 100$ the number of interconnections is 4,950. The public telephone network is probably the best example of a network where direct interconnections would reach astronomical figures.

In any particular system, all interconnections are not needed at the same time. This allows the use of switching.

Line Switching

Line switching is exemplified by the public telephone network. A temporary direct connection between the two stations seeking communication is made. At the end of the communication, the connection is broken. Figure 13–17 illustrates line switching with one switching center. If station B needs to be connected to station H or station C needs to be connected to station D, the connections are made at the switching center. Multiple switching centers may be tied together in a network of high-speed lines.

Figure 13–17
Line Switching

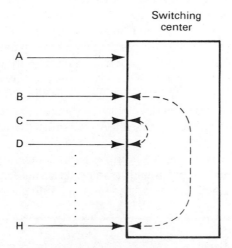

Message Switching

In a **message switching** network the transmitting station and the receiving station are not directly connected. The message along with addressing information is sent to the switching center. The switching center interprets the address and forwards it to the receiving station when a line is available. The message may pass through several switching centers and is temporarily stored at each. This concept is called **store and forward.**

An advantage of a message switching network is that the transmitting and receiving stations do not have to be available for communication at the same time (as in a line switching network). The transmitting station inserts the message into the network when it is ready; the receiving station accepts the message from the network when it is ready.

Packet Switching

Packet switching is a specialized form of message switching. It is used most often in (but not limited to) CPU-to-CPU communication. The switching centers are special purpose computers. The non-network computers are called **host computers.** A host computer transmits its message to the local network computer. The network computer breaks the message up into a number of blocks, or **packets,** that contain address information. Each packet is transmitted to another network computer closer to its destination. Each packet is transmitted when a communications line has *space* available. Each network computer decides on the routing to the next network computer. Packets from one original message may travel different routes to their final destination. Storage of all packets at a sending network computer is required until acknowledgement is received from the receiving network computer. All packets eventually reach the destination network computer. They are assembled into the original message format and transmitted to the receiving host computer. An acknowledgement of receipt is then transmitted back to the transmitting host computer.

Figure 13–18 illustrates a simple packet switching network. In this example, host computer 1 transmits a message to switching computer (SC) 1, which breaks the message into packets. One packet

Figure 13–18
Packet Switching Network

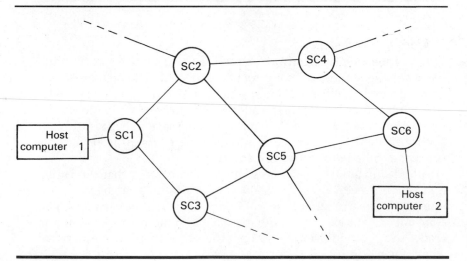

may travel the route SC1–SC3–SC5–SC6; another may travel SC1–SC2–SC5–SC6, and another SC1–SC2–SC4–SC6. Individual routings are determined by such factors as line availability and line loading. At switching computer 6 the message is reassembled and transmitted to host computer 2. An acknowledgement from host computer 2 is routed back to host computer 1. Many other host computers have access to the network.

Local Area Networks

A **local area network (LAN)** is a network interconnecting various data handling devices, usually in an office environment and within a relatively small area. A LAN may be installed to provide a network capability within an office, a building, or several buildings. Although LANs usually require proximity of the devices to be connected, Cablenet (a LAN offered by AMDAX) allows connections to the network of devices up to 50 miles apart. A LAN can be either baseband or broadband.

A **baseband LAN** provides one digital channel. Data are transmitted over this channel between devices on a time-shared basis. An example of a baseband LAN is Xerox's Ethernet.

A **broadband LAN** provides multiple analog channels that are frequency multiplexed. Some channels may provide dedicated connections between devices, and others may be switched. An example of a broadband LAN is Wang's Wangnet.

Various devices, such as CPUs, word processors, electronic copiers, etc., can be connected to the LAN. This means that data entered or produced at one device may be made available at any other device on the network.

Teleprocessing Concepts

Although some such concepts have already been discussed, **teleprocessing** is concerned with the use of telecommunications facilities by computer equipment. It is the linking of a central processing unit over telecommunications lines to remote terminals or to another central processing unit, and the operation of this combined equipment.

Synchronous and Asynchronous Operation

Synchronous transmission of data means that both the transmitting and receiving stations are operating in time phase with each other. The transmitter first sends a synchronization pattern that the receiver uses to get into phase. Once in phase, a block of data is sent in a continuous stream. Each character follows the previous character directly. Usually an error checking pattern follows each block. As an example, if a line is carrying 1,200 bps (at 1,200 baud) and each character takes 6 bits, then 200 characters per second are transmitted, and each character takes 0.005 second. Every 0.005 second one character is received.

Asynchronous transmission of data means that the transmitting and receiving stations are not in time phase with each other. This type of transmission is also called **start-stop.** A special signal indicates the start of a character, the character representation follows, and another special signal indicates the end of the character. The next character is also bracketed by the start and stop signals. The amount of time between characters is completely variable.

Asynchronous devices tend to be less expensive than synchronous devices. Synchronous devices make more efficient use of the communications line, since time for the start and stop signals with each character is not required.

Communications Controllers

A **communications controller** is a device that serves as a buffer between the central processing unit and the remote terminals. It is also called a **communications control unit.** There is a serious mismatch between communications line speed and the processing speed of the central processing unit. If the central processing unit is required to handle all communications line interface requirements, less processor time is available for its primary processing load. The communications controller relieves the central processing unit of this burden, and thus allows more efficient use of the CPU.

The controller includes buffers so that received data may be assembled and temporarily stored before transfer to the central processing unit. For example, data may be received serially (bit by bit or character by character) but processed in blocks of characters. There may also be code conversion, if the telecommunications code is different from the internal code of the central processing unit. Error checking of messages received will also be carried out. For messages to be transmitted from the CPU, buffering and, perhaps, code conversion are also required. Miscellaneous other housekeeping functions are also carried out.

If the device interfacing between the communications lines and the central processing unit has some processing capability, it can relieve the CPU of even more details. For example, data compression, data editing and formatting, collection of statistics, and more extensive error control are some capabilities that might be contained in the device. In this case, the device is called a **communications processor** or a **communications front end.** These are, in fact, specialized programmable computers. In addition to CPU front end applications, communications processors are used as switching centers in message switching networks.

Conclusions

The marriage of communication and computer technologies has resulted in an explosive growth and change in telecommunications. It has added greater flexibility and accessibility to computer based information systems for users.

The telecommunications field is currrently in a state of flux. This change is, perhaps, best exemplified by the entry of competition into parts of the communications lines market and the break up of AT&T. Traditionally, the services offered by communications common carriers have fallen under regulated monopoly. In recent years the FCC and a number of court decisions have allowed competition between the traditional and new common carriers for the data communications market. In addition, the new digital technology promises much further change in the near future.

The system designer has many decisions that must be made when a teleprocessing capability is sought. In the selection of communications lines alone, the following illustrates only some of the choices available in choosing a line between two points:

1. Use a dial-up public telephone line.
2. Lease a WATS line.
3. Use a full-time leased line.
4. Dial-up or lease a line from one of the specialized common carriers.
5. Lease a line from one of the value-added network carriers.

Geographic dispersion of processing capability is a fact of life. Distributed networks require telecommunications between CPUs and with the terminal devices attached to each CPU. Networks connecting remote users to a central CPU also require telecommunications. Hardware devices, such as multiplexors, concentrators, and communications front ends, are designed to make telecommunications in a network more feasible.

Competition among those companies offering telecommunications lines, those companies offering communications-oriented hardware, and those now introducing local area networks, promises to produce many new changes in this field. Telecommunications will continue to be one of the fastest growing areas supporting computer based information systems.

Reference

1.   Shannon, C. E. "The Mathematical Theory of Communication," in *The Mathematical Theory of Communication,* Shannon, C. E., and W. Weaver. Urbana, Ill.: University of Illinois Press, 1949.

Additional Readings

Asten, K. J. *Data Communications for Business Information Systems.* New York: Macmillan, 1973.

Brooks, C. H. P., et al. *Information Systems Design,* Chapter 8. Englewood Cliffs, N.J.: Prentice-Hall, 1982.

Doll, D. R. *Data Communications.* New York: John Wiley & Sons, 1978.

Klee, K.; J. W. Verity; and J. Johnson. "Battle of the Networkers." *Datamation* 28, No. 3 (March 1982), pp. 115–27.

Martin, J. *Introduction to Teleprocessing.* Englewood Cliffs, N.J.: Prentice-Hall, 1972.

_____. *Systems Analysis for Data Transmission.* Englewood Cliffs, N.J.: Prentice-Hall, 1972.

_____. *Telecommunications and the Computer.* 2d ed. Englewood Cliffs, N.J.: Prentice-Hall, 1976.

_____. *Future Developments in Telecommunications.* 2d ed. Englewood Cliffs, N.J.: Prentice-Hall, 1977.

_____. *Communications Satellite Systems.* Englewood Cliffs, N.J.: Prentice-Hall, 1978.

Tannenbaum, A. S. *Computer Networks.* Englewood Cliffs, N.J.: Prentice-Hall, 1981.

Review

1. Differentiate between analog and digital communications lines.
2. What is a repeater?
3. What is baseband signaling?
4. What is the function of a modem?
5. What is an acoustic coupler?
6. Briefly describe each of the following types of modulation:
    a Continuous wave.
    b Frequency shift keying.
    c Phase modulation.
7. Differentiate between PAM and PCM.

8. Does channel capacity of a communications line increase, decrease, or remain the same (assuming all other factors equal) if:

 a Bandwidth increases.

 b Signal power increases.

 c Lowest frequency passable increases.

9. Briefly explain the meaning of each of the following terms:

 a Amplitude distortion.

 b Delay distortion.

 c Impulse noise.

 d Gaussian noise.

 e Crosstalk.

 f Echo.

10. How are all of the terms in question 9 related?

11. Differentiate between the up-link and the down-link of a communications satellite.

12. Why are communications satellites placed in synchronous orbit?

13. *a* What is a common carrier?

 b What is a tariff?

14. What is conditioning?

15. Differentiate between simplex, half-duplex, and duplex lines.

16. Differentiate between a voice grade and a wideband line.

17. Differentiate between polling and contention as line disciplines.

18. Give the main rationale for multiplexing.

19. Differentiate between frequency division and time division multiplexing.

20. What is a guard band?

21. What is a concentrator?

22. *a* Differentiate between line switching and message switching.

 b Differentiate between message switching and packet switching.

23. What is a communications front end?

24. What is a LAN?

Chapter 14

Data Integrity and Security

Introduction

Computer based information systems have become such ubiquitous tools in our society that the degree to which they have penetrated the day-to-day working of organizations is not always recognized. The following describes only a few of the problems that can arise with their use.

The availability of information when needed from the organization's computer based information systems is taken for granted. The failure of such a system may result in repercussions that can range from serious inconvenience to catastrophe. An airline reservations system is an example of such an essential system.

The *checkless society* concept has already been implemented in some limited applications, e.g. direct crediting of social security payments to checking accounts. Security designed to prevent fraudulent manipulation of money transfer is paramount in such a system.

Relatively high expenses may be incurred in collecting data over a period of time. As an example, mailing lists of potential buyers in a specialized market may be both time-consuming and expensive to accumulate. Programs may involve many man-months or man-years of effort to write, debug, and thoroughly test. Copies of these data or programs may be made from a computer system, leaving no trace that such theft has occurred.

Some files may contain data of a personal or confidential nature, e.g. medical files or credit files. The access of data in such files by unauthorized users may result not only in serious legal problems for the file owner, but in damage, inconvenience, or embarrassment to the subject who has been compromised.

Although many of the concerns associated with the integrity and security of computer based data files also exist with noncomputer based systems, they take on a more critical nature in computer based systems. Since data recorded on secondary storage devices are usually represented by magnetization on a ferrite material surface, it is only necessary to change the magnetization to change data. No trace may remain to indicate that such a modification has occurred.

The failure of a critical component, e.g. the CPU, may prevent access to, or use of, any of the resources of the system. Denial of service to users over a period of time may have serious results. Potential losses may increase rapidly as down time of the system continues.

Threats to a computer based information system's integrity and security may be either accidental or deliberate. The effects of either may range from the trivial to the disastrous. A successful accidental infiltration may lead to further deliberate infiltration. Thus, the possibilities of accidental compromise cannot be ignored.

The term **work factor** refers to the effort required on the part of an infiltrator to overcome the system and accomplish his or her goal. An objective of the system designer must be to increase the work factor for such an infiltrator while limiting the effect of such design measures on authorized users. The work factor is really a measure of cost. Various measures might include:

1. Availability of required expertise.
2. Cost of obtaining required equipment, information, etc., needed to infiltrate the system.
3. Time required to circumvent the built-in safeguards of the system.

Martin[3] lists three principles in the design of a security system:

1. Minimize the probability of a compromise happening at all.
2. Minimize the damage if it does happen.
3. Design a method of recovering from the damage.

Thus, a system designed on the assumption that failure will never occur is inviting disaster.

The range of concern is wide. The following are only a few examples of the possible objectives of a system infiltrator:

1. To obtain data from a sensitive file, e.g. salary data on a particular employee.
2. To change data in such a file, e.g. to change the current balance in a particular checking account.
3. To obtain a listing of the data contents of a file, e.g. to sell as a mailing list.
4. To destroy contents of a file, e.g. an act of revenge on the part of an employee suffering real or imagined injustice.
5. To copy a valuable program, e.g. to be resold to another user.
6. To discover patterns of either individual or organizational data use, e.g. an increase in use of socioeconomic data on a particular geographic area by a planning group might indicate possible expansion into that area.
7. To obtain free use of hardware or software resources.
8. To deny the use of hardware or software resources to legitimate users.

In addition, serious threats exist from either natural or accidental causes.

It is not possible to provide a computer based information system with 100 percent security and integrity. The possible losses must be evaluated against the costs required to safeguard the system against these losses at a reasonable level of confidence. In other words, cost/benefit analysis must be applied.

Availability, Validity, Integrity, Security, and Privacy

Before proceeding further, it is necessary that some terms be defined and clarified. Some of these terms are used interchangeably in different contexts. The terms do have different meanings but are not unrelated to each other.

Availability measures that the computer system is operating correctly when needed. It is a function of both reliability and maintainability. **Reliability** measures that the computer system is operating correctly over a long period of time. **Maintainability** measures that the computer system returns to operation quickly after failure.

Availability means that the system can be used with confidence during almost all of the time in which it is scheduled. The simplest measure of availability is:

$$\frac{\text{time available to users}}{\text{time scheduled available to users}} \times 100\%$$

Thus, if in a given month the computer system is scheduled for 176 hours and, in fact, it is available 172 hours, then availability is rated at 97.7 percent. It should be pointed out that this measure of availability is subject to manipulation. By scheduling the system for more maintenance in a month, the time scheduled for users is decreased, and the percentage availability is increased. Thus, availability must be viewed both in terms of a percentage and of actual hours available.

A measure of reliability is the **mean time between failure (MTBF).** This is the expected time between the point at which a system becomes available to users and the point at which an unscheduled interruption in the system operation occurs. This measure may also be misleading. In comparing two systems, it cannot always be concluded that the system with the higher MTBF is better. Reliability must be viewed in conjunction with maintainability.

A measure of maintainability is the **mean time to repair (MTTR).** This is the expected time between the point at which a system fails and the point at which it becomes available to its users again. For example, a system with a 100 hours MTBF may require an MTTR of 10 minutes, and another system with a 150 hours MTBF may require an MTTR of 3 hours. It is, therefore, necessary to use MTBF and MTTR together.

Availability may be improved by the use of **redundancy,** that is, one or more critical system components may be duplicated. This may involve even duplication of the central processing unit.

A number of configurations involving redundancy of the CPU are possible. The primary system may be backed up by an equally powerful secondary system. An alternative is to backup the primary system with a less powerful secondary system. In this case, the secondary system may take over only the more critical jobs of the primary system in the event of a failure. Usually the backup system does not remain idle while in a standby mode, but it is used for low priority and convenience jobs. Another possible configuration is to have the two systems share the job load normally. In the event of a failure of one system, the other system picks up the full load with some degradation of performance.

Graceful degradation refers to limited operation of the computer system after a failure. Some resources may not be available, yet the system continues operating in a degraded manner with the remaining resources. The degradation may be reflected in temporary loss of some programs or data files, reduced throughput, increased turnaround times, or increased response times or reduced number of terminals accepted in an on-line system.

Validity is concerned with acceptance of data entered into the system. It involves the checking of those data and preventing those data items in error from entering further processing. Validation is a function of input control and basically discriminates between those data passing all acceptance checks and those that have failed one or more. Accepted data are forwarded for further computer processing; rejected data are returned to their source for correction or change. Chapter 4 discussed data validation in some detail.

Integrity is concerned with the prevention of the destruction or loss of data. If this primary goal is not achieved, then it is concerned with the detection that data destruction or loss has happened, with the prevention of further destruction or loss, and with taking steps to offset or correct this destruction or loss.

Security is concerned with the protection of data and programs from either accidental or deliberate destruction, unauthorized access, or unauthorized modification. Since, to be used, data and programs require further computer resources such as hardware, software, etc., these resources are also usually encompassed within the scope of data security. An additional consideration is that data security measures should ideally not interfere with use of the computer by authorized personnel.

Privacy is a broad concept that applies not to data but to individuals. It is concerned with the rights of individuals regarding collection and use of personal data.

To summarize, validity is concerned with input of data, and integrity is concerned with the preservation of these data if they are accepted. Availability is concerned with the computer system operating correctly to allow access to these data when needed. It is a function of reliability and maintainability. Security is concerned with the prevention of unauthorized manipulation of the data (or programs). There is some overlap in these, but they are all oriented around the computer system itself. Privacy is concerned with the individual, whether the data should be collected at all, and, once collected, their protection from unauthorized release. Thus, concern for privacy implies a direct concern for data integrity, validity, and security and, perhaps, an indirect concern for availability.

Disaster Planning

Natural disasters, such as flood, fire, tornado, earthquake, etc., present a threat to all aspects of an organization's operations. Computer operations are no exception.

The usual precautions against fire should be taken. Since computer installations almost always use false floors to hide cabling and air conditioning ducts, there is an increased danger if a fire should start under the false floor. Detectors should be installed under the floor as a precaution against this possibility. Fire detectors are of two types: heat detectors and smoke detectors. Both types are used. The danger of fire is greater if printer paper and punch cards are stored in a hazardous manner in the computer center. Fire in the same building on a floor above the computer center may result in water damage.

Brownouts or blackouts may occur as the result of a natural cause, e.g. a lightning strike, or a nonnatural cause, e.g. extremely high demand on a hot summer day. The computer systems cannot operate on fluctuating or lowered voltage power sources. Backup generators and voltage regulation equipment may be used to minimize the effects of such occurrences.

Air conditioning failure may prevent a computer system from further operation, since the temperature and humidity requirements on computer equipment are relatively tight.

Alternative arrangements for processing in the event of an emergency should be made in advance. This means that the same computer model or a compatible model from the same family of computers must be available. Needed compilers, assembler, primary storage, etc., must also be available. Assurance that time will be made available on this backup system must be obtained. Usually, an exchange agreement is made, that is, organization A agrees to backup organization B if B loses its processing capability and vice versa. For a multilocation organization, backup arrangements may be made at another site within the organization. Service bureaus may be available. If the disaster is widespread, there is a possibility that the alternative processing location has also been damaged.

An alternative processing site is useless, however, unless backup copies of essential programs and data files can be made available. Such backup copies should always be stored at a source location remote from the using site. What is a reasonable distance depends on the possible dangers. Several miles might be adequate for protection against fire, but not for protection against earthquake or widespread flooding. Special forms, checks, bills, etc., must also be provided at the alternative site for processing to continue.

All emergency plans for dealing with disasters must be tested periodically in order to minimize the possibility of failure when the plan is implemented in an actual emergency.

Vital Records Program

The data used by an organization in its operation range from the critical to the merely convenient. In preparing a plan to cope with an emergency, data files must be categorized by the degree of criticality that they possess. The number of categories may vary, along with the descriptive names applied to these categories. As an example, the following three categories might be established:

1. **Vital**—those data that are absolutely essential to the continued operation of the organization. Without these files the organization cannot continue to exist. These files must be fully backed up and the backup must be frequently updated.
2. **Important**—loss of these data results in serious inconvenience, delays in processing, and increased costs are incurred to compensate for the loss. These files may be fully backed up, but not as frequently updated as the vital files.
3. **Convenient**—these data simplify operations, and their loss results in some increased costs. These files will probably not be backed up, or will be backed up at relatively longer intervals of time.

Reproducing files for backup involves costs; and the more frequent the reproduction the more costly the procedure is. Thus, the backup of more vital files will involve significantly greater costs than the backup of less vital files. Purges of unnecessary data from the files should be done regularly.

Backup and Recovery

Failure in the computer system presents the possibility of the loss of data ranging from one record to all or substantial parts of a large data base. After failure the computer system must be brought back up into operation, and any data lost must be restored. This process is called **recovery,** that is, the system must recover from the failure.

The recovery problems found in an on-line system are more complex than those faced in a batch system. Each will be discussed in turn.

Batch System Recovery

Checkpoint/restart operations are well-established in batch operations to recover when the system fails during the execution of an applications program. Without such procedures, a program (even one requiring a great deal of processing time) must be restarted and run through from the beginning again. With such procedures, a checkpoint is taken at various points during the execution of the program. This **checkpoint** consists of recording on a secondary storage device the current step in the program just executed, the contents of various data holding memory locations, and the contents of various registers. If the program should fail, restart may begin at the last checkpoint taken. The registers and memory locations are restored to their status at the checkpoint, and execution proceeds from that point.

A batch environment using magnetic tape as the file storage medium employs the **grandfather-father-son** concept of backup. In a magnetic tape operation a transaction file is processed against a master file, producing a new master file and some reports. Figure 14–1 illustrates this. As an example, the master file may be a personnel file; the transaction file may consist of master file changes, such as salary increases, address changes, income tax deduction changes, etc. Output consists of a new master file incorporating the changes,

Figure 14–1
Magnetic Tape Processing

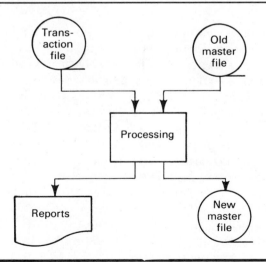

a set of management reports, and some error reports. The old master file and the transaction file are saved as backup. The old master file is called the father, and the new master file is called the son. Three generations, including the grandfather, are normally involved. If it is discovered that the new master file has not been created correctly, or it has been damaged, the old master (the father) and the transaction file may be rerun. If the old master file has also been damaged, its predecessor master file (the grandfather) and its predecessor transaction file may be used to begin a two-stage recovery.

If preservation of the data being stored is critical, two files may be created—each a duplicate of the other. If one is damaged, the other may be used to immediately provide needed data. (This approach may also be used on on-line systems.) Of course, additional time and file space is needed to create duplicate files. A programming error may damage both files, however.

On-Line System Recovery

In an on-line system, there does not directly exist both a before and an after version of an updated file. Only the records requiring updating are changed and reentered in the original file. However, at specified times, the contents of a data file may be copied or dumped onto magnetic tape. If the system fails and the original file is lost, then the file **dump** may be reloaded, and the system is restored to that point at which the dump was taken. The transactions that were entered since the dump, however, are not available in the backup file. This is accomplished through the use of logs or journals (discussed below).

Dumps may be very time-consuming. They do not have to be exact replicas of the data file, e.g. **garbage collection** (removal of data records that have been logically but not physically deleted) or moving of records from overflow areas to primary areas may be carried out at the time of the dump. Dumps are usually accomplished during off-hours. Sometimes only those parts of the files that have been changed are dumped. This is called **differential dumping.** Security of the data dumps is critical, and tapes containing them may be stored at an off-site location.

A **transaction log** may be kept that records all transactions entered into the system before further processing or updating is allowed to occur. By itself, however, this leaves the terminal user with an ambiguous updating status in the event of a failure. The failure may have occurred after the entry was made in the transaction log, but the file may or may not have been updated. As a result, a second log that records file updates is frequently kept. This is sometimes called a **file action journal.** Entries showing both the before and after status of the records updated are made. After reloading the most recent dump, these logs are used to bring the file up to date. If the dumps are not made frequently, the logs will become long.

Individual transactions must be identified uniquely. This can be done by having each operator assign a sequential code to each transaction entered, or by having the computer assign the codes. After updating the file, notification of a successful update should be given to the terminal user. Prompting of the user for the next transaction may also be made.

While the failure is being corrected and the file is being reconstructed, further transaction processing must be prevented. Depending on the circumstances, transactions occurring during this period of time are either held up until the system is ready to accept them again, or manual processing of the transactions is instituted with a later computer update.

Security of the data dumps is critical, and tapes containing them may be stored at an off-site location.

Physical Security

Data integrity and security are not possible without physical security. The installation itself must be protected from physical damage by deliberate sabotage or accident. Physical security implies that access to the computing center is limited to those with a legitimate need to be there. Nonpermanent personnel should be escorted at all times.

Basically the goals of physical security must be:

1. To minimize the possibility of an intruder gaining physical access to a computer system and/or its supporting facilities.
2. If physical access is gained, to insure that the intruder has a minimum amount of time to accomplish his objectives.
3. To minimize the possibility of accidental damage to the installation.

There are two main aspects to the dangers facing physical security: The possibility that the damage done by an intruder will be accomplished either upon or quickly after entry, and that once entry is gained a surreptitious compromise of the system will be attempted, perhaps over a period of time.

In its most elementary form, physical security is provided by the use of appropriate locks, alarms, and other detection devices. Unauthorized access through windows (if any), ducts, etc., must be prevented. Access through the normal means of entrance should be controlled. The best form of identification is personal recognition. If this is not practical, keys, badges, or other means of identification may be used. **Man-traps** are sometimes used in installations especially susceptible to sabotage. Figure 14–2 illustrates such an arrangement.

With a man-trap, the individual seeking entrance to the installation enters the trap through Door 1, which then locks. After proper identification Door 2 is opened, and entrance to the computer center gained. If identification is not accepted, the intruder is trapped.

Theft of tapes, disk packs, etc. may be hindered by attaching tags or adhesive tape that can be sensed by special detectors. These de-

Figure 14–2
Man-Trap

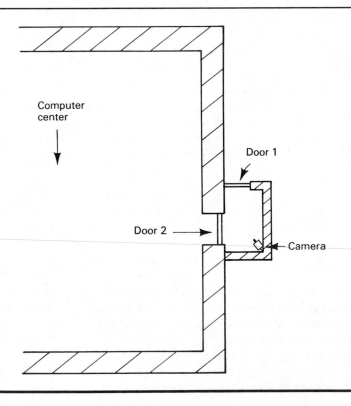

vices usually give off a low-level radiation that is sensed by the detectors. The detectors are emplaced on both sides of the exit. Such devices are now commonly used in department stores, where the tag is removed when the sale is rung up.

To hinder the intruder seeking one or more particular volumes, tapes and disk packs can be code numbered with no further identification. Thus, to obtain a particular tape or disk pack, the code itself must also be obtained.

Devices used to detect an intruder during nonoperating hours include:

1. Current-carrying tape or wire that is broken upon entry (commonly used on windows).
2. Use of a microswitch to make or break a circuit, e.g. on a door, under a carpet, etc.
3. Microphones to detect sound.
4. A beam of ultraviolet, infrared, or laser light that is interrupted.
5. Movement detectors.
6. Closed circuit television.
7. Time lapse cameras.

Alternative actions when an intruder is sensed include sounding an alarm, either in the room to perhaps frighten off the intruder before any damage is done, or at a guard station or police station. The exit might also be locked, if possible, until the arrival of a guard or police officer.

Cables leaving the installation may be shielded. Such cables require more time for an intruder to cut into. Cables internally pressurized with an inert gas are sometimes used. If the cable is broken into, the pressure drops and a monitoring system can notify the appropriate authority. Cables may also deliberately be run open to view, e.g. between buildings, so that an attempt to tap into them must be done in plain view.

Magnets can destroy data on tape or disk, but only if brought very close to the surface. Especially for tapes this may be a very time-consuming process. If such a danger exists, magnet detectors may be placed at the entrance to the installation.

Radar also has the capability of damaging data on ferrite type secondary storage devices. The potential for damage depends on the power output of the radar and its proximity to the computer installation. It would be prudent not to place an installation within the immediate vicinity of a radar.

Hardware Security

There are a number of security elements associated with the hardware itself. In multiprogrammed systems, more than one applications program with its associated data may reside in primary memory at the same time. It is critical that one program does not reference or transfer control to an area of primary memory reserved for another user. It is especially critical that an applications program not be able to successfully transfer control to any area occupied by the operating system. Thus, memory bounds on any partition must be established, and attempted violation of these bounds must generate an interrupt that returns control to the operating system. **Memory bounds** are usually established by registers holding a base address and the length of the partition assigned to a particular job.

Some commands are restricted only to the operating system. These are called the **privileged instruction set.** These instructions cannot be executed by an applications program. Any attempt to do so also generates an interrupt, which returns control to the operating system. These privileged instructions, as an example, might change the values in the memory bounds registers.

Residue control is concerned with sensitive data remaining in an area of primary memory after processing has been completed. It is possible for another user to enter this area and either deliberately or accidentally read these data. The solution is to write over the data with either zeros or random numbers, thus destroying the data before releasing the area to another program. In some instances the same area of core is always allocated to sensitive processing jobs; as a result, only this area need be overwritten. In paged systems, only areas occupied by one or more pages may have to be overwritten.

Handling of residue on secondary storage devices is more difficult. The processing time to overwrite areas on disk may be relatively high. Tapes may be degaussed (i.e. demagnetized) offline. Destruction of data in control unit buffers may also be carried out as a security precaution.

Storing files on removable media may provide some additional security, since sensitive material on a disk pack or a tape reel may then be locked in a safe or vault and removed only when needed.

All electronic and electromechanical devices give off radiation when used. This electromagnetic radiation may be intercepted by means of sophisticated equipment. The danger exists primarily with typewriter and CRT type terminals. Disadvantages are that the equipment may be expensive and difficult to obtain. In addition, it must be located relatively close to the equipment. Since the cost of such a technique is high, it would be a rare installation that would face such a threat. Countermeasures include placing the computer center and any remote teminals deep inside a building, and placing the equipment within a *screened** room. Equipment may also be designed to produce reduced radiation (but not completely eliminate it). Again, only in rare instances would such a redesign be warranted.

In an installation with no remote terminals, security is provided at the computer center and in its environment. When remote terminals are used in the system, the problem becomes more complex. Security may be provided for either the terminal or the user, or both.

Terminal devices may be secured by two general methods: The device itself may be placed in a secure location, e.g. in a locked room, or a code or an address of the device may be used as a part of a message sent to the central processor. This code or address can then be looked up in a table to determine its legitimacy and what access rights may be granted to the terminal.

There are some problems associated, however, with terminal identification. Since the identification is wired into the terminal, terminals are not interchangeable without rewiring. Thus, a terminal failure may result in a delay before it can be corrected.

The dangers of compromise on a remote terminal system are much higher than on a system limited to a central site only. As a result, in some applications sensitive data are not allowed to be accessed by remote terminals at all. If this is not feasible, then only a limited number of terminals may be authorized to access, and these may be placed under a high level of security. The Department of Defense requires on its installations that all terminals not authorized and protected for classified data must be disconnected from the system before processing begins.

After a terminal has been inactive for a specified amount of time, it is common for the system to shut the terminal off. This reduces the risk of an unauthorized person finding an unattended terminal already connected to the system.

Communication between central processing units remote from each other also requires identification procedures. Both the calling and the called CPU must be identified to each other.

In some installations, sensitive data may be processed only during certain times of the day or week. Other processing is not allowed at

* A screened room is one surrounded totally by a screen or mesh that will absorb any electromagnetic radiation (at least in a particular frequency range). Power lines, etc., may also be filtered.

these times, and special security measures may be taken. The advantage is that increased security may be provided when needed. The disadvantage is that flexibility of the users is restricted.

In some especially sensitive applications, two independent systems may be provided: One for sensitive applications and the other for nonsensitive applications. The advantages and disadvantages are clear.

User Authorization

User authorization methods are intended to minimize the possibility of an unauthorized user being granted access to the system. If the individual requesting access is identified as an authorized user, access is granted; otherwise, access is denied.

In an installation with no remote terminals, access is granted on the basis of personal recognition, usually combined with an account number and a password given to each authorized user. The account number and password are entered in the job control statements.

When remote terminals are used in the system, the problem is more complicated. Security can be provided for either the terminal, the user, or both. Terminal identification was discussed above.

Because of the limitations of terminal identification, user identification is more common. In some applications, user identification may be combined with terminal identification. User identification may be secured by two general methods:

1. By the insertion of a physical device such as a card, key, or badge into a reader connected to the terminal. The inserted device is read for a code, which may then be checked by the central processor for authorization in a table.
2. By the use of a password or code memorized by the user. The password or code is requested from the user. The user enters it, and it is checked in a table of authorized words or codes.

Additional research is being carried on in an attempt to develop means to use physical characteristics of the user as the basis for authorization. Voice prints, fingerprints, and palm geometry are possibilities.

However, in all cases involving physical characteristics, they must be coded for transmission over a telephone line and are thus subject to possible counterfeiting and deception. For example, tape recording a voice print by means of wiretapping and playing it back at a later time may result in an easy defeat of this method. Any such method will still probably have to be combined with other methods, e.g. passwords.

The use of physical devices inserted into a reader is common in factory information systems and automated bank tellers. The use of passwords and codes is more common in most other applications. Time sharing systems, for example, use this method.

Passwords and codes possess the same disadvantages as safe combinations, that is, users frequently write them down. If written down by the user, their security value is reduced almost to zero. When requested by the system, the user types in his or her password. Printing is frequently suppressed at the terminal so that no record is made on the printout. Another method involves overprinting, that is, several sequences of characters are printed over each other before the password is printed in the same position. Because of this overprinting, the password is unreadable.

As with safe combinations, passwords should be changed at intervals and whenever someone having access leaves the organization and no longer has the need for access. Sometimes passwords are given a fixed expiration date, or may be revoked after a given number of accesses have been made.

As a precaution, some systems, upon a successful access, will print out at the terminal the time the last access was made with the particular password. If the password has apparently been compromised, action may then be initiated to revoke its access rights.

In general, it is not a good practice to allow the user to select the password. Users will tend to select easy-to-remember passwords that may also be easy to compromise. The system should randomly generate passwords. Unfortunately, this is not consistent with the goal of having passwords easy to memorize. Some systems generate passwords randomly but in accordance with the single-letter, digram, and, possibly, trigram frequencies found in English. The result is a password that resembles English and is pronounceable (thus aiding memorization).

A brute force method to obtain access is to simply try all combinations of possible characters in the password until one is accepted by the system. For example, if the password consists of four alphabetic characters, try AAAA, then AAAB, etc. If the password is a legitimate word, then the number of possible combinations would be significantly reduced. In addition, if the total number of legitimate combinations was a significant percentage of the total number of possible combinations, then the number of trials would also be reduced.

Two approaches are generally taken to offset this trial and error method: The system may be designed to automatically disconnect the user after a given but small number of attempts have failed, e.g. two or three, or the password itself may be made arbitrarily long, making the number of possible combinations extremely large. The password may also be combined with a second code word. In this case, after obtaining the first word, the process must be repeated.

In practice, both methods are frequently combined. Neither, however, offsets the danger of wiretapping, or compromise resulting from a written copy of the password or words being seen by an unauthorized person. To offset this danger, a list of passwords may be provided to the user and entered in the computer. Each time the user attempts to gain access, he uses the next password in the list. The use of a previously used password will be rejected. Of course, the situation is now more complicated in that the user must either memorize or safeguard a list of passwords rather than one such password.

A second approach sometimes used to partially cope with the danger of wiretapping is to have a long password, but on any given attempted access the system randomly requests only certain characters of the password, e.g. with a 10-character password a particular access might require entering the 3d, 7th, and 8th characters. A wiretapper would require repeated interceptions before an unauthorized attempt could be made to enter the system.

Another approach is to obtain the answers to a prespecified list of questions from the user. These questions should be of a nature that only the user would reasonably be expected to know the answer, e.g. the first name of the user's mother-in-law, the name of his or her dog, etc. The questions and answers are stored in advance, and one or more may be selected randomly. The rationale is that a casual infiltrator would be unable to answer the questions, since they are individually oriented. Even after wiretapping, an infiltrator will probably receive a different random set of questions.

Yet another approach is to use a mathematical procedure known to the user and stored in the system. Upon signing on, the system generates a random number. The user must perform the mathematical operation on it and respond with the answer. If the user's answer matches the computer's calculation, access is authorized. The mathematical procedure should be simple but not obvious. For example, simply squaring the number is not very secure. Squaring the number and subtracting the current hour of the day plus two might be difficult for a wiretapper to deduce.

All of these methods have the same weaknesses. Users tend to write down passwords or procedures. Once they are written down, the system may be compromised. Badges, keys, and other inserted devices avoid this, but in turn may be lost. This is both an advantage and a disadvantage. If a badge, etc., is lost, it is obvious and action can be taken to cancel that device's authorization. With a password being compromised, it may not be known until it is too late to prevent widespread infiltration. With a lost badge or key, the system is open to unauthorized access until the device's authorization is cancelled.

Badges or keys may be combined with the use of passwords and codes. After the device has been inserted and accepted, a password or code must be provided. This password may be one authorized only for the badge or key accepted. Thus, both badge or key and the password or code must be compromised before an unauthorized user can gain access to the system.

Security of a password system requires security of the table of authorized passwords. The passwords in the table may be enciphered. Encipherment involves transforming the original set of characters into, in general, a different set of characters. This topic is discussed in greater detail below. The user enters the original password. It undergoes a transformation into its enciphered form, and this form is compared against those in the password table. Thus, even if the table is compromised, the original passwords are not.

Ideally a password should:

1. Be in use for a relatively short time (i.e. it should be changed frequently).
2. Be a relatively long character string.
3. Be easy to memorize.
4. Be one of a small number of legitimate passwords out of a large possible number.

Clearly not all of these characteristics can be achieved ideally at the same time. Some trade-offs must be made.

As discussed above, threats to data security may be of two types: accidental or deliberate. An unintentional compromise of data security is considered accidental, whereas an attempt to compromise undertaken for a specific purpose is considered deliberate. A successful accidental penetration of the system may lead to further deliberate penetrations of the system.

Deliberate attempts to infiltrate a system may consist of either passive or active techniques. **Passive infiltration** techniques do not enter directly into the system and, as a result, may be difficult to detect.

An example of a passive technique is wiretapping. This is practical and may be relatively easy to accomplish on systems that have remote terminals connected to the central processor over telephone lines. If the connection between the central processor and the terminal is made through the public telephone network, connections, in general, will differ each time they are made. As a result, wiretapping is effectively limited to the telephone lines and equipment before the first or after the last switching center. The telephone junction box entering a building is an obvious point.

Active infiltration techniques involve direct entry into the computer system. These techniques include:

1. **Browsing**—this is an infiltration involving an authorized user who seeks access to unauthorized data or programs.
2. **Masquerading**—this is an infiltration involving an unauthorized user who is using identification obtained through illegitimate means. In effect, an unauthorized user masquerades as an authorized user.
3. The use of **trapdoors**—these may be flaws introduced into either the hardware or the software accidentally or deliberately that will allow an unauthorized user to infiltrate the system or some part of it.
4. Interception and deception on a telecommunications line—a number of methods may be used including:

    (a) Using equipment on the line to pick up signals and then forwarding the signals (perhaps after modification). This is sometimes called a **piggy-back approach.**

    (b) Using equipment to cancel an authorized user's sign-off procedure and then continuing to operate in his or her place, or replacing a user on the line who has failed to sign off.
5. Other means such as the use of someone *on the inside* with the computer center, telephone company, a vendor, etc.

An additional authenticity check is sometimes built into a message. This check may be based on the content of the previous message. This may complicate some active forms of infiltration.

Cryptography

Cryptography, or **privacy transformation,** is a technique that can be used to provide additional security for either data stored on secondary storage devices or data transmitted over telecommunications lines.

Cryptography can be used as a final defense in the safeguarding of sensitive data. Even if the data become available to an unauthorized user, they are in an unintelligible form.

Data may be hidden in two general ways. These techniques are the concerns of the fields of steganography and cryptography. **Steganography** is concerned with hiding the existence of the data. The methods associated with this field are those usually associated with espionage in the popular mind. Examples are the use of invisible inks, microdots, spurt radio systems, etc.

Cryptography is concerned not with hiding the existence of data, but with making the data unintelligible to unauthorized persons by means of various transformations.

The following definitions are commonly accepted in the literature of cryptography:

Plaintext is data that are to be transformed into secret or disguised form. Plaintext data are intelligible to all knowledgeable in the language and the context.

Ciphertext is plaintext data after they have been transformed into a secret or disguised form. Ciphertext is unintelligible unless it can be transformed back into plaintext. Figure 14–3 illustrates this relationship. The transformation must be one-to-one and, obviously, must be reversible.

Figure 14–3
Cryptographic Transformations

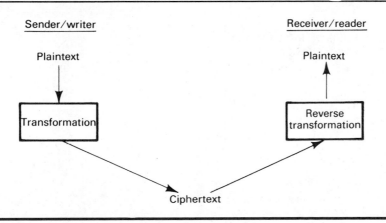

In cryptography there are two broad classes of transformations: transposition and substitution. In addition, characters in the plaintext may be substituted for one at a time (i.e. monographic) or two or more at a time (i.e. polygraphic). Before discussing each of these transformations, a code should be differentiated from a cipher.

Codes and Ciphers

A **code** involves the substitution of a set of characters for an idea, word, phrase, or entire message. There is no relationship between the length of the plaintext message and its encoded version. Nor is there a relationship between any part of the plaintext message and any part of the encoded message. In general, a code takes a variable number of characters and substitutes a fixed number of coded characters. A **cipher** takes a fixed number of characters and substitutes a fixed number of enciphered characters. Cryptography is concerned with ciphers.

The transformation between the plaintext and the encoded forms of the message and the reverse transformation cannot be accomplished by an algorithm of any kind. These are accomplished by referring to a **code book.** The plaintext message is looked up, as in a dictionary, for its encoded equivalent. A similar lookup is accomplished to reverse the transformation. As an example, code book

---

Figure 14–4
Example of Encoding

.
.
.
.

PERTINENT INFORMATION TO FOLLOW	XXABT
PREPARATIONS COMPLETE	DRILO
PREPARE GEOLOGICAL REPORT FOR	BROOZ
PREPARE TO SHIP	KAETN
PRESIDENT OF COMPANY	PORAN
PRESIDENT OF U.S.	UYMOD
PROXIMITY OF	SMIFL
QUEENSLAND	HHACK

.
.
.
.

---

entries are shown in Figure 14–4. Using these transformations, the plaintext message:

PREPARE GEOLOGICAL REPORT FOR QUEENSLAND. PERTINENT INFORMATION TO FOLLOW.

would be encoded as:

BROOZ HHACK XXABT

Decoding this message would involve referring to a codebook containing the entries shown in Figure 14–5.

Commercial codes have been in use almost since the development of the telegraph by Samuel Morse. The original purpose of these codes was not to insure security for the data transmitted over telegraph lines. Charges were based on the number of characters transmitted, and the codes represented abbreviations for longer strings of data. Thus, economics was the incentive. Related to this consideration and to security is the fact that a long message may be trans-

---

Figure 14–5
Example of Decoding

.
.
BROOZ   PREPARE GEOLOGICAL REPORT FOR
.
.
DRILO   PREPARATIONS COMPLETE
.
.
HHACK   QUEENSLAND
.
.
KAETN   PREPARE TO SHIP
.
.
PORAN   PRESIDENT OF COMPANY
.
.
SMIFL   PROXIMITY OF
.
.
UYMOD   PRESIDENT OF U.S.
.
.
XXABT   PERTINENT INFORMATION TO FOLLOW
.
.

formed into a relatively short code—thus making the breaking of the encoded message even more difficult.

A clear disadvantage of codes is that all parties must possess the code book. Codes may become rather comprehensive, running into the thousands or tens of thousands of entries. Thus, the code books may be bulky and present a security problem in their own right. The loss of a code book compromises all messages that have used it.

Transposition

In **transposition** the characters of the plaintext are rearranged into a different sequence. The characters remain the same, but their relative positions change. As an example:

COMPUTE

is transformed into:

TOUMPEC.

In normal English (or any other natural language) the letters of the alphabet do not occur with equal probability. Figure 14–6 shows the frequency distribution of the letters of the alphabet in normal English text. The frequencies range from approximately 13 percent for the letter E to 0.1 percent for the letter Z. Such frequencies can be estimated by taking a reasonable sized sample of text and making a count for each letter. The results of such samples produce remarkably similar results.

It should be noted that transposition methods do not change this frequency distribution. Therefore, an enciphered message with a frequency distribution similar to that of normal English text has probably undergone only a transposition transformation.* Transposition methods offer very little security against an unauthorized receiver of the message breaking it, that is, transforming it back into plaintext without previous knowledge of the original transformation.

Substitution

In substitution the characters of the plaintext are replaced by other characters, but each character still retains its relative position in the data.

There are two types of substitution: monoalphabetic and polyalphabetic substitution. The list of equivalents used to transform the

---

* It should also be noted that E. V. Wright in 1939 wrote a book entitled *Gadsby: A Story of over 50,000 Words Without Using the Letter E*. The book provides a precautionary note that the normal frequency distribution can be interfered with.

Figure 14–6
Frequencies of the Letters of the Alphabet in English

Alphabetical Order		Frequency Order	
A	73	E	130
B	9	T	93
C	30	N	78
D	44	R	77
E	130	I	74
F	28	O	74
G	16	A	73
H	35	S	63
I	74	D	44
J	2	H	35
K	3	L	35
L	35	C	30
M	25	F	28
N	78	P	27
O	74	U	27
P	27	M	25
Q	3	Y	19
R	77	G	16
S	63	W	16
T	93	V	13
U	27	B	9
V	13	X	5
W	16	K	3
X	5	Q	3
Y	19	J	2
Z	1	Z	1

Based on a count of 1,000.
Source: Sinkov[5]

plaintext into the ciphertext is called the **cipher alphabet. Monoalphabetic substitution** uses one cipher alphabet; **polyalphabetic substitution** uses more than one cipher alphabet.

In a monoalphabetic substitution, a plaintext character is always
transformed into the same ciphertext character. In a polyalphabetic
substitution, a plaintext character may be transformed into any one
of two or more ciphertext characters.

In a monoalphabetic substitution, there will exist a wide variation
in the character distribution of the ciphertext. This frequency distribution will approximate that found in normal plaintext English (or

that of any other natural language). The only difference between the ciphertext distribution and normal plaintext is in which characters are relatively common or uncommon. Frequency analysis is the key to the solution of this cipher. The **cryptanalyst,** that is, an individual trying to obtain the plaintext from the ciphertext without an *a priori* knowledge of the transformation, uses information on character frequencies, digram (two-letter pair) frequencies, and trigram (three-letter group) frequencies. Figures 14–7 and 14–8 show the frequency occurrences of the most common English digrams and trigrams. A monoalphabetic substitution offers little security.

In polyalphabetic substitution, there must be a rule or algorithm for selecting among the multiple cipher alphabets in the proper se-

Figure 14–7
Most Common English Diagrams

TH	1,582	RO	275
IN	784	LI	273
ER	667	RI	271
RE	625	IO	270
AN	542	LE	263
HE	542	ND	263
AR	511	MA	260
EN	511	SE	259
TI	510	AL	246
TE	492	IC	244
AT	440	FO	239
ON	420	IL	232
HA	420	NE	232
OU	361	LA	229
IT	356	TA	225
ES	343	EL	216
ST	340	ME	216
OR	339	EC	214
NT	337	IS	211
HI	330	DI	210
EA	321	SI	210
VE	321	CA	202
CO	296	UN	201
DE	275	UT	189
RA	275	NC	188

Based on a count of 25,000.
Source: Gaines[2]

Figure 14–8
Most Common English Trigrams

THE	1,182	TED	110
ING	356	AIN	108
AND	284	EST	106
ION	252	MAN	101
ENT	246	RED	101
FOR	191	THI	100
TIO	188	IVE	96
ERE	173	REA	95
HER	170	WIT	93
ATE	165	ONS	92
VER	159	ESS	90
TER	157	AVE	84
THA	155	PER	84
ATI	148	ECT	83
HAT	138	ONE	83
ERS	135	UND	83
HIS	130	INT	80
RES	125	ANT	79
ILL	118	HOU	77
ARE	117	MEN	76
CON	114	WAS	76
NCE	113	OUN	75
ALL	111	PRO	75
EVE	111	STA	75
ITH	111	INE	73

Based on a count of 25,000.
Source: Gaines[2]

quence. As the number of independent cipher alphabets increases, the character frequency distribution of the ciphertext approaches a uniform distribution. In an ideal transformation any ciphertext character has an equal probability of representing any plaintext character. In information theory terms, maximum information is needed to break such a cipher.

Polygraphic Systems

In a **polygraphic system** two or more characters are transformed as a group. In general, the security of a polygraphic system is greater than that of a monographic system. In general, it is also true that security increases as the number of characters transformed together increases. The main disadvantage of polygraphic systems is that if one character is garbled, the entire group will be garbled. Figure 14–9 summarizes the major cryptographic transformations.

Figure 14–9
Major Cryptographic Transformations

		Monographic	Polygraphic
Transposition		Plaintext characters are rearranged into ciphertext	
Substitution	Monoalphabetic	1 plaintext character always replaced by same ciphertext character.	Not Used
	Polyalphabetic	1 plaintext character replaced by different ciphertext characters.	2 or more plaintext characters replaced as a group by different ciphertext character groups.

Computer Based Systems

The most basic computer oriented approach to cryptography is built on work done by Vernam[6]. The **Vernam system** was first used in telegraphic communications. Two tapes were read into the transmitting machine: One tape contained the plaintext, the other contained a string of pseudorandom digits. A logical exclusive OR operation was performed and the ciphertext resulted.

Figure 14–10 defines the logical exclusive OR operation. This operation produces a 0 if both bits are the same, that is, both are 0 or both are 1. If the bits are different, it produces a 1.

Figure 14–10
Logical Exclusive OR Operation

String 1:	1100
String 2:	1010
Result:	0110

An advantage of the logical exclusive OR operation is that the same pseudorandom bit string is used to both encipher and decipher. This is illustrated in Figure 14–11.

Figure 14–11
Encryption/Decryption Example

Plaintext String:	0110 0001
Pseudorandom String:	1101 1010
Ciphertext String:	1011 1011
Ciphertext String:	1011 1011
Pseudorandom String:	1101 1010
Plaintext String:	0110 0001

In a computer environment the plaintext may be viewed as a bit stream that is combined with a pseudorandom bit string to produce the ciphertext. The pseudorandom bit string can be generated either by hardware or software. One approach involves storing this bit string on a demountable volume that is kept safeguarded and made available only under proper supervision.

Data Encryption Standard

The **Data Encryption Standard (DES)** is a new encryption standard required by the U.S. government to be met on all future systems that it purchases. The standard is required to be implemented in hardware for federal agencies, but may be implemented in software for nongovernment users. Implementation of the standard is required for all federal agencies except those handling classified or atomic energy data. These excepted agencies will continue to use their own cryptographic systems.

The DES uses a **product cipher,** that is, a cipher that uses alternating transposition and substitution. The system is polygraphic. It uses a 64-bit, or 8-byte, plaintext block combined with a 64-bit pseudorandom string (including 8 parity bits) to produce the ciphertext.

Public Key Cryptosystems

Diffie and Hellman[1] have introduced the concept of a **public key cryptosystem.** In such a system, the encryption algorithm and the decryption algorithm are different. The decryption must also be such that it cannot be deduced from the encryption, that is, the computational workload to do so would be prohibitive. In addition, the capability exists with a public key cryptosystem to obtain a **digital signature,** that is, authentication that the ciphertext received over a telecommunications line was, in fact, sent by the alleged transmitter and, in fact, cannot be denied by the transmitter.

In a public key cryptosystem, every member of the network has a personal cipher. The encryption algorithm for each member is published in a public directory, but the decryption algorithm is kept secret by each member. Any member of the network may encrypt data for any other member by using the receiver's public encryption algorithm. Only the receiver has the corresponding decryption capability.

A digital signature can be obtained as outlined in Figure 14–12. The sender carries out a two-stage transformation of the plaintext. First, the plaintext is *decrypted* by the sender's secret decryption

Figure 14–12
Obtaining a Digital Signature

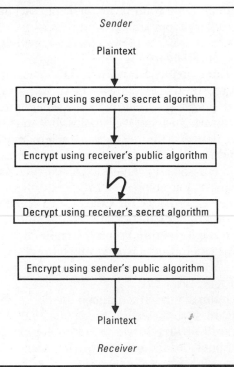

algorithm. This is not the usual meaning of decryption, but the algorithm operates on the data independent of what they represent. Second, the transformed data are encrypted, using the receiver's public encryption algorithm.

Upon receipt of the data, the receiver also carries out a two-stage transformation: The ciphertext is decrypted, using the receiver's secret decryption algorithm, and the data are then encrypted using the sender's public algorithm.

The plaintext that results is guaranteed to be from the sender, since only the sender had access to his or her secret algorithm. Similarly, only the receiver can decrypt the data with his or her own secret algorithm.

Access Management

Access management is concerned with authorization for accessing of sensitive files. Once granted access to a computer system, a user may be authorized further access only to selected programs or files. Conversely, a user may be denied access to some programs or files.

The simplest form of protection for sensitive files has already been mentioned. They may be stored on removable media, such as magnetic tapes or disk packs. These media are securely stored and mounted only at certain times when increased security and controls may be provided.

A check is frequently made at the time that a file is opened to determine that the attempted user is authorized access. A table containing all authorized users for each file may be kept by the operating system.

Another approach used in remote access systems is **dial-up and call-back.** Before a sensitive file is opened and access authorized, the computer operator is notified. The operator then telephones the alleged user and confirms by a password that the access is legitimate. Security for sensitive files may also be provided by storing a **lock-word** (password) with the file. When the file is opened as a result of a request from an applications program, the operating system may request a password from the computer operator. If it is provided and it matches the word stored with the file, access to the file may be granted to the applications program.

Access to a file may be granted to a user at various levels, e.g. file level, record level, field level, or segment (group of fields) level. Thus, the user may access the entire file if file level access is granted, but only certain records if record level access is granted. If access to a group of fields is granted, then only those fields may be accessed but in all records of the file.

Authorization for access on another dimension may also have several levels, e.g. the user may be authorized to:

1. Read records.
2. Read and change records.
3. Delete records.
4. Add records.

Operations Controls

Operations controls are those administrative or organizational procedures oriented toward data security in day-to-day operations. Though not technical in nature, they are essential for effective security and control.

Separation of responsibilities is standard practice in the handling of money. Similar division of duties should be practiced in the computer environment. Systems design, programming, and operations should be separate. Operators should not program; applications programmers should not do systems programming, etc. Program development may be separated from program maintenance. Responsibilities should always be split in such a way that attempted fraud will always require two or more persons to cooperate. There should, in general, not be any family relationships within the computer center staff. Personnel may be rotated among various duties. Thus, any suspicious activity by one individual stands an increased chance of being discovered by his or her successor. This also implies that more personnel must work together to carry out a fraud.

The tape and disk pack library must be closely controlled. All volumes should be accounted for at all times. They should be controlled and signed out for only by those with a legitimate need to use them. When not in use, all volumes should be kept under lock and key or under personal observation of the librarian.

Changes in programs must be carefully controlled and documented, or inadvertent modification or destruction of data may occur. Additionally, changes may offer the opportunity for fraud. All new production programs should undergo rigorous acceptance testing. In conversion from an old to a new system, parallel operations should be run using both systems until confidence is gained in the new system. Output from both systems should be compared.

Production programs may be randomly tested with **test decks.** The output resulting from these decks is known in advance and can be compared against the actual output. Any differences may indicate that an unauthorized (or undocumented) change in the program has been made.

A detailed **console log** may be kept and reviewed by supervisory personnel on a daily basis. The log may contain information on what programs were run, what files were accessed, actions of the computer operator, processor time used for each program run, downtime, and errors or access denials, especially from remote locations. Monitoring the use of processor time is important, since outside nonorganization work may be carried out on the computer system otherwise.

Threat monitoring is an approach in which the system records data that may be useful in determining the existence of attempted infiltration or patterns of infiltration. It can be designed to operate at various levels of detail, ranging from any simple failure to access to recording of all activities of all users.

Monitoring of system accesses may be either made known to, or kept from, users. Knowing that access attempts are monitored may discourage attempts such as browsing.

In some particularly critical or sensitive applications, the system might be designed to delay access while the operator or a security officer may be notified that a possible infiltration attempt is under way at a particular terminal.

It is to be normally expected that mistakes on the part of users will occur. These mistakes may result in an apparent infiltration attempt. If the normal number or pattern of such attempts changes, then this may be an indication that a serious attempt is being made (or has succeeded) to infiltrate the system. Of course, it may also mean that a new user is learning how to use the system. Threat monitoring may also indicate areas for additional training for users if patterns of honest errors on their part are discovered.

The ability to invalidate a password and authorize a new password quickly is essential. It is almost useless to discover that a password has been compromised if it takes days to effectively make a change to the authorized password list.

Printouts of sensitive programs or data should be destroyed, e.g. by shredding or burning, before disposal. This practice should include debugging runs. It is useless to take precautions (perhaps costly precautions) when copies of the data or programs to be protected are available in a wastebasket. Disposal of carbon paper, printer ribbons, etc., that have handled sensitive material must also be properly carried out.

Good security ultimately rests on the personnel involved with the computer system. If the personnel take their responsibilities seriously, security will be good; if they do not, security will be lax. Management must enforce security discipline for a high level of security consciousness.

Conclusions

There is a trade-off involved in data security. The tighter the security procedures are, the less convenient and the less accessible the computer system is to its users. Thus, convenience must be given up as security increases. Clearly, if security is too tight, users may make a less than optimum use of the computer facilities available. There is also an increasing temptation for users to take informal shortcuts with the system if the formal procedures become too complex. These shortcuts may result in serious compromises.

The degree of protection afforded a system depends on the possible loss incurred by its compromise. Protection incurs costs and, therefore, a balance must be achieved. Thus, a cost/benefit analysis is appropriate. After evaluating the costs of potential losses, the probabilities of their occurrence must also be estimated so that a reasonable balance between security costs and expected losses may be attained. It should be observed that not all losses are easy to estimate, e.g. the loss of public confidence in a banking institution that has been the victim of extensive fraud or embezzlement.

IBM[3] observes: "Both the casual viewer at an open door and the more sophisticated intruder with a telephoto lens or parabolic microphone can be deterred when system components are kept away from open windows, doors, and the glass walls that frequently surround machine rooms." Thus, many threats may be averted through relatively simple, inexpensive means. It may be much easier for an intruder to buy a copy of a sensitive file from a member of the computer center staff than to implement sophisticated, relatively expensive techniques to obtain a copy of the same file. If the large, obvious holes in the security net are not plugged, it is a waste of time to worry about small holes.

There is no absolutely secure system. Given enough time and enough resources, any system can be broken. An effective security system makes the cost for an intruder higher than the value of the compromise. A final general principle is that the number of persons required to be trustworthy should be minimal.

References

1. Diffie, W., and M. E. Hellman. "New Directions in Cryptography." *IEEE Transactions on Information Theory* IT-22, No. 6 (November 1976), pp. 644–54.
2. Gaines, H. F. *Cryptanalysis.* New York: Dover Publications, Inc., 1939.
3. International Business Machines Corp. *Security Considerations for Operation Management.* 1970.
4. Martin, J. *Security, Accuracy, and Privacy in Computer Systems.* Englewood Cliffs, N.J.: Prentice-Hall, 1973.
5. Sinkov, A. *Elementary Cryptanalysis.* New York: Random House and The L. W. Singer Company, 1968.
6. Vernam, G. S. "Cipher Printing Telegraph Systems for Secret Wire and Radio Telegraphic Comunications." *Journal of the American Institute of Electrical Engineers* 45 (February 1926), pp. 109–15.

Additional Readings

Bosworth, B. *Codes, Ciphers, and Computers.* Rochelle Park, N.J.: Hayden Book Company, Inc., 1982.

"Computers, Crime and Privacy—A National Dilemma. Congressional Testimony from the Industry." *Communications of the ACM* 27, No. 4 (May 1984), pp. 312–21.

Denning, D. *Cryptography and Data Security.* Reading, Mass.: Addison-Wesley Publishing, 1982.

Fernandez, E. B.; R. C. Summers; and C. Wood. *Database Security and Integrity.* Reading, Mass.: Addison-Wesley Publishing, 1981.

Hansen, J. V. "Audit Considerations in Distributed Processing Systems." *Communications of the ACM* 26, No. 8 (August 1983), pp. 562–69.

Hsiao, D. K.; D. S. Kerr; and S. E. Madnick. *Computer Security.* New York: Academic Press, 1979.

Kahn, D. *The Codebreakers.* New York: Macmillan, 1967.

Krauss, L. I., and A. MacGahan. *Computer Fraud and Countermeasures.* Englewood Cliffs, N.J.: Prentice-Hall, 1979.

Meyer, C. H., and S. M. Matyas. *Cryptography.* New York: John Wiley & Sons, 1982.

Murray, T. J. "Cryptographic Protection of Computer-Based Data Files." *MIS Quarterly* 3, No. 1 (March 1979), pp. 21–28.

Parker, D. B. *Crime by Computer.* New York: Charles Scribner's Sons, 1976.

Review

1. What does the term *work factor* mean?
2. What does the term *graceful degradation* mean?

3. Differentiate between integrity and security.
4. Describe a checkpoint/restart procedure.
5. What is the grandfather-father-son concept?
6. Briefly describe the procedures needed for on-line system recovery.
7. What is a man-trap?
8. What is the privileged instruction set?
9. *a* What is one advantage of using a physical device for user identification?
   b What is one disadvantage?
10. *a* What is one advantage of using a password for user identification?
    b What is one disadvantage?
11. Describe how a mathematical procedure could be used as a basis for user identification.
12. Differentiate between browsing and masquerading.
13. Differentiate between cryptography and steganography.
14. Differentiate between a code and a cipher.
15. Differentiate between transposition and substitution.
16. Differentiate between monographic and polygraphic systems.
17. Break the following ciphers.

    a SEDWH   QJKBQ   JYEDI   OEKXQ   LURUU
         DQRBU   JEIKS   SUIIV   KBBOR   HUQAJ
         XYIDE   JJEEI   EFXYI   JYSQJ   UTSYF
         XUH

    b BJFDM   ZPQGZ   PUJFO   XJQSZ   TAEAA
         FZEGA   PJOQB   BAOOH   QGGXE   MAZIP
         SUOCJ   MAOJK   SUOPU   BZPAR   BUKSA
         M

18. What is the Data Encryption Standard?
19. Describe how a digital signature may be obtained in a public key cryptosystem.
20. What is a lockword?
21. What is treat monitoring?

Systems Analysis

Introduction

The evolution of a systems project from the original idea to full implementation and operation can be a long and complex process. It is also a process that can be filled with many pitfalls and opportunities for mistakes.

The development of any new systems project should occur under the umbrella of the organization's EDP master plan. The **master plan** is a document that lays out those projects over the next few (perhaps five) years that are planned for development. All of the projects contained within the master plan have been selected as those that should contribute significantly to the achievement of the organization's overall goals and objectives. In addition, the projects should be consistent with each other and placed within a time frame for completion. A master plan can and does change. However, changes must be reviewed, and their implications for the overall plan and for the organization need to be recognized.

Motivation for the initiation of a systems project may come from a number of sources. These include:

1. Problems or inefficiencies may exist in a current system. This may be true whether the system is manual or computer based. The infor-

mation requirements in any organization change over a period of time. These changes must be reflected in the existing systems that produce the information. Sources of data, data collection methods, assumptions of relevancy, etc., are all subject to change. As a result, the systems that use these data may require modifications.

2. With experience the users of an information system may discover additional ways in which the system may assist them. Changes can be made in a system to serve its users better.

3. New technology may provide a means of providing information more efficiently or less expensively. In addition, new technology may make practical the extension of the current system.

4. Integration of current systems may be deemed advisable. As an example, the availability of a data base management system will lead to extensive work in preparing the data base, its schema, and the required subschemas.

5. A manual system may be converted over to a computer based system. This may be due to the greater efficiencies possible in the computer based system or to overloading of the manual system, e.g. a significant and steady increase in the number of transactions.

A system is usually thought of as undergoing a life cycle of its own. This is illustrated in Figure 15–1. The **systems life cycle** views the maturation of a system as going through the stages of systems analysis, systems design, systems implementation, and systems operation. The cycle begins with a feasibility study, which precedes a formal systems analysis. The feasibility study is frequently considered part of systems analysis and, as a result, is included in this chapter. Systems design and implementation are followed by operation of the new (or revised) system. This cycle may repeat, that is, implementation and operation of a system may be followed at some later date by a new feasibility study, which is followed by a new analysis effort, etc. The systems life cycle model essentially views systems development as an evolutionary process, that is, a process that does not reach a clear point at which further changes do not occur.

The importance of a thorough, rigorous, and objective stepping through the systems life cycle cannot be overemphasized. The starting or continuing of a project that should never have had resources assigned to it only wastes these resources. Moreover, it prevents these resources from being assigned to other projects that may provide many benefits to the organization. In a real sense, the opportunity costs of this misallocation may be very high.

Figure 15–1
Systems Life Cycle

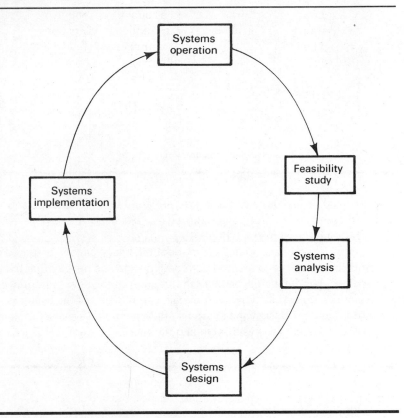

It may be unimportant how efficiently the software, the hardware, and the personnel resources are used in a system. If the system has been designed for the wrong purpose, then it is a failure.

As a general rule: *The earlier an undetected error is made in the systems life cycle, the more devastating will its impact be, and the more expensive in resources will its correction be.*

An objective of systems analysis is the development of a set of systems requirements for the new or revised system or systems under study. These requirements are then transformed into a clean and unambiguous statement of the specifications for the system to meet these requirements. These specifications outline *what* the system is to do, not

---

Figure 15–2
Main Components of the Systems Life Cycle

Feasibility study

Systems analysis
    Development of systems requirements
    Development of detailed specifications

Systems design
    Design
    Development $\left\{\begin{array}{l}\text{Data}\\\text{Hardware}\\\text{Software}\\\text{Procedures}\end{array}\right.$

Systems implementation

---

how to do it. Unless there can be agreement on the requirements, and unless these requirements can be turned into clear specifications, a systems design effort should not begin.

Systems design deals with how to meet the specifications prepared in systems analysis. It is concerned with both design and development. Systems implementation deals with the transfer of the new system over to its users. Figure 15–2 outlines the main components of the systems life cycle. Systems design and systems implementation are discussed in Chapter 16. Systems analysis, including the feasibility study, is the subject of this chapter.

The Feasibility Study

A **feasibility study** is a preliminary investigation into a proposed systems project to determine whether or not the project is practical and should be approved. The feasibility study occurs before a systems analysis effort is begun. If the feasibility study results in a positive recommendation, then the project may be phased into the master plan. The systems analysis phase may begin almost immediately or at a later date, depending on other priorities and the resources available.

Burch et al.[1] list five dimensions of feasibility:

1. Technical feasibility.
2. Economic feasibility.

3. Legal feasibility.
4. Operational feasibility.
5. Schedule feasibility.

The feasibility study must look at all five aspects in order to make a balanced and meaningful recommendation.

Technical feasibility is concerned with the practicality and availability (or development potential) of the hardware and software that will be necessary to implement the project. Of course, at the time of the feasibility study, specifications do not exist on the details of the hardware and software requirements. The evaluation, as a result, must be carried out on the basis of whether the general hardware and software resources that will be needed are within the state of the art and within the organization's technical capability.

Economic feasibility is concerned with cost/benefit analysis. This requires estimates on both the expected costs associated with, and the expected benefits in monetary terms resulting from, implementation of the project. Obviously, projected benefits must exceed projected costs to justify the project. Benefits can be divided into those that are tangible and those that are intangible. **Tangible benefits** can, with relative ease, be estimated in dollars. Examples are reduction in personnel, increased output, better cash flow, etc. **Intangible benefits** are more difficult to quantify (but may be just as real as tangible benefits). Examples are improved service, higher morale, better organizational image, etc. Although the estimation of tangible benefits is also subject to abuse, intangible benefits are particularly susceptible to manipulation to justify the acceptance or rejection of a project. Caution and objectivity are especially needed in their estimation. If a project can be justified on the basis of tangible benefits alone, it is on a much firmer basis than if it is justified on the basis of both tangible and intangible benefits.

Legal feasibility is concerned with evaluating whether a proposed system meets all legal and regulatory requirements that apply. For example, a payroll system must be able to withhold federal income tax (and state or city income tax, if applicable) and social security payments. It must also be able to produce a statement of earnings for each employee every January.

Operational feasibility is concerned with whether the proposed system can be successfully fitted into the organizational structure. Changes in the organization may be required, and these changes should be identified.

Schedule feasibility is concerned with estimating the time required from approval to final implementation of the system. Schedule constraints may dictate one development approach over another. For example, software may be obtained off-the-shelf from a vendor instead of developed in-house in order to save time on the schedule and thus meet organizational needs.

During the feasibility study, estimates must be made without the assistance of the analysis and design efforts that may follow. These estimates are *first cut* and subject to change as the project progresses. Nevertheless, the best estimates possible based on few details are needed. The outcome of the feasibility study should be a written report that is reviewed by management. Management may decide to terminate the project, approve further work (i.e entry into the systems analysis phase), call for modification of the proposal, or request further study.

Systems Analysis

If the feasibility study recommends proceeding with the project and this is approved by management, systems analysis is the next phase in the cycle. The alternative decisions may be to terminate the project or to return it for additional study.

Systems analysis is the phase of the systems life cycle concerned with study of the current system, delineation of relevant nonphysical constraints, and the production of a *statement* of the specifications required for a new system. User needs are studied during this phase, and specifications for the system required to meet these needs are laid out in detail.

Systems analysis usually involves a study of the current system (if one exists) and requires a clear understanding of that system. A new system does not, however, have to resemble an old system. Computerizing or making more efficient a system that meets the wrong requirements is not a useful undertaking. It is essential that the basic requirements of a system under development be clearly specified. Anything less than this increases the probability of failure.

The following discusses a number of techniques and tools used in systems analysis. Some of these techniques and tools may also be involved in the systems design phase.

Interviewing

Interviewing those who are involved in the current system and those who may be involved in the new system is probably one of the most important tools in gathering information for systems analysis.

The interview is sometimes conducted by a user/analyst team to provide a better balance between the technical and the user points of view. Interviewing provides an opportunity to gather information directly from users and fill in gaps in formal documentation.

It is a rare (if not nonexistent) situation in which all of the details of the operation of a system are well-documented. Poor, sloppy, or obsolete documentation makes systems analysis more difficult and more time-consuming. Even with good documentation there are always exceptions and details that can only be obtained from those directly involved in the operation of the system.

The analyst must be concerned with the flows of data within the current system and the uses to which these data are put. It is necessary to understand the decisions supported by the system and the information needed to assist in this decision making.

It is important that all facts be cross-checked. The interviewee may be in error, may have misunderstood a question, or may be protective of some local interest within the organization. There may also be a tendency on the part of the interviewee to guess at an answer rather than admit ignorance.

The interviewer must be careful that questions do not lead, or suggest the right answer. A leading question may cause the interviewee to give what is perceived to be a desired answer.

Copies of all documents referenced, e.g. report forms, invoices, etc., should be obtained. The source and the receiver of each document must be determined. For multiple copies, the destination of each copy must be confirmed.

An agenda should be at least informally prepared by the analyst before each interview. This insures that all important questions can be touched upon during the meeting. This also helps the analyst to keep the discussion on relevant matters if the interviewee verbally rambles. An individual may have to be interviewed more than once as the analyst's knowledge of the current system increases.

It is a good policy to make notes immediately after the interview, since extensive note taking during the interview may be distracting to the interviewee. Questionnaires may be used to supplement the interview. If they are used, the questions should be clear and unambiguous. Direct observation of a procedure or sampling may also be used as supplements.

System Flowcharts
Flowcharts are one method of documenting the logic and the components of a system. They may provide an overview of the old system

and may be the only documentation that exists for that system. Flowcharts fall into two categories: program flowcharts and system flowcharts.

A **program flowchart** is a graphical representation of the logic contained in a program. A **system flowchart** is a graphical representation of the programs, files, and manual procedures contained in a system. The system flowchart outlines on a macro scale the processing elements contained in a system. It identifies the programs involved in the system, but does not show the logic contained within any program. Appendix 15–1 gives the definitions of some of the more commonly used flowcharting symbols.

Figure 15–3 shows a system flowchart for a simplified order entry system. Orders are received, and a check is made to determine if they are complete. If an order is not complete, it is sent to the sales department for follow-up with the customer. If the order is complete, it is entered on a key-to-disk system. The paper orders are filed offline (in a filing cabinet). An edit routine accepts as input the output tape of orders and a disk file containing permanent validation data, e.g. part numbers, etc. The run produces a new disk file containing the valid order data and an error listing, which is sent to the data entry group for correction. The validated orders are sorted and then run against the master order file. The order entry program updates the master order file and produces hard copy shipping orders for the warehouse and a backorder report for the sales department. (A backorder covers the case where legitimate parts are temporarily out of stock. The parts are shipped later when received in the warehouse.) There are other supporting efforts not included here, e.g. updating inventory, cancelling orders, credit checking, etc. The internal logic of these three programs, that is, the edit routine, the sort routine, and the order entry routine, are contained in individual program flow charts.

Flowcharts become unwieldy for larger programs or systems. As a result, they are tending to be replaced by some of the newer structured techniques, such as data flow diagrams or Warnier/Orr diagrams (which are discussed below).

Decision Tables

A **decision table** is a tool to represent complex logic in the form of a table. An advantage of decision tables is that they allow logic to be represented compactly and in an easy-to-read tabular form. The analyst can use these as devices to understand logical decision making in a system, to find inconsistencies in that logic, and to uncover

Figure 15–3
System Flowchart

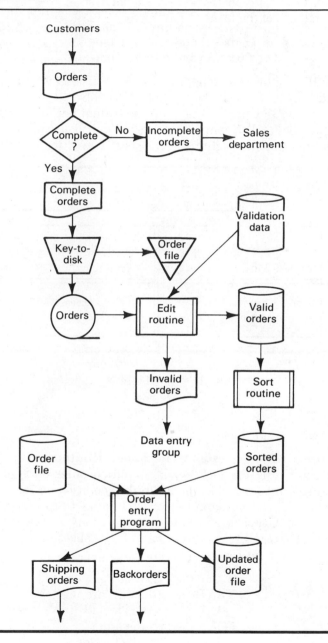

n the logic. Decision tables also tend to be understood and ᴈd more easily than flowcharts by users. As a result, they may ᴉmmunication between user and analyst.

table is of the form:

> **IF** these conditions are true
> **THEN** take the action indicated.

Figure 15–4 shows the general form of a decision table. The table is divided into quadrants. The top half of the table presents the conditions (i.e. the IF components), and the bottom half presents the actions (i.e the THEN components). The stub half consists of short descriptions, and the right half consists of a selection of entries.

Figure 15–4
General Form of a Decision Table

Condition stubs	Condition entries
Action stubs	Action entries

There are three types of decision tables:

1. A limited entry table.
2. An extended entry table.
3. A mixed entry table.

Figure 15–5 provides an example of a **limited entry decision table** containing the logic for a simplified order entry operation. There are three allowable entries in the *condition entries* quadrant: **Y** (for yes), **N** (for no), and — (for irrelevant). In the action entries quadrant an **X** appears in the relevant positions. A rule consists of a series of *ANDs* in the condition half of the table followed by one or more actions. Rule 1 reads as follows:

> **IF** the order is complete
> **AND** the order data are valid
> **AND** payment is included
> **THEN** process the order
> **AND** prepare the invoice.

Figure 15–5
Limited Entry Decision Table

	1	2	3	4	5
Order complete	Y	Y	Y	N	Y
Order data valid	Y	Y	Y	—	N
Payment included	Y	N	N	—	—
Credit approved	—	Y	N	—	—
Process order	X	X			
Hold order				X	X
Reject order			X		
Prepare invoice	X	X			

Rule 5 reads:

> **IF** the order is complete
>> **AND** the order data are not valid
> **THEN** hold the order

If a number of rules all result in the same action, one approach taken is to list all of the other rules and then encompass the common action rules in the condition entries under **ELSE.**

Figure 15–6 is an example of an **extended entry decision table.** In such a table parts of the stubs are included in the entries. Rule 2 states that:

> **IF** the quantity on hand is less than 100
>> **AND** the unit price is greater than $1.00
> **THEN** place a rush order
>> **AND** notify the Purchasing Department.

Figure 15–6
Extended Entry Decision Table

	1	2	3	4
Quantity on hand	<100	<100	<250	E
Unit price	≤$1	>$1	>$5	L
				S
				E
Place order	Regular	Rush	Regular	
Notification		Purchasing		None

An ***ELSE*** rule is also contained in this table. This rule states that for any other combination of condition stubs nothing is done. The main advantage of the extended entry table is that it can be more compact than the limited entry table for the same application.

A **mixed entry decision table** contains elements of both the limited entry and the extended entry tables. It is the most flexible of the three alternatives.

An action stub may indicate a transfer to a second table where further logic is described. As a result, logic may be represented in a hierarchy of tables.

Data Flow Diagrams

A **data flow diagram** is a graphical analysis tool that shows the various flows of data occurring within a system. It does *not* provide control information.

Figure 15–7 shows a simple data flow diagram. The diagram consists of arrows representing data flows, e.g. ***ORDER-DATA.*** The data

Figure 15–7
Data Flow Diagram

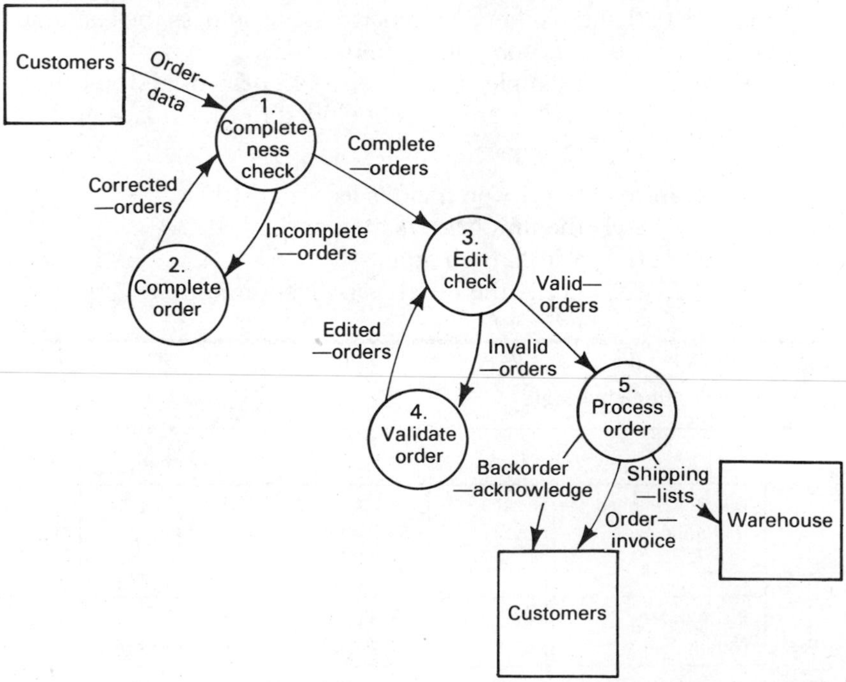

flows are transformed or converted by processes, e.g. *1. COM-PLETENESS CHECK.* Processes are represented by circles (or bubbles). A data flow diagram is sometimes also called a bubble chart. Data sources and sinks (outside the system under study) are represented by squares.

There may be more than one data flow between two processes. This implies that the two sets of data do not occur together, e.g. one data flow may occur daily, but another data flow may occur only as required. All data flows must be labelled and given a unique data name. In effect, the data flows are the interfaces between processes.

The data flow diagram may also undergo decomposition. This is the basis for establishing a hierarchical partitioning of the system. Figure 15–8 shows the decomposition of the *5. PROCESS ORDER* process of Figure 15–7. The fourth (and only remaining) symbol of data flow diagrams also appears in this figure. A straight line represents a data store. For example, *INVENTORY STATUS* is a data store. A data store may have data flowing both in and out of it. How-

Figure 15–8
Second Level Data Flow Diagram

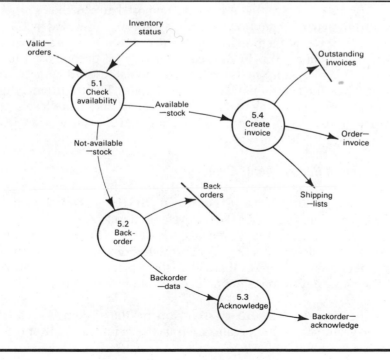

ever, minor flows are not represented. For example, although the search key (a form of data) is used to retrieve data from a file, it is not included in the data flow diagram. The data store does not necessarily represent a computer based file. It is a store for data and may be as simple as a file cabinet in a manual environment.

The decomposition approach contained in the data flow diagram methodology is highly compatible with modularization. In addition, the appropriate degree of detail is available for different viewers. Although the nontechnical user may meaningfully review the data flows at a higher level, a narrower but more detailed review may be carried out by an individual responsible for only part of the system. It is easy to match the level of detail to the reviewer. If more detail is needed for a process, the next level of that process only can be reviewed. This flexibility should be contrasted with flowcharting. With a flowchart a reviewer gets all detail or no detail. An intermediate level of detail is not practical.

If the highest level diagram contains only one process and the data flows interface it with the various external sources and sinks as in Figure 15–9, it is usually called a **context diagram.** It shows the system under study within the context of its environment.

At the lowest level the bubbles are called **functional primitives.** They are the processes that are not decomposed any further.

A variation of the data flow diagram approach is provided by Gane and Sarson[2] Using their approach, the data flow diagram is decomposed to only one level. In rare cases, it may be decomposed to a third level. As a result, the Gane and Sarson data flow diagrams are broader than the traditional data flow diagrams. The traditional diagrams are, in general, deeper, that is, decomposed to more levels. In addition, the process symbol in the Gane and Sarson version is a square with rounded corners.

Structured Requirements Definition

Structured requirements definition is the systems analysis component of the **Data Structured Systems Development (DSSD)** methodology. DSSD is a systems development technique marketed by Ken Orr and Associates, Inc. It uses **Warnier/Orr** diagrams as the basis for its graphical presentations. The Orr methodology is output-oriented; therefore, the objective of structured requirements definition is to produce the output requirements of the system.

As the first step, an **entity diagram** for the system is created. The diagram shows the organization at the center and all entities

Figure 15–9
Context Diagram

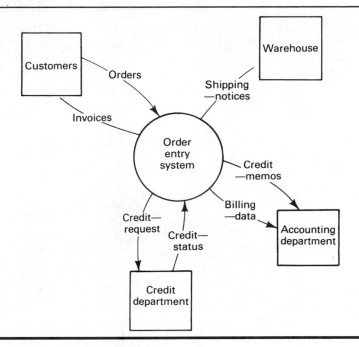

(other organizational units) with which it interacts around it. Various interactions between the organization and the other entities are defined. Figure 15–10 gives a simple illustration of this. Each of the transactions that occur between the organization and another entity is named on the diagram.

An entity diagram is created for each user in the system. These diagrams are integrated into a single user entity diagram. This boundary defines the application. Figure 15–11 illustrates this. Obviously, there are a number of additional transactions that could be included. In a real-world application, a much more complex set of diagrams would be required for this application. Those transactions crossing the application boundary define the objectives of the system.

Warnier/Orr diagrams are then used to produce an **assembly line diagram.** This diagram is a means of creating and describing the functions to be carried out in the application. This diagram incorporates the functional flows necessary to achieve the stated objec-

Figure 15–10
Entity Diagram

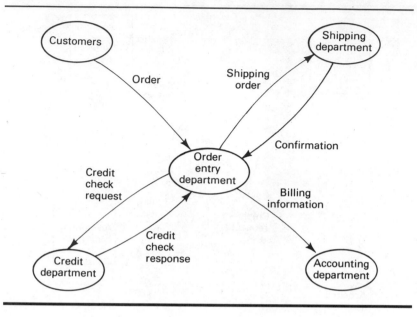

tives of the system. Figure 15–12 illustrates a simplified main-line assembly line diagram. It is main-line in the sense that it shows the main, or primary, flow through the system. The scope of the proposed system is also clarified at this stage, that is, it may be decided that the new system's boundaries may be changed to encompass a more limited application. A further and more detailed breakdown of the functional processes contained in the main-line diagram under study is made. Each process is broken into functional steps and functional subsystems. A **functional step** is a simple, well-defined task. A **functional subsystem** is a more complex set of tasks that may be broken down into greater detail.

The final phase of structured requirements definition is the definition of the system's outputs. This detailed definition of the proposed system's outputs is the final step in the systems analysis phase, and also serves as the input to the systems design phase of the DSSD (Warnier/Orr) methodology.

Figure 15–11
Integrated Entity Diagram

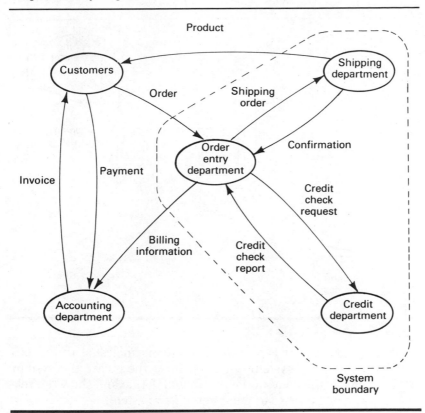

Data Dictionaries

A **data dictionary** is a reference source that contains information on data and the relationships among the data in a system. A data dictionary is always used with data flow diagrams. It can also be used in an environment without data flow diagrams. The data dictionary may be manual or computer based. For computer based systems, a number of software packages are available. It is also not uncommon for larger information systems organizations to develop their own data dictionary software. A data dictionary is also frequently used in conjunction with data base management systems.

Figure 15–12
Main-Line Assembly Line Diagram

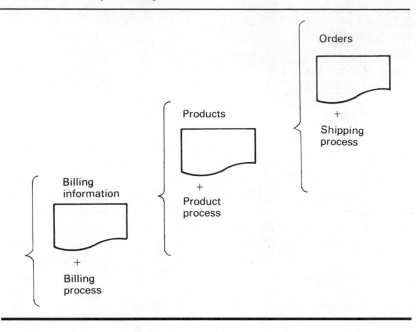

The data dictionary is built by the systems analyst as the specifications for the new system are defined. At the end of the systems analysis phase, the data dictionary should define and show the relationships among every data item in the new system.

The data dictionary contains an entry for every data flow in a data flow diagram. An entry in the dictionary lists the data components for each data flow. For example, the data flow **CUSTOMER-AC-COUNT** may be shown to consist of **CUSTOMER-NUMBER, CUSTOMER-NAME,** and **CUSTOMER-ADDRESS.** If these are not elementary data items, their components may be determined by retrieving their entries in the dictionary. As a further example, the entry **CUSTOMER-ADDRESS** may consist of **STREET-ADDRESS, CITY, STATE,** and **ZIP CODE.** For each elementary item, a data description is provided. This description is most frequently made in a COBOL-like manner. For example, **CUSTOMER-NUMBER** may be described as **9(6),** meaning it is a six-digit numeric data item. **STATE** may be described as **AA,** that is, as a two–alphabetic character data item. The data in the dictionary are decomposed in a manner analogous to the decomposition carried out in the data flow diagrams.

The use of a data dictionary also prevents redundant data naming. When a new data name is assigned, it is entered in the data dictionary. If that name has already been assigned, the new assignment is rejected. If the name is unique, the assignment is made and entered in the dictionary for future reference. At any time, the data components of a data flow may be easily determined. Changes in data definitions can also be controlled.

The data dictionary can also show that the same data are called by different names, e.g. two user groups may use different terms for the same data. With the data dictionary, both terms can be used and recognized as referring to the same data.

In the context of a data base management system, the data dictionary also provides to the user or the analyst a reference of all available data contained in the data base. This serves as a guide to what data are available and under what data name access is possible.

In addition to the data flows, the contents of data stores are also contained in the data dictionary. Data flows into a data store and data flows out of that store must be reconciled. If a data element enters the store and never leaves, it is useless. Similarly, if a data element is required in a flow out and it never enters the store, a modification is required in the diagram.

Scheduling

Within the systems analysis phase, the project is progressively defined in greater detail. Scheduling is carried out only after sufficient details on the project are known and a detailed work plan can be created. There are two commonly encountered scheduling tools: Gantt charts and PERT networks.

Gantt Charts

A **Gantt chart** is a bar chart that plots tasks in a project against time. Figure 15–13 shows a sample Gantt chart. In this example there are five tasks in the project, labelled A through E. The entire project is estimated to take 13 weeks. The schedule calls for task B to begin when task A is completed. Task C overlaps the end of task B and the beginning of task D. Task D will begin at week 7 and will end at week 10. At some points in the schedule, work on more than one task will be undertaken at the same time. Manpower scheduling must obviously reflect this.

Figure 15–13
Gantt Chart

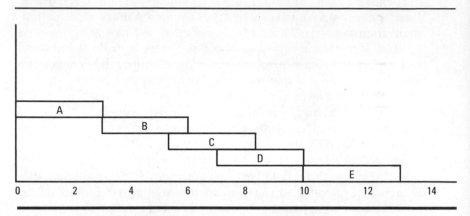

The Gantt chart shows the time relationship between tasks but does not directly show any dependency relationships between tasks. For example, whether task B in Figure 15–13 could be started earlier, that is, before task A has been completed, cannot be answered from the Gantt chart.

PERT Networks

The **Program Evaluation and Review Technique (PERT)** is a network-oriented model that was first used by the U.S. Navy in the Polaris project. A PERT network consists of the interconnection of events and activities. Figure 15–14 illustrates these constructs. An **event** is a point in time. It does not represent any work and does not take any time itself. An event is represented by a circle. Events 1 and 2 are shown. An **activity** is a task that, in general, does take time and is a contribution toward the completion of the total project. All activities begin and end on an event. An activity is represented by a straight line with an arrow pointing from its beginning event to its ending event. Activity A is shown.

Figure 15–14
PERT Symbols

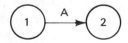

A rule at the very heart of the PERT concept is that: *All of the activities entering an event must be complete before any activity exiting that event can begin.* Figure 15–15 illustrates this rule. Neither activity C nor activity D can begin until both activity A *and* activity B are complete.

Figure 15–15
Precedence in a PERT Network

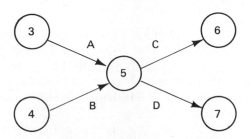

Another concept encountered is that of the dummy activity. A **dummy activity** is an activity that takes no time and carries out no task, but is required in order to maintain correct precedence relations within the network. Figure 15–16 presents an example using a dummy activity. In Figure 15–15 both activities A and B must be completed before either activity C or D can begin. In Figure 15–16 both activity A and the dummy activity must be completed before activity C can begin. But the dummy activity is complete as soon as activity B is complete (since the dummy takes no time). As a result, activity C is constrained by activities A and B, but activity D is constrained only by activity B.

Figure 15–16
Dummy Activity

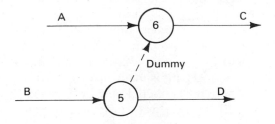

Time estimation for a task has been handled two ways. The first (and the traditional) method combines three estimates using the relationship:

$$t_e = \frac{t_o + 4 \cdot t_m + t_p}{6}$$

where t_o = optimistic time

t_m = most likely time

t_p = pessimistic time

t_e = expected time

All three time estimates are made by the manager responsible for the task. The optimistic time is that required to complete the task if it proceeds smoothly and efficiently without any unforeseen difficulties. The pessimistic time is that required if unforeseen difficulties and delays are encountered. The **most likely time** is the best overall estimate. The **estimated time** is a weighing of these three estimates. It is assumed that statistically the time estimate falls within a beta distribution.

The second method for estimating task completion time is to simply make one best managerial estimate. This would be analogous to the most likely time in the traditional approach.

Figure 15–17 shows a project consisting of a number of tasks and the associated PERT network. Every network begins and ends on a single event. The total time to complete the project can be calculated. This is done by assuming that the beginning event (i.e. event 1) occurs at time 0. Event 2 is two weeks later and, as a result, is at time 2. There are two activities ending at event 3. Activity D cannot begin until both activities (i.e. activity B and the *dummy* activity) are complete. This can occur only at two weeks, since the *dummy* cannot occur until activity A is complete, and this requires two weeks. In general, for multiple activity paths into an event the controlling path is the longest time path. Using this methodology, the time to complete the entire project is 12 weeks.

Another concept is that of the critical path. The **critical path** is that sequence of activities that cannot be delayed without a delay occurring in the final conclusion time for the entire project. The critical path is continuous from the beginning event to the ending event, that is, there are no breaks in the path. In the example of Figure 15–17, the critical path is made up of activities A, the *dummy*, D, G, I, and J. If activity G should slip by 1 week, then the final completion time will slip by 1 week to 13 weeks. Some slippage can

Figure 15–17
PERT Example

Activity	Required Preceding Activity	Estimated Time (weeks)
A	—	2
B	—	1
C	A	2
D	A, B	3
E	C	1
F	C	1
G	D	2
H	E	2
I	F, G	3
J	H, I	2

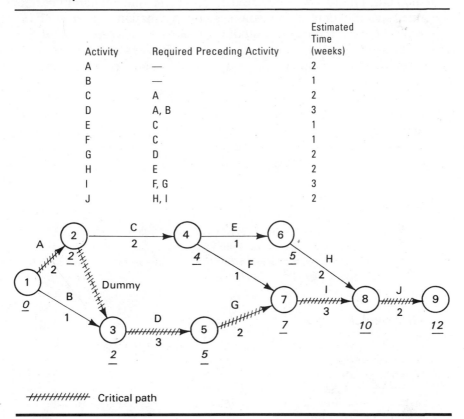

########## Critical path

be tolerated in an activity not on the critical path. **Slack** is the maximum amount that an activity can slip (assuming that all other activities remain on schedule) without causing the final project time to slip. As an example, activity B has a slack of one week.

Conclusions

The systems life cycle is the model describing the creation, maturation, and rejuvenation of any computer based system. It is a cycle that describes systems development as stepping through analysis, design, implementation, and operational phases. It recognizes that development is not a one-time event, but an evolutionary process.

Systems analysis is concerned with the decomposition of a current system into its constituent parts so that the analyst may understand in detail the inner workings of the system. This understanding leads to the specification of the new system. A detailed outline of the requirements of the new system is prepared. It is essential that this set of specifications is understood by both users and systems analysts. It is this document that is approved by both groups that will be the basis for the systems design phase.

The current trend is to greater detail in the requirements specification. This greater detail frequently serves to expose problem areas and misunderstandings between the user and the technical community. In addition, a more detailed specification serves as a better starting point for the systems design effort.

References

1. Burch, J. G. Jr.; F. R. Strater; and G. Grudnitski. *Information Systems: Theory and Practice.* 2d. ed. New York: John Wiley & Sons, 1979, pp. 259–60.
2. Gane, C., and T. Sarson. *Structured Systems Analysis.* Englewood Cliffs, N.J.: Prentice-Hall, 1979.

Additional Readings

DeMarco, T. *Structured Analysis and System Specification.* Englewood Cliffs, N.J.: Prentice-Hall, 1978.

Hurley, R. B. *Decision Tables in Software Engineering.* New York: Van Nostrand Reinhold, 1983.

Martin, J. *Application Development Without Programmers.* Englewood Cliffs, N.J.: Prentice-Hall, 1982.

Orr, K. *Structured Requirements Definition.* Topeka: Ken Orr and Associates, Inc., 1981.

Ward, P. T. *Systems Development Without Pain.* New York: Yourdon Press, 1984.

Review

1. Describe the systems life cycle. Why is it necessarily repetitive?
2. What is the purpose of a feasibility study?
3. What is systems analysis?
4. Some interviewees may give an answer to a question that they think the interviewer wants to hear. How can the effects of this problem be minimized?

5. Give the flowcharting symbol for each of the following:
   a Annotation.
   b Offline storage.
   c Disk storage.
   d Magnetic tape.
   e Sort.
   f Predefined process.
6. Differentiate between a limited entry decision table and an extended entry decision table.
7. Describe the use of the ELSE rule in a decision table.
8. How is control information presented in a data flow diagram?
9. In a data flow diagram, what is a functional primitive?
10. What is an assembly line diagram?
11. What is a data dictionary?
12. The Warnier/Orr technique is output-oriented. Explain.
13. What is the primary advantage of the PERT methodology over Gantt charts?
14. In PERT, what is a dummy activity?
15. Using the three time estimates methods in PERT, when will the expected time not be equal to the most likely time?

Appendix 15–1
Flowcharting Symbols

Symbol	Definition

Processing

Predefined process
—details of process are contained on a different flowchart

Input/output

Decision

Annotation
—explanatory comments entered on flowchart

Document

Punched card

Symbol	Definition

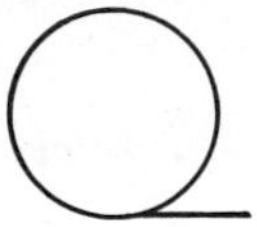

Magnetic tape

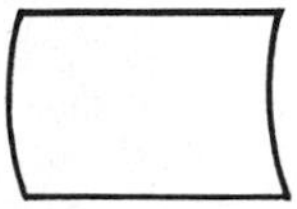

On-Line storage
—general symbol

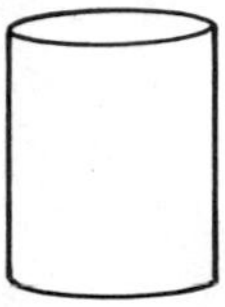

Disk storage

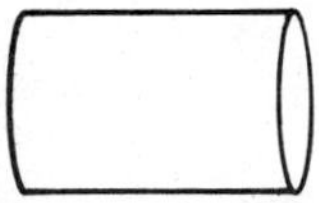

Drum storage

Off-Line storage

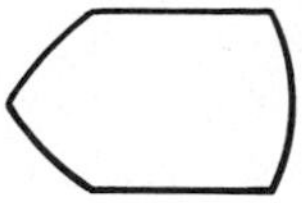

Display
—non-hard copy output or output to be used
   immediately

Manual Input
—e.g., badge, light pen, switch, etc. input

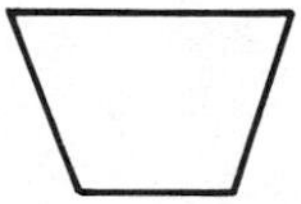

Manual Off-Line Operation
—speed of operation is that of equipment

Symbol	Definition
	Auxiliary Off-Line Operation —speed of operation is that of equipment
	Merge —Creation of one set of data from two sets of data in the same sequence
	Extract —Reverse of merge
	Sort —sequencing of data on a key
	Communication Link —telecommunications connection

Chapter 16

Systems Design and Implementation

Introduction

The systems analysis phase of the systems life cycle is concerned with developing the specifications for the new system. Systems design is concerned with the development of the system that meets these specifications. If systems analysis is concerned with *what* a system is to do, then systems design is concerned with *how* it is to be done. Whereas systems analysis involves a close working relationship between the technical staff and the users, systems design is primarily a responsibility of the technical staff. There are some aspects of the design that require close user involvement, e.g. report or screen formatting. It is possible that questions or decisions faced in the systems design phase may require additional systems analysis.

Systems implementation is that phase of the systems life cycle concerned with the incorporation of a new system into the organization. Once the systems design phase is complete, required hardware obtained, and new software developed or contracted, the system cannot be introduced into day-to-day operations without careful preparation.

Normalization

The contents of all data stores proposed for the system should have been simplified in the systems analysis phase. This essentially means that no data are stored that are not needed, and all data are stored that are needed in a data flow.

Even though data have been simplified, certain insertion and deletion anomalies, that is, unintended results, may occur. The designer must normalize the data so that users will not encounter these unexpected actions.

Normalization further simplifies the contents of all data files to be used in the computerized portions of the system by removing unwanted functional dependencies. Functional dependencies exist between fields (or attributes). Field 1 is functionally dependent on field 2 if the value of field 1 is determined by the value of field 2. For example, current age is functionally dependent on date of birth. There are seven levels of normalization. These are identified as first normal form (1NF), second normal form (2NF), third normal form (3NF), Boyce-Codd normal form (BCNF), fourth normal form (4NF), fifth normal form (5NF), and domain-key normal form (DKNF). Only the first three normal forms will be discussed, since they are the most commonly used. It has been shown that a relation in DKNF produces no update anomalies. DKNF, therefore, is the design ideal. How DKNF can be reached, and if it can be reached in any given case, remains unclear.

The terminology used in normalization is that of relational data bases. As a result, data are viewed as a relation.

First Normal Form (1NF)

A relation is in 1NF if it contains no repeating groups of data. Since the definition of a relation does not permit repeating groups, all relations are in 1NF. For example, assume that a grouping of data **STUDENT** exists:

```
STUDENT

    STUDENT - NO
    STUDENT - NAME
    MAJOR
    COURSE
       COURSE - NO ⎫
       GRADE       ⎬ repeats
       CREDITS     ⎪
       GPA - POINTS⎭
```

The key in the example is underlined, that is, the key is **STUDENT - NO.** Since each student has, in general, taken more than one course, **COURSE** data repeat. To achieve 1NF status, the data grouping **STUDENT** must be broken into two relations:

STUDENT	COURSE - TAKEN
STUDENT - NO	STUDENT - NO
STUDENT - NAME	COURSE - NO
MAJOR	GRADE
	CREDITS
	GPA - POINTS

No repeating groups are allowed in a data structure in 1NF. The key in the original relation was **STUDENT - NO.** This remains the key in the new relation **STUDENT** and is concatenated with **COURSE - NO** in the new relation **COURSE - TAKEN** to produce a unique identification.

Second Normal Form (2NF)

A relation is in 2NF if it is in 1NF and none of the nonkey fields in the relation can be uniquely identified with only part of the key. For example, the contents of the field **CREDITS** can be determined by knowing only **COURSE - NO** in the relation **COURSE - TAKEN.** The concatenated key is not required. This assumes that any course has a fixed number of credits associated with it. The example is not in 2NF. This can be transformed into 2NF by breaking the relation **COURSE - TAKEN** into two relations:

COURSE - TAKEN	COURSE
STUDENT - NO	COURSE - NO
COURSE - NO	CREDITS
GRADE	
GPA - POINTS	

GRADE is dependent on both **STUDENT - NO** and **COURSE - NO.** **CREDITS** is dependent only on **COURSE - NO.**

Third Normal Form (3NF)

A relation is in 3NF if it is in 2NF and no nonkey field is dependent on another nonkey field. For example, in the relation **COURSE - TAKEN** the field **GPA - POINTS** is dependent on the concatenated key **STUDENT - NO COURSE - NO,** but it is also dependent on **GRADE.** Therefore, the relation **COURSE - TAKEN** is not in 3NF.

COURSE - TAKEN can be transformed into 3NF by removal of the field **GPA - POINTS,** which is uniquely identified by **GRADE.**

The example now consists of three relations:

STUDENT   COURSE - TAKEN   COURSE

STUDENT - NO   STUDENT - NO   COURSE - NO
STUDENT - NAME   COURSE - NO   CREDITS
MAJOR   GRADE

Relation **STUDENT** still has a hidden dependency: **MAJOR** (a non-key field) can be determined by **STUDENT - NAME** (a nonkey field). Therefore, **STUDENT** must be broken into two relations to remove this dependency:

STUDENT   STUDENT - MAJOR

STUDENT - NO   STUDENT - NO
STUDENT - NAME   MAJOR

Third normal form simplifies data relationships and avoids subtle inconsistencies and update anomalies within the data.

File Design and Organization

Once data stores have been simplified and normalized, there may be some further reorganization made. For example, two files that have the same key may be combined, if that makes sense in terms of the data flows.

Access requirements must be defined, and from these access requirements file search techniques and access methods are selected. Consideration of file activity, file volatility, update requirements, response times, etc., are used to achieve a file organization that will meet the requirements of its users. There may be some trade-off between user requirements made at this point.

Software

The computerized component of the system is divided into programs. There are two general sources of software: in-house development and outside sourcing.

In-house development is carried out by the organization's own staff. The main advantage is that the organization obtains programs that should exactly meet users' requirements. The disadvantages are that software development takes time and money. If there is no outside source, in-house development is the only choice.

Software can also be obtained from outside sources. The primary advantages are savings in time and probably a substantial savings in cost. These savings in cost are probable because the development cost can be spread over mutiple users by the vendor. The cost of outside software is also certain, whereas the cost of in-house development is uncertain. The disadvantage is that a package may not exactly fit the users' needs. It may, however, be possible to contract with the software vendor for modifications to the package to make it more closely meet system requirements. If the modifications are minor, the in-house technical staff can probably make the changes.

There is general agreement that a good program should meet most (if not all) of the following characteristics. Programming practice has not always resulted in products meeting these goals. There is now a more serious concern for good practice because of the labor intensive nature of programming. A good program should:

1. Work. It should carry out the purpose for which it was written. It should be capable of performing under the full range of operating conditions that can reasonably be expected.

2. Be capable of being tested. Although no nontrivial program can be proven to be free of errors, it should be capable of being thoroughly tested before it becomes operational. The program should have been designed with testing in mind, and test data should be available.

3. Be documented well. This implies that not only is the logic flow of the program presented clearly, but the purpose of individual sections of coding is made clear with appropriate comments or supporting notes. In addition, restrictions on data input, interface requirements with other programs, and input/output requirements must be clearly stated.

4. Be maintained easily. This means that a qualified programmer should be able to make changes, additions, or deletions to the program with a reasonable amount of effort. This requires good documentation, but also implies that clever, subtle, or tricky logic has been avoided.

5. Make efficient use of resources. This implies that scarce resources such as processor time and primary memory space should not be wasted. To a certain extent, there is a trade-off between processor time and primary storage. The goal should be to not unnecessarily allow requirements for either to increase without a decrease in the other. In addition, peripheral devices should be used efficiently.

A major and expensive resource is the human resource. There is another trade-off between the amount of additional human program-ming effort required to make an improvement in resource usage and the value of the savings resulting from that improved program. The pendulum has swung in this area from a concern in earlier computer based systems for improved hardware usage to a greater concern in more recent systems for improved utilization of both programmer and user time.

6. Provide good error checking. This applies especially to testing all input data. These tests should provide a reasonable assurance that further processing is carried out on only valid data. Under some circumstances, checks may also be made on interim or final results.

7. Be delivered on time. It has unfortunately been the exception rather than the rule when a program (or a set of programs) has been completed on schedule.

8. Be simple. A program should reflect simple, clean logic. Sim-plicity in design also tends to increase reliability. As any system becomes more complex, the possibility of hidden errors or logic flaws increases. A conceptually simple program may be understood more easily and tested more thoroughly.

Top-Down Concepts

Major components of current software design philosophy are the top-down concepts. The introduction of these concepts has imposed some additional structure on a previously ill-structured activity. The top-down approaches use successive efforts of system decomposition. There are three top-down techniques:

1. Top-down design.
2. Top-down coding.
3. Top-down testing.

Top-down design decomposes a complex software requirement into successively smaller and simpler software modules. At the lowest level, the modules are manageable and clear in their purpose. A main, or first-level, module is designed. This module in turn calls, or trans-fers control to, second-level modules, which in turn may call third-level modules, etc. As examples, these transfers may be accom-plished in FORTRAN by use of subroutines or in COBOL by use of the PERFORM verb.

The top-down approach should be constrasted with the more tra-ditional bottom-up approach. In the **bottom-up approach** lower-level modules are first designed, coded, tested, and debugged. They are then integrated together and tested. As more and more modules are integrated into the system, the testing requirements become more sophisticated. The final stage is called the system test, in which the entire system is tested.

Top-down coding is concerned with the coding of the modules designed during top-down design. Coding of the higher-level modules may be carried out while lower-level modules are still being designed. This is possible since each module is relatively self-contained, and entry to and exit from it are tightly controlled.

Top-down testing is concerned with testing of the higher-level modules even before lower-level modules are designed or coded. **Testing** is a systematic approach to determining that a module, in fact, operates correctly. Since modules at one level call modules at a lower level, a mechanism must be available to call modules that have not yet been coded or, perhaps, even not yet designed. A **program stub** is a dummy module that exists only to allow testing of a higher module. The stub performs minimal work. It may, for example, provide simply an entrance to, and an immediate exit back to, the calling module. It might provide dummy data as output, or it might print out a simple message to the tester that entrance to the module was successful. The program stub is eventually replaced with a fully designed and coded module that, in turn, may call new program stubs at the next lower level.

Figure 16–1 illustrates these top-down concepts. The development does not have to progress at the same pace on all branches of the design chart. For example, the middle branch is farther along in the figure than either of the side branches.

Probably the primary advantage of the top-down approach is that testing of major modules and interfaces occurs early in the development phase. Problems that occur in these modules will have the most far-reaching consequences and will be caught early in testing. Problems found in the lowest-level modules will be caught late in the testing effort, but will have fairly limited effect on the system. In an environment in which CPU time is scarce, spreading out the testing effort over a longer period of time can be useful. In the traditional approach, the greatest amount of testing is required at the end of the design. This testing is all too frequently compromised if there has been schedule slippage. In the top-down approach, testing is not carried out primarily at the end of the project—it is spread out throughout the project, and the most critical modules and interfaces are tested early in the project.

Figure 16–1
Top-Down Concepts

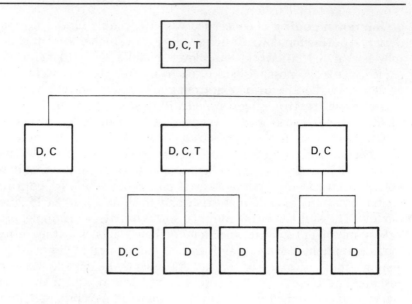

D = designed
C = coded
T = tested

Software Maintenance

The total cost for software consists of development and maintenance costs. The development cost is one-time and is incurred in the
design, coding, and testing of new software. The maintenance cost,
however, is ongoing and is spread over the life of the software. The
maintenance cost may significantly exceed the development cost
when the entire life cycle of the software is viewed.

Since some maintenance programming is inevitable, software engineering must provide for ease of maintenance. A difficult-to-main-
tain program will incur high maintenance costs over its life. A well-
designed, well-coded, and thoroughly tested program will minimize
software errors and design flaws. As a result, maintenance effort
(and costs) will not have to be devoted to correcting them later.

Structured programming and the top-down concepts are techniques that result in easier-to-maintain software. Changes to the software do not produce unexpected results requiring additional maintenance efforts. Maintainability is now a design goal of good software engineering.

Hierarchy Charts

A **hierarchy chart,** or **structure chart,** is a means of showing the logical relationships among modules of a program by means of a graphical device similar to an organization chart. The hierarchy chart is a tool that is compatible with the top-down design approach.

Figure 16–2 gives an example of a hierarchy chart. Each box in the chart is concisely described by a verb and a brief phrase. There is successively more detailed specification as one progresses further down the chart. A hierarchy chart does not indicate the number of

Figure 16–2
Hierarchy Chart

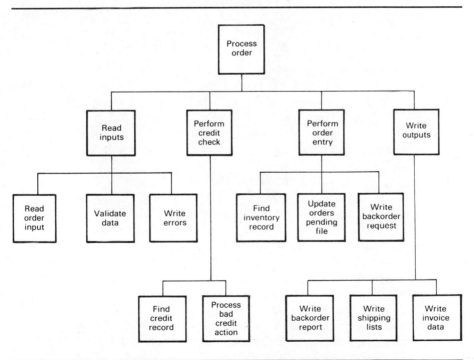

times a module is executed, or even if a module is executed. For example, in the figure under ***READ INPUTS*** data are validated. Only data that fail validation are processed under **WRITE ER-RORS.** For clearer presentation of the overall logic, hierarchy charts are usually supplemented with clarification in the form of a narrative description, decision tables, etc.

IBM has developed a hierarchical methodology called **HIPO,** that is, **Hierarchical Input Processing Output.** HIPO consists of three diagrams:

1. A table of contents that consists of a hierarchy chart and a legend defining various symbols used.
2. Overview diagrams that define the input, process, and output elements of higher-level modules.
3. Detail diagrams that define in more detail the components of a module. An extended description table is used to further clarify details.

None of the hierarchy chart types indicate directly details such as the number of times a module is executed, the decision rule for determining if a module should be executed, etc. Data interfaces between modules are also not defined.

Warnier/Orr Diagrams

Warnier/Orr diagrams are used as a tool for systems design. The method is based on original work by Warnier[7] and extended by Orr[6]. Appendix 16–1 briefly outlines the basic concepts of Warnier/Orr diagrams. The Warnier/Orr technique is output-oriented. Using structured requirement definition, the end result is a definition of the required outputs. The systems design phase begins with this definition.

A goal of the Warnier/Orr technique is to provide a minimal system, that is, one that does only what is required to produce the required outputs. Although the starting point for the design effort may be one or more reports, the first step is to define in complete detail the structure of these reports. The logical data base required by the system to produce these reports is next defined. This data base should not contain redundant or unnecessary data elements. At this stage of the design effort, redundant data elements are not permitted. At the later stage of physical design, the designer for good reasons, such as improved retrieval time, may introduce some redundancy. The basic underlying data structure of the system is derived from the outputs.

For example, Figure 16–3 shows an inventory status report that has been determined in the structured requirements definition phase to be a required output. The report's inherent hierarchical data structure can be represented by Warnier/Orr as shown in Figure 16–4. Each report consists of data for one week. Each week's entry provided data on S stockrooms, and each stockroom set of data consists of I inventory items. Each inventory item entry is, in turn, divided into data elements of number, units on hand, and reorder point. Detailed definition continues until the design of this report and all other reports in the system is complete.

A complete Warnier/Orr specification may be converted into structured English. If a data flow diagram has been produced as the basic set of specifications from the systems analysis phase, the logic

---

Figure 16–3
Example of Output Report

World Wide Widget Company
Inventory Status Report

Week of: January 17, 1986

	Item Number	Units on Hand	Reorder Point
Stockroom 1:			
	123	120	60
	345	84	90
	672	35	20
Stockroom 2:			
	123	57	40
	306	22	15
	672	18	20
	711	161	100

Figure 16–4
Warnier/Orr Representation of Output Report

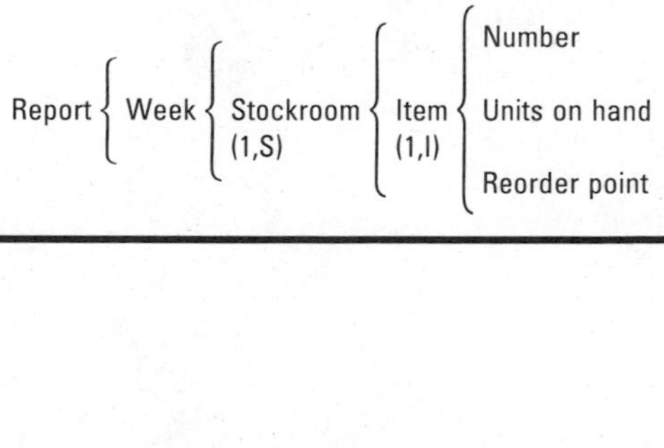

Report { Week { Stockroom (1,S) { Item (1,I) { Number / Units on hand / Reorder point

required to implement the process in each of the lowest-level bubbles can also be represented in structured English. In either the Warnier/Orr or the data flow diagram case, structured English can then be converted into source code.

Structured English

Structured English, or **pseudocode,** is an artificial language used to write specifications in an unambiguous fashion. It is also sometimes called **Program Design Language,** or **PDL.** Both the vocabulary and the syntax of structured English are limited. Structured English is a means of written expression that lies between the informality and ambiguity of narrative English and the detailed requirements of a programming language. It is a step on the way to detailed coding.

There are three logical constructs in structured English:

1. The sequence construct.
2. The decision construct.
3. The repetition construct.

Each of these constructs has only one entry point and only one exit point. This enforced simplicity allows easier formulation and easier understanding of the logical framework. All structured English formulations consist of combinations of these three constraints.

Figure 16–5 gives an example of structured English. The logic states that inventory records in a file are read one at a time until the end-of-file is reached. For each record, the number of items on hand

---

Figure 16–5
Structured English Example

```
REPEAT UNTIL the end-of-file is reached
   Read inventory record
   IF the number-of-items-on-hand is less than the reorder-point
      Move EOQ to order-outstanding
      Add EOQ to total items
      Set order-flag to 1
      Write purchase order record
   ELSE (number-of-items-on-hand is greater than or equal to the reorder-point)
      Write inventory-status-OK record
   END-IF
END-REPEAT
```

---

is compared against the reorder point. If the number on hand is less than the reorder point, four steps are taken to place an order; if the number on hand is not less than the reorder point, a record is written out indicating that the status is satisfactory. The **REPEAT UNTIL** is a repetition construct. The **END-REPEAT** specifies the end of the **REPEAT.** The **IF. . . ELSE . . .** is a decision construct, and the four statements following the **IF** are sequential and form a sequence construct. A **THEN** is sometimes included in the decision construct to more clearly set out the logic required in the event that the **IF** is true. The **ELSE** component of the decision construct may optionally be followed by a statement in parentheses specifying the conditions under which it applies. Indentation is used to make the logic clearer to a reader. The **END-IF** statement clearly specifies the end of the **IF** statement. The three constructs used are the basis for structured programming, which is discussed in more detail below.

Chief Programmer Concept

IBM[2, 3] has also pioneered in the concept of the chief programmer. This was introduced in a project for the *New York Times*. The ability of programmers covers a very wide range. A good programmer may be 10 times as productive as a mediocre programmer. In addition, a programmer spends relatively little time programming. He or she spends much more time attending meetings, waiting for runs, waiting for tapes or disk packs, finding and/or updating documentation, etc. The **chief programmer concept** organizes a programming team around a chief (or super) programmer who controls all technical decisions and assignments. In addition, there is full-time administrative support provided for the team. As a result, programmers devote their time to programming and increase productivity. The chief programmer concept is centered on one very highly competent programmer who is supported by a less experienced but competent staff. The concept has been compared to a surgical team by Brooks[4]. The surgical team is centered on one highly specialized surgeon who is supported by other surgeons and medical specialists.

Structured Programming

Structured programming is a way of writing programs that limits itself to a few basic structures. Since these programming structures can be understood easily, their use as building blocks in a program leads to a better understanding of the logic of the entire program.

Structured programming involves the elimination of the **GO-TO** statement. In practice **GO-TO** statement use is minimized; in exceptional cases it may be allowed if it makes the logic clearer. The elimination of the **GO-TO** statement was first advocated by Dijkstra[5]. His rationale was that its elimination made proving the correctness of a program mathematically easier.

Structured programming uses three basic constructs that are assembled into more complex arrangements to form a working program. The two main arguments for structured programming are that the source code is more understandable and, therefore, more maintainable, and is capable of being tested more thoroughly. There is one entrance to, and one exit from, each of the basic building blocks.

Figure 16–6 illustrates the three basic constructs of structured programming. A **process** (or **sequence**) **construct** involves a simple entry and exit with no branching or repetition in the construct. A **decision** (or **selection**) **construct** involves a test that determines which of two paths is taken. This construct is also called an IF-THEN-ELSE construct, that is, if the decision criterion proves true, then one path is taken; otherwise a second path is taken. This is illustrated as follows:

> **IF** decision criterion
> **THEN** take true path
> **ELSE** take false path

A **repetition** (or **iteration**) **construct** involves the repetition of a process until some termination condition is met. Two versions of the construct are encountered: the **DO-WHILE** and the **DO-UNTIL.** The **DO-WHILE** version of the repetition construct makes the termination check before processing. As a result, the logic in this construct will not be carried out if the terminating condition is present upon logical entry to the construct. The **DO-UNTIL** checks for the terminating condition at the end of the process. As a result, the process is executed at least once upon logical entry to the construct. These constructs are the same as those described under structured English.

A structured program forms a nest of these basic constructs. Figure 16–7 illustrates this. The dashed lines represent basic constructs, which in turn are made up of other basic constructs. In all cases, one entrance to, and one exit from, each construct exist.

Structured Walkthroughs

A structured walkthrough is another IBM concept. It is frequently used in connection with the chief programmer concept (but is not limited to that concept). A **structured walkthrough** is a formal

Figure 16–6
Structured Programming Constructs

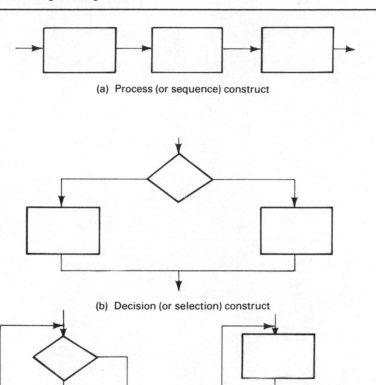

(a) Process (or sequence) construct

(b) Decision (or selection) construct

DO-WHILE   DO-UNTIL

(c) Repetition (or iteration) construct

review procedure by a programming team. When a programmer has completed a module (or small group of modules), the team *walks through* the logic with the responsible programmer at the review. The purpose of the review is not only to discover any logic error, but also to ensure that all programming standards of the organization have been met. Criteria, such as clarity in design, maintainability, etc.,

Figure 16–7
Nested Structured Constructs

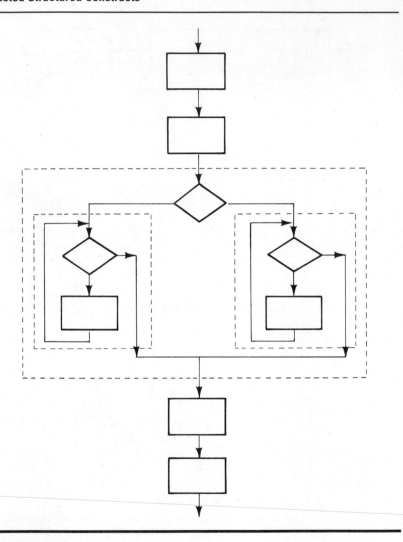

are judged. The goal is to produce a higher quality product through the efforts of the entire programming team. Any problem uncovered at a later time in the module is a failure of the entire team and not only of the individual programmer. Obviously, it is not always easy for every programmer to subject his or her work to the rigorous review of peers. When successful, the structured walkthrough can be an extremely valuable and cost effective tool for achieving quality software.

Hardware

Hardware should not be allowed to dictate system requirements. Instead, hardware should be selected that will meet the specifications of the system designer. Of course, any system design must be technically feasible, that is, implementable within the available hardware constraints.

Once the specifications for the required hardware are set, vendors are contacted. A **request for proposal (RFP)** is a formal document submitted to a number of vendors that outlines in detail the specifications of the required hardware. The RFP will have a cutoff date for vendor responses. Once the responses for the RFP are received they are reviewed, and any reponses that do not meet the specifications are eliminated from further consideration. A comparative analysis is then made. Since all proposals at this point meet the minimum specifications, comparisons and trade-offs must be based on multiple criteria. For example, proposal A may include a higher speed printer, whereas proposal B may include a higher capacity disk. All other inclusions in the proposal are approximately equal.

In the evaluation of the proposals, user references are highly recommended for smaller vendors or for any vendor offering a relatively new product. User experience is probably the single best basis for judging a vendor's claims. A number of independent agencies, such as Datapro, and trade magazines, such as *Infoworld*, also rate various products. These sources can be used to supplement other information obtained on the proposal. Miscellaneous other factors have to be considered also. For example, maintenance costs must be considered in addition to the initial purchase price. Training and documentation available are also important criteria.

Leasing versus Purchasing

In general, hardware may be either leased or purchased. Some small vendors may only offer their products for sale. There is a trade-off involved in the lease/purchase decision. Purchasing hardware will prove to be less expensive if the hardware is kept over a longer period of time. However, if the hardware is replaced in a shorter period of time, it will be less expensive to lease it.

Because of rapidly changing technology, the residual value of much equipment is very low after only a few years. Leasing allows an organization to update its equipment, e.g. to increase capacity or take advantage of new technology, without having to write off virtually all of the value of its replaced hardware. Of course, this flexibility costs the leasee more over a longer period of time.

It may also be easier to get money approved out of the operating budget for a lease than out of the capital budget for the purchase of computer equipment. Taxes and cash flow considerations may also be involved in the decision.

A system that is leased can usually only be operated for a fixed number of hours per month. Any use beyond this limit involves a surcharge. Purchased equipment may, of course, be used as the organization deems necessary. The payments on a lease are usually based on a full payment to the leasor in from three to five years.

Third party leasing involves a middleman organization between the vendor and the user. The third party purchases the hardware and then leases it to the ultimate user. The advantage to the user is that the lease is written so as to recover full payment over a longer period of time. This means that monthly lease payments are less than those required in a direct lease from the vendor. Maintenance contracts may still be purchased from the original vendor.

Some organizations also offer short term (i.e. one- or two-year) leases. The user may want to lease equipment only for a short period of time until other equipment that is on order is delivered. The lease payments are greater than with the usual lease. The leasor must re-lease the equipment upon its return. This involves some additional risk on the leasor's part.

Information Centers

An **information center** is an organizational unit that is staffed by technical personnel and oriented toward supporting users in meeting their information systems needs. The information center is not set up to carry out systems analysis and design on major systems. Instead, the personnel of the center are knowledgeable in user-oriented languages, easy-to-use packages, etc. They would usually provide support for the one-time inquiry and the repetitive, but changing, report. Information center personnel are, in effect, consultants to end users.

The main advantage of the information center is that users may obtain assistance for single requests. The waiting time for systems development work may be many months or even years. The information center personnel can provide assistance to users on a more timely basis.

The resources of the information center may also be used to build prototypes. **Prototyping** involves building a simple, *quick and dirty* version of a proposed system. This allows a number of trial and error design approaches at little cost, since the prototype may be designed with a very high-level, or fourth-generation, language. Use of this high-level capability may be limited to designing reports or screens for terminal output. The design of output usually involves a long iterative process. This approach can produce an agreed-upon, final version of the output or terminal dialog before beginning the more formal systems analysis and design effort.

Obviously, the personnel assigned to the information center must possess not only the requisite technical knowledge and applications experience, but also strong interpersonal and communications skills.

Systems Implementation

Systems implementation is that phase of the systems life cycle concerned with the incorporation of a new system into the organization. Once the systems design phase is complete, required hardware obtained, and new software developed, the system cannot be introduced into day-to-day operations without careful planning. Argyris[1] points out that even though a new system may be an excellent vehicle to assist in managerial decision making, it may still be rejected by its users. It may even appear to the outside observer that this opposition is not rational. This resistance to a new information system can arise from several sources. Managers may have learned to hide and manipulate data so as to protect their own interests. There is fear that the introduction of a new information system will expose these practices. There is, of course, the usual *empire building* and the *protection of one's own domain,* which may be more difficult with an information system not under the control of the using managers. Problems exposed by the information system may be known to a manager's supervisor before the manager has an opportunity to investigate and correct these problems. Another common problem is communication between the users and the systems analysts. These two groups do not speak the same language. The users do not really understand the new system and, as a result, fear it. Users sometimes see the introduction of a new system as a constraint on their freedom of action, and oppose it.

There are also some very legitimate concerns. Many information systems have been introduced that do not work. Promises of real-time on-line strategic information systems, total management information systems, and other concepts have proven in the past to be more fantasy than reality. Many managers are sceptical of new promises.

The best way to minimize implementation problems is for the users and the systems personnel to work closely together on the development of a new system from the very beginning. If the users are introduced to a new system only during the systems implementation phase, failure is virtually assured.

Training and Staffing

In conjunction with the introduction of a new system new personnel may have to be added, and current personnel may have to be trained to use the system. Training will probably begin during the systems design phase. There may be a wide range of personnel that must be involved in this training. For example, data entry operators must be familiarized with any source documents that will be introduced with data entry formats, and new screens used, and with the handling of any new data validation messages received during on-line data entry. Various manual procedures used to support the computer-oriented operation must be introduced, and the importance of accuracy and timeliness must be stressed. As another example, computer operators must be trained in the running of new programs and systems and the handling of new data files. Error procedures and recovery sequences must be reviewed and understood by all who may be involved in their implementation. Managers using the information output of the system must understand the underlying assumptions built into the system, and they must be able to intelligently evaluate the output from that system. They must control the information system by understanding its limitations and its potentialities.

The new system may require additional staff. Recruitment and hiring must be carried out so that required personnel are in place and trained when they are needed. Specialists in some technical areas may be difficult to attract and to hire. As a result, the lead time needed to hire such personnel may be relatively long. Perhaps the most overlooked source of skilled personnel is the organization's own employees. They have friends and professional contacts who form a potential recruiting pool.

Testing

Although program testing is carried out during the design phase and is interspersed throughout the programming effort if a top-down philosophy is used, some testing is also involved in the implementation phase. The manual procedures complementing the computer-based system must be tested. Forms required must be designed, printed, and made available to users. Hardware and any new software, such as an operating system or a telecommunications package, required with it must be tested before acceptance.

Recovery and backup procedures in the event of a system failure must be designed and tested before reliance is placed on the new system. This includes arranging for the storage of critical files and programs. These precautions for the new system will probably be incorporated into the current recovery and backup procedures. However, a backup facility may not be able to handle the increased workload in the event of an emergency. As a result, the new system may trigger an extensive overhaul of the entire recovery and backup plan. Any new forms needed must also be supplied to the backup facility.

File Creation

A new computer based system requires the use of data files. These files must be initialized before the system can be implemented. Master files containing data on customers, products, inventories, etc., must all be loaded. The loading of these files may be a time-consuming and labor intensive activity. In some cases, temporary data entry personnel are hired specifically to assist in this effort. A high degree of accuracy and tight quality control are essential for this file creation activity to be successful. These files must be in place before conversion is implemented.

Site Preparation

When new equipment is to be installed as a part of the system, a number of preparations are required to be made at the installation site. For a small minicomputer or for terminal equipment, this may consist of simply reserving floor space and ensuring that adequate power and outlets are available. For larger installations, site preparation will be more extensive. Heavy equipment may require that the floor be strengthened. Almost all medium and larger computer installations use false floors under which cabling and air conditioning ducts connect the various cabinets. Fire and smoke detectors, fire extinguishers, etc., must be installed. Air conditioning capacity may need to be expanded. Even the width of doors may be a factor in getting the equipment to its site. Various security requirements, e.g. locks, television monitors, man-traps, etc., must be planned and installed before the implementation date.

Documentation

Complete documentation on the system must be provided before the system implementation phase can be considered as finished. Documentation developed during systems analysis should include:

1. The feasibility study report.
2. Any formal systems analysis report submitted at the end of that phase.
3. Copies of all forms and reports reviewed during systems analysis.
4. The functional specifications laid out at the end of that phase.
5. Any other data collected, e.g., sampling results, etc.

The systems design phase documentation includes:

1. Hardware and software design details.
2. Record and file layouts.
3. Source document layouts.
4. Report layouts.
5. System flow chart.
6. Structured source code.
7. A narrative description of the purpose of the system and the functions of the individual programs in the system.
8. Any RFP issued.

In addition, it must include detailed instructions for the users and the operators who will interact with the system. In addition to recovery and backup procedures, detailed instructions for a computer operator will be included in the **console run book.**

Documentation to support change control procedures and authorization for changes in programs must also be established and strictly maintained.

Clearly written nontechnical instructions for all users who must interact directly with the system must also be provided. All options available to users must also be clearly stated, along with the means of selecting one from a set of options.

Conversion

Conversion is the process of changing over from the old system to the new system. There are four major approaches:

1. Direct conversion.
2. Parallel conversion.
3. Modular conversion.
4. Phased conversion.

Direct conversion involves the termination of the old system at the same time as the startup of the new system. It is common for any new system to encounter problems, bugs, or overlooked conditions. These situations may be minor or so critical that the final implementation of the entire system must be postponed. In the case of delay, the old system must continue in operation. As a result, it is usually considered too risky to use direct conversion. This conversion approach is usually used only when the old system is completely inadequate or a total failure.

Parallel conversion involves running both the old system and the new system at the same time until the new system proves itself reliable. The output of the old system is compared to that of the new system. If the new system produces values, where appropriate, that are identical to those produced by the old system, some confidence is established in the new system. A full cycle of data input and report generation is usually run in parallel. If problems are discovered in the new system, its use is discontinued and the old system continues to operate until the problems are corrected.

Modular conversion involves the installation of the new system in only one location in the organization. It is also called the **pilot approach.** The problems of the new system are worked out at this one installation. When confidence is gained in the new system, it is then installed at other locations within the organization.

Phased conversion involves installing the new system in phases. Whereas modular conversion partitions the organization, phased conversion partitions the new system. Each phase (or piece) of the new system is implemented in all organizational units involved, and problems are corrected before the next phase is introduced. Familiarity with the new system is gained by the users over a period of time.

Conversion approaches may be combined. For example, in a phased conversion each phase may be implemented in parallel with its old counterpart.

Postimplementation Audit

After a new system has been in operation for some period of time and the users of the system are familiar with it, a review of the operation should be made. A **postimplementation audit** is a formal review with the users of the operation of the new system. There are a number of advantages to this:

1. An evaluation of the actual costs and benefits associated with the introduction of the new system can be made. With feedback, future cost/benefit analysis may be made more accurately.
2. Small problems that still exist in the system can be brought to the attention of the systems group for correction.
3. There may be difficulty on the part of some classes of users in taking advantage of the full potential of the system. Minor modifications to the system may allow those users to more fully utilize its capabilities.
4. With experience, users may make recommendations for future improvements. These recommendations should be put in writing and filed for review and possible incorporation into the system during the next loop through the systems life cycle.
5. Psychologically, a review by the group responsible for the system gives the users a feeling that their needs are being served.

Conclusions

The systems life cycle is the model describing the creation, maturation, and rejuvenation of any computer-based system. It views systems development as an ongoing process.

Design is concerned with constructing the details and interfaces necessary to carry out the objectives of a new system. It involves the meshing of the hardware, software, and manual procedures necessary to meet the specifications of the system.

Systems analysis and design are becoming more and more oriented around structured techniques. Decomposition techniques in analysis and modularity in design are the key underpinnings of successful systems work. The decomposition resulting from a structured analysis methodology such as data flow diagrams forms the framework for modularization and the software design of a new system. Modularity makes possible the top-down techniques of design, coding, and testing with their resulting efficiencies. Modularity and close control of the module interfaces are helped by structured programming. With structured programming the inherent simplicity of the logic flow results in easier debugging and, more importantly, easier maintenance. It should be remembered that even though the design of a system may cover a relatively short period of time, the maintenance of the system must be carried out over the life of the system. Although efforts to improve maintainability in the design phase may increase costs, savings over the life of the system will almost certainly more than compensate for these increases.

Successful implementation involves careful planning for the new system. Detailed planning begins long before the cutover date. Long lead times on some phases of the implementation may be required, e.g. the hiring of technically specialized personnel, purchase or lease of new hardware, or extensive site preparation.

The ultimate test of any system is its ability to assist users to make better decisions with the information provided by the system. Any computer based information system is only a tool to assist its users. It must always be judged in this context.

References

1. Argyris, C. "Resistance to Rational Management Systems." *Innovation,* No. 10 (February 1970), pp. 28–35.
2. Baker, F. T. "Chief Programming Team Management of Production Programming." *IBM Systems Journal* (January 1972), pp. 56–73.
3. _____, and H. D. Mills. "Chief Programmer Teams." *Datamation* 19, No. 12 (December 1973), pp. 58–61.
4. Brooks, F. P. Jr. *The Mythical Man-Month.* Reading, Mass.: Addison-Wesley Publishing, 1975.
5. Dijkstra, E. W. "GO-TO Statement Considered Harmful." Letter to the Editor, *Communications of the ACM* 11, No. 3 (March 1968), pp. 147–48.
6. Orr, K. T. *Structured Systems Development.* New York: Yourdon Press, 1977.
7. Warnier, J. D. *Logical Construction of Programs.* New York: Van Nostrand Reinhold, 1976.

Additional Readings

Boehm, B. *Software Engineering Economics.* Englewood Cliffs, N.J.: Prentice-Hall, 1981.

Bohl, M. *Tools for Structured Design.* Palo Alto, Calif.: Science Research Associates, 1978.

Gilb, T. *Software Metrics.* Cambridge, Mass.: Winthrop Publishers, Inc., 1977.

Hammond, L. W. "Management Considerations for an Information Center." *IBM Systems Journal* 21, No. 2 (1982), pp. 131–61.

Higgins, D. A. *Program Design and Construction.* Englewood Cliffs, N.J.: Prentice-Hall, 1979.

Martin, J., and C. McClure. *Software Maintenance.* Englewood Cliffs, N.J.: Prentice-Hall, 1982.

Myers, G. J. *Reliable Software Through Composite Design*. New York: Van Nostrand Reinhold, 1975.

————. *Composite/Structured Design*. New York: Van Nostrand Reinhold, 1978.

Page-Jones, M. *The Practical Guide to Structured Systems Design*. New York: Yourdon Press, 1980.

Senn, J. A. *Information Systems in Management*. Belmont, Calif.: Wadsworth, 1978.

Shneiderman, B. *Software Psychology*. Cambridge, Mass.: Winthrop Publishers, Inc., 1980.

Stevens, W. P. *Using Structured Design*. New York: John Wiley & Sons, 1981.

Weinberg, G. M. *The Psychology of Computer Programming*. New York: Van Nostrand Reinhold, 1971.

Yourdon, E. *Techniques of Program Structure and Design*. Englewood Cliffs, N.J.: Prentice-Hall, 1975.

————. *Structured Walkthroughs*. New York: Yourdon Press, 1977.

————. *Managing the Structured Techniques*. 2d ed. New York: Yourdon Press, 1979.

————, and L. L. Constantine. *Structured Design*. Englewood Cliffs, N.J.: Prentice-Hall, 1979.

Review

1. What is normalization?
2. What is systems design?
3. Differentiate between top-down design and bottom-up design.
4. What are the advantages of the top-down approach?
5. *a* Give an advantage of hierarchy charts.
   b Give a disadvantage of hierarchy charts.
6. Describe the chief programmer concept.
7. Give the three basic constructs of structured programming.
8. Differentiate between the DO-WHILE and the DO-UNTIL.
9. What is a structured walkthrough? What is its advantage?
10. What is an RFP?
11. *a* What is the primary advantage of purchasing hardware?
    b What is the primary advantage of leasing hardware?
12. What is third party leasing?
13. What is a fourth-generation language?
14. What is the purpose of an information center?
15. What is systems implementation?
16. Give some reasons why a manager may oppose a well-thought out and well-designed information system.
17. What is the primary problem in initializing files for a new information system?

18. Briefly explain each of the following conversion approaches.
    a Direct conversion.
    b Parallel conversion.
    c Modular conversion.
    d Phased conversion.
19. What is a postimplementation audit? What is its primary purpose?

Appendix 16–1
Warnier/Orr Diagrams

Sequence is from top to bottom, left to right.

$$\text{Step 1} \begin{cases} \text{Step 1A} \\ \text{Step 1B} \end{cases}$$

Interpretation; Step 1 consists of first Step 1A and then Step 1B.

$$\text{Step 1} \begin{cases} \text{Step 1A} \\ \oplus \\ \text{Step 1B} \end{cases}$$

Interpretation: Step 1 consists of Step 1A or Step 1B. This is the exclusive OR operation.

$$\text{Step 1} \begin{cases} \text{Step 1A} \\ \oplus \\ \overline{\text{Step 1A}} \end{cases}$$

Interpretation: Step 1 consists of Step 1A or not Step 1A exclusively.

$$\text{Step 1} \begin{cases} \text{Step 1A} \\ (0,1) \\ \\ \text{Step 1B} \\ (1,N) \end{cases}$$

Interpretation: Step 1 consists of 0 through 1 repetitions of Step 1A and 1 thru N repetitions of Step 1B.

Index

This book has been set Linotron 202, in 10 point Primer, leaded 2 points, and 8 point Primer, leaded 3 points. Part numbers and chapter numbers are 16 point Univers italic. Part titles are 36 point Univers italic and chapter titles are 30 point Univers italic. The size of the type page is 25½ by 44 picas.